T0340365

The Role of Law and Regulation in Sustaining Financial Markets

This book explores the role of law and regulation in sustaining financial markets in both developed and developing countries, particularly the European Union, the United States and China. The central argument of this book is that law matters for the operation of financial markets, which in turn significantly influences the performance of firms, industries and economies.

The Role of Law and Regulation in Sustaining Financial Markets is divided into four parts. Part I addresses the connection between law, financial development and economic growth. Part II deals with the role of financial regulation, which can be used to correct market failures, such as negative externalities, information asymmetries and monopolies. Part III focuses on the design, functioning and performance of different financial instruments. Part IV examines the topic of corporate social responsibility (CSR). This book contributes to the 'law and finance' literature by studying certain conventional issues, such as the relationship between finance and economic growth, and the effects of regulatory quality on financial development, from new perspectives and/or with new evidence, data and cases. It also explores novel topics that have been overlooked in the current literature, such as project finance contracts, insurance and climate change and the shadow banking system.

This book is meaningful not only for the EU and the US, which have suffered considerably from the financial crisis of 2008, but also for China, which is struggling to build a sound institutional infrastructure to govern its increasingly complicated financial system. By comparing the regulatory philosophies and practices of the EU, the US and China, this book will help the reader to understand the diverse nature of the global 'law and finance' nexus, and avoid succumbing to the myth of 'one-size-fits-all'.

Niels Philipsen is Associate Professor of Law and Economics, and Vice-Director of the Maastricht European Transnational Legal Research (METRO) Institute, in the Faculty of Law, Maastricht University, the Netherlands.

Guangdong Xu is Associate Professor of Law and Economics at the China University of Political Science and Law, Beijing, China.

The Economics of Legal Relationships
Sponsored by Michigan State University College of Law
Series editors:
Nicholas Mercuro, *Michigan State University College of Law*
Michael D. Kaplowitz, *Michigan State University*

**The first three volumes listed above are published by and available
from Elsevier*

The Role of Law and Regulation in Sustaining Financial Markets

Edited by Niels Philipsen and Guangdong Xu

Routledge
Taylor & Francis Group

LONDON AND NEW YORK

Firstpub lished 2015
by Routledge
2 Park Square, Milton Park, Abingdon, Oxon OX14 4RN

and by Routledge
52 Vanderbilt Avenue, New York, NY 10017

First issued in paperback 2020

Routledge is an imprint of the Taylor & Francis Group, an informa business

British Library Cataloguing in Publication Data
A catalogue record for this book is available from the British Library

Library of Congress Cataloguing in Publication data
The role of law and regulation in sustaining financial markets / Edited by Niels Philipsen and Guangdong Xu.
p. cm.
Includes bibliographical references and index.
1. Capital market–Law and legislation 2. Financial services industry–Law and legislation. I. Philipsen, Niels, 1975– editor. II. Xu, Guangdong, editor.
K1114.R65 2014
332'.0415–dc23
2014011801

ISBN 13: 978-0-367-66924-9 (pbk)
ISBN 13: 978-0-415-74900-8 (hbk)

Typeset in Times New Roman
by Out of House Publishing

Contents

Figures

Tables

Notes on contributors

Jianwei Chen, Center for Law and Economics at the China University of Political Science and Law, Beijing, China.

Nicolas de Sadeleer, Saint-Louis University, Brussels, Belgium.

Yanqiang Ding, Shandong University School of Economics, Jinan, China.

Michael Faure, Maastricht University School of Law, Maastricht and Erasmus School of Law, Rotterdam, the Netherlands.

Binwei Gui, Center for Law and Economics at the China University of Political Science and Law, Beijing, China.

Lars Hansson, International Institute for Industrial Environmental Economics at Lund University, Lund, Sweden.

Qihao He, University of Connecticut School of Law, Hartford, United States of America.

Jiye Hu, Center, for Law and Economics at the China University of Political Science and Law, Beijing, China.

Wenjing Li, Center for Law and Economics at the China University of Political Science and Law, Beijing, China.

Jingyuan Ma, Erasmus School of Law, Rotterdam, the Netherlands and Institute of Law and Economics, University of Hamburg, Germany (European Doctorate in Law and Economics Programme).

Niels Philipsen, Maastricht University, School of Law, Maastricht, the Netherlands.

Shouji Sun, University of International Business and Economics, Beijing, China.

Constantijn van Aartsen, Maastricht University, School of Law, Maastricht, the Netherlands.

Federico Wesselhoefft, Institute of Law and Economics, University of Hamburg, Germany (European Doctorate in Law and Economics Programme).

Tao Xi, Center for Law and Economics at the China University of Political Science and Law, Beijing, China.

Guangdong Xu, Center for Law and Economics at the China University of Political Science and Law, Beijing, China.

Tianshu Zhou, Center for Law and Economics at the China University of Political Science and Law, Beijing, China.

Acknowledgements

As editors, we are grateful to the many people who made this book and the preceding seminar possible. We are especially grateful to all the contributors for their willingness to participate in this highly interesting and challenging project, and for meeting the strict deadlines that we imposed upon them.

We are especially grateful to the organizers of the seminar on 'Law and Finance: The Role of Law and Regulations in Sustaining Financial Markets'. Our thanks in this respect go to Professor Tao Xi, Director of RCLE, for his continuous support, and to Ms Liang and Ms Wang for their efficient practical support in organizing the seminar. We also owe thanks to the Ministry of Education of the People's Republic of China (PRC) for financially supporting the CUPL Chair of Michael Faure as *Haiwaimingshi* (Distinguished Foreign Professor), as it is within this framework that the seminar took place, and that this volume was consequently assembled. We equally owe thanks to the administrative centre of METRO, and to the METRO student fellows Christopher Mondschein and David Rüetschi for their excellent work on the review and proofreading of all chapters. Finally, we are grateful to our publisher Routledge for their kind support in the publication of this book.

Abbreviations

ABC	Agricultural Bank of China
ABCP	asset-backed commercial paper
ABS	asset-backed security
ADF	augmented Dickey-Fuller
AIC	Akaike information criterion
AIG	American International Group
AML	Anti-Monopoly Law (China)
BAT	best available technology
BEPG	broad economic policy guidelines
BOC	Bank of China
BOT	build-operate-transfer
BP	British Petroleum
BREF	best available techniques reference document
CAFE	Clean Air for Europe (Programme)
CBA	cost-benefit analysis
CBRC	China Banking Regulation Commission
CCB	China Construction Bank
CDO	collateralized debt obligation
CEO	chief executive officer
CIRC	China Insurance Regulation Commission
CJEU	Court of Justice of the European Union
CNY	Chinese Yuan
COREPER	Committee of Permanent Representatives
CPI	consumer price index
CRED	Centre of Research on the Epidemiology of Disasters
CRESTA	catastrophe risk evaluating and standardizing target accumulations
CSC	China Scholarship Council
CSR	corporate social responsibility
CSRC	China Securities Regulatory Commission
DOJ	Department of Justice
EC	European Commission
ECB	European Central Bank

ECHR	European Convention for the Protection of Human Rights and Fundamental Freedoms
ECJ	European Court of Justice
Ecofin	Economic and Financial Affairs Council
EDP	excessive deficit procedure
EEA	European Economic Area
EFSF	European Financial Stability Facility
EFSM	European Financial Stability Mechanism
EMU	European Monetary Union
EPA	Environmental Protection Agency
EPCM	engineering-procurement-construction-management
E-PRTR	European Pollutant Release and Transfer Register
ESFS	European System of Financial Supervisors
ESM	European Stability Mechanism
ESRB	European Systemic Risk Board
ETS	Emissions Trading System
EU	European Union
EUA	EU Allowances
FCA	Financial Conduct Authority
FDIC	Federal Deposit Insurance Corporation
FEMA	Federal Emergency Management Agency
FIAP	International Federation of Pension Funds Administrators
FSB	Financial Stability Board
FSDI	financial sector development indicators
FSF	Financial Stability Forum
FSOC	Financial Stability Oversight Council
GDP	Gross Domestic Product
GFI	Global Financial Integrity
GLS	generalized least squares
GNP	Gross National Product
GSE	government-sponsored enterprise
ICBC	Industrial and Commercial Bank of China
ICN	International Competition Network
IMF	International Monetary Fund
IPO	initial public offering
IRF	impulse response function
JCCE	Jilin Corn Centre Exchange
LDP	legal disciplinary partnership
LLP	limited liability partnership
LPFC	limited-purpose finance company
MBI	market-based instrument
MBS	mortgage-backed securities
MDP	multi-disciplinary partnership
MMMF	money market mutual fund
MTO	medium-term budgetary objective

NASDAQ	National Association of Securities Dealers Automated Quotations
NBFI	non-bank financial institution
NBS	National Bureau of Statistics (China)
NDRC	National Development and Reform Commission
NFIP	National Flood Insurance Program (US)
NGO	non-governmental organization
NPL	non-performing loan
NPV	net present value
NRP	National Reform Programme
NYSE	New York Stock Exchange
OECD	Organisation for Economic Co-operation and Development
OFIs	other financial intermediaries
OLS	ordinary least squares
OTC	over the counter
PAYG	pay as you go
PBOC	People's Bank of China
PC	private credit
PCBC	People's Construction Bank of China
PES	payment for environmental services
PFI	private finance initiative
PFC	project finance contract
PICC	People's Insurance Company of China
PRA	Prudential Regulatory Authority
PWT	Penn World Table
QE	quantitative easing
QMV	qualified majority voting
R&D	research and development
REIT	real estate investment trust
RMB	Renminbi
RQMV	reverse qualified majority voting
SAIC	State Administration of Industry and Commerce
SCAV	Standing Committee on the Assessment of Vulnerabilities
SD	Sustainable Development
SEC	Securities and Exchange Commission (US)
SEK	Swedish Krona
SGP	Stability and Growth Pact
SHSE	Shanghai Stock Exchange
SIV	structured investment vehicle
SMC	stock market capitalization
SME	small- and medium-sized enterprise
SMP	securities market programme
SOB	State-owned bank
SOE	State-owned enterprise
SPV	special purpose vehicle

SZSE	Shenzhen Stock Exchange
TEU	Treaty on European Union (Maastricht Treaty) 1993
TFEU	Treaty on the Functioning of the European Union
TFP	total factor productivity
TSCG	Treaty on Stability, Coordination, and Governance in the EMU ('Fiscal Compact') 2012
UDIV	urban development investment vehicle
UK	United Kingdom
UN	United Nations
UNCTAD	United Nations Conference on Trade and Development
UNFCCC	United Nations Framework Convention on Climate Change
USA / US	United States of America / United States
VAR	vector autoregression
VD	variance decomposition model
WBCSD	World Business Council for Sustainable Development
WBWDI	World Bank's World Development Indicators
WHO	World Health Organization
WTO	World Trade Organization

1 Introduction

Niels Philipsen and Guangdong Xu

1.1 Reasons for this book

The goal of this book is to explore the role of law and regulation in sustaining financial markets in both developed and developing countries, particularly the European Union (EU), the United States (US), and China, from a law and economics perspective. The financial system is praised as "the brain of the economy" (Mishkin 2006: 25). In the absence of a financial system, it is difficult or even impossible to transfer idle funds to more efficient uses; new ideas, innovative products, and productive investments will therefore have to be abandoned, and the society will, in turn, be trapped in the status quo.

The development of a financial system requires certain mechanisms, in particular a well-designed and effectively operating regulatory regime to address certain problems that may cripple the operation of financial markets, such as serious market failures, high transaction costs, and systematic risks. Without these mechanisms, financial markets will inevitably decline and shrink. The connections between financial markets and their legal and regulatory underpinnings therefore constitute a theoretically attractive and practically important topic – a topic that will be systematically examined in this book from a law and economics perspective.

Law and economics – or economic analysis of law – has been regarded as "one of the most important and productive innovations in legal scholarship of the twentieth century" (Ulen 1996). By applying rational choice theory and a behavioral approach to legal and regulatory issues, law and economics scholars have successfully revealed the economic and social consequences of different legal and regulatory institutions, explained the logic behind legal change and regulatory reform, and provided feasible policy and institutional suggestions for improving legal and regulatory frameworks. We believe that the law and economics approach is an effective tool for studying the law and finance nexus, and this belief will be tested in this book.

This book will contribute to the law and finance literature by studying certain conventional issues, such as the relationship between finance and economic growth, the effects of regulatory quality on financial development, and so forth, from new perspectives and/or with new evidence, data, and cases. This book will further explore some novel topics, such as project finance contracts, insurance and climate change, the shadow banking system, and others, that have been overlooked to some extent in the existing literature.

The conclusions reached in this book are meaningful not only for the EU and the US, which have suffered considerably from the financial crisis of 2008, but also for China, which is struggling to build a sound institutional infrastructure to govern its increasingly complicated financial system. The experiences with financial development in these countries, whether satisfying or frustrating, are consistent with the central argument of this book, i.e., law matters for the operation of (financial) markets, which, in turn, significantly influences the performance of firms, industries, and economies.

1.2   History and origins of this book

This book is the second volume in a series of books that originate from a long-standing cooperation between various Chinese and European institutions. The editors have worked together for a long time through collaboration between, on the one hand, the Research Center for Law and Economics (RCLE) of the China University of Political Science and Law (CUPL), to which Guangdong Xu is connected, and, on the other hand, the Maastricht European Institute for Transnational Legal Research (METRO), where Niels Philipsen is Vice-Director. Guangdong Xu is recently obtained a doctoral degree in law at the Erasmus School of Law under the supervision of Professor Michael Faure, Director of METRO (and *Haiwaimingshi* (Distinguished Foreign Professor) at CUPL). Niels Philipsen is involved in teaching activities at the China-EU School of Law (CESL) at CUPL and regularly gives guest lectures at CUPL in the field of law and economics.

It is within the framework of this collaboration that a first joint seminar entitled "Using Economics to Improve Regulation" was organized in May 2012 in Beijing. The papers that were presented at this seminar were later compiled into a book titled *Economics and Regulation in China*, which was published by Routledge in 2013 (Faure and Xu 2013). A follow-up seminar entitled "Law and Finance: The Role of Law and Regulations in Sustaining Financial Markets" was organized on 13 May 2013, in Beijing. The contributions to this book comprise a selection of the papers that were presented at the second seminar. The papers were subsequently rewritten and intensively edited before they were included in this volume.

Compared with Faure and Xu (2013), which focuses on how economic tools can be used to improve the quality of regulation in general, the current volume focuses almost exclusively on a specific type of regulation, i.e., financial regulation, and therefore addresses questions related to the economic consequences of different types of financial regulation, the enforcement strategies of regulatory authorities, and so forth.

1.3 Methodology

1.3.1 Multidisciplinary and interdisciplinary approach

In addition to law and economics, which will be relied upon in the current book as the main tool for studying the law and finance nexus, other disciplines, such as financial economics, political science, and sociology, will also be applied. Given that law and finance are embedded in highly sophisticated institutional environments in which political, economic, and social factors influence, complement, and strengthen one another, a monodisciplinary approach may fail to provide relevant answers. Therefore, a multidisciplinary and interdisciplinary approach is desirable.

1.3.2 Positive analysis and policy recommendations

Most of the studies in this volume can be classified as positive analyses, in the sense that these studies attempt to explain legal rules and outcomes as they are, rather than to evaluate them on the basis of subjective criteria or to provide some institutional proposals to improve them. With no intention of underestimating the importance of normative analysis, this book prefers factual issues that are related to positive analysis to the value judgments that are associated with normative analysis, which inevitably generates controversy owing to its subjectivity. Furthermore, convincing positive analysis studies may contribute to clarifying existing normative issues and hence make it more likely that a consensus will be reached. Nevertheless, some contributions go beyond a mere positive analysis and provide some carefully defined policy recommendations, e.g. indicating how particular legal rules may be better able to stimulate the functioning of the market mechanism.

1.3.3 Comparative perspective

This book not only discusses general theory on financial regulation but also – and perhaps more importantly – compares the regulatory philosophies and practices of the EU, the US, and China. This comparative approach will provide opportunities for mutual learning and understanding. The formation, operation, and evolution of financial regulation in both the EU and the US may be used as a reference source for policymakers in China as they design and implement their own regulatory framework. Conversely, the lessons that the Chinese have learnt from their financial reform and development may enrich the understanding of their counterparts in the EU and US regarding the connection among law, finance, and economic growth. In brief, a comparative approach may help us to understand the diversified nature of the law and finance nexus worldwide, and help us to avoid succumbing to the myth of 'one-size-fits-all'.

1.4 Structure of this book

This book is divided into four Parts. Part I addresses the connection between law, financial development, and economic growth. Chapter 2 by Nicolas de Sadeleer describes the architecture of the new economic governance in the EU as a response to the financial crisis of 2008 and explains its institutional underpinnings. Chapter 3 by Shouji Sun and Jiye Hu reveals the impact of the pension system on financial development (particularly stock market development) and therefore makes an important contribution to the debate regarding the so-called 'legal origin' hypothesis. Chapter 4 by Guangdong Xu and Binwei Gui discusses the logic behind the coexistence of a repressed financial system and a fast-growing economy in China, and reveals the Janus-faced role played by financial repression in China's economic growth. Chapter 5 by Tao Xi and Jianwei Chen offers a theoretical framework to analyze the main endogenous factors that influence the money supply in China and subsequently proposes some policy suggestions for reforming China's monetary policy.

Part II deals with the role of financial regulation, which can be used to correct market failures, such as negative externalities, information inequalities, and monopolies. Chapter 6 by Niels Philipsen discusses recent developments in the regulation of auditors, in the light of recent accounting and corporate scandals and the current lack of competition in the market for statutory audits. Chapter 7 by Tianshu Zhou evaluates the enforcement strategies (public versus private) of controlling public companies' misrepresentation in China's stock markets and claims that public and private enforcement mechanisms serve different (and perhaps complementary) functions in addressing agency problems. Chapter 8 by Wenjing Li describes the development of the shadow banking system in China and analyzes the consequent challenges faced by China's regulatory authorities in attempting to regulate and supervise the shadow banking system.

Part III focuses on the design, functioning, and performance of different (financial) instruments. Chapter 9 by Michael Faure and Jingyuan Ma investigates whether criminalization can be used as an effective instrument to improve the enforcement of antitrust law in China and ultimately doubts the feasibility of criminalizing antitrust violations in China. Chapter 10 by Qihao He studies the role of insurance in covering catastrophic disasters in China and proposes that insurance, particularly mandatory multi-year insurance, should be considered as a possible solution to the problem of catastrophe risk distribution. Chapter 11 by Federico Wesselhoefft explores the essential components of project finance contracts and argues that certain features of project finance contracts keep them free of the well-known agency conflicts in corporate settings.

Part IV examines the interesting and important topic of corporate social responsibility (CSR). Chapter 12 by Lars Hansson and Yanqiang Ding shows that compared with environmental regulation, market-based instruments, such as green taxes, may be more efficient and more effective tools for encouraging enterprises to take environmental responsibility for their actions. Chapter 13 by Constantijn van Aartsen argues that the current legal framework for CSR has failed to produce satisfactory economic and social outcomes because free markets, on which current CSR is based, do not provide a feasible basis for a sustainable framework for CSR.

Part V contains in Chapter 14 a set of comparative and concluding remarks by the Editors, in cooperation with Michael Faure.

1.5 Contributors

The contributors to this book are from various universities in China, Europe, and the US. Many of the Chinese scholars, including Jianwei Chen, Binwei Gui, Jiye Hu, Wenjing Li, Tianshu Zhou, Tao Xi, and Guangdong Xu, are connected to the RCLE of CUPL. Shouji Sun is associated with the University of International Business and Economics (UIBE). Yanqiang Ding is associated with Shandong University. Qihao He is associated with the University of Connecticut, USA. He is one of the Chinese contributors who do not currently reside in China. This is also the case for Jingyuan Ma (who is connected to the Erasmus School of Law in the Netherlands and the University of Hamburg in Germany via the European Doctorate in Law and Economics programme).

Constantijn van Aartsen is associated with Maastricht University (the Netherlands). Michael Faure and Niels Philipsen are connected to METRO (at Maastricht University, the Netherlands). Lars Hansson is associated with Lund University (Sweden). Nicolas de Sadeleer is associated with Saint-Louis University (Brussels, Belgium). Federico Wesselhoefft is associated with the University of Hamburg (Germany) via the European Doctorate in Law and Economics programme.

References

Faure, M. and Xu, G. (eds) (2013) *Economics and Regulation in China*, London and New York: Routledge.

Mishkin, F. S. (2006) *The Next Great Globalization: How Disadvantaged Nations Can Harness Their Financial Systems to Get Rich*, Princeton, NJ: Princeton University Press.

Ulen, T. S. (1996) 'The Comparative Law and Economics of Federalism', *Cardozo Law Bulletin*. Available online at: http://www.jus.unitn.it/cardozo/review/Comparative/Ulen-1996/ulen1.htm (accessed 6 May 2014).

Part I
Law, financial development and economic growth

2 The new architecture of European economic governance

Nicolas de Sadeleer

2.1 Introduction

Due to the accumulation of structural deficits by certain EU Member States, bail-outs of debt-ridden banks and fiscal stimulus plans intended to relaunch growth, budget deficits started rapidly expanding after 2009. Accordingly, the 2008 financial crisis was followed by a substantial fiscal crisis that compromised the financial stability of the Eurozone as a whole.

Among the different reasons for the crisis that is undermining the European construction, many authors have been highlighting the asymmetry of the Economic and Monetary Union (EMU). On the one hand, there is a single currency falling under an exclusive competence with its own independent central bank (the European Central Bank (ECB)), which has permitted the monetary Europe to speak with one single voice, whilst on the other hand, there is the prevailing disorder where national economic policies are not integrated but only set within limits.[1] As far as the latter is concerned, as it is known the Member States retain their sovereignty subject to compliance with a certain number of headline principles, such as sound public finances and an 'open market economy with free competition' (Treaty on the Functioning of the European Union Article 119(1)). The ECB has therefore been required to determine monetary policy without being able to count on the support of a genuine European economic government. This situation has persisted since the German authorities for many years considered that the establishment of a European economic government would end up leaving a sword of Damocles hanging over the independence of the ECB (Jabko 2011: 12). Nevertheless, the framers of the Maastricht Treaty took greater care to prevent a feeling of impunity from developing within the Member States that did not keep public expenditure under control, which would have had the effect of subjecting monetary policy to uncontrolled budgetary policies. Against this backdrop, the TFEU contains a no bail-out clause (Article 125) and a prohibition on the ECB and the central banks from granting overdraft facilities or any other type of credit facility (Article 123).

Although the EMU has been able to avoid any fundamental change during the various reviews of the fundamental treaties (Amsterdam, Nice, Lisbon), the crisis has brought to light the fragile and asymmetrical nature of this union.

The lack of any effective coordination of economic policies and the weak nature of budgetary discipline has thus drawn the EMU into a vicious circle. Initially, it was only possible to prevent its fall thanks to the implementation by the ECB of "non-conventional measures to support the banking sector and the sovereign debt market" (Allemand and Martucci 2012: 21).

Whilst this new crisis laid bare the weaknesses within economic integration, it has not, however, sounded the death knell for political union, which has to some extent been reinforced.

In the wake of the financial crisis, the EU has implemented various mechanisms in incremental stages in order to stop the financial and the budgetary crisis from spreading. In an attempt to remedy inadequacies within the organisation of the prudential oversight system for financial establishments which the 2008 crisis had laid bare, it first adopted a European System of Financial Supervisors (ESFS) comprised of three sector authorities (banks, insurance and pension companies, and markets and financial services) as well as a European Systemic Risk Board (ESRB) (Moloney 2010: 1317–83; Martucci *et al.* 2011: 4–9; Van der Mensbrugghe 2011: 165–83; Louis 2012a). Since this chapter is focused on macroeconomic and fiscal control, the oversight of financial establishments will not be addressed, even though we are all aware of the role that the ESFS is required to play within the new control structure within the system of economic governance.[2]

From 2011 onwards, a range of new mechanisms have risen out of the depths of the European Union: the Euro Plus Pact, the European Semester, the 'six-pack', the 'two-pack', the Treaty on Stability, Coordination and Governance (Fiscal Compact) and several financial capacities (the European Financial Stabilization Mechanism (EFSM), the European Stability Mechanism (ESM) and the European Financial Stability Facility (EFSF)). All in all, these mechanisms are intended to bring significant changes to the economic governance of the EU.

The discussion within this chapter will be structured in the following manner. The first part of the chapter summarises the succession of mechanisms that have made economic governance possible and discusses their contribution to the reinforcement of fiscal discipline. There is indeed a question as to whether this reform masks a deep-seated crisis of identity within the EU institutions that are simply at a loss what to do, or should one see here a real desire to reinforce the EMU, which recently fell victim to a congenital defect? The second part shows how this flurry of treaties and secondary acts is impinging on the principle of institutional balance (Jacqué 2004: 383).

2.2   The architecture of the new economic governance

2.2.1   *Introductory comments*

The financial crises and the turmoil in sovereign debt markets have clearly highlighted challenges in the EU's economic governance. Taking account of the unprecedented scope of this crisis, the European Council of 25–26 March 2010 established a Task Force on Economic Governance in the EU. The Task Force was called on to devise proposals for better budgetary discipline in improving the Stability and Growth Pact (SGP), and an improved crisis resolution framework.[3] The recommendations addressed the high economic interdependence of the euro area, while preserving national sovereignty on fiscal and economic policies.

At the first stage, taking account of the recommendations made by the Task Force as well of the unprecedented scale of this crisis, the European Parliament and the Council of the European Union adopted six legislative measures (five Regulations and a Directive (the 'six-pack')) during the Autumn of 2011 intended to remedy deficiencies in the SGP, in particular by reinforcing and expanding the range of preventive and corrective mechanisms. Four acts deal with fiscal issues and two aim at detecting and addressing emerging macroeconomic imbalances with the EU and the Eurozone.

At the second stage, with a view to reinforcing the 'six-pack', on 9 December 2011 the heads of State and government meeting within the European Council, with the exception of the British Prime Minister and later the Czech authorities, decided to sign an intergovernmental agreement on 1 March 2012 on Stability, Coordination and Governance in the EMU (Treaty on Stability, Coordination, and Governance (TSCG) or Fiscal Compact).

At the third stage, treaties concluded between the Eurozone countries have been setting up financial facilities (EFSF and ESM).

At the fourth stage, given that the edifice was far from being complete, the European Parliament and the Council adopted on 21 May 2013 two additional Regulations, known as the 'two-pack', with a view to reinforcing the 'six-pack'.

All in all, the 'six-pack', the 'two-pack', as well as the Fiscal Compact, are intended to reinforce fiscal and macroeconomic discipline – whereas the ESM, replacing the EFSF, provides for a permanent crisis resolution framework.

In order to highlight more clearly the impetus provided by the Task Force established by the European Council of 25–26 March 2010, the left-hand column in Table 2.1 lists its propositions, whilst the right-hand column identifies each of the regulatory results achieved.

The first section will be dedicated to crisis management mechanisms (2.2.2). The second section will provide an indepth analysis of the economic and employment coordination (2.2.3). The third section will deal with the frameworks of fiscal and macroeconomic surveillance (2.2.4). Finally, in the fourth section there will be a discussion of the added value of the Fiscal Compact (2.2.5).

2.2.2 First approach: improved and permanent crisis management mechanisms

2.2.2.1 EFSM and EFSF

In the wake of the financial crisis, in the course of 2010 financial rescue mechanisms were activated with the aim of rescuing highly indebted

Table 2.1 EU approaches to tackle the 2008 financial crisis

2010 Task Force on Economic Governance Proposals	*Implementation*
Enhancing fiscal discipline	Euro Plus Pact 'six-pack' 'two-pack' Fiscal Compact
Broadening multilateral surveillance	Regulations 1174 and 1176/2011 on macroeconomic surveillance and Directive 2011/85
Policy coordination	European Semester
Crisis management	EFSF EFSM ESM
Reinforcement of economic governance	Euro Plus Pact 'six-pack' Fiscal Compact

Euro-area Member States. In this connection, bilateral agreements were concluded between the Eurozone States. The financial assistance granted to Greece, for instance, was supervised by the Commission, the ECB and the International Monetary Fund (IMF).

Additionally, in 2010 the Council adopted a Regulation establishing the EFSM that provided financial assistance to EU Member States in financial difficulties (Council Regulation No. 407/2010 of 11 May 2010 that was adopted on the basis of Article 122(2) TFEU). Under EFSM, the Commission was allowed to borrow up to a total of EUR60 billion in financial markets on behalf of the EU under an implicit EU budget guarantee. The Commission was then lending the proceeds to the beneficiary Member State.

However, the financial capacity of the EFSM was not enough to be credible on the grounds that it could not be increased for the small size of the EU budget (De Streel 2013: 349–51). Due to the fact that Spain, Portugal, Italy and Ireland were facing budgetary difficulties, a more ambitious approach was needed. It was therefore necessary to do more. However, any far-reaching change to the basic rules of the EMU with a view to incorporating a permanent crisis management mechanism is inconceivable, as it would without doubt be at odds with the principle of the division of competences (Article 5(1) of the EU Treaty). The EU has powers of coordination and not harmonisation in relation to the economy. The need to uphold the division of competences thus obliges the Members States to act on the margins of EU action and, in the absence of soft law, to complete it with the use of satellite treaties. Thus, the adoption of satellite treaties is justified in the area of crisis management. This initially involved the adoption of the EFSF, which was subsequently replaced by the ESM. This calls for a closer analysis.

The 17 Member States of the Eurozone set up a common debt fund on 9 May 2010 in the form of a limited company incorporated in Luxembourg (EFSF) with a lending capacity of EUR440 billion.[4] The German Constitutional Court delivered an ambivalent verdict as to the compatibility of the EFSF with the budgetary rights of the German parliament that is embedded in the so-called eternity clause of Article 79(3) of the Basic Law (Calliess 2012: 402–15).[5]

One further point may be of relevance. The EFSM and the EFSF could only be activated after a request for financial assistance has been made by the concerned Member State and a macroeconomic adjustment programme, incorporating strict conditionality, has been agreed with the European Commission (EC), in liaison with the ECB. By way of illustration, the EC has been empowered to contract borrowings on behalf of the EU for the purpose of funding loans made under the EFSM (Article 2 of Council Regulation 407/2010) contributing to the overall loan packages for Ireland and Portugal, which were co-funded by the EU, the EFSF and the IMF, each acting independently but in a coordinated way.[6] As discussed below, strict conditionality is clearly of central importance.

What is more, in order to assuage the markets, the ECB adopted the securities market programme (SMP) allowing the purchase of government bonds on the secondary market with a ceiling of EUR209 billion.[7]

2.2.2.2   ESM Treaty

The Greek crisis highlighted that financial distress in one Member State can rapidly threaten macro-financial stability of the EU as a whole. Accordingly, the Task Force considered the need to establish a credible crisis resolution mechanism capable of avoiding contagion.[8]

That recommendation has been taken over by the Eurozone States. Since January 2013, the ESM, a new inter-governmental agreement concluded by the 18 Member States of the Eurozone, is replacing both the EFSM and the EFSF.[9] The ESM aims at permanently providing financial assistance to the Member States of the Eurozone. In contrast to the other funds, the ESM is a permanent international financial institution with a lending capacity of EUR500 billion. It has full legal personality. The ESM's purpose is to mobilise funding and provide stability support under strict conditionality, appropriate to the financial assistance instrument chosen, to the benefit of ESM Members which are experiencing, or are threatened by, severe financial problems. That support may be granted only if indispensable to safeguard the financial stability of the Euro area as a whole and of its Member States.

In line with the previous crisis management frameworks, the granting of any required financial assistance under the ESM is subject to strict conditionality. By the same token, the new Article 136(3) TFEU recalls that obligation. The strict conditionality to which any support must be subject may take the form, notably, of a macroeconomic adjustment programme or the obligation continuously to respect pre-established eligibility conditions.

Given that the founding treaties did not provide for any legal basis allowing permanent financial assistance mechanisms, the intergovernmental fund had to be based on a treaty between the Eurozone countries. Against this background, Germany requested the revision of Article 136 TFEU (Louis 2012a: 284–319) in order to circumvent the no bail-out rule enshrined in Article 125 TFEU (Louis 2010: 971–86).

The European Council took the view that the simplified revision procedure provided for under Article 48(6) TFEU was sufficient to achieve such a revision of Article 136 TFEU. On 25 March 2011, the European Council adopted Decision 2011/199/EU,[10] which amends Article 136 TFEU with regard to a stability mechanism for Member States whose currency is the euro. The third paragraph added to Article 136 TFEU reads as follows: 'The Member States whose currency is the euro may establish a stability mechanism to be activated if indispensable to safeguard the stability of the euro area as a whole. The granting of any required financial assistance under the mechanism will be made subject to strict conditionality'.

The ESM Treaty has been challenged before the German Constitutional Court[11] and before the Irish Supreme Court. Regarding the second challenge, it must be noted that the Irish Supreme Court has decided to refer to the Court of Justice pursuant to Article 267 TFEU the question of the validity of the European Council Decision and the question of whether Ireland, by entering into and ratifying the ESM Treaty, would undertake obligations incompatible with the Union Treaties. The full Court of Justice ruled on the validity of the European Council Decision on 27 November 2012. Given that a complete discussion on this case is beyond the scope of this chapter, a bare outline of this judgment will be given.

Given that the European Council used the possibility of amending the TFEU by a simplified revision procedure, the Court of Justice of the European Union (CJEU) had to verify whether the conditions were fulfilled and in particular whether the EMS did not increase the competences conferred on the EU in the Treaties. Among these conditions, it must be noted that the modifications are limited to the provisions related to internal policies and the actions of the EU (TFEU, third section) and that they cannot increase the competences of the Union.

First, the Court took the view that the challenged amendment did not encroach on the exclusive competence held by the EU in the area of monetary policy for the Member States whose currency is the euro. Given that the primary objective of the EU's monetary policy is maintaining price stability (§ 54 and 94), the Court stressed that ESM pursues an objective which is clearly distinct, namely to safeguard the stability of the Eurozone as a whole. The Court justified its interpretation on the grounds that an economic policy measure cannot be treated as equivalent to a monetary policy measure for the sole reason that it may have indirect effects on the stability of the euro (§ 56 and 96) (Craig 2013: 3; Louis 2013).

Second, the claimant argued that the challenged amendment did affect the competences held by the EU in the area of the coordination of national economic policies. In his view, the EU has already pre-empted the area. The CJEU rejected this second contention on the basis that the EU Treaties do not confer any power on the EU to set up such a stability mechanism. As a result, the area was not pre-empted. Accordingly, the Court upheld Decision 2011/199.

Further, in response to the question of whether certain provisions of the Treaty on European Union (TEU) and TFEU and the general principle of effective judicial protection preclude the conclusion between the Member States whose currency is the euro of an agreement, such as the ESM Treaty, the Court held that the founding treaties and the general principle do not preclude the conclusion and ratification of the ESM Treaty.

One of the claimant's key contentions was the violation by the Eurozone countries of the 'no bail-out' clause enshrined in Article 125 TFEU. That clause provides that neither the EU nor a Member State are to be liable for the commitments of another Member State, or assume those commitments. The *raison d'être* of this clause is to secure that indebted Member States 'are sanctioned via the financial market by higher interest rates on their government bond' (Calliess 2012: 408). As a result, the clause enhances financial responsibility.

Though the interpretation of the 'no bail-out' clause has been dogged by controversy, the CJEU asserted that such a clause is not intended to prohibit either the EU or the Member States from granting any form of financial assistance to another Member State (§ 130 and 131). Admittedly, the Court held that the aim of Article 125 TFEU is to ensure that the Member States follow a sound budgetary policy by ensuring that they remain subject to the logic of the market when they enter into debt (§ 135). Accordingly, the clause does not prohibit the granting of financial assistance by one or more Member States to a Member State that remains liable for its commitments to its creditors provided that the conditions attached to such assistance are such as to prompt that Member State to implement a sound budgetary policy (§ 137, 143 and 146). In effect, the budgetary responsibility is enhanced by the strict conditionality requirements imposed by the fund which have to be fulfilled before successive tranches of funding can be released. Admittedly, neither the ESM nor the Member States who participate in it are liable for the commitments of a Member State which receives stability support and do not assume liability within the meaning of the 'no bail-out' clause. Account must also be taken of the fact that the CJEU ruled that the revision of Article 136 TFEU was not a necessary condition for the validity of the Treaty on the ESM with regard to EU law (§ 120).

2.2.3   Second approach: improved economic and employment policies coordination

As stressed in the introduction, the principal weakness of the EMU is that it is not based on a pillar but rather on an economic crutch, whilst monetary competence is based on solid foundations (Article 3(1)(c) TFEU). Initially, coordination prevailed over the harmonisation of economic rules. Subsequently, their coordination did not necessarily enable the different economies to converge, as had been conceived by the founders of the EMU. By contrast, the macroeconomic differences accentuated as the crisis progressed. Over the course of these last years, several mechanisms have been adopted with a view to remedying the weaknesses within the coordination of economic policies. We are shedding light on the EU 2020 Lisbon Strategy (2.3.1), the Euro Plus Pact (2.3.2), the Compact for Growth and Jobs (2.3.3) and the Fiscal Compact of 1 March 2012 (2.3.4). In contrast to budgetary and macroeconomic frameworks that are analysed in the third section, these texts only generate soft law.

2.2.3.1   *The Europe 2020 Strategy*

By replacing the Lisbon Strategy whilst retaining the open coordination method, the 2020 Strategy adopted by the European Council in 2010 is principally aimed at enhancing competitiveness. Its success is conditional upon the means implemented by the Member States. The Strategy has three priorities:

- intelligent growth
- based on knowledge and innovation
- which is sustainable and inclusive (high employment rates and economic, social, and territorial cohesion).

National reform programmes (NRP) must be presented at the same time as stability and convergence programmes within the context of the European Semester, which will be discussed below. In contrast to convergence and stability programmes which pursue the sustainability of public finances, the NRP implement major planks of economic and social policy.

2.2.3.2   *The Euro Plus Pact*

At their meeting on 11 March 2011, the heads of State and government from the Eurozone as well as six other Member States which do not use the euro as their currency adopted the idea initially mooted by Germany of a competitiveness pact. Following a non-binding inter-governmental approach aimed at reinforcing the treaty mechanisms on the fight against excessive deficits, the Euro Plus Pact is based on four leading rules:

- the reinforcement of economic governance
- the improvement of competitiveness and convergence of States' levels of competitiveness
- the integrity of the single market
- the involvement of the Member States.

It may be recalled in particular that the Euro Plus Pact invites the parties and national Parliaments to establish the 'budgetary golden rule' that is already written into certain national constitutions (Louis 2012b[12]) which will now be imposed on the parties to the Fiscal Compact.

Moreover, this Pact applies to matters that in some cases are amenable to harmonisation under EU law (e.g. tax harmonisation pursuant to Article 113 TFEU), whilst in other cases fall under national jurisdiction (agreements between social partners on wage moderation). Control over the commitments made by the States' parties to the Pact is assured by their peers. Each year, the State parties will report on the projects adopted in order to honour their commitments. Their implementation must be incorporated into the NRP provided for under the EU 2020 Strategy, as well as into stability and convergence programmes provided for under the SGP. The Commission is also required to play a role in assessing compliance with these commitments.

2.2.3.3   *Compact for Growth and Jobs*

The Compact for Growth and Jobs that was agreed at the European Council in June 2012 aims at relaunching growth, investment and employment. Under this Compact, EU Member States are committed to tackling unemployment and addressing the social consequences of the crisis effectively. The promotion of employment is encouraged by the Fiscal Compact (Article 9). Another aim of the Compact is faster progress towards the goals set out in the EU 2020 Strategy. This Compact is accounted for under secondary law: the priorities of economic partnership programmes seeking to ensure the correction of excessive deficits must be consistent with this strategy (Article 9(1) of Regulation (EC) No. 473/2013).

2.2.3.4   *Coordination of economic policies under the Fiscal Compact Treaty*

As regards the coordination of economic policies, Articles 9 to 11 of the Fiscal Compact specify in greater detail the obligations provided for under Articles 120 and 121 TFEU on economic policy. These provisions are more statements of good intentions rather than new obligations. Since the role of these new obligations is to provide an impetus, they do not impose new tasks on the EU institutions (10th Recital Treaty on Stability, Coordination, and Governance (TSCG) in the EMU ('Fiscal Compact')) (Pernice 2012: 18), as the extension of tasks is reserved exclusively to the Court of Justice (Article 273 TFEU).

In its final report, the Future of Europe Group is proposing to make 'economic policy coordination between Member States more binding in selected areas which are key for sustainable economic growth and employment and essential for the stability of the Eurozone'. Such coordination should 'help overcome existing imbalances and strengthen overall competitiveness'.

2.2.4   Third approach: reinforcement of the preventive and corrective dimensions of the SGP

2.2.4.1   Introductory remarks

2.2.4.1.1   THE SGP PREVENTIVE AND CORRECTIVE DIMENSIONS

Mindful of the fragility of this construction and of the risk that the Member States will relax their budgetary discipline due to the protective function of the Euro, in 1997 the European Council and the Council of the European Union adopted an alternative form of European governance: the SGP. Concluded after the Maastricht Treaty once EMU had become a reality, the SGP had the merit of setting out guideline rules within the Euro area. It consists formally of a Resolution of the European Council of 17 June 1997 and two Regulations adopted by the Council on 7 July 1997 (Louis 2009: 108–15).[13]

The SGP is based on two pillars: a preventive approach involving multilateral surveillance and a corrective dimension relating to the sanctions procedure for excessive deficit procedure (EDP). The preventive and corrective limbs should not be regarded in isolation.[14] Indeed, both mechanisms are intended to force Member States to reduce the ratio between their forecast or actual public deficit as a percentage of gross domestic product (GDP) to 3 per cent and to lower their public debt as a proportion of GDP to 60 per cent (Article 126(2) TFEU and Protocol no. 12 on the EDP). The intention of these thresholds is to ensure that, assuming 5 per cent growth, a deficit of 3 per cent will then lead debt to stabilise at 60 per cent (Lefeuvre 2011: 27). In thereby guaranteeing sustainable levels of public debt, compliance with these two thresholds could have led to a harmonisation of fiscal policies without feeling the need, following the spirit of the framers of the SGP, to establish genuine economic governance (Fitoussi 2010: 253).

2.2.4.1.2   THE 2005 REFORM

The Council of the EU reformed the surveillance mechanisms in 2005 (Regulation (EC) No. 1055/2005), in particular by introducing medium-term budgetary objectives (MTOs).[15]

Since 2005 the Member States have been subject to an obligation to achieve their MTOs in a differentiated manner along the adjustment trajectory. As far as Eurozone countries are concerned, MTOs have to be specified within a defined range between 1 per cent GDP and balance or surplus (Article 2 bis (2) of Regulation (EC) no. 1466/97 as amended by Regulation (EC) no. 1055/2005). MTOs pursue three main aims:

* providing a safety margin with respect to the 3 per cent of GDP deficit limit
* ensuring rapid progress towards sustainability
* allowing room for budgetary manoeuvre, in particular taking into account the needs for public investment.[16]

Accordingly, the MTOs are differentiated for individual Member States according to the diversity of economic and budgetary positions and developments, the fiscal risk to the sustainability of public finances and the prospective demographic changes. As a result, the country-specific MTOs may diverge from the SGP requirement of a close-to-balance or in-surplus fiscal position (Articles 2a(2), 3(2) and 7(2) of Regulation (EC) No 1466/97). They are likely to be more stringent where the level of debt and estimated costs of an ageing population are higher.

The MTOs are reviewed every three years (Article 2 (a)(3) of Regulation 1466/97 as amended by Regulation (EU) No 1175/2011). They are set out within a stability programme (for Member States in the Eurozone) or a convergence programme (for Member States outside the Eurozone), which is updated every year. These programmes serve as a basis for multilateral surveillance by the Council, which by virtue of Article 121 TFEU should ward off, at an early stage, the occurrence of EDP and promote the coordination of economic policies. Accordingly, the annual stability or convergence programmes must demonstrate how the Member States are intent on achieving sound fiscal positions in the medium term. In the context of their assessment, the Commission assesses these programmes and the Council gives its opinion on them. Where the Council considers that the MTO should be strengthened, it can invite the Member State concerned to adjust its programme. Pursuant to Article 121 TFEU, a rapid alert system enables the Ecofin Council to address a recommendation to a State in the event of budgetary overrun.

2.2.4.1.3   THE SHORTCOMINGS OF THE SGP

The preventive virtues of the SGP were not able to prevent the growth in public deficits, especially after the 2008 economic downturn. Whereas they should have been close to equilibrium, certain budget deficits continued to grow significantly. The legislation in place was flawed for three reasons.

First, the SGP has not produced the expected effects since the Council enjoyed broad discretionary powers as to compliance by national authorities with the criteria which, following the difficulties encountered by France and Germany in respecting them (Case C-27/04 *Commission* v. *Council* [2004] ECR I-6649), were relaxed in 2005.[17]

Second, the SGP approach focusing exclusively on the debt and deficit criteria can account for the fiscal crises in Ireland and Spain, where public debt, levels as a proportion of GDP lay at around 30 per cent in 2007. In effect, this narrow approach prevented the Commission from detecting problems at an early stage. Indeed, the surveillance mechanisms put in place were not able to detect the rapid increase in debt levels for these two Member States. Compared to the 30 per cent of GDP in 2007, Spain's debt had doubled by 2010. As regards Ireland, whilst the Commission had forecast public sector debt at less than 30 per cent of GDP in 2008, in 2010 it suddenly rose to more than 80 per cent. In retrospect, it is clear that the economic and budgetary crises are interlinked. In fact, price increases, salary indexation, low levels of worker mobility and qualifications, competitiveness losses, over-emphasis on certain economic sectors (the financial sector in the United Kingdom and construction in Spain), bubbles (such as the housing bubble) and the failure to diversify the tax base are all factors fuelling public deficits.

Third, any application of the regime of fines provided for under the sanctions procedure for excess public deficits would have been tantamount to using a sledgehammer to crack a nut; when the nuclear option is available one tends not to use it.

2.2.4.1.4   THE SIX-PACK REFORM

The subprime crisis that resulted from inadequate surveillance of the banking and financial sectors did not immediately call into question the budgetary limits laid down in the SGP. Two dynamics operated in opposition to one another. The Member States that had room for budgetary manoeuvre called for the maintenance of fiscal orthodoxy, whilst those that did not have such room for manoeuvre conversely called for the suspension of compliance with these criteria due to the exceptional economic circumstances with which they were confronted (Allemand and Martucci 2012: 28).

To a certain extent, the basic tenets of budgetary orthodoxy prevailed. In effect, the exceptional circumstances relied on by the Member States running deficits did not prevent the implementation of the EDP under Article 126 TFEU (Allemand and Martucci 2012: 28). Consequently, between April 2009 and July 2010, 22 of the 27 Member States were subject to EDP. Nevertheless, due to the deterioration of the economic situation between 2009 and 2011, the Commission and the Council displayed greater flexibility, in particular by granting extra time in order to correct certain national deficits.[18]

Such circumstances inevitably led the institutions to reinforce the requirement to comply with the criteria laid down in the SGP and, as the case may be, to adopt a more strict approach against Member States that were not able to reduce their budget deficit and public debt at the same time. Accordingly, as will be shown below, budgetary rigour finally carried the day over flexibility.

Thanks to the 2011 'six-pack', which was completed by the 2013 'two-pack', additional rigour was finally imposed under secondary law.

Seeking to reinforce economic governance within the EU and more specifically within the Eurozone, the fiscal discipline has been reinforced significantly by the 'six-pack', which is comprised of five Regulations and one Directive. These six acts, which were adopted by the Parliament during the first reading on 28 September and by the Council on 4 October 2011, entered into force on 16 December 2011. The architecture of the 'six-pack' is somewhat complicated.

Two Regulations (1175/2011 and 1177/2011) contain significant amendments to the preventive and corrective mechanisms of the SGP provided for under Regulations 1466/97 and 1467/97 (subsections 2.4.2 and 2.4.3). A third Regulation (1173/2011) concerning the effective implementation of fiscal surveillance of the Eurozone reinforces the two limbs of the SGP.[19] A Directive (2011/85) harmonises the budgetary frameworks of the Member States with a view to avoiding excessive deficits (subsection 2.4.7). Moreover, two additional Regulations on macroeconomic surveillance (1176/2011 and 1174/2011) are introducing a new mechanism for macroeconomic surveillance entailing an excessive imbalance procedure (subsection 2.4.5).

In addition to strengthening fiscal discipline with the intention of reducing public debt levels, the 'six-pack' will also guarantee enhanced coordination of surveillance and evaluation rules which had proved to be indispensable due to the accumulation of the programming process. Since the programming and assessment of several national programmes by different institutions raises important coordination problems, enhanced coordination has proved to be indispensable, in particular through the 'European Semester' (subsection 2.4.6). All in all, four of these acts are related to fiscal control and macroeconomic convergence.

Finally, in order to add additional teeth to the 'six-pack', the European Parliament and the Council adopted a new regulatory package on 21 May 2013, known as the 'two-pack'. Under the first Regulation, the Member States from the Eurozone have to present their draft budgets to the Commission, which may, if appropriate, issue an opinion.[20] The Commission is entitled to require that the draft budgets be amended if it considers that the terms of the budget exceed the SGP criteria. However, it does not amount to a veto power. The second Regulation seeks to reinforce the surveillance of those Member States which benefit from a financial assistance programme thanks to bilateral loans, the EFSF or the ESM, or which are seriously threatened by financial instability.[21] This Regulation therefore appears to offer a common framework and a gradualist approach to surveillance requirements.

2.2.4.2   Enhancing fiscal discipline through the reinforcement of the preventive arm of the SGP

As stated above, the SGP is focused on a preventive dimension under Regulation 1466/97 based on multilateral surveillance of States from the

Eurozone, which are required to present their MTOs in order to ensure public finance sustainability. Let us turn to the more fundamental questions that arise here: the criteria underpinning the budgetary surveillance framework and the sanctions.

So far, the implementation of the SGP has focused mainly on the *deficit criterion*. However, in the past, certain governments have run up public debts during periods of growth, whilst they should have taken advantage of such periods in order to reduce their debts. In doing so they voluntarily deprived themselves of the ability to adopt stimulus policies during subsequent periods of deep recession. In other words, the debts became so high that it was no longer possible to increase them in order to deal with emergency situations.

Admittedly, there has been a growing awareness of the need to broaden the scope of the multilateral surveillance. In this connection, the Task Force on Economic Governance established by the European Council of 25–26 March 2010 took the view that 'the high indebtedness is a drag on medium- and long-term growth prospects, aggravates the risk of financial instability and reduces the ability to run counter-cyclical fiscal policies when the need arises'.[22]

In placing henceforth the focus on public debt and fiscal sustainability in the budgetary surveillance framework, the 'six-pack' marks a turning point. In effect, the priority will now focus on *debt reduction*, in particular through the allocation to future years of exceptional debt reduction measures.[23] This should make it possible to avoid situations in which measures are not allocated as a priority to reducing the debt, which had occurred in the past. In other words, indebted Member States will have to start putting aside after years of lavish spending.[24]

In addition, the 'six-pack' defines a new 'expenditure benchmark' to assess progress towards the country-specific MTOs. This benchmark places a cap on the annual growth of public expenditure according to a medium-term rate of growth. For Member States that have not yet reached their MTOs, the rate of growth of expenditure should be below this reference rate with a view to ensuring adequate progress. In particular, if that norm is not matched, the Member States are called on to increase government revenues. Conversely, discretionary revenue reductions have to be compensated by reductions in expenditure (Recital 20 of Regulation 1466/97 as amended by Regulation (EU) No 1175/2011).

That being said, as far as the fiscal positions of the Member States are concerned, the MTO can still be watered down. In effect, Member States may disregard it, while providing a safety margin with respect to the 3 per cent of GDP government deficit ratio (Article 2 bis(2) of Regulation 1466/97 as amended by Regulation (EU) 1175/2011).

It must also be noted that the MTOs have to be included in the national medium-term budgetary frameworks in accordance with Chapter IV of Council Directive EU 2011/85 of 8 November 2011 on requirements for budgetary frameworks of the Member States, as will be elaborated on below

(Article 2 bis(4) of Regulation 1466/97 as amended by Regulation (EU) No 1175/2011).

The new regime of sanctions also merits special note. As discussed above (see the discussion in Section 2.4.1.3), the SGP has been suffering from a credibility problem for a long time. Indeed, during the first decade, when the violation of the EDP was chronic, no fines were imposed against the offending Member States. From now on, however, the preventive arm will be reinforced by the adoption of a regime of progressively increasing sanctions starting from an early stage. If a Member State in breach fails to adopt measures following a recommendation by the Council identifying a significant departure of its fiscal position from the country-specific MTO, the Council may require it to lodge an interest-bearing deposit of 0.2 per cent of GDP (Article 4(1) of Regulation (EU) 1173/2011[25]) with it, as a precursor to infringement proceedings, which may be transformed at a later stage (corrective limb) into a non-interest-bearing deposit (Section 3). These sanctions have been put in place in order to reinforce the credibility of the prevention measures (Louis 2012b: 6). Moreover, the reverse qualified majority procedure guarantees henceforth that these sanctions will be applied almost automatically (Article 4(2) of Regulation (EU) No 1173/2011). It follows that the Council's powers are in actual fact extremely limited because the Commission's proposals can only be amended or rejected within a specific time limit by qualified majority. At the outset the European Parliament supported this reform, whereas Germany and France opposed it. The Commission is fully aware of its new prerogatives.

2.2.4.3 *Enhancing fiscal discipline through the reinforcement of the corrective arm of the GDP*

Article 126 TFEU lays down an EDP. Since 1997, this procedure is further specified in Council Regulation (EC) No. 1467/97 on speeding up and clarifying the implementation of the EDP, which is part of the SGP. The EDP is triggered by the deficit exceeding the 3 per cent of GDP threshold. In case the deficit is deemed to exceed this threshold, the Council issues a recommendation to the Member States concerned to correct their excessive deficits and gives a time frame for doing so. Today, 17 out of 28 Member States are still in EDP; Germany, Luxembourg, Finland, Sweden, Bulgaria, Hungary, Romania, Lithuania and Estonia are not subject to an EDP.

The changes brought to the corrective arm of the SGP by the 'six-pack' originated in response to the concern that the EDP has not been effective in curbing debt development. As far as the corrective aspect is concerned, the debt surveillance framework has been strengthened: in addition to the public sector deficit criterion (3 per cent), the debt criterion (60 per cent) will now be applied (Article 2 (1bis) 2nd al. of Regulation 1467/97 as amended by Regulation (EU) 1177/2011).

Table 2.2 Debt reduction obligations
(Belgium) 2013–33

Fiscal year	Ratio debt-GDP (%)
2013	104.0
2014	101.8
2015	99.6
2016	97.4
2017	95.2
2018	93.0
2019	90.8
2020	88.6
2021	86.4
2022	84.2
2023	82.0
2024	79.8
2025	77.6
2026	75.4
2027	73.2
2028	71.0
2029	68.8
2030	66.6
2031	64.4
2032	62.2
2033	60.0

Accordingly, the Member State must reduce by one-twentieth annually (on average over three years) the gap between its debt level and the 60 per cent reference for the debt-to-GDP ratio.[26] As emphasised below, Article 4 TSCG enshrines the same requirement. In other words, the ratio of the difference between public debt and the 60 per cent debt-to-GDP threshold must fall by 5 per cent annually (Article 2 (1bis) 1st al. of Regulation 1467/97 as amended by Regulation (EU) No 1177/2011).

As far as Belgium is concerned, Table 2.2 illustrates the budgetary efforts that need to be accomplished with a view to achieving in 2033 the ratio debt-GDP of 60 per cent.

It must be noted, however, that the possibility to alter efforts to reduce the debt over the course of a three-year cycle increases the flexibility granted to the Member States. As the rate of reduction of one-twentieth must be reached at the end of the period, the Member State is able to defer most of its efforts to the end of the three-year cycle, or to do the opposite. As regards the Member States whose debt is lower than the fateful threshold of 60 per cent of GDP, they are free to decide whether it is convenient to reduce their level of debt any further. However, they are not subject to any obligation to improve their structural budget balance (Allemand and Martucci 2012: 58–9).

What is more, even Member States that respect the public deficit criteria will now be required to adopt measures in order to bring their public debt below the 60 per cent threshold. Accordingly, bringing the deficit below 3 per cent of GDP is not sufficient any more for the abrogation of the EDP, unless the debt has been put on a satisfactory declining path. As a result, an EDP may be launched where the Member State does not comply with the debt-reduction pace requirement. Nonetheless, Member States already in EDP in January 2012 having to comply with agreed fiscal consolidation paths, benefit from a transitional period of three years. The Council of the European Union and the Commission are called on to examine whether the Member State concerned is improving its budget situation in applying such standards.

It should be added that the Fiscal Compact and one of the 'two-pack' Regulations require Eurozone countries that are subject to EDP to submit to an 'economic partnership programme' setting out the policy measures and structural reforms intended to correct excessive deficits.[27] The 'two-pack' provides in relation to Member States in serious financial difficulties for the replacement of the 'economic partnership programme' intended to guarantee the correction of an economic deficit (Article 9 of Regulation (EU) No 473/2013) with an 'economic adjustment programme' (Article 7 of Regulation (EU) No 473/2013).

What is more, financial sanctions provided for in Article 126(11) TFEU must henceforth constitute a real incentive for compliance with the notices under Article 126(9) TFEU (Recital 21 of Regulation 1467/97 as amended by Regulation (EU) No 1177/2011).

As far as the Eurozone members in breach of their SGP obligations are concerned, this change in scale will further imply a new set of gradual financial sanctions that can be imposed throughout the procedure. The Council may require the Member State concerned to lodge an interest-bearing deposit of 0.2 per cent of GDP with it, which may be transformed into a non-interest-bearing deposit (Articles 4 and 5 of Regulation (EU) No 1173/2011[28]). The interest-bearing deposit imposed should be released to the Member State concerned together with the interest accrued on it once the Council has been satisfied that the situation giving rise to the obligation to lodge that deposit has come to an end. Besides deposits, fines may be imposed. In effect, if no action is taken in order to correct the excessive deficit, in a third stage the Council may, acting on the basis of a Commission recommendation, impose a fine of up to 0.2 per cent of GDP on the State concerned (Article 6(1) of Regulation (EU) No 1173/2011). The effectiveness of these sanctions should be buttressed by the new reverse qualified majority procedure (Article 5(2) of Regulation (EU) No 1173/2011). What is more, the parties to the Fiscal Compact are committing themselves to support the proposals submitted by the Commission where it considers that a Member State whose currency is the euro is in breach of the deficit criterion in the framework of an EDP procedure (Article 7 TSCG).

Table 2.3 describes the new enforcement measures underpinning the SGP in the Eurozone.

In contrast, for non-Eurozone members in breach of their SGP obligations, the Council is empowered to adopt decisions (qualified

Table 2.3 Sanctions for Eurozone members in breach of their SGP obligations

Trigger for sanction	Sanction	Voting procedure
Council decision establishing failure to take action in response to a Council recommendation under Article 121(4) TFEU	Interest-bearing deposit in virtue of Article 4 of Regulation 1173/2011 (as a rule 0.2% of GDP)	Reverse qualified majority voting (RQMV)
Council decision based on Article 126(6) TFEU	Non-interest-bearing deposit in virtue of Article 5 of Regulation 1173/2011 (as a rule 0.2% of GDP)	RQMV
Council decision based on Article 126(8) TFEU (i.e. non-effective action in response to the recommendation to correct the excessive deficit under Article 126(7))	Fine in virtue of Article 6 of Regulation 1173/2011 (as a rule 0.2% of GDP)	RQMV
Council decision based on Article 126(11) TFEU (i.e. non-effective action in response to the notice to correct the excessive deficit under Article 126(9))	Fine in virtue of Article 11 of Regulation 1467/97 as amended (0.2% of GDP + variable component)	Qualified majority voting (QMV)

majority) imposing fines based on Article 126(11) TFEU with respect to non-effective action in response to the notice to correct the excessive deficit under Article 126(9) TFEU (Articles 10 and 11 of Council Regulation (EU) No 1177/2011). Therefore, the Commission has to reckon upon the suspension of Cohesion Fund commitments for non-Eurozone Member States, subject to an EDP, which are not taking effective action at an early stage to correct it. For instance, in January 2012 the Commission threatened Hungary with a freeze on its EU development funds for the year 2013 if it did not comply with the new rules.[29]

2.2.4.4 Broadening economic surveillance to encompass macro-imbalances and competitiveness

The SGP also suffered from other faults. In effect, the debt crisis has uncovered gaps within the surveillance both of fiscal and economic policies. Since healthy public finances may mask excessive levels of household debt, housing bubbles, lack or loss of competitiveness, price and salary growth, unbalanced patterns of trade and investment, the deficit threshold is certainly not the only bulwark against the risk of insolvency. Indeed, in focusing exclusively on fiscal aspects, the surveillance regime disregarded macroeconomic questions. It is therefore necessary to enlarge the horizon.

As was provided for under the 2020 EU Strategy, the 'six-pack' broadens the SGP to macro-structural surveillance for individual countries. To this effect, Regulation 1176/2011 addresses macroeconomic imbalances and divergences in competitiveness in all Member States.[30] In line with the SGP, this Regulation reckons upon a preventive and a corrective mechanism. It introduces a procedure applicable to 'excessive macroeconomic imbalance' based on an alert mechanism entailing a scoreboard. This mechanism is designed to detect macroeconomic imbalances quickly by using a limited number of economic indicators. The imbalances will be picked up using a scoreboard and a detailed balance sheet, and may, upon the detection of imbalances, result in the adoption of preventive measures.

In the case of particularly serious imbalances, the Council may decide to place the Member State in an 'excessive imbalances position' based on a recommendation by the Commission. This would trigger the 'corrective arm' of the mechanism (Article 121(4) TFEU).

Twelve Member States have already been subject to an in-depth assessment.[31] That being said, the 2013 Annual Growth Report of the Commission is stressing that the Alert Mechanism Report adopted alongside this Survey shows that developments in price and non-price competiveness are contributing positively to improving external imbalances ... (Commission Communication, Annual Growth Survey 2013, COM (2012) 750 final).

The 'two-pack' provides, in relation to Member States in serious financial difficulties, for the replacement of the economic partnership programme with an economic adjustment programme (Article 7 of Regulation (EU) No 472/2013).

As far as the Eurozone is concerned, Regulation 1174/2011 reinforces Regulation 1176/2011 by making provision for different sanctions in the event of failure to comply with Recommendations regarding the correction of excessive macroeconomic imbalances from the Council of the Union.[32] The Council decisions concerning the sanctions based on Article 136 TFEU will be restricted to Eurozone Member States (the vote of the member of the Council representing the Member State concerned by the decisions shall not be taken into account). These sanctions may indeed be cumulated with those laid down in relation to budgetary surveillance (Allemand and Martucci 2012: 74).

Last but not least, there is a question as to whether EU lawmakers were able to extend the regime of sanctions applicable to excessive public debts to the new excessive macroeconomic imbalance procedure. Indeed, there are several stumbling blocks to overcome. Given that Article 352 TFEU requires a vote of unanimity, neither the Commission nor the Council have considered that provision as a relevant legal basis to endorse such mechanisms. What is more, Article 136 TFEU does not contain any specific provision to this effect (Ruffert 2011: 1800). For Louis, everything has happened as if this provision amounted to a simplified amendment of the Treaty by way of legislative provisions enacted to bolster the effects of Article 121 on the

surveillance and coordination of economic policies and Article 126 on excessive deficits (Ruffert 2011: 1801; Louis 2012b; Allemand and Martucci 2012:
72). Louis takes the view that Article 136 TFEU has been conceived more on
the model of reinforced cooperation, in line with Article 20 of the TEU and
Articles 326 to 334 TFEU.

Finally, this new form of multilateral surveillance is, moreover, completed
by the Euro Plus Pact, which requires commitments from its parties in the
areas of priority action, such as the reduction of labour costs, productivity
increases, labour market reforms, etc. (see the discussion in Section 2.4.1.3).
EU law thus intersects with the non-binding commitments made by certain
Member States.

2.2.4.5   *The European Semester: deeper and broader coordination*

2.2.4.5.1   THE SUBMISSION OF ALL MEMBER STATES TO THE FIRST 'EUROPEAN SEMESTER'

The synchronisation of political and macroeconomic budgetary calendars
is now assured through the European Semester. Given that the surveillance
is conducted over the first semester of the year, whilst the directions and
recommendations issued by the EU institutions are implemented during
the second semester, the new procedure has been coined as the 'European
Semester'.

The European Semester indubitably constitutes the great novelty of the
reform (Louis 2011: 58–61; De Sadeleer 2012: 364–66). From now on, the
cycle of surveillance and coordination will operate within a synchronised
framework. The first European Semester was organised in an informal manner in 2011 on the basis of a decision of the Ecofin Council of 6 September
2010. A second and a third European Semester have been implemented during
2012 and 2013 under Regulation (EU) No 1175/2011 amending Regulation
(EU) No 1466/97 (Articles 11 and 12 of Regulation 1466/97 as amended
by Regulation (EU) No 1175/2011). The objective of these procedures is to
ensure closer coordination of economic policies and a sustained convergence
of economic performance of the Member States within the context of multilateral surveillance under the preventive part of the SGP (Article 2 bis (1) of
Regulation 1466/97 as amended by Regulation (EU) No 1175/2011).

This will make it possible to monitor in particular the implementation of
broad economic policy guidelines (BEPG) (Articles 5(1) and 121(2) TFEU)[33]
as well as guidelines for employment (Article 148(2) TFEU, see Council
Decision 2010/707 of 21 October 2010 on guidelines for the employment policies of the Member States [2010] OJ L 308/46). It also includes the stability[34]
or convergence programmes provided for under Regulation 1466/97[35] and the
surveillance may prevent and correct macroeconomic imbalances in accordance with Regulation (EU) No 1176/2011 (see the discussion in Section 2.4.5).
Furthermore, the NRP intended to implement the EU's growth and employment strategy has to be assessed with the other documents (see the discussion

section in 2.3.1). For countries that are subject to a regime of enhanced surveillance, the rules providing for surveillance of the sustainability of public finances are suspended (Article 12 of Regulation (EU) No 472/2013).

Since the European Semester is more a matter of rationalisation than of innovation synchronisation does not entail a merger of procedures. Indeed, each initiative continues to be subject to self-standing procedural arrangements (Allemand and Martucci 2012: 51). In other words, the SGP does not have to be incorporated into the surveillance of macroeconomic policies, or vice versa. However, convergence does actually occur where the Council no longer limits its action to issuing distinct recommendations to the Member States relating on the one hand to their stability or convergence programmes, and on the other hand to their NRPs. Henceforth, the two issues will be incorporated into one single recommendation, adopted on the dual basis of Article 121(2) and Article 148(4) TFEU (Conclusion of European Council, Brussels, 25 and 26 March 2010, EUCO, 7/10).

This coordination certainly has the merit of increasing interdependence between the different programming processes, which appears to be justified given that structural policies are closely related to fiscal policies. On the one hand, the former must be financed by the latter, whilst on the other hand; the EC States are entitled to expect tax revenues to climb following increases in growth.

Though they remain separate, the existing surveillance processes are henceforth aligned in terms of timing. The European Semester commences at the start of the year with a horizontal assessment by the Commission based on an annual report on growth (January)[36] that enables the European Council to formulate strategic guidance (March). Starting from April, this guidance has to be taken into account within medium-term budget strategies as part of stability programmes (for the 18 Member States of the Eurozone) or convergence programmes (for the ten other States) as well as in NRP seeking to guarantee the objective of the Europe 2020 Strategy. The last stage of the European Semester is concluded during June and July with the formulation of political guidelines by the Council and the Commission for each country. Moreover, the budgetary criteria specified for the following year will be required to comply with the guidelines specified during the Semester.

- January: the Commission publishes its annual report on growth, setting priorities for the EU in order to stimulate growth and create employment over the coming year.
- March: the European Council adopts the EU guidelines on national policies.
- April: the Member States submit their stability or convergence programmes, as well as their NRP.
- June: the Commission evaluates the programmes and addresses its own recommendations to each State. The Ecofin Council examines these recommendations and the European Council approves them.
- July: The Ecofin Council formally adopts the recommendations for each country.

Is the coordinated assessment at EU level likely to ensure that the EU/Euro area dimension is better taken into account when Member States prepare their budgets and their NRP? Whether this coordination will contribute to a higher degree of policy coordination among Member States still remains to be seen.

That being said, the Member States must take due account of the recommendations issued by the European Council when drawing up their economic, employment and fiscal policies before taking any major decision concerning their national budgets for the coming years. The failure by the State authorities to respond to the guidelines that are issued to them could result in new recommendations from the Council of the EU, a warning from the Commission under Article 121(4) TFEU on multilateral surveillance, or in economic control measures (Article 2 bis (3) of Regulation (EC) 1466/97 as amended by Regulation (EU) No 1175/2011).

2.2.4.5.2   THE SUBMISSION OF EUROZONE COUNTRIES TO THE SECOND
EUROPEAN SEMESTER

The 'two-pack', as the two Regulations adopted by EU lawmakers on 21 May 2013 have been baptised, constitutes the last plank of the reform of the EU's economic governance. One of these regulations is dedicated to the monitoring and assessment of draft budgetary plans and the correction of excessive deficit of the Member States in the Euro area.[37] Regulation 473/2013 is predicated upon the assumption that Member States whose currency is the euro are particularly subject to spill-over effects from each other's budgetary policies (Recital 19). With the aim of strengthening the coordination and surveillance of the Eurozone budgetary discipline, the specific measures laid down by Regulation 473/2013 in the Euro area go beyond the provisions applicable to all Member States. Accordingly, its legal basis is Articles 121(6) and 136 TFEU, which authorise the Parliament to 'strengthen coordination and surveillance' of the fiscal discipline of Member States of the Eurozone.

Given that 'biased and unrealistic macroeconomic and budgetary forecasts can considerably hamper the effectiveness of budgetary planning and, consequently, impair commitment to budgetary discipline', Regulation 473/2013 sets up 'a common budgetary timeline' for Eurozone States (Recitals 10–11). Admittedly, these States are called on to better synchronise the key steps in the preparation of national budgets, thus contributing to the effectiveness of the SGP and of the European Semester for economic policy coordination (Recital 12).

As a first step in that common budgetary timeline, Member States have to make public their national medium-term fiscal plan at the same time as their stability programmes, preferably by 15 April and no later than by 30 April. Those fiscal plans should include indications on how the reforms and measures set out are expected to contribute to the achievement of the targets and national commitments established within the framework of the EU's strategy for growth and jobs (Recital 13). What is more, the national medium-term fiscal plan and the stability programme can be the same document.

As a second step, Member States are required to publish the draft central government budget by 15 October. The Commission must adopt an opinion on the draft budgetary plan in any event by 30 November. Where the Commission identifies particularly serious non-compliance with the budgetary policy obligations laid down in the SGP, the Commission may request that a revised draft budgetary plan be submitted.

As a third step, Member States are called on to adopt their budget by 31 December.

The following template sets out the deadlines of the new budgetary framework:

- By 15 April but no later than 30 April each year: submission of the medium-term fiscal plans in accordance with the medium-term budgetary framework. Such plans are presented together with the NRP and the stability programmes.
- By mid-October: submission to the Commission of draft budgetary plan for the forthcoming year.
- By 30 November: European Commission adopts its opinion.
- By 15 December: submission of the revised draft budgetary plan where the Commission has been identifying particularly serious non-compliance with the budgetary policy obligations laid down in the SGP.
- By 31 December: the budget for the central government shall be adopted or fixed.

One is struck by the sheer complexity of the review processes. For the sake of clarity, Table 2.4 describes the different mechanisms underpinning the SGP's preventive branch.

2.2.4.6   *Harmonisation of the requirements applicable to national fiscal frameworks*

The Directive on the requirements applicable to the national fiscal frameworks of Member States, which was adopted by the Council following consultation with the European Council – due to the fact that it was based on Article 126(14) TFEU – contributes to reinforcing both the preventive and the corrective approach of the SGP by requiring the Member States to comply with their obligations relating to fiscal matters.[38] Effective and timely monitoring of compliance with these rules must be based on reliable and independent analyses assured by the 'institutions or independent fiscal offices' (Article 6(b)).

Given that most fiscal measures have budgetary implications that go well beyond the annual budgetary cycle, annual budget legislation has to incorporate the multiannual budgetary perspective of the budgetary surveillance

Table 2.4 SGP's preventive branch arrangements

	Acts	Measures	Obligations placed on Member States	Obligations placed on institutions
SGP 1997	European Council 1997	Orientations regarding the SGP enforcement	Debt and deficit criteria	European Council and Commission
Europe 2020	European Council 2010	Intelligent growth	NRP	Commission and Council recommendations
Euro Plus Pact	European Council March 2011	Coordination economic policies	Golden rule and additional commitments	Member States Assessment by the Commission
Compact for Growth and Jobs	European Council June 2012	Enhancing investments	National investments	Assessment by the Commission
First European Semester	Specifications SGP and Guidelines ECOFIN 7/9/2010, Article 2 bis Régl. 1466/97	Cycle of surveillance and coordination operates within a synchronised framework	Stability/convergence programmes NRP, macroeconomic data and medium-term budgetary framework	UPSTREAM • Commission report • ECOFIN • European Council orientations DOWNSTREAM • Commission project • Council approval • ECOFIN orientations
Second European Semester	Regulation 473/2013	Common budgetary timeline	Submission of draft budgetary plan, revised draft budgetary plan and adoption of the budget	Non-binding opinion from the Commission

framework of the EU. In other words, in order to be consistent with both the preventive and the corrective parts of the SGP, the planning of annual budget legislation should adopt a multi-annual perspective stemming from the MTOs framework. Against this backdrop, in accordance with Article 5 of the Directive, Member States are called on to adopt numerical fiscal rules over a multiannual horizon with a view, on the one hand, to comply with the reference values on deficit and debt and, on the other, to promote a multi-annual fiscal planning horizon, including adherence to the Member State's MTOs.

Furthermore, MTOs go hand in hand with a medium-term budgetary framework providing for the adoption of a fiscal planning horizon of at least 3 years. This new framework must ensure that national fiscal planning follows a multiannual fiscal planning perspective (Article 9(1)). It follows that annual budget legislation must be consistent with the provisions of the medium-term budgetary framework (Article 10).

2.2.4.7   *Enhanced control of Member States facing serious financial difficulties*

As stated above, the two-pack, as the two Regulations adopted by EU lawmakers on 21 May 2013 have been baptised, constitutes the last plank of the reform of the EU's economic governance. A second Regulation (No 472/2013) of this supplementary plank applies to Member States facing serious financial difficulties: the Member States in receipt of financial assistance flowing from bilateral loans or under the ESM, or those that are seriously threatened by financial instability. Regulation No 472/2013 tightens up the procedural arrangements by a notch.[39] It is more demanding than Article 5 of the Fiscal Compact, which also provides for an enhanced surveillance mechanism for States subject to an EDP. The legal basis for Regulation 472/2013 are Articles 121(6) and 136 TFEU, which authorise the Parliament and the Council to 'strengthen coordination and surveillance' of the fiscal discipline of the Member States of the Eurozone.

2.2.5   *Reinforcement of the SGP by the Fiscal Compact*

2.2.5.1   *Introduction*

Will the range of mechanisms intended to guarantee balanced national budgets bear fruit? In the eyes of certain heads of government, since the edifice put in place over the previous years had remained incomplete, something additional had to be done in order to reassure the markets. Accordingly, in 2011 the German authorities – backed up by the French – proclaimed their intention to amend the TFEU which, having been concluded at Lisbon on 18 and 19 October 2007, only entered into force two years later on 1 December 2009, despite the urgent need to find a response to the crisis which had resulted from the termination of the defunct European Constitution. For a long time there had been questions as to whether the reforms planned should be applied to the 18 (Eurogroup), the 23 (Euro Plus Pact) or the 28 (EU) and whether they should bring the coordination of economic policies under genuine shared competences where EU law exercises its primacy.

Taking account of the opposition of the UK's representative,[40] the European Council held on 9 December 2011 finally decided to conclude an inter-governmental agreement between an initial 26, which later fell to 25 Member States. The negotiations, which were swiftly initiated under the aegis of the President of the European Council, resulted in a political agreement on 30 January 2012. The Fiscal Compact Treaty was signed on the fringes of the European Council of 1 March 2012.

Contrary to the wishes of the German authorities, this new inter-governmental agreement does not result in an amendment of the fundamental treaties to which the 27 Member States were parties. As a treaty concluded between the 17 Member States of the Eurozone (18 since 2014), and 8 other Member States which do not use the euro as their currency, it constitutes a self-standing legal framework which is superimposed on EU law, whilst borrowing various techniques from EU law. To put it simply, although the Treaty aims at fostering the implementation of the SGP, it is not part of the *acquis communautaire*. This piece of legal wizardry that could be described as an 'Economic Schengen' – due to the British veto – therefore, for the moment, prevents the adoption of a fully fledged amendment treaty.

The Fiscal Compact entered into force on 1 January 2013 (Louis 2012c; De Streel and Etienne 2012; Martucci 2012; Craig 2012) following its ratification by Finland, the twelfth Euro area Member State to ratify the Treaty (Article 14(2) TSCG). Given the misadventures to which the Treaties amending the founding treaties (including the Maastricht, Nice and Lisbon Treaties) have been subject, the path of the Fiscal Compact is littered with pitfalls. By way of illustration, in a referendum that took place on 31 May 2012, 60 per cent of Irish voters have been backing the Treaty, most of whom were aware that its rejection would hurt Ireland's chances of attracting further EU bailouts. It must be noted that, for several Member States, the ratification of the Fiscal Compact went hand in hand with the granting of financial assistance by the ESM. In effect, starting from 1 March 2013, any assistance has been conditional upon the prior ratification of this Treaty (Recital 5 TSCG). In December 2013, Belgium finally ratified it, though some regional sub-entities requested various reservations regarding the implementation of several budgetary obligations.

The 16 provisions of the Fiscal Compact are grouped under five titles. The titles on the Fiscal Compact (Title III, Articles 3–8), on the coordination of economic policies (Title IV, Articles 9–11) and on the governance of the Euro area (Title V, Articles 12–13) are of central importance. Since it is not possible to provide a detailed commentary on this Treaty, this chapter shall be limited to briefly highlighting some of the relationships that it will have with the measures discussed above.

2.2.5.2   *Fiscal Compact*

The core obligations are found in Title III of the Fiscal Compact. It is the aim of this subsection to explore some of the key issues arising in discussion of Article 3 (golden rule), Article 7 (reversed qualified majority (RQM)) and Article 8 (control of the obligation to balance budgets).

2.2.5.2.1   GOLDEN RULE

Article 3 enshrines the golden rule, according to which 'the budgetary position of the general government of a Contracting Party shall be balanced or in surplus' (Article 3(1)(a) TSCG). This requirement is deemed to have been met where the structural deficit does not exceed 0.5 per cent of GDP at market prices, or 1 per cent for countries with a debt above 60 per cent of GDP (Article 3(1)(b) and (d) TSCG).

Four separated, albeit related issues, must be distinguished. The first issue concerns the golden rule. It must be noted that the new inter-governmental golden rule does not match the traditional definition of a golden fiscal rule, which requires that public authorities borrow only to cover investments, and not to fund current spending (Artis 2002: 101–16).

The second issue concerns the added value of the so-called golden rule. This provision is less innovative than certain heads of State have asserted on the account that it reasserts the commitments made in the Euro Plus Pact of 11 March 2011 (Supra B). The essential difference consists in the fact that the 2011 Pact is not binding. Second, it was only signed by 23 Member States and not the 25 Member States that undertook to ratify the Fiscal Compact. Another difference should also be highlighted: compared to the Euro Plus Pact, the new Treaty limits the States' powers of appreciation.

The third issue concerns the relationship between Article 3 and the obligations stemming from the 'six-pack'. As regards its relations with secondary law, Article 3 restates the obligation as laid down by Regulation 1476/97 amended by Regulation 1177/2011, whilst also reinforcing it. A first difference must be noted: the deficit threshold may not exceed 0.5 per cent of GDP at market prices or 1 per cent for States whose debt is lower than 60 per cent. Given that these thresholds are more stringent than those established under the 'six-pack', the Treaty imposes significantly stricter fiscal rigour. In practice, future MTOs will have to be in line with the 0.5 per cent limit imposed by the golden rule (Verhelst 2012). Another difference relates without doubt to the fact that the preventive approval of the SGP has previously been based on a permanent tension between automatism (the application of the thresholds on an arithmetical basis) and the capacity for judgment (the discretionary power exercised by the Commission). How will things work under the Fiscal Compact? In providing for an automatic correction mechanism, will the new Article 3(1)(e) remove this capacity for judgment?

The fourth issue concerns the implementation of the golden rule which will have to be set in constitutional stone, or failing that, in a rule of equivalent standing (Article 3(2) TSCG). Since only the German, Italian and Spanish constitutions contain such a rule, 22 other States will have to cross the proverbial Rubicon. Moreover, the national rule will have to provide for an automatic correction mechanism that will be engaged if there is a sustained imbalance (Article 3(2) TSCG). This mechanism should aim at correcting deviations from MTOs, or the adjustment path.

Furthermore, it should be added that the 'national appropriation' of the requirement of a balanced budget, in particular through its incorporation into the Constitution or a provision of equivalent nature, is destined to shift control from EU level to State level. It goes without saying that this obligation should, depending upon the circumstances, permit opposition parties to initiate proceedings before the Supreme Courts, with controls thus being shifted from EU to national level. However, this move will raise various questions: Will such laws be subject to actions for annulment? Who will have standing? Will it be easy to correct a budgetary law that has been annulled by national courts? Will they take sufficient time in order to rule on such applications with the aim of not compromising the proper implementation of the contested budget? How will the automatic correction mechanism work? It can easily be imagined that in 2014 this international law obligation will cause upheaval within constitutional circles.

Will the findings reached within the case law of the German Federal Constitutional Court relating to the constitutionality of the Lisbon Treaty and the EFSM act as an inspiration for other Supreme Courts? In these two judgments, the Court held that since the principle of democratic self-determination can only be exercised on the level of the Nation State, the EU cannot deprive the Member States of essential powers in relation to the latter, including fiscal powers.[41] In particular, in the Lisbon judgment the Court went on to say:

> A transfer of the right of the *Bundestag* to adopt the budget and control its implementation by the government which would violate the principle of democracy and the right to elect the German *Bundestag* in its essential content would occur if the determination of the type and amount of the levies imposed on the citizen were supranationalized to a considerable extent. The German *Bundestag* must decide, in an accountable manner *vis-à-vis* the people, on the total amount of the burdens placed on citizens. The same applies correspondingly to essential state expenditure.
>
> Budget sovereignty is where political decisions are planned to combine economic burdens with benefits granted by the State. Therefore the parliamentary debate on the budget, including the extent of public debt, is regarded as a general debate on policy. Not every European or international obligation that has an effect on the budget endangers the

viability of the *Bundestag* as the legislature responsible for approving the budget. The openness to legal and social order and to European integration which the Basic Law calls for, include an adaptation to parameters laid down and commitments made, which the legislature responsible for approving the budget must include in its own planning as factors which it cannot itself directly influence. What is decisive, however, is that the overall responsibility, with sufficient political discretion regarding revenue and expenditure, can still rest with the German *Bundestag*.

However, the German constitutional case law is not as clear-cut as one might believe. In the first place, EU obligations with a budgetary impact do not compromise the freedom of action of the *Bundestag*. Second, the Constitutional Court indicated that international budgetary rules cannot call into question 'the general responsibility' of the *Bundestag*, which 'to this effect must have a sufficient margin of political appreciation, both over revenues as well as expenditure' (§ 256). Accordingly, in the same manner as the SGP, the Fiscal Compact offers the Contracting Parties a certain degree of flexibility, provided that they respect the thresholds specified, although they may depart from them in exceptional cases.[42] Consequently, this Treaty does not appear to have the effect of annulling the fiscal self-determination of its signatory States.

Article 8 enshrines the jurisdiction of the Court of Justice to verify the implementation of this rule on national level (Article 8 TSCG). In expanding the jurisdiction of the Court, which is possible under Article 273 TFEU, the framers of the Fiscal Compact have done more than redrafting substantive law. Absent of any power to control the implementation of Article 3 by the Commission, the State parties to the Treaty take on responsibility to implement it. Admittedly, on the basis of the applications initiated by the national authorities, the Court of Justice will be required to rule on the compatibility of national law with the golden rule, and not of national budgets as desired by German Chancellor Merkel. This operates alongside the 'double infringement' mechanism in the event that the State in breach, fails to comply with the judgment against it (Article 3(2) TSCG). Whilst the enshrinement of this new competence results from a compromise of jurisdiction, in accordance with Article 273 TFEU, it does not however modify EU law. Formally speaking it will be the Member States that take action before the Court of Justice.[43] That being said, the borderline between a genuine settlement mechanism and the EU legal order is a fine one. Though the control of the implementation of the golden rule is not an EU legal issue in its own rights, it is likely to involve considerations of EU legal problems.[44]

2.2.5.2.2 DEBT CRITERION

The Fiscal Compact is also less innovative than has been asserted, since it expressly or implicitly consolidates obligations under secondary law. For example, Article 4 on the reduction of debt levels for Contracting Parties with a debt exceeding 60 per cent of GDP reasserts the obligation provided for under Article 2 Regulation 1467/97, as amended by Regulation 177/2011 (the preventive limb of the SGP) (see Section 2.4.2). In effect, the ratio of the gap between public debt and the 60 per cent debt-to-GDP threshold must be reduced by 5 per cent annually.

2.2.5.2.3 SANCTIONS AND REVERSE QUALIFIED MAJORITY

With respect to sanctions against States in breach of their SGP obligations, the Fiscal Compact is also less innovative than has been asserted. Proof of this lies in the reinforcement of fiscal discipline through the means of sanctions that are almost automatic. In this regard, Article 7 of the Treaty reinforces the considerable powers which the Commission exercises over the Council of the Union, as the latter must establish a 'blocking qualified majority' in order to oppose sanctions proposed by the Commission, whilst at present a blocking minority is sufficient. This Copernican Resolution will guarantee the semi-automatic nature of sanctions (see the discussion above in Section 2.4.3). Account must be made of the fact that Article 7 has not been amended by Article 126(6) TFEU.

2.2.5.3 *Added value of the Fiscal Compact*

The Fiscal Compact is certainly not a pure copy of existing law. Although it does not amend either primary or secondary EU law, the fact remains nonetheless that it adds new elements to EU law in order to guarantee its efficacy. This is the case for example, where it reinforces the budget deficit thresholds, as specified in Article 3. It is also apparent in the possibility for the Court of Justice to review the correct transposition of the golden rule into national law. On a strict interpretation of the principle of the attribution of competences enshrined in Article 13(2) TEU it may appear that these additions may constitute an amendment to applicable law and would therefore be illegal. However, a pragmatic interpretation is called for. Pursuant to Article 4(2) TEU, the Fiscal Compact provisions have the sole objective of facilitating compliance with the goal of achieving a balanced budget, and avoiding excess deficits (by analogy, see Joined Cases C-181/91 and C-248/9 *Parliament* v. *Council and Commission* [1993] ECR I-3713).

Has this Treaty really been worth it? On the one hand, the answer is affirmative if the Treaty is placed within its political context. Whilst undeniably betraying a certain scepticism regarding the classical mechanisms of EU law contained in the 'six-pack', it will be clear with hindsight that the adoption of such a Treaty was really necessary. Moreover, by playing the card of 'national appropriation', its framers certainly sought to reassure the financial markets and the electorates of various Member States. Furthermore, a link is established with the ESM, which was revised on 2 February 2012.

On the other hand, the answer is negative if one considers its contents objectively, since the Fiscal Compact does not introduce practically anything new into EU law (Carrera Hernandez 2012; Hinajeros 2012; Vitorino 2012). Whilst it certainly does guarantee greater efficacy for various mechanisms, nonetheless, no supplementary powers are granted either to the Commission or the Court of Justice, which would in any case have run contrary to Articles 5(2) and 13(2) TEU. Moreover, the integrity of the market has been maintained. At worst, according to some critics, the Fiscal Compact will have the effect of ossifying rules which would undoubtedly have been better placed within secondary law than in an inter-governmental agreement.

In summary, it is a pointless Treaty, which is without doubt insufficient in order to stave off a budgetary crisis, the end of which is still not in sight, although it is certainly indispensable within the current crisis situation.

2.3 The impacts of the reforms on the institutional equilibrium

2.3.1 Introductory remarks

As was stressed at the outset, the institutional balance in relation to budgetary and economic matters has always been atypical. On the one hand, the coordination of economic policy has been a matter for national sovereignty, whilst on the other hand budgetary control has been based on an equilibrium which is highly skewed in favour of the Council, where a blocking minority can easily stand in the way of Commission proposals. The European Parliament has only played a secondary role in such matters.

Does the reform enshrine the victory of the Community method over inter-governmentalism or the opposite? As is known, the recourse to multilateral cooperation has proved to be necessary in order to adopt the Euro Plus Pact and to set up the EFSF, the ESM as well as the Fiscal Compact. Control by fellow signatories has become more significant in the implementation of the commitments under the Euro Plus Pact and Europe 2020 Strategy which in a clear departure from the Community method, is based on the good will of the States. Finally, compliance with the implementation of the golden rule into constitutional law or a rule of equivalent effect will be approved by the Court of Justice on the basis of applications introduced not by the Commission but by other Contracting Parties to the Fiscal Compact.

However once again, the developments have been contradictory. In effect, the crisis has enabled a gradual improvement in the efficacy of this institutional framework by reinforcing the role of the Euro Group, the Council of the Eurozone and the Commission to the detriment of inter-governmentalism.

2.3.2 European Commission

Needless to say the 'six-pack' and the 'two-pack' significantly increase the powers of the Commission over the surveillance and evolution of the

Member States' public finances (Recital 12 of the preamble of Regulation 1466/97 as amended by Regulation (No 1175/2011). In effect, the implementation of programmes detailing structural reforms, and annual fiscal plans will be monitored both by the Commission and the Council.

Moreover, the Commission henceforth disposes of considerable powers with regard to the Council of the European Union, which must now establish a 'blocking qualified majority' in order to oppose sanctions proposed by the Union executive, whereas before, the entry into force of the 'six-pack', a blocking minority was sufficient.[45] This Copernican Revolution, which was strongly supported by the European Parliament, guarantees the semi-automatic nature of sanctions.

Finally, both the Fiscal Compact (Article 5(1) and (2); Article 6; Article 8(2) TSCG) and the ESM (Article 4(4); Article 5(3); Article 6(2); Article 13(1), (3) and (7); see Case C-370/12 *Pringle*, para. 158) confer various tasks on the Commission. In *Pringle*, the Court of Justice held that the tasks vested by the ESM in the Commission do not distort the powers of that institution under the fundamental treaties. Various questions spring to mind. Should one see within the new governance a Leviathan wearing down national sovereignty to the benefit of increased EU powers over economic matters? Often decried as the quintessence of technocratic power, surely the European Commission is itself the best placed, in terms of legitimacy, to exercise a right to monitor the contents of national budgets (Regulation (EU) No 73/2013) or to control highly political functions in a neutral manner? However, surely the mere fact of asking the question already implies an answer. Within a Europe in which it is necessary to put out one fire after another, without being able to count on a sufficient number of firemen, surely the role of the legislature will have to be reviewed? Moreover, the Ecofin Council, which does not lack any legitimacy whatsoever (Jacqué 2010: 82), has the last word. Nonetheless, as has been seen with Greece, Portugal and Ireland, budgetary constraints now appear to determine the scope of the substantive law implementing policies which have not, however, been harmonised on EU level (Triantafyllou 2011: 195–208). In effect, financial assistance was granted to these Member States on the strength of their commitment to implement significant reforms to their fiscal, social, employment and health policy, as well as public finance law, commercial law and their public administrations.[46]

2.3.3 *Euro Group*

As an *ad hoc* structure for informal coordination established with the implementation of the EMU, the Euro Group is not one of the ten formations of the Council of the Union (Louis 2009: 127–31; Kasel 2012) (see Protocol no 4). It is comprised of the finance ministers of the Member States that have adopted the euro as their currency. The President of the ECB is invited to attend its meetings, whereas the Commission participates as of right. It is certain that the Euro Group has been called upon to play a decisive role in the implementation of the European Semester for the Member States from the Euro area. It is charged with the preparation and follow-up of the Euro Summit meetings. Moreover, its President may be invited to attend these meetings (Article 12(4) TSCG). In contrast to other formations, it has the advantage of having a stable Presidency with terms of two-and-a-half years. On the other hand, due to its informal nature, it cannot issue Recommendations since it is for the Ecofin Council to formally ratify these acts.

2.3.4 Council of the euro area

The Euro Summit Meeting of 26 October 2011 concluded that the different heads of State and governments from the Euro area will meet 'informally' twice per year and elect a President for a term of two-and-a-half years. The President of the ECB is invited to attend its meetings, whereas the Commission participates as of right. The Summit should meet at key moments of the annual governance cycle, where possible, after meetings of the European Council. This will accordingly seek to prevent the official institution from being short-circuited by the decisions taken by the 18 Member States of the Euro area.

In providing for similar institutional arrangements, the Fiscal Compact formally provides for the existence of this Council (Article 12(1) TSCG). This parallel council will be called upon to determine strategic guidelines on the conduct of economic policy, the improvement of competitiveness and the reinforcement of governance within the Eurozone (Article 12(2) TSCG).

2.3.5 Economic and Financial Committee

As a body that engages in studies, preparation, dialogue and consultation, the Economic and Financial Committee plays a central role in the preparation of decisions relating to the functioning of the EMU.[47] Pursuant to Article 134(2) TFEU the EFC's tasks are, among others, to contribute to the preparation of the work of the Council, particularly as regards recommendations required as part of the multilateral surveillance and decisions required as part of the EDP (Article 126(4) TFEU) as well as to promote policy coordination among the Member States. It provides opinions at the request of the Council of the EU or the European Commission. The EFC shall be consulted within the framework of the European Semester (Article 2 bis (4) of Regulation (EC) No 1466/97 as amended by Regulation (EU) No 1175/2011). As a serious competitor to the Committee of Permanent Representatives (COREPER), this Council plays a key role in the preparation of Ecofin meetings. In particular, its preparatory work for the Council includes the assessment of the economic and financial situation, the coordination of economic and fiscal policies, contributions on financial market matters, exchange rate polices and relations with third countries and international institutions. In order to ensure a consistent application of the principles mentioned above for defining the country-specific MTOs, regular methodological discussions take place in the Economic and Financial Committee (Ecofin Council, Specifications on the Implementation of the SGP). It may also represent a threat for the Commission's prerogatives by standing between it and the Council. Its penchant for secrecy and the complete lack of political responsibility raise difficulties in terms of democratic control (Louis 2009: 119).

The 'two-pack' reinforces this body even further. The EFC has in effect been charged with numerous missions relating to the control of Eurozone Member States faced with financial stability difficulties (Recital 14, Article 3, par. 1st and Article 7, par. 4 of Regulation (EU) No 472/2013) or which are subject to an EDP (Article 10, par. 3 et 11, par. 2 of Regulation (EU) No 473/2013).

2.3.6   European Central Bank

Various tasks are conferred on the ECB by the 'six-pack' and the 'two-pack' Regulations. What is more, the ECB is an integral part of the ESM regime (Article 13(1), (3) and (4)). In *Pringle*, the Court held that the allocation by the ESM Treaty of new tasks to the ECB is compatible with its powers. The Court stated, inter alia, that the duties conferred on the ECB within the ESM Treaty do not entail any power to make decisions of its own, and that the activities pursued by this institution within the ESM Treaty solely commit the ESM.

2.3.7   Respective roles of the European Parliament and the national parliaments

The progress made under the Treaty of Lisbon for parliamentary institutions was welcomed by most commentators (Piris 2011: 113–14). There is now a question as to whether the European Parliament[48] and the national parliaments have missed out on the reform (Ruffert 2011: 1801).

Legitimacy of the fiscal approach is indeed becoming a touchstone issue. In this connection, two examples will suffice. First, the European Council held in the conclusions of its 18/19 October 2012 meeting that:

> Strong mechanisms for democratic legitimacy and accountability are necessary. One of the guiding principles in this context is to ensure that democratic control and accountability take place at the level at which decisions are taken and implemented. In this spirit, ways to ensure a debate in the context of the European Semester, both within the European Parliament and national parliaments, should be explored.
>
> (EUCO 156/12, para. 17)

Second, in its final report, the Future of Eurogroup stress that: 'a fundamental deepening of the EMU must go hand in hand with greater democratic legitimacy. Wherever new competences are created at European level or closer coordination of national policies is established, full democratic control has to be ensured'.

Needless to say, it is likely that these political commitments will enhance parliamentary participation in the decision-making process.

2.3.7.1 The European Parliament

The European Parliament did indeed adopt five of the six principles from the 'six-pack' on their first reading. Nevertheless, both the definition and assessment of objectives as well as the control of national policies and budgets is the prerogative of an institutional network within which the European Council, the Ecofin Council, the Euro Group and the Commission divide up these roles. Is the European Parliament entirely absent from this network? This again calls for a nuanced response.

First and foremost, the European Parliament is required to take action at the start of the annual cycle of surveillance before the European Council has defined the strategic guidelines for macro-economic and micro-budgetary policy within the context of the European Semester. In effect, there must be discussions within the Parliament.[49]

Moreover, according to Article 121 TFEU, the President of the Council, the Commission and, depending upon the circumstances, the President of the Euro Group must report to the European Parliament on the results of the multilateral surveillance and the implementation of EDPs (Article 2 bis(4) al. 2 of Regulation (EC) No 1466/97 as amended by Regulation (EU) No 1175/2011). Exchanges of opinion with the Member State that has been the object of a recommendation by the Council may occur within the competent parliamentary committee.[50] Similarly, the Euro Summit Councils may invite the President of the European Parliament to be heard (Article 12(5) TSCG). Last, Article 13 of the Fiscal Compact provides for the oversight of the budgetary policies and other issues covered by this Treaty by both the European Parliament and national parliaments.

2.3.7.2 National parliaments

By the same token, national parliaments warrant special attention (Clerc 2012: 759). Given that following the entry into force of the Lisbon Treaty the national parliaments dispose of the power to control the correct application of the principle of subsidiarity, have the tables now been turned on them? In accordance with the principle 'no taxation without representation', one of their main functions is to approve annual budget legislation. Has their autonomy been seriously cut back?

It is certain that national parliaments must be fully involved with the European Semester and the preparation of the various programmes.[51] However, in the final analysis, national budgets will now be drawn up within a framework that leaves decidedly less room for manoeuvre than in the past (see Regulation (EU) No 473/2013).

First, the European Semester is called upon to reinforce the powers of the Prime Minister and the Finance Minister to the detriment of those of Parliament, just at it enhances the Economic and Monetary Affairs portfolio within the Commission, currently held by the Commissioner Oli Rehn.

Second, on the account that most fiscal measures have budgetary implications that go well beyond the annual budgetary cycle, Member States are now required by Directive 2011/85 to base their annual budget legislation on multi-annual fiscal planning stemming from the medium-term budgetary framework. Any departure from this framework shall be duly explained (Article 10 of Directive 2011/85/EU of the Council of 8 November 2011 on requirements for budgetary frameworks of the Member States, [2011] OJ L306/41). As a matter of course, the Directive does not prevent a Member State's new government from updating its medium-term budgetary framework to reflect its new policy priorities.

Whilst in the wake of the constitutional litigation it has ended up embracing the positions adopted by German Ministers within European institutions (Dechâtre 2011: 321[52]) the *Bundestag* will in any case have to pass beneath the Caudian yoke and accept the constraints introduced by the new budgetary arrangements.

2.3.8   Concluding remarks

The Euro Plus Pact, the ESM and the Fiscal Compact are testament to a move towards inter-governmentalism. Nonetheless, neither the Fiscal Compact nor the ESM call into question the primacy of EU law. Since they were not able to amend either the TEU or the TFEU, the parties to the Fiscal Compact ensured that it would be consistent with EU law. Given that there is no question of its encroachment upon the competences of the EU (Article 2(2) TSCG, see also Articles 3 and 7 stating that the Treaty is to be applied without prejudice to EU law), the principle of primacy remains unaffected. Moreover, with the Fiscal Compact obligations strengthening pre-existing mechanisms of primary and secondary law calling for reinforced cooperation (Article 20 TEU and Articles 326 to 34 TFEU), the Community method need not give ground to any inter-governmental method (Louis 2012c: 4). On the contrary, the parties to this Treaty are making full use of the existing EU institutional mechanisms.

Moreover, the adoption of the 'six-pack' is testament to the fact that Directives and Regulations have not been dwarfed by these inter-governmental arrangements. Moreover, the 'two-pack' appears as an appropriate vehicle to flesh out the economic partnership programmes set out by the Fiscal Compact.

At the end of the day, all EU institutions except for the European Parliament appear to be much stronger, given that they were granted more competences. In particular, the new powers conferred on the Commission and the Council are likely to give real teeth to economic governance in the EU. The Fiscal Compact confirms some of the surveillance mechanisms introduced by the 'six-pack' and the 'two-pack'. Whether the balance of power has tilted in favour of one institution remains to be seen. Some institutional developments have been contradictory. Besides, the crisis has shown the extent to which informal mechanisms are likely to prevail over formal mechanisms. Lastly, given that an avant-garde of countries whose currency is the euro is likely to foster more integration in the field of economic policies, this might be the beginning of a permanent 'two-class' EU (Piris 2012: 13).

2.4 Conclusions

Whilst the financial crisis highlighted the inadequacies in the surveillance and regulation of markets, the debt crisis has brought to the fore the gaps within the structuring of economic and fiscal policies. In order to remedy this, EU institutions have not tarried in reforming and beefing-up the Stability and Growth Pact (SGP) and, absent of any power to amend any provisions of the TFEU, in adopting several inter-governmental agreements overarching EU law (the EFSF, the ESM, the Fiscal Compact).

Needless to say, the budgetary surveillance framework currently in place, defined in the SGP, remains broadly valid. Indeed, the SGP is still an essential part of the fiscal and macroeconomic framework of the EMU, which contributes to achieving macroeconomic stability in the EU and safeguarding the sustainability of public finances.

Nonetheless, the modifications brought to the SGP by the 2011 'six-pack' and the 2013 'two-pack' reflect a significant shift towards greater focus on debt and fiscal sustainability, with a view to reinforcing compliance and ensuring that national fiscal frameworks reflect the EU's fiscal rules. In particular, the criterion of public debt is henceforth better reflected in the budgetary surveillance mechanism. Accordingly, the Commission and the Council will be able to scrutinise the Member States' public finances much more carefully and pre-emptively than before. By the same token, the introduction of a new mechanism for macroeconomic surveillance is broadening the EU fiscal surveillance. Moreover, to increase the effectiveness of the SGP, a wider range of sanctions and measures are provided for in both the preventive and the corrective arms of the SGP. The financial sanctions range from interest-bearing deposits to fines. For Euro area countries, the Commission will be able to enforce more strongly than before the Council's recommendations by proposing sanctions at an earlier stage. What is more, the introduction of a reverse majority rule for the adoption of enforcement measures is likely to reinforce the effectiveness of the sanctions. In addition, the European Semester (a reinforced *ex-ante* coordination) allows a simultaneous assessment of both fiscal discipline (stability and convergence programmes), macroeconomic stability and structural reforms, fostering growth and employment. Needless to say, the 'six-pack' represents hitherto the most drastic reinforcement of economic governance since the launch of the EMU (Rehn 2011; de Sadeleer 2012).

Last but not least, the TSCG, better known as the Fiscal Compact, represents a step forward in providing 'national appropriation' of the fiscal control mechanisms. It buttresses some of the 'six-pack' obligations. In particular, it reinforces the two nominal anchors of the SGP: the GDP reference value for the deficit ratio (from a 3 per cent to a 1 or 0.5 per cent threshold) and confirms the 60 per cent of GDP reference value for the debt ratio (through a reduction at an average rate of one-twentieth per year as a benchmark) as well as the control of the medium-term budgetary objectives which are the centrepiece of multilateral surveillance.

At this stage, various observations may be made. The crisis undeniably and very clearly renders the need to replace the rules at the heart of economic governance, following decades of deregulation. Measures taken in soft law or the control over fiscal policies through the sanctioning of markets are no longer sufficient.

Nevertheless, one has the impression of meandering through an English-style park rather than a classic French garden. Indeed, one can only be struck by the heterogeneous nature of the texts setting out the new structure of governance, which is based on provisions forming part of international law (the EFSF, the ESM and the Fiscal Compact), treaty (Articles 121, 126 and 136 TFEU) and secondary law, hard law (the 'six-pack' and the 'two-pack'), soft law (the 2020 EU Strategy and Euro Plus Pact), Directives, and Regulations.

Competences are not clear-cut: the 2020 EU Strategy and the Euro Plus Pact stand astride EU and national competences, whereas the Fiscal Compact requirements reckon upon EU competences.

Moreover, the scope of these measures varies. As shown below, some rules are applicable to the 18 States with the euro as their common currency (Regulation (EU) No 1174/2011), whilst others apply to the whole of the EU (Regulation (EU) No 1173/2011 and No 1176/2011; Directive 2011/85/EU), and others still to the 23 States (Euro Plus Pact). This has led to a balkanisation of economic governance.

Moreover, these measures seek to proliferate the regimes of preventive control and sanctions (notices, reports, warnings, deposits, fines, etc.).

In addition to its Byzantine structure, the new governance also involves an accumulation of coordination and evaluation procedures (the European Semester, the Euro Plus Pact and the 2020 EU Strategy), with all of the problems of scheduling and overlap which this entails for a public service operating under budgetary constraints.

It also results in an increase in informal decision-making procedures, whether this may be with the Euro Group – an informal grouping within the Council – or more recently with the Council of the Euro area which, following its creation by the European Council on 26 October 2011, has now been called upon to play a significant role in economic integration within the Euro area. One also has the feeling that the informal procedures will progressively replace formal decision-making procedures, even if this involves formalising them as well.

Table 2.5 Economic governance in the EU

Measures	Member States
'Six-pack' Regulations 1175/2011, 1176/2011 and 1177/2011	28 EU Member States
Reference values mentioned in the Protocol No 12 on EDP and Numerical Fiscal Rules (Articles 5 to 7 Directive 2011/85)	27 (all EU Member States except UK)
'Six-pack' Regulations 1173/2011 and 1174/2011 and 'two-pack' Regulations 472/2013 and 473/2013	18 Member States having the euro as currency
Fiscal Compact	25 (all EU Member States, except UK, Cz and Croatia)
SEM	18 Member States having the euro as currency
Euro Plus Pact	23 (all EU Member States, except Sw, Hu, Cz and UK)

Furthermore, this governance still resembles a flat-footed colossus since it is liable to fall foul of the principle whereby powers must be allocated (Article 5(1) TEU). There is also a valid question as to whether the rules adopted by the Euro area (Article 136 TFEU) enable the sanctions applicable to excessive public deficits (EPDs) (Article 126 TFEU) to be extended to other pillars of the SGP, including in particular macroeconomic surveillance. Or is this a false problem? Only time will tell.

Will the accumulation of these processes distract us by throwing sand in our eyes? Will the application of the 'six-pack' and the 'two-pack' rules in a strict manner make sense in the face of a significant economic downturn? Is the new Treaty sufficient in order to set up a new economic governance whilst respecting the powers of the national parliaments and the European Parliament? Would the Fiscal Compact be any more effective than the reformed SGP? Will these reforms live up to the task? Will they be able to reduce imbalances in terms of indebtedness and competitiveness? In any case, will the waves of reform be able to reassure the markets, or will it all be necessary to do more in order to reassure the financial markets? Given that fiscal challenges differ among the Member States, the question arises as to whether a 'one-size-fits-all' approach fits the need for a differentiated speed of consolidation.

By themselves, the 'six-pack', the 'two-pack' and the Fiscal Compact will not bring the EU out of the crisis that started with Greece, spread to other peripheral Eurozone Member States and is likely to continue to challenge the future of the monetary union, let alone the EU itself.

Nevertheless, the grey areas remaining must not mask the will to bolster fiscal discipline through an enhanced coordination and a range of sanctions. Despite all the imperfections within the edifice which we are now describing, the signal given by the EU and the parties to the Fiscal Compact is as clear as crystal.

Be that as it may, that is still not the full story. Since the EU has been backed into a corner, the identity crisis that is undermining the integration project will at any cost have to lead to significant progress in terms of economic governance. The monetary federation has now been complemented by a budgetary federation, which in the end will inevitably lead the EU towards a tax federation. One day, with or without the UK authorities, it will be necessary to reform the Treaties establishing the EU, and that reform will certainly no longer be limited only to Articles 121 and 126 TFEU.

Notes

1 The powers of the EU are shared in the area of coordination of economic and employment policies as well as of social policies (Articles 4(1) and 5 TFEU). Unlike shared competences listed in Article 4(2), these competences are only the subject of coordination measures, and not of legislative harmonisation (Article 5 TFEU). On the other hand, the EU enjoys exclusive competence in the area of monetary policy for Member States whose currency is the euro (Article 4(1)(c) TFEU).

2 The work of the ESRB shall be taken into due consideration in the drafting of indicators relevant to financial market stability. The Commission shall invite the ESRB to provide its views regarding draft indicators, relevant to financial market stability. See Article 4(5) Regulation (EU) No 1176/2011 of the European Parliament, and of the Council of 16 November 2011 on the prevention and correction of macroeconomic imbalances, [2011] OJ L306/25.

3 Final report of the Task Force to the European Council, *Strengthening Economic Governance in the EU*, Brussels, 21 October 2010.

4 Decision of 10 May 2010 of the Representatives of the Governments of the Euro area Member States Meeting within the Council of the European Union establishing the European Financial Stability Facility, doc. 9610/10 and the EFSF Framework Agreement of 7 June 2010 between the participating Member States.

5 BVerfG, 7 September 2011, 2 BVR 987/10, *et al.*

6 The EFSM has been activated for Ireland and Portugal, for a total amount up to EUR48.5 billion (up to EUR22.5 billion for Ireland and up to EUR26 billion for Portugal), to be disbursed over three years (2011–13).

7 Decision 2010/281 of the European Central Bank of 14 May 2010 establishing a securities markets programme, [2010] OJ L 124/8.

8 Final Report of the Task Force to the European Council, *Strengthening Economic Governance in the EU*, para. 48.

9 Council Regulation (EU) No 407/2010 of 11 May 2010 establishing a European financial stabilisation mechanism, [2010] OJ L118/1.

10 On 25 March 2011, the European Council adopted in virtue of Article 48(6) TFEU, under the heading *Simplified revision procedures*, Decision 2011/199/EU. See the Decision of the European Council of 25 March 2011, OJ [2011] L 91/1.

11 In an interim ruling, the Court allowed the German authorities to ratify the Treaty. See BVerfG, 12 September 2012, BVR 1390/12. The final decision is still pending.

12 Article 109 of the *Grundgesetz* provides that 'In managing their respective budgets the Federation and the Länder shall take due account of the requirements of the overall economic equilibrium'. Spain was the second country after Germany to approve a golden rule of budget stability in the Constitution. On 7 September 2011,

the Spanish Senate approved an amendment to Article 135 of the Constitution introducing the requirement of a balanced budget provision and a strict limit on the indebtedness that both the national government and the regional governments may incur. On 7 September 2011, the Italian Lower House approved a constitutional reform introducing a balanced budget obligation (Article 81).

13 Regulation (EC) No 1466/97 of the Council of 7 July 1997 on the strengthening of the surveillance of budgetary positions and the surveillance and coordination of economic policies, [1997] OJ L209/1; Regulation (EC) No 1467/97 of the Council of 7 July 1997 on speeding-up and clarifying the implementation of the EDP, [1997] OJ L209/6.

14 Recital 19 of Directive 2011/85/EC of the Council of 8 November 2011 on requirements for budgetary frameworks of the Member States, [2011] OJ L306/41. See in particular Regulation (EU) No 1173/2011 of 16 November 2011, which sets out a system of sanctions for enhancing the enforcement of the preventive and corrective parts of SGP in the Euro area.

15 Regulation (EC) No 1055/2005 of the Council of 27 June 2005 amending Regulation (EC) No 1466/97 on the strengthening of the surveillance of budgetary positions and the surveillance and coordination of economic policies, [2005] OJ L 174/1.

16 Ecofin Council, *Specifications on the implementation of the Stability and Growth Pact and Guidelines on the format and content of Stability and Convergence Programmes* (2010), p. 4.

17 Regulation (EC) No 1055/2005 of the Council of 27 June 2005 amending Regulation (EC) No 1466/97 on the strengthening of the surveillance of budgetary positions and the surveillance and coordination of economic policies, OJ [2005] L174/1.

18 Regulation (EC) No 1467/97, which enacted more detailed legislation on the EDP on the basis of Article 126 TFEU, contains a flexible element that enables negative and unexpected economic shocks to be taken into account. It follows that the Council may decide, acting on a recommendation by the Commission, to extend the time limit granted in order to correct an excessive deficit, initially by one year. Accordingly, on the basis of '*special circumstances*', in 2009 the Council granted Ireland and Greece a supplementary period of two years beyond the normal time limit in order to enable them to correct their budget deficits.

19 Regulation (EU) No 1173/2011 of the European Parliament and of the Council of 16 November 2011 on the effective enforcement of budgetary surveillance in the Euro area, [2011] OJ L306/1.

20 Regulation 473/2013 of European Parliament and of the Council on common provisions for monitoring and assessing draft budgetary plans and ensuring the correction of excessive deficit of the Member States in the Euro area, [2013] L140/11.

21 Regulation 472/2013 of European Parliament and of the Council on the strengthening of economic and budgetary surveillance of Member States experiencing or threatened with serious difficulties with respect to their financial stability in the Euro area, [2013] L140/1.

22 Final report of the Task Force to the European Council, *Strengthening economic governance in the EU*, Brussels, 21 October 2010, p. 7.

23 Recital 18 and Article 5(1), 2nd al. of Regulation 1466/97 as amended by Regulation (EU) No 1175/2011; Recital 18 of Directive 2011/85/EU of the Council of 8 November 2011 on requirements for budgetary frameworks of the Member States, [2011] OJ L306/41.

24 It must be noted that in its 2010 *Specifications on the Implementation of the SGP*, the Ecofin Council already invited the Member States to use unexpected extra

revenues for deficit and debt reduction. See Ecofin Council, *Specifications on the Implementation of the Stability and Growth Pact* (2010), p. 5.

25 Article 4(1) of Regulation (EU) No 1173/2011 16 November 2011 on the effective enforcement of budgetary surveillance in the Euro area, [2011] OJ L306/1.

26 Article 5(1) al. 1 and 2 of Regulation 1466/97 as amended by Regulation (EU) No 1175/2011. It ought to be remembered that in accordance with the report on the SGP reform endorsed by the European Council on 22 March 2005, Euro area and ERM II Member States that have not yet reached their MTOs should achieve an annual adjustment in cyclically adjusted terms, net of one-offs and other temporary measures of 0.5 per cent of GDP as a benchmark. By the same token, in its *2010 Specifications on the Implementation of the SGP*, the Ecofin Council invited the Member States subject to an EDP procedure to achieve a minimum annual improvement in its cyclically adjusted balance of at least 0.5 per cent of GDP as a benchmark. See Ecofin Council, *Specifications on the implementation of the Stability and Growth Pact* (2010), p. 8.

27 Article 9 of Regulation (EU) No 473/2013 and Article 5 TSCG. See Section IV, Specifications of 1 July 2013 on the implementation of the Two Pack and Guidelines on the format and content of draft budgetary plans, economic partnership programmes and debt issuance reports.

28 Regulation (EU) No 1173/2011 of 16 November 2011 on the effective enforcement of budgetary surveillance in the Euro area, [2011] OJ L306/1.

29 However, in May 2012 the Commission has concluded that Hungary has taken the necessary corrective action to correct its excessive deficit for the lifting of the suspension of its Cohesion Fund commitments amounting to EUR500 million.

30 Regulation (EU) No 1176/2011 of the European Parliament and of the Council of 16 November 2011 on the prevention and correction of macroeconomic imbalances, [2011] OJ L306/25.

31 Commission, *Alert Mechanism Report prepared in accordance with Articles 3 and 4 of the Regulation on the prevention and correction of macro-economic imbalances*, COM(2012) 68 final.

32 Regulation (EU) No 1174/2011 of the European Parliament and of the Council of 16 November 2011 on enforcement measures to correct excessive macroeconomic imbalances in the Euro area, [2011] OJ L306/8.

33 See Council Recommendation 2008/390/EC of 14 May 2008 on the BEPG for the Member States and the Community (2008–10), [2011] OJ L 137/13.

34 Eurozone Member States that are subject to a macroeconomic adjustment procedure need not submit stability programmes under the terms of the European Semester. See Article 10(1) of Regulation (EU) No 472/2013.

35 See the Code of Conduct of the Ecofin Council of 7 September 2010. (See, *Specifications on the implementation of the Stability and Growth Pact and Guidelines on the format and content of Stability and Convergence Programmes*.)

36 The 2012 Commission Report was adopted on 23 November 2011 and not in January 2012. See Communication from the Commission, *Annual Growth Survey 2012*, COM(2011) 815 final.

37 Regulation (EU) No 473/2013 of the European Parliament and of the Council of 21 May 2013 on common provisions for monitoring and assessing draft budgetary plans and ensuring the correction of excessive deficit of the Member States in the Euro area, OJ L140/11.

38 Directive 2011/85/EU of the Council of 8 November 2011 on requirements for budgetary frameworks of the Member States, [2011] OJ L306/41.

39 Regulation (EU) No 472/2013 on the strengthening of economic and budgetary surveillance of Member States in the Euro area experiencing or threatened with serious difficulties with respect to their financial stability, [2013] OJ L 140, p. 1.

40 The UK Prime Minister vetoed the treaty, largely on the grounds that he had not managed to secure a guarantee that it would not affect the UK's financial services industry. See House of Commons, *The Treaty on Stability, Coordination and Governance in the Economic and Monetary Union*: political issues, Research Paper 12/14, 27 March 2012.

41 Lisbon Case, BVerfG, 2BvE 2/08, 30 June 2009, §§ 250 and 256; aid measures for Greece and against the euro rescue package Case, 2BvR 987/10, 2BvR 1485/10, 2BvR 1099/10, 7 September 2011, § 124. With respect to the guarantees in the framework of the ESM, the Constitutional Court ruled that by adopting this act, the German *Bundestag* did not impair in a constitutionally impermissible manner its right to adopt the budget and control its implementation by the government or the budget autonomy of future Parliaments. Nonetheless, the Federal Government is obliged to obtain prior approval by the Budget Committee before giving guarantees.

42 Pursuant to Article 3(1)(c), the Contracting Parties may temporarily deviate from their medium-term objective or the adjustment path towards it only in exceptional circumstances.

43 The Commission is merely called on to submit a report regarding the implementation of Article 3(2). Accordingly, the initiators of the infringement proceeding are the Member States, not the Commission.

44 Council Legal Service Opinion on the compatibility with EU law of draft Article 8 TSCG, 26 January 2012.

45 Article 6(2) al. 5 of Regulation 1466/97 as amended by Regulation (EU) No 1175/2011; Article 6(2) of Regulation (EU) No 1173/2011 on the effective enforcement of budgetary surveillance in the Euro area; Article 3(3) of Regulation (EU) No 1174/2011 on enforcement measures to correct excessive macroeconomic imbalances in the Euro area, [2011] OJ L306/8, (TSCG. Article 7).

46 Decision 2010/320/EU of the Council of 10 May 2010 addressed to Greece with a view to reinforcing and deepening fiscal surveillance and giving notice to Greece to take measures for the deficit reduction judged necessary to remedy the situation of excessive deficit, [2010] OJ L145/1; Council implementing decision 2011/77/EU of 7 December 2010 granting EU financial assistance to Ireland, [2011] OJ L30/4; Council implementing decision 2011/344/EU granting EU financial assistance to Portugal, amended by decision of 2 September 2011, [2011] OJ L240/8.

47 The Committee is composed of senior officials from national administrations, and central banks, the ECB, and the Commission. See Council decision 2003/476/EC of 18 June 2003 on a revision of the Statutes of the Economic and Financial Committee, [2003] OJ L 158.

48 Ever since the entry into force of the Maastricht Treaty, the institutional arrangements regarding MEU are specific. In sharp contrast with other EU economic policies such as internal market, the role of the European Parliament has always been belittled. The Lisbon Treaty does not bring any improvement.

49 14th Recital of the preamble and Article 2 bis (4) and 2 bis of Regulation 1466/97 as amended by the Regulation (EU) No 1175/2011. In this connection, the Future of Europe Group proposes that the European Parliament 'should, among other things, be consulted within the scope of the European Semester before the formulation of fundamental aspects (e.g. the Annual Growth Survey) or on concrete recommendations affecting the EU, or the euro area as a whole'.

50 Article 2 bis ter (3) of Regulation (EC) No 1466/97 as amended by Regulation (EU) No 1175/2011. See also Article 8(4) on the strengthening of economic and budgetary surveillance of Member States experiencing or threatened with serious difficulties with respect to their financial stability in the Euro area, COM(2011) 819 final.

51 Regulation (EU) No 1175/2011 modifying the Regulation (EC) No 1466/97 under-
scores the association of national parliaments in drafting different programmes. See
the 16th Recital of the Preamble of Regulation 1466/97 as amended by Regulation
(EU) No 1175/2011. See also Article 8(4) of the proposal for a regulation on the
strengthening of economic and budgetary surveillance of Member States experiencing or threatened with serious difficulties with respect to their financial stability
in the Euro area, COM(2011) 819 final.
52 See also BVerfG (2BvE 2/08), of 11 September 2011 on the MESF, § 128, by virtue
of which the *Bundenstag* is called on to give its assent to the considered aids.

References

Allemand, F. and Martucci, F. (2012) 'La nouvelle gouvernance économique
européenne', *Cahiers de droit européen*, 1, 21.
Artis, M. (2002) 'The Stability and Growth Pact: Fiscal Policy in the EMU', in Breuss,
F., Fink, G. and Griller, S. (eds), *Institutional, Legal and Economic Aspects of the
EMU*, Vienna: Springer, 101–16.
Calliess, C. (2012) 'The Future of the Eurozone and the Role of the German Federal
Constitutional Court', *Yearbook of European Law*, Oxford: Oxford University
Press, 402–15.
Carrera Hernandez, J. (2012) 'El Tratado de Estabilidad, coordinación y gobernanza
en la Unión económica y monetaria: un impulso a la realización de la política
económica de la unión europea o un tratado superfluo e innecesario?', *Revista
General de Derecho Europeo*, 28.
Clerc, O. (2012) 'Les traités SCG et MES et la participation des Parlements nationaux
à la gouvernance économique de l'Union: déclin confirmé ou potentiel renouveau?',
Revue des Affaires Européennes—Law & European Affairs, 4, 759.
Craig, P. (2012) 'The Stability, Coordination and Governance Treaty: Principles,
Politics and Pragmatism', *European Law Review*, 3, 231.
Craig, P. (2013) 'Guest Editorial. Pringle: Legal Reasoning, Text, Purpose and
Teleology', *Maastricht Journal*, 20 (1), 3.
Dechâtre, L. (2011) 'La décision de Karlsruhe sur le MESF: une validation sous
condition et une mise en garde sybilline pour l'avenir', *Cahiers de droit européen*,
1, 321.
De Sadeleer, N. (2012) 'The New Architecture of the European Economic Governance:
A Leviathan or a Flat-Footed Colossus', *Maastricht Journal*, 19 (3), 354–82.
De Streel, A. (2013) 'The Evolution of the EU Economic Governance since the Treaty
of Maastricht: An Unfinished Task', *Maastricht Journal*, 20 (3), 349–51.
De Streel, A. and Etienne, J. (2012) 'Le TSCG au sein de l'UEM', *Journal de droit
européen*, 182.
Fitoussi, J-P. (2010) 'Politiques macroéconomiques et réformes structurelles: bilan et
perspectives de la gouvernance économique au sein de l'UE', *Revue d'économie
publique*, 120 (2), 253.
Hinajeros, A. (2012) 'The Euro Area Crisis and Constitutional Limits to Fiscal
Integration', *Cambridge Yearbook of European Legal Studies*, 256.
Jabko, N. (2011) 'Which Economic Governance for the EU?', *SIEPS*, 2, 12.
Jacqué, J. P. (2004) 'The principle of Institutional Balance', *Common Market Law
Review*, 41, 383.
Jacqué, J. P. (2010) *Droit institutionnel de l'UE*, 6th edn, Paris: Dalloz.

Kasel, A. (2012) *'Le président de l'euro groupe et la gouvernance économique de la zone euro'*, Paris: EMA.

Lefeuvre, E. (2011) *Sortir de l'Euro? Une idée dangereuse*, Paris: Eyrolles, 27.

Louis, J. V. (2009) *Commentaire J. Mégret. L'Union européenne et sa monnaie*, Brussels: Presses de l'ULB, 108–15.

Louis, J. V. (2010) 'The No-Bailout Clause and Rescue Packages', *Common Market Law Review*, 47, 971–86.

Louis, J. V. (2011) 'The Enforcement of Economic Governance', in Lepoivre, M., Keller-Noëllet, J. and Verhelst, S. (eds), *The European Union and Economic Governance. Studia Diplomatica*, 64 (4), 58–61.

Louis, J. V. (2012a) 'The Unexpected Revision of the Lisbon Treaty and the Establishment of a European Stability Mechanism', in Ashiagbor, D., Contourids, N., and Lianos, I. (eds), *The European Union after the Treaty of Lisbon*, Cambridge: Cambridge University Press, 284–319.

Louis, J. V. (2012b) 'La nouvelle 'gouvernance' économique de l'espace euro', in *Mélanges en hommage au professeur Joël Molinier*, Paris: Lextenso éditions.

Louis, J. V. (2012c) 'Un traité vite fait, bien fait? Le traité du 1er mars 2012 sur la stabilité, la coordination et la gouvernance dans l'Union économique économique', *Revue trimestrielle de droit européen*, 2, 4.

Louis, J. V. (2013) 'La sentencia *Pringle*', *Revista General de Derecho Europeo*, 29.

Martucci, F. (2012) 'Traité sur la stabilité, la coordination et la gouvernance, traité instituant le mécanisme européen de stabilité. Le droit international public au secours de l'UEM', *Revue des Affaires Européennes—Law & European Affairs*, 4, 716–31.

Martucci, F., Lasserre Capdeville, J., and Kovar, J-P. (2011) 'Le système européen de surveillance financière', *Europe*, 6, 4–9.

Moloney, N. (2010) 'EU Financial Market Regulation after the Global Financial Crisis: "More Europe" or More Risks?', *Common Market Law Review*, 47, 1317–83.

Pernice, I. (2012) *Legal opinion of on the International Agreement on a Reinforced Economic Union*.

Piris, J-C. (2011) *The Lisbon Treaty*, Cambridge: Cambridge University Press.

Piris, J-C. (2012) 'Avanti tutti, Europa!', *EuropeanVoice*, 29 March 2012, 13.

Rehn, O. (2011) 'EU's new 'six-pack' shows just how tough Europe will be on national governments', *The Telegraph*, 20 October 2011, London, UK.

Ruffert, M. (2011) 'The European Debt Crisis and European Union Law', *Common Market Law Review*, 48, 1800.

Triantafyllou, D. (2011) 'Les plans de sauvetage de la zone Euro et la peau de chagrin', *RDUE*, 2, 195–208.

Van der Mensbrugghe, Fr. (2011) 'New Pan-European Regulators for the Financial Sector', *Annales d'études européennes de l'UCL (2011)*, 165–83.

Verhelst, S. (2012) 'Will the National 'Golden Rule' Eclipse the EU Fiscal Norms?', *Vox EU*.

Vitorino, A. (2012) 'Le TSCG: beaucoup de bruit pour rien?', *Notre Europe*.

3 The impact of pension systems on financial development

An empirical study

Shouji Sun and Jiye Hu

3.1 Introduction

What are major factors that affect a country's economic and financial development? This question is always bewildering scholars. A large number of economists find that economic growth is positively associated with financial development (Goldsmith 1969; Levine 1997), and recently a growing literature has examined the links between legal origins and financial development and has found that legal system development affects access to external finance, and that differences in financial development between countries are caused by different legal origins. At the same time, the endowment hypothesis argues that financial development is indirectly dependent on natural resources, climate and other resource endowments through the property system. In the past 30 years, confronting an aging population crisis worldwide, countries have adopted different measures and policies to manage this issue. In this chapter, we assume that the pension system determines financial development and present this as the pension fund hypothesis. Specifically, this applies to those countries that use an accumulated pension fund system. On the one hand, they accumulate considerable pension assets, which can supply stable investment capital to financial markets. On the other hand, as institutional investors, pension funds can improve corporate governance, promote innovation in financial products and improve the efficiency of financial markets. For the countries with a pay-as-you-go (PAYG) pension system, pension funds are paid in the current pay period, which will limit the surplus on the balance sheet or may even potentially result in a deficit. The pension fund thereby makes little contribution to financial markets.

This chapter analyses the relationship between pension funds and financial development using cross-sectional, time series and panel data. The first academic contribution of this chapter is that it is one of the first studies to consider three factors: legal origin, resource endowment and the pension system, in a cross-sectional analysis of financial development. We find that these three factors do not conflict but instead interact with financial development. The second contribution is derived from the empirical research conducted with panel data. We find that different pension systems have different impacts on financial development. Large pension funds bring a greater positive influence on the financial development of non-common law countries with underdeveloped financial markets and low economic growth. The result shows that with the current aging population crisis, countries could reform and redesign their pension systems and try to use the accumulation system to enlarge the size of their pension funds, which could then be used for financial and economic development with the restriction of legal origins and resource endowment.

The structure of this chapter is as follows. Section 3.2 will propose the topics and review the related literature. Section 3.3 will introduce pension systems from an international perspective and explain how pension funds can influence financial development. Section 3.4 will present the empirical results, and several conclusions are reached in Section 3.5.

3.2 Research topics and literature review

Economists have extensively studied the factors contributing to financial, and economic development (Beck *et al.* 2003). John R. Hicks, a Nobel Prize winner, studied how finance stimulated the industrial revolution and found that the industrial revolution was not triggered by technological innovations but by financial reform because most new technology was invented or discovered before the revolution. Hicks (1969) believes that the legal and monetary systems are the foundations of a market economy. Goldsmith (1969) compares the financial interrelation ratios of 100 years and finds that financial development, to a large extent, reflects the country's economic development and that the two components are positively correlated. King and Levine (1993) analyze the data of 80 countries over the period from 1960–89, and their results show that more developed financial markets tend to experience faster economic growth. Financial intermediaries are positively associated with economic development. The development of financial sectors could induce the development of other sectors, and financial development is a predictor of economic development.

Apart from the positive relationship between financial development and economic development, La Porta *et al.* (1998, 1999) propose the legal origin hypothesis. Different legal origins lead to differences in financial development: in common law countries, investors and creditors are better protected than in civil law countries. Accordingly, their financial development is better. More specifically, compared with civil law countries, especially French civil law countries, the English common law countries tend to provide stronger legal protection to shareholders and creditors. The common law has a capacity and flexibility that is oriented towards financial development. Britain's former colonies inherited the common law system; thus, their financial development began from an advantageous starting position. However, if a country was colonized by France, Spain, Portugal or other civil law countries, it will have a civil law tradition. Its financial market development level is therefore relatively low on average.

Acemoglu *et al.* (2001) propose the endowment hypothesis: during colonial expansion, European colonists adjusted the colonization according to the geographical and resource endowments. In those regions that shared a similar latitude to Europe and in which European colonists had low mortality rates, European settlers chose a resident-colonization style to prevent the State from plundering individuals. The resident style also emphasizes freedom of contract, which helps to protect private property and benefits the development of financial markets. In epidemic regions at low latitudes, because of the harsh environment and high mortality, the European colonists had no intentions to create settlements; thus, the style of predatory colonization was applied. A few controllers were allowed to take advantage of their privilege and private property was less effectively protected, which slowed financial development. Therefore, different resource endowments led to different colonial policies, which in turn produced different legal systems in terms of property protection and thus determined the level of financial development.

In addition to the legal origin hypothesis and the endowment hypothesis, Stulz and Williamson (2003) have discussed the question of financial development from a religious and cultural point of view. They find that different religions have different attitudes towards the rights of creditors, resulting in different levels of financial development. Compared with Christian Protestant-oriented countries, Catholic and Islamic countries have negative attitudes regarding interest, and their credit is therefore at a relatively underdeveloped level. Using Switzerland as an example, Roe (2006) proposes a view that regards politics and war issues as the driving forces behind the government's willingness to open and develop capital markets, which subsequently determines the development of financial markets in different countries. Differences are therefore created for political reasons rather than driven by legal systems. Switzerland has a prosperous financial sector, though it is a civil law country, in part because it suffered lower losses during the First and Second World Wars. Moreover, Cheffins (2001) studies the history of the securities market in England and finds that ownership and control rights in terms of law have not been as important as the implications of the legal origin hypothesis. Coffee (1999, 2007) believes that although the relationship between the protection of investors' rights and the development of the stock market appears to be convincing, the legal origin hypothesis misplaces the causation as being the other way around.

3.3 Pension funds' impact on financial development: a new hypothesis

From the above discussion, many example countries can be identified that support the legal origin hypothesis and the resource endowment hypothesis. However, these hypotheses cannot explain the differences across countries, and some countries such as Switzerland can only be regarded as exceptions. The critics of the legal origin and endowment hypotheses, who take religious, cultural, political and war points of views, are reasonable. For example, the legal origin hypothesis cannot be applied to the Netherlands, Denmark and Switzerland, where financial markets are well developed. The endowment hypothesis does not work for Chile, which has a geography and a mortality rate similar to its neighbors but a stock market that performs well. Neither of the two hypotheses can explain why the Chilean stock market is much better than that of New Zealand when the former is a French civil law country with a high death rate. Davis and Hu (2008) have compared 18 Organisation for Economic Co-operation and Development (OECD) countries and 19 transforming countries. Their results indicated that the size of pension funds could be an explanatory variable for the differences in economic growth between countries, particularly for the transforming countries. If an accumulated scheme could be integrated into the system as part of a pension system reform, it will bring significant returns in the stock market and also to the national economy of a country. Therefore, based on the contribution of pension funds to economic growth, the legal origin hypothesis introduced by La Porta *et al.* should be revised to address the fact that pension funds can drive economic growth by providing financial support to the real economy. Following this point, the present chapter argues that in addition to the religious and cultural view and the political and militaristic view on the differences in financial development, the pension fund view can provide another explanation that is particularly useful for these exceptional countries.

Figure 3.1 shows a comparison of the financial development between the UK, the US and some civil law countries. Switzerland is a German civil law jurisdiction, the Netherlands is a French civil law jurisdiction, and Denmark and

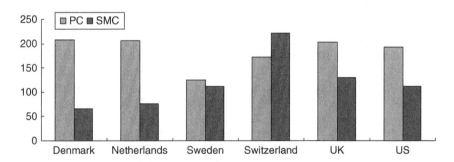

Figure 3.1 Comparison of financial development in civil law countries and in Anglo-American countries

(Source: World Bank 2012: New Database on Financial Development and Structure. Available online at: http://econ.worldbank.org/WBSITE/EXTERNAL/EXTDEC/EX TRESEARCH/0,,contentMDK:20696167~pagePK:64214825~piPK:64214943~theSi tePK:469382,00.html (accessed 31 January 2014).)

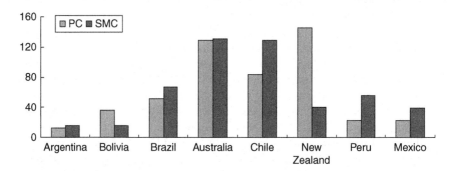

Figure 3.2 Comparison of financial development in Australia and in Chile and their neighbours

(Source: World Bank 2012: New Database on Financial Development and Structure. Available online at: http://econ.worldbank.org/WBSITE/EXTERNAL/EXTDEC/EX TRESEARCH/0,,contentMDK:20696167~pagePK:64214825~piPK:64214943~theSi tePK:469382,00.html (accessed 31 January 2014).)

Sweden are Nordic civil law countries. The indicators are the ratios of private credit (PC) and stock market capitalization (SMC) over gross domestic product (GDP). In Figure 3.1, the financial development of Switzerland outperforms that of the UK and the US. Denmark, the Netherlands and Sweden have development levels similar to the UK and the US. The legal origin hypothesis can only regard this situation as an exception because it does not capture the difference between these countries. Roe's politics and war hypothesis works only for Switzerland, but not for the Nordic countries.

Figure 3.2 displays a comparison of Chile and its neighboring countries together with Australia and New Zealand in the southern hemisphere. Chile and its neighbors not only share similar geography but also the same French legal tradition. According to data from Acemoglu *et al.* (2001), the death rates of the first group of settlers in those countries were more or less equal: 68.9 per thousand in Chile and Argentina and 71 per thousand in Bolivia, Brazil, Peru and Mexico. However, in terms of financial development, the PC/GDP ratio of Chile is 6.6 times that of Argentina, 2.3 times that of Bolivia and 3.7 times that of Peru. The SMC/GDP ratio of Chile is 8.6 times that of Argentina, 8.4 times that of Bolivia, 2.3 times that of Peru and 1.9 times that of Brazil. Neither the legal origin hypothesis nor the endowment hypothesis can properly interpret those figures.

Similarly, the legal origin hypothesis and the endowment hypothesis do not address the fact that the Chilean stock market performs better than New Zealand's. New Zealand has a common law system and low settler mortality (8.55 per 1,000 per year) compared with Chile (68.9 per 1,000 per year). However, the SMC/GDP ratio in Chile is 2.2 times larger than that of New Zealand. These two theories cannot even address the differences between

Australia and New Zealand, which have the common geography, language and legal origin. Nevertheless, the financial development of Australia is nearly the same as Chile and far better than New Zealand. What is the reason behind these differences?

If these hypotheses do not hold true in many cases, this elicits natural doubts about them in addition to new ideas: do any other factors address these exceptions? This is the key question of this research. Based on an understanding of pension funds and economic development, this chapter presents a new hypothesis to address this issue.

3.3.1 Social security systems and pension funds

Almost all countries in the world have established various social security systems to meet the needs of an aging population. The accumulated size of pension funds varies under different systems and policies. There are primarily five types of pension systems in terms of whether the funds are accumulated and how they are accumulated (Zheng 2005).

The Anglo-American model: in countries such as the UK and the US, the national pension scheme takes low fees and therefore provides a low substitution rate. The majority of pension funds come from corporate voluntary annuities.

The Continental model: in European countries as represented by Germany and France, the national public pension funds are PAYG. There is little surplus, and the retirement pension is frequently substituted. The corporate annuity contribution is relatively small; thus, the size of the accumulated funds is limited.

The Nordic European model: in the northern countries, aside from the corporate annuity, the government has established mandatory pension systems through legislation or work unions, which accumulate large pension funds. This system can be considered a mandatory pension model.

The Chilean model: in Latin America, the Middle East and Eastern Europe, the social security system requires people to have a personal account and to accumulate on a compulsory basis. The funds are completely tradable in the markets. In these countries, pension funds come from self-accumulated personal accounts.

The Singaporean model: the government has both a national, and a personal pension system. The central government controls the interest and announces it regularly, but the interest cannot reflect the real return. The Singaporean pension system is fully funded.

The different methods of raising and managing funds have resulted in different sized pension funds. According to data from international financial services organizations, global pension funds have grown from US$16.9 trillion to US$31.4 trillion, which is an increase of 85.8 per cent from 2001 to 2007. The largest four countries, the US, the UK, Canada and Ireland, accounted for 78 per cent (US$24.5 trillion) of the total pension assets. The

Table 3.1 Different social security models

Anglo-American model	Continental model	Nordic European model	Chilean model	Singaporean model
USA, UK, Canada, Ireland	France, German, Spain	Austria, Iceland, Switzerland	Chile, Peru, Argentina	Singapore

Anglo-American model takes the majority shares of all global funds (Xiong and Gao 2010).

3.3.2   Impact of pension funds on financial development

Pension funds have both quantitative and qualitative impacts on financial development. Quantitatively, pension funds increase the capital supply to financial markets. Larger financial markets are located in countries with large pension funds to GDP ratios. Qualitatively, the managing organizations of pension funds are institutional investors who influence corporate governance and information disclosure, and therefore help establish financial markets and improve the efficiency and depth of information. There is evidence supporting this point. In 2011, the weighted average ratio of pension funds to GDP for all OECD countries was 72.4 per cent, while the civil law countries, the Netherlands, Iceland and Switzerland, took the top three places with over 100 per cent. Other countries such as Australia, the UK, Finland, the US, Canada and Chile all exceeded 60 per cent. Greece has nearly no private pensions, but it has the highest public pension replacement rate (110 per cent); therefore, the Greek government's debt as related to public pensions aggravated its fiscal situation. Other European countries with a sovereign debt crisis such as Spain, Portugal and Italy (which, together with Greece, were called the 'PIGS') had private pension assets only accounting for 7.8 per cent, 7.7 per cent and 4.9 per cent of their GDP, respectively. Hence, these countries must pay the public pensions for their retirees, which worsens fiscal sustainability (OECD 2012). Compared with individual investors, pension funds as institutional investors have four advantages when promoting financial development as described below.

First, pension fund portfolios are held over a long period of time, which provides abundant funds to the financial market in the long term rather than providing short-term speculative capital. These funds are thus good for the stability of financial markets. For example, in the US, the 401k pension scheme brings substantial long-term investment capital to Wall Street, which provides IT companies such as Microsoft, IBM and Apple with the opportunity to grow into industry leaders by taking advantage of the capital market.

The pension-holding organizations become shareholders of the world's most promising companies. At the same time, the organizations obtain constant returns from these high-quality companies. The pension and capital markets interact positively and profitably.

Second, pension funds as large institutional investors are also large share-holders. Their influence on the board can help improve the governance structure of listed companies. Pension-holding organizations can participate in nominating directors and amendments, proxy voting and drafting motions, all of which make information disclosure more transparent and improve corporate governance and financial conditions. For example, pension funds in California have been actively involved in corporate governance through an investment committee composed of an affiliated group of lawyers. This group participates in investment analysis, monitoring investment targets and the management team, and rejecting unfavorable motions together with small shareholders in general meetings (Hebb 2006). The positive impacts of institutional investors on corporate governance result in investment returns in the stock market, which once again enhances investor confidence in the financial markets.

Third, pension funds indirectly stimulate financial innovation. Bodie (1990) studies the relationship between pension funds and financial innovation and finds that pension funds in the US play a significant role in asset securitization, derivatives, debt and other financial innovations. Many new financial products in the US such as zero-coupon bonds, options and futures, guaranteed securities, guaranteed mortgages and forward contracts are being created to meet the demands of pension funds.

Finally, pension funds as managed by the government are supervised, and the financial markets they enter are also regulated by the government. The returns on investment of pension funds are essential for both the State and for individuals. In this context, supervision and regulatory systems receive widespread attention, which is helpful for developing sound regulatory systems and policies for financial market development, such as more flexible taxation, more efficient and transparent transactions, and more risk management departments and advisory intermediaries. Thus, the development of pension funds is good for a country's financial innovation, the modernization of the infrastructure for security exchanges and the establishment of a sound settlement system.

3.4   Empirical results

Earlier in the chapter we found that pension funds have different impacts on financial markets, particularly on security markets among different countries. Because the legal origin and endowment hypotheses do not support the observations, we proposed the pension hypothesis to explain these differences. Here, we use empirical analysis on cross-sectional data, panel data and time series data; the results show that our hypothesis is valid.

3.4.1   Cross-sectional data analysis

3.4.1.1   Data description

Two indicators measure financial development. The first indicator is the ratio of PC to GDP, which measures the development of financial intermediaries. Private credit is defined as the credit issued by banks and other financial institutions to the private sector. The second indicator is the ratio of SMC to GDP. In the regression equation, the logarithms of the average values for these two variables from 2003 to 2005 are used; they are denoted by LPC and LSMC, respectively. The data are extracted from the New Database on Financial Development and Structure in the World Bank.

LPAP represents the logarithm of PAP, which is the value of pension funds over GDP in 2002. The data from OECD countries are sourced from *Pension Market in Focus* 2003. The data from other countries come from Hu's 2005 research.

ENGLISH is a dummy variable that is equal to 1 when the country's legal system originated from English common law and 0 otherwise. LGNP is the logarithm of the average gross national product (GNP) from 1970 to 1995. Both ENGLISH and LGNP are from the data of La Porta *et al.* (1999).

LPR measures property protection in 2002; it is the logarithm of the index of economic freedom which comes from The Heritage Foundation (2001). There are only 24 cases with mortality rates in the sample of Acemoglu *et al.* (2001) and this chapter thus uses property protection to replace mortality rate as a measure of endowments.

LINFL is the logarithm of the standard deviation of the inflation rate from 1980 to 1999. This variable measures the stability of macroeconomic policy, and is sourced from the Penn World Table (PWT) 6.1 (Heston *et al.* 2002).

3.4.1.2   Results

Table 3.2 presents the results of the ordinary least square (OLS) regression models. There are two groups of models based on the dependent variables LSMC and LPC. We can draw several conclusions from the regression results.

First, considering financial intermediaries, the impact of pension funds on the stock market is larger and stronger. In the LSMC models, the variable LPAP is significant in all five models, and the coefficients indicate that the elasticity of pension funds on the market value ranges from 0.15 to 0.23. In other words, when controlling for legal origin, property protection, GNP per capita and the standard deviation of the inflation rate, an increase of 1 per cent in pension fund assets will increase the stock market value by 0.15 to 0.23 per cent. In the LPC models, the elasticity of pension funds is much smaller, ranging from 0.09 to 0.036. If controlling for the legal origin and property protection, LPAP is no longer significant.

Table 3.2 OLS estimation results

Explanatory variables	Model A: dependent variable (LSMC)					Model B: dependent variable (LPC)				
	A1	A2	A3	A4	A5	B1	B2	B3	B4	B5
LPAP	0.23***	0.15**	0.17**	0.21***	0.15**	0.09**	0.06	0.05	0.07	0.036
	(3.57)	(2.05)	(2.46)	(2.99)	(2.09)	(2.04)	(1.20)	(1.05)	(1.53)	(0.74)
ENGLISH	—	0.46*	0.60**	—	0.59**	—	0.34*	0.33*	—	0.28
		(1.84)	(2.19)		(2.12)		(1.95)	(1.71)		(1.50)
LPR	—	0.96***	—	0.34	0.28	—	1.07***	—	0.62**	0.57**
		(3.34)		(0.84)	(0.72)		(5.53)		(2.46)	(2.30)
LGNP	0.29***	—	0.35***	0.22*	0.29**	0.27***	—	0.31***	0.14*	0.18**
	(3.32)		(3.97)	(1.75)	(2.34)	(4.67)		(5.05)	(1.80)	(2.22)
LINFL	-0.29	—	-0.10	-0.26	-0.08	-0.48***	—	-0.38***	-0.41***	-0.34**
	(-1.55)		(-0.52)	(-0.52)	(-0.42)	(-3.86)		(-2.80)	(-3.51)	(-2.62)
Constant	0.24	-0.67	0.07	-0.53	-0.51	0.60	-0.53	0.50	-0.67	-0.66
	(0.30)	(-0.60)	(0.09)	(-1.38)	(-0.46)	(1.19)	(-0.70)	(1.00)	(-0.94)	(-0.95)
Obs	55	55	55	55	55	56	56	56	56	56
Adjusted R^2	0.42	0.42	0.46	0.42	0.46	0.54	0.51	0.56	0.58	0.59

Notes: ***, **, * indicate significance at the 1%, 5% or 10% confidence level; the t value is shown in brackets

Second, similar to pension funds, the results show that the legal origin is more significant for the stock market value. When controlling other variables, if a country is a common law country, the ratio of stock market capital to GDP could increase as much as 59 per cent, while the ratio of private capital to GDP will increase by 30 per cent. In other words, the legal origin has nearly twice the impact on the stock market as that of financial intermediaries, which is consistent with the conclusion of La Porta *et al.* (1999).

Third, if GNP per capita is the control variable, the variable of property protection is no longer significant because these two variables are highly correlated (0.73). When controlling for pension funds and legal origin only, the elasticity of property protection on stock market capital is 0.96, while its effect on PC is 1.07, and both are statistically significant. When controlling for pension funds, legal origin, GNP per capita and the standard variance of the inflation rate, the impact of property protection on stock market capitalization becomes insignificant, but the impact on PC remains significant with a lower confidence level.

Fourth, the variable of GNP per capita is significant in all models, which means that economic development is one of the most important factors in financial development. The impact of the standard deviation of inflation rates on private credit is significant, but not the impact on stock market capitalization. This finding means that macroeconomic policy is very important to the development of financial intermediaries.

3.4.2   Panel data analysis

In subsection 3.4.1, the cross-sectional models test the legal origin, endowment and pension hypotheses on financial market development with a focus on the security market. As the sample size is limited to 55 or 56, it is not feasible to further examine the different types of pension systems. In this section, a panel dataset is used for empirical analysis on this point.

3.4.2.1   Regression model

Following the result of the previous OLS equations, this section regards the ratio of SMC to GDP as the dependent variable. The explanatory variables are the ratio of PAP to GDP, GDP per capita and government expenses to GDP (CG). Theoretically, the first two variables are positively associated with financial development, and the last variable is negatively associated with financial development. For the convenience of calculating the elasticity, the logarithms of all items are taken, and we have the estimated equation:

$$\text{LSMC}_{it} = \alpha_i + \beta_1 \text{LPAP}_{it} + \beta_2 \text{LGDP}_{it} + \beta_3 \text{LCG}_{it} + u_{it}$$

where: i is the country,
t is the year,
α_i is the intercept,
β_1, β_2, β_3 are the coefficients of variables, and
u_{it} is the error term.

The panel dataset is built on the data of 26 OECD countries from 2001 to 2008. The stock market capital data sourced from the World Bank's New Database on Financial Development and Structure (2012), the ratio of pension funds to GDP is sourced from OECD *Pension Market in Focus* (2012) and GDP per capita and government expenses to GDP are sourced from the PWT Table 7.1 (Heston *et al.* 2012).

In the sample of 26 countries, there are seven of the Anglo-American model, nine of the Continental model, five of the Chilean model and five of the Nordic European model. This sample represents short panel data because the number of cases is fewer than the number of years. The F ratio rejects the hypothesis of mixed-effect models but accepts that fixed-effect models should be applied. Furthermore, the Hausman test shows that the model with all countries pooled, the model with only the Anglo-American pension countries and the model with the Nordic European pension countries should be applied to a fixed-effect model. The Continental and Chilean models should be applied to a random-effect model. In the estimate of the fixed-effect, considering the differences in financial development across countries, the GLS method (cross-section weights) is used.

3.4.2.2 Results

The results of the panel regression are displayed in Table 3.3. If GDP per capita and the government expense ratios are held constant, the sizes of the pension funds are significant in all models, with coefficients between 0.28 and 0.73. This result means that an increase of 1 per cent in the value of the pension funds will result in an increase of 0.28 to 0.73 per cent in the total value of stock market capital. It is noted that this impact on financial development is less significant in the Anglo-American countries where the financial markets are well developed and pension assets are at a larger scale. To the contrary, the impact is stronger in the less developed countries with smaller pension funds and less developed financial markets, such as the Continental countries, emerging Latin American countries and Middle Eastern countries. Without the effect of GDP per capita and government expenses, every unit of percentage increase will lead to an increase of 0.28 per cent in the Anglo-American model, 0.33 per cent in the Continental model, 0.58 per cent in the Chilean model and 0.73 per cent in the Nordic European model. This result means that the size of the pension funds has a more significant impact on the stock market in

Table 3.3 Estimation results from panel data

	All countries	Anglo-American model	Continental model	Chilean model	Nordic European model
LPAP	0.46***	0.28**	0.33***	0.58***	0.73**
	(7.08)	(2.26)	(3.26)	(9.93)	(2.56)
LGDP	0.96***	0.87***	2.27***	0.55**	0.24
	(4.79)	(3.10)	(4.33)	(2.52)	(0.31)
LCG	−0.85***	−2.28***	−0.74	−0.09	−1.45***
	(−4.24)	(−6.12)	(−1.44)	(−0.43)	(−2.68)
Constant	−5.48***	−1.31	−18.76***	−2.97	2.30
	(−2.63)	(−0.49)	(−3.49)	(−1.53)	(0.27)
Countries	26	7	9	5	5
Obs	208	56	72	40	40
Adjusted R²	0.97	0.96	0.36	0.81	0.82

Notes: ***, **, * indicate the significance at the 1%, 5% or 10% confidence levels; the t value is shown in brackets

non-common law countries and in countries with less developed financial markets.

Additionally, GDP per capita is significant in the first four models. The elasticity on financial development is between 0.55 and 2.27, which means that the economic level is one of the most important factors in financial development. In the Nordic European countries, GDP per capita is not significant because it is highly correlated with the other variable, government expenses to GDP ratio. The significance is reduced in the Chilean model for the same reason.

The variable of government expenses is significant in three of the five models, with coefficients ranging from −0.74 to −2.28. The negative sign shows that if the government interferes more substantially with social economic activities, financial development is more restrained. This result is consistent with the past literature. Once again, the collinearity in variables causes the government expense variable to be insignificant in the Chilean model.

3.4.3   Time series data analysis

The panel analysis shows that pension funds contribute more to financial development when they accumulate. For instance, from the view of legal origin, Chile is a French civil law country and has a similar geographic endowment to its neighboring countries. The pension reform in 1981 was a special case implemented by the Pinochet military government, but it inadvertently became a very successful and typical case in global pension reform. The pension reform was an exogenous shock to the Chilean financial market. Therefore, in this context, Chilean pension reform provides a good case study for the impact on financial development.

Generally, after the 1981 pension reform, two fundamental features of Chile's social security system were established: first, personal accounts transformed the financing method from the traditional PAYG system to a funded system; and second, pension management companies called *Administradoras de Fondos de Pensiones* shifted centralized management to decentralized management. The pension reform has not only provided adequate pensions, supported retirees' lives and maintained social stability, but it has also brought prosperity and stability to the capital markets and enhanced economic vitality.

To further test the 'pension hypothesis', cointegration and vector autoregression analyses are applied to the data from after the pension reform in Chile from 1981 to 2009, for a total of 29 years. In this empirical study, the data sources are similar: the SMC data is from the World Bank; the value of pension funds (PAP) data is from the International Federation of Pension Management (FIAP) and is converted to ratios to GDP according to the PWT Table 7.1 (Heston *et al.* 2012); and GDP per capita data is from the International Monetary Fund (IMF) World Economic Outlook 2012 database.

3.4.3.1 Cointegration and error correction model

In the Unit Root tests, these two variables are non-stationary but in the first order. This chapter uses a cointegration test based on vector autoregression (VAR) from Johansen (1988). The optimal lag is determined by the smallest SC statistic. For the first order series, LSMC, LPAP and LGDP, the Johansen cointegration test is applied. The results show that the two variables are stable in the long term. The cointegration equations are:

$$\text{ecm}_t = \text{LSMC}_t - 0.82\text{LPAP}_t - 0.13\text{LGDP}_t - 0.54$$

which can be rewritten as:

$$\text{LSMC}_t = 0.54 + 0.82\text{LPAP}_t + 0.13\text{LGDP}_t + \text{ecm}_t$$

The equation above shows the relationship between stock market capital, the value of pension funds and GDP per capita, in which the coefficients are the elasticity of the value of pension funds, and GDP per capita. Specifically, if GDP remains constant, stock market capital will increase 0.82 per cent for each increase of 1 per cent in pension funds; if the size of pension funds remains constant, stock market capital will increase 0.13 per cent for each increase of 1 per cent in GDP per capita.

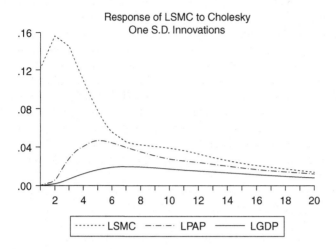

Figure 3.3 Impulse responses of the stock market to shocks

In the short term, these variables are not in equilibrium, although they are in equilibrium in the long term. However, they can be adjusted using the error correction model as below:

$$\Delta LSMC_t = 0.28\Delta LPAP_t + \Delta 0.82LGDP_t - 0.27ecm_{t-1}$$

(2.70) (4.29) (−2.05)

3.4.3.2   *VAR model and IRF and VD*

Based on the test above, the VAR model is built on the endogenous variables of stock market capital the value of pension funds and GDP per capita. According to the Lag Length Criteria, this chapter uses the second order VAR model. As it passes the stationarity test, the model shifts to the impulse response function (IRF) and variance decomposition (VD) models.

The IRF is used to describe the effect that the random error term is applied to an external shock that equals the standard deviation and provides the current and future values of endogenous variables. This function captures the dynamic interactions between the variables. Figure 3.3 shows the response function of the stock market value to the external shocks of the pension funds and GDP per capita.

The first curve in Figure 3.3 is the stock market under the change to itself. The middle curve is the impulse function of pension funds to external shocks caused by changes in stock market value. On this curve, when the current pension fund is shocked by a change in the standard deviation, the value of the stock market capital increases rapidly, reaching a peak in the fifth period.

Table 3.4 Variance decomposition of LSMC

Period	SE	LSMC	LPAP	LGDP	Period	SE	LSMC	LPAP	LGDP
1	0.12	100.00	0.00	0.00	11	0.32	86.15	11.47	2.38
2	0.20	99.95	0.05	0.00	12	0.32	85.64	11.80	2.55
3	0.25	98.52	1.40	0.07	13	0.33	85.21	12.09	2.70
4	0.27	96.41	3.34	0.25	14	0.33	84.84	12.33	2.82
5	0.29	93.76	5.68	0.56	15	0.33	84.53	12.54	2.93
6	0.30	91.49	7.58	0.93	16	0.33	84.28	12.70	3.02
7	0.30	89.70	8.99	1.31	17	0.33	84.07	12.83	3.09
8	0.31	88.41	9.94	1.65	18	0.33	83.90	12.94	3.16
9	0.31	87.47	10.59	1.94	19	0.33	83.76	13.03	3.21
10	0.32	86.74	11.08	2.18	20	0.33	83.64	13.10	3.25

Then the value gradually declines, finally converging to zero. This process takes a long time. The bottom curve is the impulse function of GDP per capita to external shocks caused by changes in the stock market value. This curve shows that when the current GDP per capita suffers a shock reflected in its standard deviation, the stock market value starts to increase, but more slowly than the increase in pension funds, reaching a peak in the seventh period. The impulse is less intense. Thus, the impact of pension funds on stock market value is not only stronger, but also longer.

The IRF describes the impact of the endogenous variables on other endogenous variables in a VAR model, while VD demonstrates the importance of different structural shocks by analyzing the contributions of endogenous variables on the changes from each structural shock.

From the VD of the stock market value in Table 3.4, among all factors that change the stock market value, the first one is the market itself. However, the stock market shows an attenuating trend that declines to 83.64 per cent by the twentieth period. In other words, the stock market is self-developing and self-reinforcing. The second factor, the impact of pension funds, is also significant; it becomes stronger, reaching 13.10 per cent in the twentieth period. The stock market value increases together with the pension funds but declines naturally with the attenuation, which shows that pension funds are becoming an increasingly important investor in the security market from another point of view. Finally, the influence from GDP per capita is minor, as it reaches 3 per cent in the twelfth period. The result is consistent with the theoretical analysis that the impact of pension funds on the stock market is positive in both quantity and quality, such as the innovation of financial products and the improvement of corporate governance.

3.5 Conclusion

Against the background of the aging population crisis, many countries have applied different pension systems. The pension system changes financial development. An increase in the value of pension funds not only supplies the financial markets with more capital, but also produces innovations in financial products, improves corporate governance, and improves the supervision and regulatory system, which are all good for financial development. This chapter tested different hypotheses by modeling the impact of pension funds on financial development using cross-sectional, panel and time serial data.

The empirical analysis uses cross-sectional data for 55 countries and regions in the regression model. The results show that the pension system and its value can explain differences between countries with respect to financial development and, more specifically, differences in stock markets. This is the first study to consider the legal origin, endowment and pension systems at the same to time analyse their influence on financial development. Next, the panel regression models investigate financial development under different pension models. The results show that an increase in the size of pension funds signifies a greater boost in the development of financial markets for non-common law countries with underdeveloped financial and economic systems. Finally, this chapter uses the Chilean case between 1981 and 2009 in a time series analysis using a cointegration and VAR model. The results also confirm the positive impact of pension funds on financial development. In all of these empirical studies, we have found that the legal origin, endowment and pension fund theories are not in conflict but complement one another. The implication of the pension hypothesis is that when the legal system and resource endowments are inherent and cannot be changed, given an aging population, applying a funded pension system is possibly a solution. A funded pension system also benefits the accumulation of pension funds, stimulates financial markets and accelerates economic growth.

These findings are of great value for China's pension system reform and development, and China's financial development. China is not a common law country. Other theories such as resource endowments, religious and cultural differences, politics and war do not properly address China's financial development and rapid economic growth. These theories imply that China cannot perform well in its financial development. However, if China follows the pension theory, it has the potential to grow stronger in the future, as the benefits from pension funds are greater in non-common law and developing countries. In the developing country Chile, after pension system reform in the 1980s, its financial and economic achievements established it as a miracle in Latin America. Accordingly, Chile has become the first South American country to join the OECD.

In 1997, China formally established a pension system that is a combination of an overall social pooling and individual accounts. The individual pension accounts are mostly in deficit, and there is no legal support for their investment in the capital market. Since 2004, China has had an enterprise annuity scheme; however, its size is relatively small and the participation rate is low.

The annuity, as the second pillar in the pension system, has not been functional. Without the investment of pension funds, the Chinese capital market is far behind in the development of the real economy. As the world's second largest economy, China will outperform Chile if it focuses on pension reform, and economic development and the security market will benefit. Therefore, China should provide an opportunity to invest in personal pension accounts, encourage corporate annuities, provide more methods for investment, supply more financial products and improve the investment environment. All of these changes will prompt pension funds and financial markets to interact in a positive manner. Based on this chapter, future work could focus on how to reform and improve China's pension system. A strong pension system will promote capital markets, financial development and economic growth and will also solve the problem of growing old before becoming rich.

References

Acemoglu, D., Johnson, S. and Robinson, J. A. (2001) 'The Colonial Origins of Comparative Development: An Empirical Investigation', *American Economic Review*, 91(5), 1369–1401.

Beck, T., Demirgüç-Kunt, A. and Levine, R. (2003) 'Law, Endowments and Finance', *Journal of Financial Economics*, 70(2), 137–81.

Bodie, Z. (1990) 'Pension Funds and Financial Innovation', *Financial Management*, 19(3), 11–22.

Cheffins, B. R. (2001) 'Does Law Matter? The Separation of Ownership and Control in the United Kingdom', *Journal Legal Studies*, 30(2), 459–84.

Coffee, J. (1999) 'The Future as History: The Prospects for Global Convergence in Corporate Governance and its Implications', *Columbia Law School Centre for Law and Economic Studies*, Working Paper, no. 144.

Coffee, J. (2007) 'Law and the Market: the Impact of Enforcement', *University of Pennsylvania Law Review*, 156(2), 229–311.

Davis, E. P. and Hu, Y-W. (2008) 'Does funding of pensions stimulate economic growth?', *Journal of Pension Economics and Finance*, 7, 221–49.

Goldsmith, R.W. (1969) *Financial Structure and Development*, New Haven, CN: Yale University Press.

Hebb, T. (2006) 'The Economic Inefficiency of Secrecy: Pension Fund Investors' Corporate Transparency Concerns', *Journal of Business Ethics*, 63(4), 385–405.

Heritage Foundation (2001) *2002 Index of Economic Freedom*, 8th edn, Heritage Foundation.

Heston, A., Summers, R. and Aten, B. (2002) *Penn World Table Version 6.1*, Center for International Comparisons of Production, Income and Prices at the University of Pennsylvania, USA.

Heston, A., Summers, R. and Aten, B. (2012) *Penn World Table Version 7.1*, Center for International Comparisons of Production, Income and Prices at the University of Pennsylvania, USA.

Hicks, J. R. (1969) *A Theory of Economic History*, Oxford: Clarendon.

Hu, Y-W. (2005) 'Pension Reform, Economic Growth and Financial Development – An Empirical Study', *Economics and Finance Discussion Papers*, Brunel University, Uxbridge, Middlesex.

International Monetary Fund (2012) World Economic Outlook database. Available online at: http://www.imf.org/external/pubs/ft/weo/2012/02/weodata/index.aspx (accessed 30 January 2014).

Johansen, S. (1988) 'Statistical analysis of cointegration vectors', *Journal of Economic Dynamics and Control*, 12(2–3), 231–54.

King, R. G. and Levine, R. (1993) 'Finance and Growth: Schumpeter Might Be Right', *Quarterly Journal of Economics*, 108(3), 717–37.

La Porta, R., Lopez-de-Silanes, F., Shleifer, A. and Vishny, R. (1998) 'Law and Finance', *Journal of Political Economy*, 106(6), 1113–55.

La Porta, R., Lopez-de-Silanes, F., Shleifer, A. and Vishny, R. (1999) 'The Quality of Government', *Journal of Law, Economics, and Organization*, 15, 222–79.

Levine, R. (1997) 'Financial Development and Economic Growth: Views and Agenda', *Journal of Economic Literature*, 35(2), 688–726.

OECD (2012) *Pension Markets in Focus*, Issue 9, September.

Roe, M. J. (2006) 'Legal Origins, Politics, and Modern Stock Markets', *Harvard Law Review*, 120(2), 460–527.

Stulz, R. M. and Williamson, R. (2003) 'Culture, Openness, and Finance', *Journal of Financial Economics*, 70(3), 313–49.

Xiong, J. and Gao, Q. (2010) 'Jin rong wei ji dui quan qiu yang lao ji jin de ying xiang (The Impact of the Financial Crisis on Global Pension Funds)', *Guo ji jin rong yan jiu (Studies of International Finance)*, 4, 54–9.

Zheng, B. (2005) 'Fu li mo shi bi jiao yan jiu yu fu li gai ge shi zheng fen xi:zheng zhi jing ji xue de shi jiao (Comparative Studies on Welfare Regimes and Empirical Studies on Welfare Reforms: A Political Economy Perspective)', *Xue shu jie (academe)*, 3, 31–46.

4 Does financial repression retard China's economic growth?

An empirical examination

Guangdong Xu and Binwei Gui[1]

4.1 Introduction

It has long been argued that financial repression is detrimental to economic growth. In their seminal works, McKinnon (1973) and Shaw (1973) show that a repressed financial sector discourages both savings and investment because the rates of return are lower than what could be obtained in a competitive market. In such a system, financial intermediates do not function at their full capacity and fail to channel savings into investment efficiently, thereby impeding the development of the overall economic system.

The influence of financial repression, especially interest rate distortion, has been tested by numerous empirical studies, many of which have identified a negative association between interest rate repression and certain fundamental macroeconomic variables, such as savings rates, investment, and economic growth (Fry 1978, 1997; Roubini and Sala-i-Martin 1992). Other repression policies, such as entry restrictions and state ownership in the banking sector, have also proven to be harmful to financial development (Barth *et al.* 2006; World Bank 2001).

There are certain anomalies to the predication of financial repression theory, however. For example, China's financial system conforms to the stereotype described by financial repression theory: interest rates are still controlled by the government and credit allocation is heavily influenced by political factors rather than commercial motives. A puzzle emerges: although theory indicates that financial repression is harmful to economic growth, China has achieved remarkable success in economic development over the past several decades in spite of its repressed financial system.

In this chapter, we will try to solve this puzzle. We will show that the connection between financial repression and economic growth is more complicated than has been suggested by previous studies. On the one hand, financial repression could arguably promote China's economic growth by lowering the cost of capital, thereby encouraging investment and production. On the other hand, evidence shows that financial repression endangers China's economic health by damaging its economic efficiency, slowing job creation, and distorting the country's economic structure. A repressed financial system therefore acts as a double-edged sword for economic growth in China.

The rest of the chapter is organized as follows. Section 4.2 describes the historical development of China's financial system. Section 4.3 discusses the repressed nature of China's financial system and the channels through which financial repression may influence economic growth in China. Section 4.4 empirically examines of the connections between financial repression and economic growth in China. Finally, Section 4.5 concludes.

4.2   China's financial development

When economic reforms began in the late 1970s, it could hardly be said that there was a real financial system in China. The situation has changed drastically since the beginning of economic reforms. The People's Bank of China (PBOC), which served as both a central bank and a commercial bank during the planned economy era, was gradually stripped of its corporate finance functions and began operating as the country's central bank. Four state-owned banks, namely, the Agriculture Bank of China (ABC), the Bank of China (BOC), the People's Construction Bank of China (PCBC, renamed the China Construction Bank, or CCB, in 1996), and the Industrial and Commercial Bank of China (ICBC), then emerged to function as financial intermediaries, and provide commercial banking services.

Given their magnitude[2] in China's financial system, the four state-owned banks (later known as the 'Big Four') have always been the focus of financial reform and appear to undergo an overhaul every ten years. In 1994, the government created three new policy banks – the Agricultural Development Bank, the China Development Bank, and the Export-Import Bank – which were expected to assume responsibility for policy lending, relieving the Big Four of the obligation to extend loans for policy purposes. In 1995, China enacted the Commercial Bank Law, which laid the legal foundation for the commercialization of the state-owned banks by, for example, mandating that banks should be responsible for their own profits and losses, as well as stipulating technical requirements such as capital-adequacy ratios in line with international banking practice. Another round of banking reforms was launched in 2004, which ultimately led to the limited privatization of the Big Four through the recruitment of strategic investors and listing on stock exchanges (Walter and Howie 2011).

Beginning in the mid-1980s, the state began to increase competition in the financial sector by allowing the entry of new financial institutions, including new commercial banks and non-bank financial entities. By the end of 2012, China had 12 joint-stock banks[3], 144 city commercial banks, 337 rural commercial banks, 147 rural cooperative banks, 1,927 rural credit cooperatives, 1 postal savings bank, 4 banking asset management firms, 42 locally incorporated foreign banking institutions, 67 trust companies, 150 finance companies owned by corporate groups, 20 financial leasing companies, 5 money brokerage firms, 16 auto financing companies, 4 consumer finance companies, 800 village or township banks, 14 lending companies, and 49 rural mutual cooperatives. Overall, there were 3,747 banking institutions employing 3,362 million people and holding financial assets of CNY133.6 trillion.[4] It can therefore be argued that China's financial system is much more diversified and competitive than before.

Compared with its banking sector, China's financial markets, including both stock and bond markets, are less developed and less important. Following their creation in 1990, China's domestic stock exchanges, the Shanghai Stock Exchange (SHSE) and Shenzhen Stock Exchange (SZSE), grew quickly, if unsteadily. At the end of 2012, there were 2,494 companies listed on the SHSE and SZSE, and the total market capitalization reached CNY23.04 trillion, equivalent to 44.36 per cent of GDP in fiscal year 2012.[5] By the same year, the SHSE was the seventh largest exchange in the world in terms of market capitalization and the fourth largest in terms of the value of shares traded.[6]

Following decades of development, however, the level of market depth remains quite low. While the total market capitalization was equivalent to 44.36 per cent of GDP in 2012, part of the total market capitalization was represented by non-tradable shares owned by 'legal persons' or government entities. Excluding the value of these non-tradable shares left China with an equity depth of only 35 per cent of GDP, which was very low compared with other countries. In fact, before 2006, the ratio of the market capitalization of tradable shares to GDP had never been higher than 20 per cent.[7]

The underdevelopment of the bond market, especially the corporate bond market, relative to the banking sector further diminishes the role played by direct financing in serving the economy. The largest component of the bond market is the government bond. Compared to the market for government-issued bonds, the corporate bond market is minuscule: in terms of the amount of outstanding bonds at the end of 2004, the corporate bond market is less than one-twelfth of the size of the government bond market (CNY2577.76 billion) (Allen *et al.* 2008). The ratio of corporate bonds to GDP in China in 2004 was only 1 per cent, giving the country a lower ranking on an international comparison.

In general, after three decades of reform and development, China's financial system has been fundamentally changed. On the surface, China has virtually all the institutions of a modern financial system: a central bank in charge of setting monetary policy, a diversified banking system that consists of, for example, commercial banks and policy banks, and a capital market on which over 2,000 companies are listed.

However, China's financial system has lagged behind the rest of the economy in the transition process. The most serious problem faced by China's financial system is the dominance of its banking sector, which, according to Naughton (2007: 459) "has been one of China's most protected industries, overregulated, dominated by state ownership, and protected from international competition." The scarce capital is thus allocated inefficiently and unproductively. Consequently, China's financial system is claimed to be "both distorting China's growth and holding it back" (McKinsey Global Institute 2006) and is regarded as the "economy's Achilles' heel" (Dobson and Kashyap 2006).

4.3   Is financial repression detrimental to China's economic growth? A theoretical discussion

4.3.1   Financial repression in China

Interest rate controls stand out as the most salient component of the Chinese version of financial repression. The PBOC maintains the cap on deposit rates for all financial institutions and, until 20 July 2013, also maintained the floor on loan rates. More importantly, the central bank appears to adjust the benchmark interest rates in an asymmetric manner in response to inflation (Liu *et al.* 2009). Thus, the central bank is quicker to adjust deposit and lending rates downward than upward. When inflation increases, the rigidity of interest rates leads to lower or even negative real interest rates. This trend has become more obvious since 2004 (Lardy 2012).

The direct result of the central bank's approach to setting nominal interest rates is that household interest earnings, on average, have been far less than they would have been in a more liberalized financial environment, where market forces play a major role in determining interest rates. In contrast, the corporate sector benefits greatly from such a monetary policy. The low real interest rates mean that the cost of capital for firms is artificially reduced and investment in projects that have low returns is encouraged. The low cost of capital in China has made it an anomaly in comparison with other countries, developed or developing (Geng and N'Diaye 2012)

In addition to interest rate controls, China's economy suffers from other financial repression policies, namely, credit misallocation, the dominance of state ownership, and exchange rate distortion. Credit misallocation means that scarce financial resources have been systematically and continually allocated to less profitable but more politically preferable entities, especially state-owned enterprises (SOEs), whereas private firms, which have become the driving force of China's economic growth, are forced to rely on informal and even underground credit channels to finance their survival (Huang 2006).

After several decades of economic reform, China's non-State sector has replaced SOEs as the key driver of China's economic growth (World Bank 2012). However, the non-state sector, especially private enterprises, has been intentionally discriminated against in terms of credit access and availability. For example, Huang (2006) shows that domestic private firms in China are among the most financially constrained in the world. In addition, Brandt and Zhu (2007) find that over the period from 1998 to 2003, the state sector, defined to include shareholding companies in which governments have significant ownership shares, continued to absorb between one-half and two-thirds of new bank lending.

China has the highest level of state ownership of banks of any major economy in the world. For example, Barth *et al.* (2006: 148–9) report that, by the end of 2001, while 87 countries had some government ownership of banks, in only 15 countries did the percentage of bank assets at government-owned banks exceed 50 per cent; China was identified as having the highest level of government ownership (98 per cent of bank assets were held by state-owned banks (SOBs)). China's situation also stands in contrast to the experience of Eastern Europe's transitional economies and other emerging markets. The McKinsey Global Institute (2006) shows that SOBs accounted for 83 per cent of bank assets in China in 2004, compared with 33 per cent in Brazil, 18 per cent in South Korea, 20 per cent in Poland, and 16 per cent in Chile. Similarly, Deng *et al.* (2011) claim that 18 of the 20 largest banks are directly state controlled and, at the end of 2009, accounted for CNY58.58 trillion, or approximately 73 per cent, of total bank assets.

Notwithstanding some significant institutional changes such as corporatization and public listings, China's SOBs for the most part continue to be governed as before. The top executives in Chinese SOBs are confronted with two different and often conflicting missions, namely, to advance the government's political objectives, and to optimize the bank's financial performance. When these two missions contradict each other, the former always dominates. In addition to the "policy burden" or "multitasking" problem, China's SOBs have been further criticized for a lack of effective internal risk management and control systems, for weakness in information collection, data analysis, and credit assessment, and for their failure to integrate their local branches into unified national systems (McKinsey Global Institute 2006).

Finally, China's currency policy has always been criticized for its pursuit of mercantile advantage by devaluing the RMB and hence stimulating exports. For example, Goldstein and Lardy (2008) conclude that "any methodology that defines the equilibrium exchange rate for the renminbi as the real effective exchange rate that would produce 'balance' in China's global current account position, or in its basic balance, or in its overall balance-of-payment position, yields the qualitative conclusion that the renminbi is significantly undervalued and most likely by an increasing margin over time." Similarly, a report issued by the International Monetary Fund (IMF) claims that "the renminbi remains moderately undervalued against a broad basket of currencies" (IMF 2013).

An inflexible exchange rate, in turn, requires a large set of distortionary policies for its maintenance over long periods. For example, Prasad (2009) shows that China's monetary policy independence has been severely weakened by the undervalued currency strategy. More specifically, as a result of China's undervaluation of its currency, the volume of export continually increases, capital inflows steadily grow, and a dramatic accumulation of foreign exchange reserves has been observed. In order to sterilize the liquidity generated by this growth pattern (and to address the corresponding inflation problem) the PBOC has to set interest rates administratively at very low levels so that its sterilization costs can be minimized and the speculative capital inflows can be discouraged. Distorted interest rates, as we have argued, will in turn lead to inefficient consequences.

4.3.2   The complicated connections between financial repression and economic growth

4.3.2.1   The dark side of financial repression

According to the conventional theory, financial repression is harmful to economic growth. When the interest rate is set at a level below the market-clearing equilibrium rate, the demand for credit greatly exceeds the available supply. This excess demand calls for rationing of the limited supply, which in turn leads to inefficient economic outcomes.[8] Interest rate controls further distort the economy in other ways (Fry 1997). First, low interest rates produce a bias in favor of current consumption and against future consumption. Therefore, these rates may reduce savings below the socially optimal level. Second, potential lenders may engage in relatively low-yielding direct investment instead of lending by way of depositing money in a bank. Third, bank borrowers able to obtain all their desired funds at low loan rates will choose relatively capital-intensive projects. Fourth, the pool of potential borrowers includes entrepreneurs with low-yielding projects, who would not wish to borrow at the higher market-clearing interest rate.

In summary, interest rate controls reduce savings and hence investments, encourage capital-intensive rather than labor-intensive technologies (and hence slow the pace of job creation), and damage economic efficiency by attracting unqualified borrowers to join financial markets. Therefore, the adoption of interest-rate controls hurts economic growth, which has been confirmed by numerous empirical studies (Fry 1978, 1997; Roubini and Sala-i-Martin 1992).

As a consequence of credit misallocation, enormous numbers of non-performing loans (NPLs) will be generated, and the bank system faces a high risk of insolvency. In addition, economic growth will be retarded because capital cannot be allocated to its best use and cannot be used in a cost-effective way. In China, a large amount of loans extended to SOEs, who are the most favored clients of the banking sector, eventually turn into NPLs. Using official figures, Allen *et al.* (2008) compare NPLs in China, the US, and other major Asian economies from 1998 to 2006. They report that, measured as a fraction of GDP, China's NPLs are the largest in the group from 2000 to 2006, reaching levels as high as 20.0–22.5 per cent of GDP in 2000 and 2001.

Internal and informal finance, such as retained earnings, trade credit, and private loans, have played a more important role in financing the growth of private firms in China (Huang 2003; Allen *et al.* 2005; Héricourt and Poncet

2009; Poncet *et al.* 2010). Whereas internal finance and informal lending can be expected to help private entrepreneurs start their businesses, the continued development of private firms will ultimately outgrow the support offered by these informal financial mechanisms. Without access to formal finance, private firms will inevitably be trapped in an inefficient state of small size, simple and outmoded technologies, and short life spans (Huang 2006). Given the importance of private firms in driving China's economic growth, their cloudy future endangers the long-term sustainability of the economy.

State ownership has long been argued to be detrimental to financial development. For example, using data on the government ownership of banks from 92 countries around the world, La Porta *et al.* (2002) find that increased government ownership of banks in 1970 is associated with slower subsequent financial development and lower growth of per capita income and productivity. The World Bank (2001: 128) further argues that state ownership of banks tends to reduce competition and limits access to credit, and may even increase the risk of crisis. State-owned banks are inherently prone to be unproductive because government ownership tends to politicize resource allocation. In other words, state ownership of banks facilitates the financing of politically attractive projects but does not necessarily do the same for economically efficient projects. In addition, state ownership can lead to a conflict of incentives: governments are exposed to an incentive conflict when they have significant state ownership, as one part of government is then charged with monitoring another, most likely leading to weak official supervision (World Bank 2001: 130).

China does not seem to be an exception to the 'bad state-owned bank' story. For example, using Chinese provincial data from 1991 to 1997, Park and Sehrt (2001) find that economic fundamentals such as industrial growth, agricultural growth, and GDP per capita have had little effect on total lending by state banks, whereas the responsiveness of lending to policy concerns, such as SOEs' output, is significant. Based on data from 1997 to 2004, Podpiera (2006) reports that the pricing of credit risk by SOBs remains undifferentiated and that bank lending decisions continue to be driven by the availability of funds and do not appear to consider enterprise profitability. In addition, compared with the joint-stock banks, SOBs are less profitable (Ferri 2008), less prudent in lending (Jia 2008), and less X-efficient (Fu and Heffernan 2007).

The role of exchange rate distortion seems to be more controversial. While the disastrous effects of overvaluation on economic growth are widely documented in the empirical literature (Ghura and Grennes 1993; Acemoglu *et al.* 2003; Gala 2008), there are more disagreements over the effects of undervaluation on economic growth. After systematically reviewing the available literature, Magud and Sosa (2010) conclude that "[r]egarding the effect of undervaluation of the exchange rate on economic growth, the evidence is mixed and inconclusive."

Even if undervaluation may promote economic growth in the short or medium term, maintaining this policy for too long will have significant adverse consequences, such as an excessive accumulation of low-yielding foreign reserves, high and destabilizing liquidity growth and inflation, etc. (Haddad and Pancaro 2010). Eichengreen (2008) therefore concludes that "there is the earlier point that a relatively undervalued real exchange rate can have costs as well as benefits and that the cost/benefit ratio will tend to rise with the general level of economic and financial development" and countries that seek to use devaluation to accelerate economic growth "need to develop an exit strategy to avoid getting locked into a strategy that has outlived its usefulness."

4.3.2.2   The bright side of financial repression

Financial repression may not be as detrimental to economic growth as suggested by conventional literature. For example, in a study of the financial policies in East Asian economies, Hellmann *et al.* (1998) argue that modest financial repression, or in their terms "financial restraint," is beneficial to economic growth because under financial restraint, the government can create rent opportunities in the private sector through a set of financial policies. These rents may induce private sector agents to increase the supply of goods and services that might be underprovided in a purely competitive market, such as the monitoring of investments and the provision of deposit collection.

The complicated role of financial repression can be further illustrated by referring to the production function, $Y = AF (K, L)$, where Y is output, K is capital, L is labor, and A is a productivity parameter. Clearly, *ceteris paribus*, the lower the cost of capital, the stronger the incentive to undertake capital accumulation (investment $I = \Delta K$), and the more capital accumulation is undertaken, the greater the potential for economic growth. Therefore, financial repression may arguably promote economic growth by lowering the cost of capital (through, for example, interest rate control) and hence encouraging investment conducted by the corporate sector.

This phenomenon is exactly what we see in China today. Financial repression policies subsidize the corporate sector at the cost of households' welfare. In China, enterprises, particularly SOEs, may be the primary beneficiaries of interest rate controls. Ma and Wang (2010) find that net interest payments as a share of GDP by the non-financial corporate sector dropped by 50 per cent between 1992 and 2007. In particular, SOEs benefit disproportionately from such financial repression. For example, Ferri and Liu (2010) show that the costs of financing for SOEs are significantly lower than those for other companies, particularly private enterprises; if SOEs had to pay the same interest rates as private enterprises, their existing profits would be entirely wiped out.

The low cost of financing has led to a significant increase in the profitability of enterprises since the early 1990s. Whereas nominal firm profits increased more than 15-fold from 1992 to 2007, the ratio of profits to increased industrial value also improved remarkably, from approximately 21 per cent in the late 1990s to close to 30 per cent in 2007 (Yang *et al.* 2011). The lack of attractive financial investments implies that firms will either choose to spend their retained earnings on investment projects to expand capacity or put them in a low-yielding bank deposit. Thus, the implication of the distorted interest rate structure is that firms face a very low hurdle rate when deciding whether to pursue a given investment project. In summary, restricted bank lending rates and retained earnings have kept the cost of investment funds very low and thus have helped China achieve one of the highest ratios of investment to GDP in the world (Aziz and Dunaway 2007; Lardy 2007).

Investment has therefore, as Prasad (2009) concludes, "been a major contributor to growth during this decade." For example, Perkins and Rawski (2008) find that capital formation dominated China's growth picture during the decade following 1995, accounting for 52.7 per cent of GDP growth during 1995–2000 and 57.1 per cent of GDP expansion during 2000 to 2005. Similarly, Knight and Ding (2012: 117) show that an increase in domestic investment of 1 percentage point raises GDP per capita growth by 0.2 percentage points.

In summary, the overall influence of financial repression on economic growth is theoretically uncertain. On the one hand, financial repression promotes economic growth by subsidizing and hence encouraging investment ($I = \Delta K$). On the other hand, financial repression hurts economic growth by damaging economic efficiency (A), slowing down the pace of job creation (L), and distorting the country's economic structure. The real effect of financial repression on economic growth is, therefore, a question that should be answered by empirical investigations.

4.4 Is financial repression detrimental to China's economic growth? An empirical examination

Based on the aforementioned discussion, we will investigate the following four relationships in this section:

Relationship 1: the relationship between financial repression and investment;
Relationship 2: the relationship between financial repression and employment;
Relationship 3: the relationship between financial repression and economic efficiency (particularly, TFP);
Relationship 4: the relationship between financial repression and economic growth.

Additionally, we will examine the relationship between financial repression and inflation (*Relationship 5*) as well as the relationship between financial repression and economic volatility (*Relationship 6*) because we believe financial repression may exacerbate inflation (for example, via a devaluation strategy that may encourage excessive capital inflows) and increase economic volatility (for example, by generating massive NPLs and hence endangering the viability of the banking system).

In accordance with our theoretical discussions, in this section we will use four indicators to proxy China's financial repression: the real interest rate ('reali'), which can be relied upon to measure the level of interest control; the ratio of the volume of credit extended to private enterprises to that extended to SOEs ('relative'), which can be used to estimate the level of credit misallocation; the significance of SOBs ('sob'), which can be used to estimate the role of SOBs versus other financial institutions such as joint-stock banks in the allocation of financial resources; and the real effective exchange rate ('reer'), which can be relied upon to measure the level of exchange rate distortion.

4.4.1   Financial repression indicators

4.4.1.1   The real interest rate ('reali')

We calculate the real interest rate by subtracting the GDP deflator from the nominal interest rate, which can be obtained from the *China Financial Yearbook*. We focus on the one-year deposit interest rate; if there were interest rate adjustments in a year, the mean value of the interest rate during that year will be calculated and accepted as the interest rate of that year. The GDP deflator is calculated from nominal and real GDP data, which can be obtained from the *China Statistical Yearbook*. The relationship between nominal interest rates, GDP deflators, and real interest rates can be seen in Figure 4.1.

As we can see from Figure 4.1, prior to 1998, the nominal interest rate in China fluctuated at around 7.3 per cent, whereas after 1998, the interest rate remained at approximately 2.4 per cent. Because the inflation level before 1998

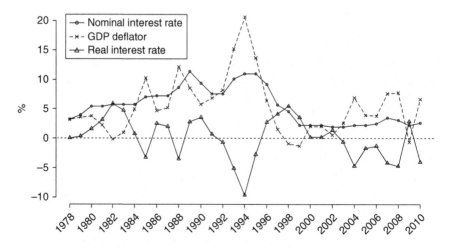

Figure 4.1 The nominal interest rates, GDP deflators, and real interest rates in China (1978–2010)

was much higher than that after 1998, the real interest rate has not changed significantly, and has fluctuated at around 0 per cent.

4.4.1.2 Ratio of volume of credit extended to private enterprises to that extended to SOEs ('relative')

Because current data sources such as the *China Statistical Yearbook* do not provide detailed information on the relative proportion of credit provided to the private sector, we must first estimate the volume of credit extended to the private sector versus that extended to the State-owned sector based on the approach of Xu and Gui (2013). The basic model is as follows.

Domestic enterprises can be divided into two types, namely, private enterprises and SOEs. The credit coefficient (the ratio of credit volume to output; a higher credit coefficient indicates that more credit is required for each unit of output) of SOEs can be defined as $\beta = C_S/Y_S$, and the credit coefficient of private enterprises can be defined as $\alpha = C_P/Y_P$. Here, C_S and Y_S are credit extended to SOEs and output generated by SOEs, respectively, and C_P and Y_P are credit extended to private enterprises and output generated by private enterprises, respectively.

The total credit volume of a region can therefore be denoted as $C = C_S + C_P = \beta Y_S + \alpha Y_P$, and the level of financial depth (the credit-to-GDP ratio) in a region can be expressed as follows:

$$\frac{C}{Y} = \frac{\beta Y_S + \alpha Y_P}{Y} = \beta\frac{Y_S}{Y} + \alpha\left(1-\frac{Y_S}{Y}\right) = \alpha + (\beta - \alpha)\frac{Y_S}{Y} = \alpha + \varphi\frac{Y_S}{Y} \qquad (1)$$

where $\varphi = \beta - \alpha$ is the difference between the two credit coefficients, which indicates the difference in the credit efficiency between state-owned and private enterprises. For example, $\varphi > 0$ means that SOEs require more credit to produce the same volume of output. Based on equation (1), we can further construct a panel data model that includes fixed-period effects as follows:

$$depth_{i,t} = \alpha_t + \varphi_t state_{i,t} + \varepsilon_{i,t} \qquad (2)$$

In equation (2), for each year, $depth_{i,t}$ and $state_{i,t}$ indicate, respectively, the level of financial depth and the proportion of output (GDP) that is produced by SOEs in a region of interest. Because obtaining regional data on the proportion of GDP produced by SOEs is difficult, we use the proportion of the gross industrial output value that was produced by SOEs as a proxy variable. From the *China Statistical Yearbook* and the *China Financial Yearbook*, we can obtain annual data on the credit-to-GDP ratio and the proportion of the gross industrial output value that was produced by SOEs for 31 Chinese

Table 4.1 The mean values of 'depth', 'state', and 'relative' for various regions in China from 1978 to 2010

Region	depth	state	relative	Region	depth	state	relative
Anhui	0.714	0.565	0.391	Jiangxi	0.753	0.615	0.352
Beijing	1.353	0.675	1.152	Jilin	1.053	0.697	0.558
Chongqing	0.898	0.654	0.496	Liaoning	0.945	0.58	0.749
Fujian	0.695	0.38	1.568	Ningxia	1.079	0.714	0.568
Gansu	0.932	0.801	0.17	Qinghai	1.013	0.804	0.234
Guangdong	0.878	0.342	2.304	Shaanxi	0.966	0.719	0.366
Guangxi	0.723	0.613	0.295	Shandong	0.705	0.418	0.944
Guizhou	0.821	0.735	0.13	Shanghai	1.176	0.578	1.322
Hainan	1.074	0.624	0.922	Shanxi	0.899	0.603	0.552
Hebei	0.625	0.478	0.462	Sichuan	0.945	0.57	0.833
Heilongjiang	0.84	0.765	0.127	Tianjin	1.186	0.511	1.601
Henan	0.726	0.512	0.564	Tibet	0.6	0.702	−0.136
Hubei	0.848	0.59	0.547	Xinjiang	0.841	0.822	0.019
Hunan	0.65	0.57	0.259	Yunnan	0.811	0.742	0.123
Inner Mongolia	0.779	0.678	0.239	Zhejiang	0.804	0.276	3.267
Jiangsu	0.697	0.312	1.998				

(Source: *China Statistical Yearbook* and *China Financial Yearbook*.)

regions from 1978 to 2010. The data are then regressed to estimate α_t (the credit coefficient of private enterprises each year) and φ_t (the difference in the credit coefficient between SOEs and private enterprises each year). The credit coefficient for SOEs can then be calculated as $\beta_t = \alpha_t + \varphi_t$.

Based on the credit coefficients and the proportion of output that was produced by SOEs, we can calculate the credit-to-GDP ratio for private enterprises and SOEs in different regions and finally obtain the second financial repression indictor ('relative'), which can be defined as the ratio of the volume of credit extended to private enterprises to that extended to SOEs:

$$\frac{C_s}{Y} = \frac{C_s}{Y_s}\frac{Y_s}{Y} = \beta \cdot state; \quad \frac{C_p}{Y} = \frac{C}{Y} - \frac{C_s}{Y} = depth - \beta \cdot state$$

$$relative = \frac{C_p}{C_s} = \frac{C_p}{Y} \Big/ \frac{C_s}{Y} = (depth - \beta \cdot state)/\beta \cdot state \tag{3}$$

Table 4.1 presents the mean values of financial depth ('depth'), the proportion of output that was produced by SOEs ('state'), and the ratio of the volume of credit extended to private enterprises to that extended to SOEs ('relative') for various regions in China from 1978 to 2010.

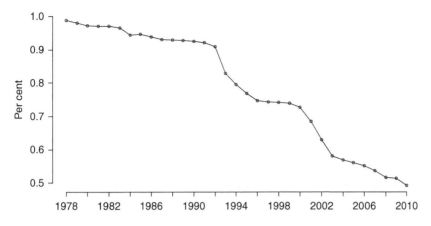

Figure 4.2 The ratio of assets of SOBs to total bank assets (1978–2010)

4.4.1.3 The significance of state-owned banks ('sob')

Data on assets and liabilities of all banks for each year come from the *China Financial Yearbook*. We then define the significance of SOBs, as the ratio of assets of SOBs (the Big Four plus the Bank of Communication) to total bank assets. As we can see from Figure 4.2, this ratio has decreased significantly over the last three decades, from 99 per cent in 1978 to 49 per cent in 2010.

4.4.1.4 The real effective exchange rate ('reer')

Data on China's real effective exchange rate ('reer') for the period from 1980 to 2010 is abstracted from the World Bank's World Development Indicators (WBWDI) dataset (2005=100).[9] As we can see from Figure 4.3, at the beginning of economic reforms, China maintained an overvalued currency under which it was generally unprofitable to export. Over the course of the reform period, the authorities devalued the official exchange rate in stages, from CNY1.5 to the US dollar in 1981 to 8.7 in 1994. Following a modest appreciation, the government effectively fixed the exchange rate at CNY8.3 to the US dollar in 1995, a rate that was not significantly changed until 2005.

4.4.2 The regression model

As specified, we will study the relationship between financial repression and investment, employment, economic efficiency, economic growth, inflation, and economic volatility. Therefore, we construct the regression equation as follows:

$$y_{i,t} = \beta_1 reali_t + \beta_2 relative_{i,t} + \beta_3 sob_t + \beta_4 reer_t + \beta_5 depth_{i,t}$$
$$+ \beta_6 state_{i,t} + \beta_7 gov_{i,t} + \beta_8 trade_{i,t} + \beta_9 edu_{i,t} + \beta_{10} urban_{i,t} + u_t + \varepsilon_{i,t} \tag{4}$$

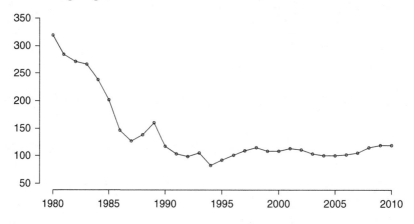

Figure 4.3 China's real effective exchange rate (1980–2010)

Here: i = 1, 2, ..., 31, representing each of the 31 provinces (or municipalities or autonomous regions) that will be examined in this study. Variable t = 1, 2, ..., 33, which represents each year from 1978 to 2010. Variable 'y' represents six dependent variables of interest:

- 'inv/gdp': The variables 'inv' and 'gdp' represent the nominal value of the gross fixed capital formation and GDP, respectively, for a particular region and year. The ratio 'inv/gdp' therefore refers to the rate of investment in fixed assets.
- 'ΔL/invc': The variable 'invc' is the amount of investment calculated in terms of 1978 fixed prices. 'ΔL' is the annual increase in the labor force, and 'ΔL/invc' represents the employment absorptive capacity of investment.
- 'TFP': is the total factor productivity (the calculation of which will be explained below).
- 'pgdp': is the real GDP per capita (calculated in terms of fixed prices of 1978) for each region.
- 'cpi': is the inflation rate for each region each year.
- 'volat': is the level of economic volatility and will be measured by the absolute value of the difference between the growth rate of two consecutive years.

With respect to the independent variables, 'reali' refers to the real interest rate, 'relative' is the ratio of the volume of credit extended to private enterprises to that extended to SOEs, 'sob', is the ratio of assets of SOBs to total bank assets and 'reer' is the real effective exchange rate. All of these indicators indicate financial repression. In addition, we use financial depth ('depth'), the proportion of the state-owned sector ('state'), the scale of government expenditures ('gov'), the scale of foreign trade ('trade'), education ('edu'), and the level of urban employment proportions ('urban') as control variables. Descriptions of the variables can be found in Table 4.2.

In this chapter the production function method is used to estimate the TFP. More specifically, we use the value of GDP in each region (expressed in terms of 1978 fixed prices) as the indicator of output, the number of employees in each region as the indicator of labor input, and fixed capital stock in each region as the indicator of capital input. The perpetual inventory method is used to calculate the fixed capital stock, and the fixed capital stock of 1978 in each region (as estimated by Zhang *et al.* 2004) is used as the stock in the base year. In addition, a 10 per cent depreciation rate is employed.

In this study, a Cobb-Douglas production function ($Y = AK^\alpha L^{1-\alpha}$) is assumed, and the TFP can therefore be expressed as $A = Y/(K^\alpha L^{1-\alpha})$. Before we estimate the TFP, it is necessary to set a value for α, the capital-output elasticity. Although in most studies that focus on countries outside of China, α is typically set to a value of approximately 0.3, this elasticity is relatively high in China (0.35–0.5) (Gui and Chen 2012). In the next section, we will use $\alpha = 0.4$ to conduct an estimation. We find that, for different values of α between 0.35 and 0.5, the estimated correlation coefficient remains greater than 0.94, which means that the choice of value of α has no significant influence on relative levels of the TFP.

4.4.3   Regression results

Before conducting a panel regression, we run stationarity tests on the variables. The approach of Maddala and Wu (1999) is used to perform an Augmented Dickey-Fuller (ADF) unit root test on the variables. We choose a maximum lag of six years and use the Akaike Information Criterion (AIC) to choose the optimal lag items. A model with an intercept and trend is employed. The results show that the aforementioned variables are stationary, with the p-values of the Chi-square statistics being less than 0.01.

Moreover, to avoid endogeneity bias, we include a one-period lag of 'reali', 'relative', 'depth', and 'state' as instrumental variables and therefore further set the model as a random-effects model, which may help us estimate the influence of individual-invariant variables, such as the real interest rate ('reali') more accurately. However, we are unable to integrate individual effects and time effects into the model simultaneously because of the introduction of instrumental variables. Given the great variance of statistical criteria among different years in China, we choose to include time-effects into the model. An 'LM test' reveals that time-effects are significant (p-value<0.01). The regression results of the models are as follows.

In model 1 (inv/gdp), a decrease in the 'reali' and an increase in credit extended to SOEs ('relative') will stimulate investment. As we have argued, the lower the cost of capital (real interest rate), the stronger the incentive to undertake investment. Moreover, compared with private enterprises, SOEs have a stronger tendency to invest because of the problem of 'soft budget constraints.' An appreciation (rather than depreciation) of China's currency seems to be accompanied by an increase in investment, a phenomenon that is not consistent with the prediction that exchange rate distortion contributes to investment. Similarly, a decrease in the ratio of the assets of SOBs to total bank assets

Table 4.2 Description of the variables

Variables	Variable definition	Mean	Median	SD	Min	Max	No. of obs
inv/gdp	rate of investment	0.355	0.326	0.142	0.045	1.106	1023
Linvc	employment absorptive capacity of investments (person/CNY 10,000)	0.563	0.193	0.959	-1.749	10.915	1023
log(TFP)	log(total factor productivity)	-1.014	-1.027	0.492	-2.183	0.385	1023
log(pgdp)	log(real per capita GDP) (CNY 10,000)	-2.035	-2.085	0.944	-4.054	0.695	1023
cpi	inflation rate	105.8	103.4	6.84	96.4	129.7	960
volat	economic volatility	0.042	0.03	0.04	0	0.316	992
reali	real interest rate	0.001	0.004	0.035	-0.096	0.059	33
depth	ratio of credit to GDP	0.872	0.829	0.305	0.199	2.585	1023
relative	ratio of volume of credit extended to private enterprises to that extended to SOEs	0.741	0.429	1.17	-0.588	10.75	1023
sob	ratio of assets of SOBs to total bank assets	0.79	0.80	0.17	0.49	0.99	33
reer	real effective exchange rate	141.40	113.20	64.7	82.65	319.20	31
State	proportion of State-owned sector	0.601	0.649	0.205	0.094	0.939	1023
gov	ratio of government spending to GDP	0.163	0.131	0.113	0.049	1.086	1023
trade	ratio of foreign trade to GDP	0.034	0.016	0.044	0.001	0.277	1023
edu	proportion of university graduates in the population	0.006	0.002	0.007	0	0.04	1023
urban	proportion of the population that is employed in an urban area	0.328	0.278	0.16	0.119	0.81	1023

(Source: *China Compendium of Sixty Years of Statistics, China Compendium of Fifty Years of Statistics* and *China Statistical Yearbook*.)

('sob') is not associated with a decrease in investment, which may reflect the fact that the difference between SOBs and other types of banks such as joint-stock banks should not be overestimated, and therefore the proportion of SOBs does not matter as much for the level of investment (but they may hurt economic efficiency, such as TFP, as we will show). Finally, there is a positive correlation between financial depth and the investment rate, a positive correlation between the scale of government expenditures and the investment rate and a negative correlation between the development of foreign trade and the investment rate.

In model 2 (ΔL/invc), we find a positive (but not significant) relationship between the interest rate and employment because an increase in the interest rate will raise the cost of capital, inhabit the preferences of enterprises for capital-intensive technologies, and therefore increase the employment absorptive capacity of investment. In addition, compared with SOEs, private enterprises are more market oriented and hence would prefer labor-intensive technologies that are more congruent with the comparative advantage of China. An increase in credit extended to private enterprises should therefore improve the employment absorptive capacity of investment, which is also confirmed by our empirical evidence (although the influence is not significant).

Exchange rate distortion seems to be harmful to employment. We find that there is a positive and significant relationship between real effective exchange rate and employment, which may reflect the fact that China's export sector is more capital-intensive than we expect and therefore has limited employment absorptive capacity. In that case, when the renminbi is devalued, the expansion of the export sector cannot be translated into employment growth (in fact, we find that there is a negative relationship between the development of foreign trade and employment growth).

The role of SOBs is confusing. We find a positive relationship between the proportion of SOBs and employment growth, which is not consistent with our theoretical argument and needs further investigation in the future. Finally, increases in the ratio of credit to GDP, the proportion of SOEs in a region, and the scale of government expenditures are harmful to the employment effects of investment.

In model 3 (log(TFP)), an increase in the interest rate has an insignificant positive impact on the TFP, which is consistent with our previous prediction that a low interest rate will damage economic efficiency. Similarly, more credit extended to private enterprises has a significant positive influence on the TFP, and the higher ratio of assets of SOBs to total bank assets has a significant negative impact on TFP. The correlation between the real effective exchange rate and TFP, however, is negative, which means that devaluation helps to improve efficiency (by stimulating exports and hence leading to export enterprises facing greater international competition).

Finally, increases in the ratio of credit to GDP, the proportion of SOEs in a region, and the scale of government expenditures have a negative effect on the TFP, whereas the expansion of foreign trade, improvement of education, and acceleration of urbanization have a positive effect on the TFP.

Table 4.3a Panel regression results (a)

Explanatory variables	Model 1: inv/gdp		Model 2: ΔLiinvc		Model 3: log(TFP)	
reali	−0.368* (0.175)	−0.367* (0.172)	0.377 (4.018)	—	0.587 (1.061)	—
relat	−0.021*** (0.004)	−0.021*** (0.003)	0.012 (0.03)	—	0.026*** (0.008)	0.025*** (0.008)
sob	−0.6*** (0.142)	—	2.817*** (1.066)	2.814*** (1.055)	−0.917*** (0.281)	−1.093*** (0.227)
reer	0.022 (0.032)	—	0.456* (0.235)	0.461** (0.232)	−0.086 (0.062)	—
depth	0.071*** (0.016)	0.068*** (0.014)	−0.198 (0.128)	—	−0.257*** (0.033)	−0.252*** (0.032)
state	−0.009 (0.033)	—	−0.463* (0.259)	−0.52** (0.219)	−0.663*** (0.066)	−0.673*** (0.065)
gov	0.353*** (0.027)	0.352*** (0.026)	−0.453** (0.216)	−0.457** (0.215)	−0.36*** (0.055)	−0.361*** (0.055)
trade	−0.233*** (0.081)	−0.226*** (0.078)	−1.859*** (0.642)	−1.804*** (0.626)	1.427*** (0.163)	1.42*** (0.163)
edu	−2.022** (0.939)	−1.953** (0.93)	30.945*** (7.403)	30.611*** (7.343)	3.741** (1.881)	3.516* (1.874)
urban	0.335*** (0.052)	0.331*** (0.051)	−3.178*** (0.409)	−3.167*** (0.408)	2.361*** (0.104)	2.368*** (0.104)
adj. R^2	0.32	0.32	0.125	0.125	0.755	0.756
obs.	1023	1023	1023	1023	1023	1023

Table 4.3b Panel regression results (b)

Explanatory variables	Model 4: log(pgdp)		Model 5: cpi		Model 6: volat	
reali	-1.043	—	-126.673***	-126.707***	-0.044	—
	(-2.716)	—	(24.73)	(21.13)	(0.062)	—
relat	0.033***	0.033***	-0.152*	-0.17***	-0.001	—
	(0.008)	(0.008)	(0.078)	(0.055)	(0.002)	—
sob	-2.485***	-2.903***	28.649***	30.138***	0.065***	0.059***
	(0.692)	(0.537)	(6.312)	(5.343)	(0.024)	(0.015)
reer	-0.193	—	-3.589**	-3.595***	0.006	0.006*
	(0.157)	—	(1.432)	(1.22)	(0.004)	(0.003)
depth	-0.305***	-0.302***	0.098	—	0.001	—
	(0.034)	(0.033)	(0.34)	—	(0.007)	—
state	-0.845***	-0.856***	0.714	—	0.001	—
	(0.068)	(0.065)	(0.692)	—	(0.015)	—
gov	-0.021	—	0.196	—	0.046***	0.045***
	(0.057)	—	(0.625)	—	(0.013)	(0.011)
trade	2.032***	2.024***	2.306	—	0.041	—
	(0.168)	(0.168)	(1.74)	—	(0.038)	—
edu	10.586***	10.59***	-29.691	—	0.171	—
	(1.948)	(1.932)	(19.712)	—	(0.407)	—
urban	4.397***	4.4***	1.706	1.457**	-0.019	—
	(0.107)	(0.107)	(1.078)	(0.651)	(0.023)	—
adj. R^2	0.883	0.886	0.092	0.113	0.056	0.058
obs.	1023	1023	960	960	992	992

Notes:

The numbers in parentheses are the standard errors.

'***', '**', and '*' indicate 1%, 5%, and 10% levels of significance, respectively.

For each regression model, we report two types of results: the first type is the initial regression results with all explanatory variables included, and the second is the results with significant explanatory variables.

In model 4 (log(pgdp)), we examine the overall influence of each variable on economic growth. The results show that a low interest rate has a positive (but not significant) effect on economic growth; however, more credit extended to SOEs has a significant negative influence on economic growth. The correlation between the SOB indicator ('sob') and economic growth is negative, which means that a higher market share of SOBs will bring about slower economic growth. Finally, devaluation helps to promote economic growth, which is reflected by the negative relationship between exchange rate indicator ('reer') and economic growth.

In addition, increases in the ratio of credit to GDP, the proportion of SOEs in a region, and the scale of government expenditures have a negative effect on economic growth, whereas the expansion of foreign trade and improvement of education have a positive influence on economic growth.

In summary, the connection between financial repression and economic growth is more complicated than suggested by conventional studies. On the one hand, interest rate controls contribute to economic growth by lowering the cost of capital, and exchange rate distortion promotes economic growth by stimulating exports; on the other hand, credit misallocation and state ownership in the banking sector retards economic growth by damaging economic efficiency. The apparent puzzle that a repressed financial system has not retarded China's economic growth can therefore be solved: when the pro-growth effects of financial repression outweigh its anti-growth effects, the overall influence of financial repression may be beneficial, rather than harmful, to economic growth.

In model 5 (cpi), we examine the relationship between financial repression and inflation. It seems that financial repression will worsen inflation. Both a decrease in the real interest rate ('reali') and increased credit extended to SOEs ('relative') will increase the level of inflation. Similarly, devaluation and a higher market share of SOBs also contribute to inflation. In addition, increases in the ratio of credit to GDP, the proportion of SOEs in a region, and the scale of government expenditures have a positive effect on inflation.

In model 6 (volat), we investigate the connection between financial repression and economic volatility. Most of our financial repression indicators contribute to economic volatility. The only exception is the exchange rate indicator. There is a positive correlation between this indicator and economic volatility, which means that devaluation of China's currency will reduce economic volatility. In addition, increases in the ratio of credit to GDP, the proportion of SOEs in a region, and the scale of government expenditures have a positive effect on economic volatility.

4.5   Concluding remarks

It has long been argued (and to a large extent proven) that financial repression, with its nature of preventing financial intermediaries from functioning at their full capacity, is detrimental to economic growth. In this chapter, we have shown that China is a more complicated version of the 'bad financial repression' story. The apparent paradox of the coexistence of a repressed financial sector and a high-growth economy in China can be solved by exploring the dual role played by China's financial system: while financial repression may help China to accomplish extraordinary economic growth by subsidizing investment and production, it also endangers China's economic health by damaging economic efficiency, slowing job creation, and distorting the country's economic structure.

The inescapable problem encountered with China's input-driven growth model is that there are diminishing returns associated with the addition of any one factor of production. With a given labor force, the addition of more and more machines will produce more output but at a steadily declining rate. Therefore, further investment can raise the level of an economy's total output but not its long-term growth rate. As the famous Solow Model shows, regardless of the level of capital with which an economy begins, without technological progress, the economy will end up at a steady state in which there is no per capita growth (Solow 1956).

China's investment-driven growth seems to face a similar destiny. China has one of the highest ratios of investment to GDP in the world, which has resulted in some serious economic and social problems, such as environmental degradation, slower job creation, urban-rural inequality, and production capacity overexpansion (Xu 2012). In addition, as Kuijs and Wang (2006) show, if China's current economic growth pattern continues, an investment to GDP ratio at the unprecedented level of 55 per cent on average in 2014–24 will be required to maintain GDP growth at 8 per cent per year. Financing such a high level of investment in the long run is impossible; under these circumstances, the investment-driven economy will finally reach a dead end.

A more market oriented financial system is therefore called for to rebalance China's distorted economy, improve the social welfare of ordinary citizens, and make China's economic growth more sustainable. Financial liberalization is undoubtedly desirable given its positive effects on savings, investment, and economic development; however, without an effective system of prudential regulation and supervision, financial liberalization will inevitably lead to financial volatility, economic instability, and even social disturbance. Therefore, a well-designed and effectively operating regulatory and supervisory framework is a precondition for further financial reform that aims to end repression policies and practices in China's financial system. Among other actions, the government must strengthen the independence, effectiveness, staffing, and funding of regulatory bodies; insist on higher standards of disclosure, auditing, and accounting; and streamline the court system to address troubled banks and firms in a timely fashion (World Bank 2012). Building such a framework demands time, resources, and, most importantly, the determination of the government.

Notes

1 This chapter is an extension of our earlier study (Xu and Gui 2013) and a follow-up study to Xu (2013). Compared with Xu and Gui (2013), this chapter adds more financial repression indicators, and discusses the influence of financial repression on inflation and economic volatility, in addition to economic growth. The focus of Xu (2013) is on the relationship between financial repression and China's distorted macroeconomic structure (investment-driven growth pattern), rather than the connection between financial repression and China's growth performance that is addressed by Xu and Gui (2013) and this chapter. This study is sponsored by the Program for Young Innovative Research Team at China University of Political Science and Law, and by the Beijing Municipal Program for Interdisciplinary Studies (Program of Law and Economics).

2 By the end of 2012, the Big Four together with the Bank of Communication held 44.9 per cent of total financial assets. See the *2012 Annual Report of the China Banking Regulatory Commission*, available online at http://zhuanti.cbrc.gov.cn/subject/subject/nianbao2012/English/Part1.pdf (accessed 14 May 2014).

3 There is another joint-stock bank, the Bank of Communication, which has been classified by the China Banking Regulatory Commission (CBRC) as a "large commercial bank" just like the Big Four.

4 See the *2012 Annual Report of the China Banking Regulatory Commission*, available online at: http://zhuanti.cbrc.gov.cn/subject/subject/nianbao2012/English/Part1.pdf (accessed 14 May 2014).

5 *China Securities Regulatory Commission Annual Report 2012*, available online at: http://www.csrc.gov.cn/pub/newsite/zjhjs/zjhnb/201307/P020130722553207507219.pdf (accessed 14 May 2014).

6 *2012 World Federation of Exchanges Market Highlights*, available online at: http://www.world-exchanges.org/files/statistics/2012%20WFE%20Market%20Highlights.pdf (accessed 14 May 2014).

7 *China's Securities and Futures Markets 2007*, China Securities Regulatory Commission, available online at: http://www.csrc.gov.cn/pub/csrc_En/about/annual/200812/P020090225529643752895.pdf (accessed 14 May 2014).

8 According to Shaw (1973: 86) "[r]ationing is expensive to administer. It is vulnerable to corruption and conspiracy in dividing between borrowers and officers of the intermediary monopoly rent that arise from the difference between low, regulated loan rate and the market-clearing rate. Borrowers who simply do not repay loans and keep their place in the ration queue by extending maturities can frustrate it. The rationing process discriminates poorly among investment opportunities … and the social cost of this misallocation is suggested by the high incremental ratios of investment to output that lagging economies report."

9 Available online at http://data.worldbank.org/country/china (accessed 29 May 2014).

References

Acemoglu, D., Johnson, S., Robinson, J. and Thaicharoen, Y. (2003) 'Institutional Causes, Macroeconomic Symptoms: Volatility, Crises and Growth', *Journal of Monetary Economics*, 50, 49–123.

Allen, F., Qian, J. and Qian, M. (2005) 'Law, Finance, and Economic Growth in China', *Journal of Financial Economics*, 77, 57–116.

Allen, F., Qian, J. and Qian, M. (2008) 'China's Financial System: Past, Present, and Future', in Brandt, L. and Rawski, T. G. (eds), *China's Great Economic Transformation*, Cambridge: Cambridge University Press, 506–68.

Aziz, J. and Dunaway, S. (2007) 'China's Rebalancing Act', *Finance and Development*, 44(3), 27–31.

Barth, J., Caprio, G. and Levine, R. (2006) *Rethinking Bank Regulation: Till Angles Govern*, New York: Cambridge University Press.

Brandt, L. and Zhu, X. (2007) 'China's Banking Sector and Economic Growth', in Calomiris, C. (ed), *China's Financial Transition at a Crossroads*, New York: Columbia University Press, 86–143.

Deng, Y., Morck, R., Wu, J. and Yeung, B. (2011) 'Monetary and Fiscal Stimuli, Ownership Structure, and China's Housing Market', *NBER Working Paper*, no. 16871, Washington, DC.

Dobson, W. and Kashyap, A. K. (2006) 'The Contradiction in China's Gradualist Banking Reforms', *Brookings Papers on Economic Activity*, 37(2), 103–62.

Eichengreen, B. (2008) 'The Real Exchange Rate and Economic Growth', *Commission on Growth and Development Working Paper*, no. 4. Available online at http://www.kantakji.com/media/4637/c361.pdf.

Ferri, G. (2008) 'Are New Tigers Supplanting Old Mammoths in China's Banking System? Evidence from a Sample of City Commercial Banks', *Journal of Banking and Finance*, 33(1), 131–40.

Ferri, G. and Liu, L. (2010) 'Honor Thy Creditors Before Thy Shareholders: Are the Profits of Chinese State-Owned Enterprises Real', *Asian Economic Papers*, 9(3), 50–71.

Fry, M. (1978) 'Money and Capital or Financial Deepening in Economic Development', *Journal of Money, Credit, and Banking*, 10(4), 464–75.

Fry, M. (1997) 'In Favour of Financial Liberalisation', *Economic Journal*, 107, 754–70.

Fu, X. and Heffernan, S. (2007) 'Cost X-efficiency in China's Banking Sector', *China Economic Review*, 18, 35–53.

Gala, P. (2008) 'Real Exchange Rate Levels and Economic Development: Theoretical Analysis and Econometric Evidence', *Cambridge Journal of Economics*, 32, 273–88.

Geng, N. and N'Diaye, P. (2012) 'Determinants of Corporate Investment in China: Evidence from Cross-Country Firm Level Data', *IMF Working Paper*, WP/12/80, Washington, DC.

Ghura, D. and Grennes, T. J. (1993) 'The Real Exchange Rate and Macroeconomic Performance in Sub-Saharan Africa', *Journal of Development Economics*, 42, 155–74.

Goldstein, M. and Lardy, N. (2008) 'China's Exchange Rate Policy: An Overview of Some Key Issues', in Goldstein, M. and Lardy, N. (eds), *Debating China's Exchange Rate Policy*, Washington, DC: Peterson Institute for International Economics, 1–60.

Gui, B. and Chen, Y. (2012) 'Biased Technology, Dual Structure and Research of Labor Income Share in China', *Working Paper Series*, CUPL: China University of Political Science and Law, China.

Haddad, M. and Pancaro, C. (2010) 'Can Real Exchange Rate Undervaluation Boost Exports and Growth in Developing Countries? Yes, But Not for Long', *Economic Premise*, 20, 1–5.

Hellmann, T., Murdock, K. and Stiglitz, J. (1998) 'Financial Restraint: Towards a New Paradigm', in Aoki, M., Kim H-K. and Okuno-Fujiwara, M. (eds), *The Role of Government in East Asian Economic Development: Comparative Institutional Analysis*, Oxford: Clarendon University Press, 163–207.

Héricourt, J. and Poncet, S. (2009) 'FDI and Credit Constraints: Firm-Level Evidence from China', *Economic Systems*, 33, 1–21.

Huang, Y. (2003) *Selling China: Foreign Direct Investment during the Reform Era*, New York: Cambridge University Press.

Huang, Y. (2006) 'Do Financing Biases Matter for the Chinese Economy?', *Cato Journal*, 26(2), 287–306.

IMF (2013) 'People's Republic of China: Staff Report for the 2013 Article IV Consultation', *IMF Country Report*, no. 13/211. Available online at http://www.imf.org/external/pubs/ft/scr/2013/cr13211.pdf (accessed 28 January 2014).

Jia, C. (2008) 'The Effect of Ownership on the Prudential Behavior of Banks – The Case of China', *Journal of Banking and Finance*, 38(1), 77–87.

Knight, J. and Ding, S. (2012) *China's Remarkable Economic Growth*, Oxford: Oxford University Press.

Kuijs, L. and Wang, T. (2006) 'China's Pattern of Growth: Moving to Sustainability and Reducing Inequality', *China and World Economy*, 14(1), 1–14.

La Porta, R., Lopez-de-Silanes, F. and Shleifer, A. (2002) 'Government Ownership of Banks', *Journal of Finance*, 57, 265–301.

Lardy, N. (2007) 'China: Rebalancing Economic Growth', in Bergsten, C. F., Gill, B., Lardy, N. and Mitchell, D. J. (eds), *The China Balance Sheet in 2007 and Beyond*, Washington, DC: The Center for Strategic and International Studies and the Peterson Institute for International Economics, 1–24.

Lardy, N. (2012) *Sustaining China's Economic Growth After the Global Financial Crisis*, Washington, DC: Peterson Institute for International Economics.

Liu, M., Margaritis, D. and Tourani-Rad, A. (2009) 'Monetary Policy and Interest Rate Rigidity in China', *Applied Financial Economics*, 19, 647–57.

Ma, G. and Wang, Y. (2010) 'China's High Saving Rate: Myth and Reality', *Bank for International Settlements Working Paper*, no. 312, Basel.

Maddala, G. S. and Wu, S. (1999) 'A Comparative Study of Unit Root Tests with Panel Data and a New Simple Test', *Oxford Bulletin of Economics & Statistics*, 61, 631–52.

Magud, N. and Sosa, S. (2010) 'When and Why Worry About Real Exchange Rate Appreciation? The Missing Link between Dutch Disease and Growth', *IMF Working Paper*, WP10/271, Washington, DC.

McKinnon, R. (1973) *Money and Capital in Economic Development*, Washington, DC: Brookings Institution.

McKinsey Global Institute (2006) *Putting China's Capital to Work: The Value of Financial System Reform*. Available online at http://www.mckinsey.com/Insights/MGI/Research/Financial_Markets/Putting_Chinas_capital_to_work (accessed 28 January 2014).

Naughton, B. (2007) *The Chinese Economy: Transitions and Growth*, Cambridge, MA: The MIT Press.

Park, A. and Sehrt, K. (2001) 'Tests of Financial Intermediation and Banking Reform in China', *Journal of Comparative Economics*, 29, 608–44.

Perkins, D. and Rawski, T. (2008) 'Foresting China's Economic Growth to 2025', in Brandt, L. and Rawski, T. G. (eds), *China's Great Economic Transformation*, Cambridge: Cambridge University Press.

Podpiera, R. (2006) 'Progress in China's Banking Sector Reform: Has Bank Behavior Changed?' *IMF Working Paper*, WP/06/71, Washington, DC.

Poncet, S., Steingress, W. and Vandenbussche, H. (2010) 'Financial Constraints in China: Firm-Level Evidence', *China Economic Review*, 21, 411–22.

Prasad, E. (2009) 'Is the Chinese Growth Miracle Built to Last?' *China Economic Review*, 20, 103–23.

Roubini, N. and Sala-i-Martin, X. (1992) 'Financial Repression and Economic Growth', *Journal of Development Economics*, 39, 5–30.

Shaw, E. (1973) *Financial Deepening in Economic Development*, New York: Oxford University Press.

Solow, R. (1956) 'A Contribution to the Theory of Economic Growth', *Quarterly Journal of Economics*, 70, 65–94.

Walter, C. and Howie, F. (2011) *Red Capitalism: The Fragile Financial Foundation of China's Extraordinary Rise*, Singapore: John Wiley & Sons (Asia) Pte. Ltd.

World Bank (2001) *Finance for Growth: Policy Choices in a Volatile World*, New York: Oxford University Press.

World Bank (2012) *China 2030: Building a Modern, Harmonious, and Creative High-Income Society*. Available online at: http://www.worldbank.org/content/dam/Worldbank/document/China-2030-complete.pdf (accessed 29 May 2014).

Xu, G. (2012) 'Law and China's Economic Growth: A Macroeconomic Perspective', *Dovenschmidt Quarterly*, 1, 3–15.

Xu, G. (2013) 'Financial Repression, Economic Distortion, and China's Growth Miracle', in Faure, M. and Xu, G. (eds), *Economics and Regulation in China*, London: Routledge.

Xu, G. and Gui, B. (2013) 'The Connection between Financial Repression and Economic Growth: The Case of China', *Journal of Comparative Asian Development*, 12(3), 385–410.

Yang, D., Zhang, J. and Zhou, S. (2011) 'Why Are Saving Rates so High in China?' *NBER Working Paper*, no. 16771, Washington, DC.

Zhang, J., Wu, G. and Zhang, J. (2004) 'zhongguo shengji wuzhi ziben cunliang gusuan: 1952–2000' (An Estimation of China's Provincial Capital Stock: 1952–2000), *jingji yanjiu (Economic Research Journal)*, 10, 35–44.

5 Law, money and price

The case of China

Tao Xi and Jianwei Chen[1]

5.1 Introduction

Article II of the Law of the People's Republic of China on the People's Bank of China (the Law on PBOC) stipulates that the PBOC 'formulates and implements monetary policies, prevents and mitigates financial risks and safeguards financial stability', clearly defining the responsibilities of the PBOC. Article III states that 'the objective of monetary policy is to maintain the stability of currency value, so as to promote economic growth', which defines the goal of the PBC's monetary policy. The Law on PBOC, the Law of the People's Republic of China on Commercial Banks, the Law of the People's Republic of China on Banking Regulation and Supervision, Securities Law of the People's Republic of China, the Regulations on Exchange Control of the People's Republic of China and other laws and regulations together constitute a specific framework for execution of the law on PBOC. What are the results of the execution of the law on PBOC?

Monetary policy is one of the tools employed by the State to regulate the macroeconomy and is mainly manifested through the central bank's (or government's) control and administration over currency, credit loans and the banking system, thereby influencing many financial and economic variables through changing the money supply. Therefore, the study of monetary policies, including policy targets, tools, transmission mechanisms and effects, must proceed from the determination of the money supply.

Since 1996, the PBOC began to regard money supply as the intermediate target of its monetary policy, adopting the quantity theory of money and a money supply principle that the growth of the money supply should be basically consistent with economic growth and the inflation rate and roughly equal to the growth of output. However, this principle has nearly never realised because the actual growth rate of the money supply is always faster than the combined value of economic growth rate and the inflation rate.[2] Therefore, to clearly understand how to practically determine the money supply, important factors must be considered. Specifically, in determining the money supply, the PBOC must consider the relationship between the money supply and the real economy,[3] the fictitious economy[4] and the international economy and balance the relationship between savings, investment and imports and exports to achieve macro-regulation targets. This issue will be discussed in this chapter. The structure of the chapter is as follows: First, we briefly review the development of money supply theories and note the problems that exist with China's current money supply. Second, we propose a law and economics framework to analyse the main endogenous factors that influence the money supply by exploring the relationship between the money supply and the real economy, the fictitious economy, the international economy, private savings and enterprise loans. Finally, we summarise and propose some policy suggestions.

5.2 Money supply theories

In the field of monetary economics, money supply theories underwent a series of changes. The academic viewpoints can be divided into exogenous supply theories, and endogenous supply theories.

Exogenous supply theories strongly emphasise a central bank's power to control the money supply, postulating that the money supply can be determined by a central bank at its sole discretion. Keynes (1971), who is one of the most important founders of modern macroeconomics, adopted the hypothesis that the money supply is exogenous and advocated that money is the unique product of the country. This became the mainstream theory for a long period of time, and it was later supplemented and developed by the neoclassical synthesis school, the monetarism school, the rational expectation school, etc. (Wang 2008). Friedman represents the exogenous supply theories. He believed that over the short term, money supply has a large impact on the real economy and that the change of money stock is jointly determined by three factors: high-powered money (H), the ratio of commercial bank deposits (D) to reserves (R) (D/R) and the ratio of commercial bank deposits to the currency (C) held by the public (D/C) (Friedman and Schwartz 1963: 123–35). The central bank has the power to control the money supply 'as long as the monetary authority is able to control or change H, it is surely able to determine the change of money supply while influencing D/R and D/C' (Wang 1992: 68). He also proposed that the growth of money supply should be maintained at a fixed rate according to the quantity theory of money. His view provided an early theoretical basis for central banks to reasonably determine the money supply. However, as the development of the global economy and the financial industry became more complicated, especially because central banks of major western market economies missed their money supply targets many times in the 1980s, exogenous supply theories seemed to conflict with reality and were challenged theoretically, and consequently endogenous supply theories attracted more attention from economists.

Endogenous supply theories hold that central banks are not able to control such key factors as the speed of money circulation and the money multiplier, so the quantity of the money supply should be endogenously determined by demand from economic entities, and a central bank's issuance of currency should be only a passive act. The classical school first proposed the theory that the necessary quantity of money in circulation in a country depends on the value of the commodities in circulation in that country. Later, money supply theories were developed further by money and finance theorists, including Gurly, Shaw and Tobin. With the rise of the post-Keynesian school in the 1970s, endogenous supply theories became the cornerstone for theorists such as Weinteaub, Kaldor, Moore and Lavoie.

> On the one hand, they took the domestic financial system, especially the evolution of the banking system, as their study object, proving that with the development of the financial industry, the endogeneity of the money supply will gradually be strengthened and replace its exogeneity; on the other hand, they broadened the horizon of the study of the money supply issue, considering not only domestic money supply, but also international money supply.
>
> (Chen 2005: 81)

Meanwhile, consensus was reached to take into consideration the relationship between money supply and the real economy, the fictitious economy and the international economy when determining money supply. Of course, most of the scholars explored the determination of money supply from the perspective of the money creation process, namely, the internal transmission mechanism of monetary policies, and they focused on the causes or leading factors of the money supply. However, these scholars seldomly conducted in-depth studies on the external factors that influence monetary policies and rarely discussed the specific relationship between money supply and economic risk prevention.

Since the outbreak of the financial crisis in 2008, which was triggered by the subprime crisis in the US, there has been heated discussion in academic circles regarding the relationship between the money supply and systemic financial risks. Attention has been focused on the factors that have a direct bearing on the money supply, such as monetary policies, bank loans and the shadow banking system. Many scholars have studied methods and measures to monitor systemic risks, and significant reforms of money supply theories have occurred. Schwarcz (2008) analysed 'systemic risks', discussed and assessed a series of possible regulatory methods, and proposed methods to ensure liquidity by providing liquidity for financial institutions to prevent breach of contract and for capital markets to maintain their operations. Such measures can significantly help to reduce systemic risks. After the release of the Dodd-Frank Wall Street Reform and Consumer Protection Act 2010 (hereinafter referred to as Dodd-Frank), Coffee (2011) analysed the inevitability and periodicity of the loosening of financial regulations, believing that Dodd-Frank would impair the ability of regulatory authorities to conduct direct bailouts. Coffee proposed to adopt the reserve withdrawal method to address the vulnerability and liquidity risks of financial institutions. Barr (2012) argued that Dodd-Frank endows regulators with the power to monitor systemically important financial institutions and systemic risks and strengthens the monitoring over such shadow banking mechanisms as over-the-counter (OTC) derivatives, repurchase agreements and asset securitisations, which have a significant impact on the money supply but had been ignored in the past. Barr believed that Dodd-Frank and its supporting regulatory reforms would provide guarantees with financial stability and economic growth. Rose and Walker (2012) argued that since the release of Dodd-Frank, financial regulatory measures have experienced an exponential increase. To strengthen the rationality and effectiveness of these measures and in order to lower the possibility of regulatory capture, regulators should employ a cost-benefit analysis approach. These studies shed light on the inherent connection between monetary policies, financial stability and prudent macro-management, further defined the systemic risks involved in the money supply, and made useful proposals on how to monitor, and manage such risks.

In China, there are many scholars who have conducted useful research on money supply theories. Most domestic scholars favour the endogenous supply theories. After conducting an empirical analysis, Wan and Xu (2001) argued that China's money supply is strongly endogenous. They found that 'the reaction made by banks and residents to the economy changes the money multiplier and the central bank's power of control over the monetary aggregate, thus influencing money supply' (Wan and Xu 2001: 43–4). Their research paid special attention to the impact of the economic behaviour of the private sector (including banks and the public) on the money supply (Wan and Xu 2001). Geng and Zeng (2006) have tested the endogenous money supply hypothesis in China and found that during the study period 'there exists a one-way causality between loans and money supply and a two-way causality between gross domestic product (GDP) and money supply, between loans and base money, and between loans and the M_2 money multiplier over the long term and also a one-way causality between loans and the M_2 money multiplier over the short term' (Geng and Zeng 2006: 73). They found that China's money supply is endogenous, that loans create deposits and that the money supply is determined by the money demand of economic entities (Geng and Zeng 2006). By breaking down the models of money supply theories, Lu and Cao have concluded that China's money supply is becoming increasingly endogenous. 'Money supply is closely integrated with the entire macro-economy; not only do families, enterprises and commercial banks influence the money supply with their respective behaviour, but the central bank's creditor's rights over the central government, various financial institutions and foreign exchange assets can also generate money demand to influence the money supply' (Lu and Cao 2007: 35–6). Their study once again showed that the influence of deposits, loans, the central bank's creditor's rights and foreign exchange reserves should be considered in determining the money supply. After the outbreak of the financial crisis in the US in 2008, Liu and Sui have attempted to identify the source of uncertainties in the growth of China's money supply, and found that 'in most historical periods, the uncertainties in China's money supply growth are triggered by macro-economic impacts, and in only some periods are they triggered by the central bank's active moves' (Liu and Sui 2010: 85). Meanwhile, 'with the deepening of economic opening and financial globalisation, the possibility of international financial risk transfers, speculative financial attacks and spreading financial crises have significantly increased' (Liu and Sui 2010: 85). The authors noted that the trend in domestic economic operations and the external impacts triggered by the international economy have become the main reason for the aggravated uncertainties currently observed in the growth of China's money supply. It is especially necessary to note that most domestic Chinese scholars proceed from the perspective of the money creation process in analysing the main factors influencing the money supply, similar to the approaches of mainstream scholars abroad.

However, scholars hold different views regarding the choice of monetary policy objectives and operating tools. Guo (2006) argues that because the basis for determining asset prices is difficult to grasp and the tools are less operable, it is not yet feasible for China's central bank to incorporate asset prices into its monetary policy objectives. Zhao and Gao (2009) believe that monetary policies that take asset prices as an endogenous variable would enable the central bank to have more power to control the realisation of its objectives. They suggest that the central bank perceives the fluctuation of asset prices as an endogenous factor and incorporates it into its prospective interest rate rules to promote the sound development of the real estate market, the stock market and the derivatives market. According to Zhou (2011), President of the PBOC, a social financing scale that measures the total capital which the real economy obtained through the financial medium over a certain period of time can reflect the relationship between finance and the economy more comprehensively, is more significantly correlated with the financial objectives of monetary policies and is also in line with the market orientation of financial macro-regulation. Using total social financing instead of credit indexes to serve as an intermediate objective of financial macro-control is a kind of innovation. Further exploration still needs to be made to reasonably determine the ultimate objectives, intermediate objectives and operational tools in practice.

It is worth mentioning that after the outbreak of the financial crisis in 2008, the domestic field of law has witnessed increased studies on monetary policies and financial stability, and many legal scholars began to provide solutions that involve standardising and improving legal institutions to prevent systemic risks. Wu (2008), observing the process of crisis formation from a legal perspective, believes that the fundamental cause of such crises is that 'the laws governing the real economy are not applicable to the fictitious economy' (Wu 2008: 29). The author argues that the limited liability system should not be applied to investment banks, and traditional legal agency relations should not be applied between companies and the senior executives of investment banks. He proposes that efforts should be made to accelerate the revision of laws and to formulate laws that are suitable for both the fictitious economy and financial derivative products to prevent market risks. Luo (2009: 91), after reflecting on the dilemma of financial regulation in the US, notes that China should step out of the trap of 'blindly following the model of the United States' in the formulation of financial laws, thoroughly reflect on and reconstruct its financial laws and regulations that are incompatible with the fictitious economy, promote the improvement of its financial regulatory framework with political wisdom and truly restore financial regulatory rules as technical market rules. Li (2012) has analysed the legal issues regarding the systematically important financial institutions that are 'too big to fail', proposing that scale, connections and replaceability have become commonly recognised criteria for these financial institutions. He suggests that proper regulation should be established to effectively incorporate these financial institutions into the realm of strict regulation and monitoring to ensure the expected safety of the financial system.

Data show that in the past decade, the actual growth rate of China's money supply has far exceeded the combined value of economic growth rate, and inflation. Moreover, because macro-regulatory policies are formulated in contrast to the general trend of economic development, the trend in growth of the money supply should be the opposite of the trend in economic growth and inflation (see Figure 5.1).

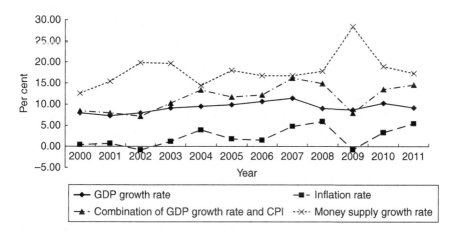

Figure 5.1 Actual growth of money supply
(Source: official websites of the National Bureau of Statistics and the People's Bank of China.)
Note: The money supply here refers to broad money (M_2)

Indeed, this phenomenon has been observed for some time, and many studies have examined it. Lei has found that 'the growth of China's money supply, M_2, has continuously exceeded the combination of GNP growth rate and inflation rate in most years' (Lei 1999: 33). The author introduces the concept of monetisation degree as an explanation and notes that 'China's broad money demand (M_2) is mainly affected by the GNP growth rate, an increase in the monetisation degree ratio and the inflation rate, all of which have a positive influence on money demand' (Lei 1999: 36). Xia and Liao (2001), after comparing the target value and actual value of China's money supply growth, have found that since 1996, when the central bank took the money supply index as the intermediate objective of monetary policy 'the target value of money supply has never been realised' (Xia and Liao 2001: 35). The authors propose that money supply should no longer be used as the intermediate objective in the central bank's monetary policy (Xia and Liao 2001). Zhang (2010) also used the target values and actual values of the central bank's money supply from 1994–2004 to conduct an empirical study. He found that 'during the 11 years, the actual growth of the money supply often deviates from the planned target value, and in particular, there are 7 years when the actual growth of M_1 is more than 2.5 percentage points away from its planned target growth and 6 years for M_2. Meanwhile, in most years, the inflation rate was also far away from the ideal regulation goal of 2 to 3 per cent' (Zhang 2010: 48). Wang (2012b: 80–1) has carried out an in-depth analysis of the causes of the deviation and argues that there are many difficulties in the formulation and implementation of China's monetary policies, which mainly manifest themselves in the following attributes: as the PBOC lowers the proportion of its allocation to domestic total assets, its power to regulate and control is lowered accordingly; the conditions for the transition from quantity regulation to price regulation are not yet mature; the operational space for the hedging of foreign exchange is narrowing; the indexes for the intermediate objectives are still difficult to choose; and the pressure from price increases is still severe. The author concluded that a series of institutional and systemic innovations are needed to address these problems.

In light of the above, it is necessary to adjust the principles used to determine China's money supply to make them more suitable to the actual conditions of economic development and to better serve the macro-objectives of maintaining currency stability and promoting economic development.

5.3   Main endogenous factors influencing money supply

This chapter holds that traditional, quantity-type money supply principles no longer suit China's economic and social development, and it also recognises the argument that the endogenous nature of the money supply is becoming increasingly dominant. Against the background of China's economic transformation, it seems inadequate to review the factors that influence the money supply only from the perspective of money creation, and the objectives of

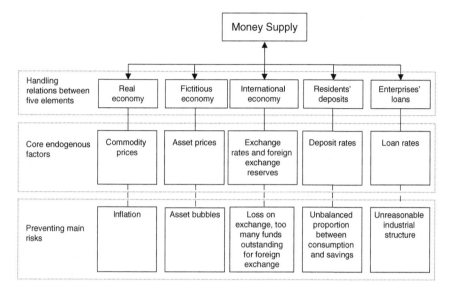

Figure 5.2 A law and economics framework for the analysis of China's money supply

making the money supply serve macroeconomic regulation and controlling economic risk must be emphasised. Therefore, based on endogenous supply theories and oriented toward risk prevention, this chapter proposes that in determining the money supply, we should consider the relationship between the development of the real economy, the fictitious economy and the international economy and balance the relationship between the money supply and residents' deposits and enterprises' loans. In addition, we should comprehensively consider the influence of such endogenous factors as commodity prices, asset prices, exchange rates, foreign exchange reserves and interest rates for deposits and loans and be committed to reducing inflation, curbing asset bubbles and preventing external market impacts and other economic risks. On this basis, we propose a law and economics framework for the analysis of China's money supply. The specific analysis framework in this chapter is shown in Figure 5.2.

According to the characteristics of China's economic development and operation and oriented toward risk prevention, this chapter holds that five factors should be comprehensively considered when determining the money supply.

5.3.1 *Money supply and the real economy*

The size and structural changes in the real economy are the primary factors to be considered when determining the money supply. Analysing the conditions for equilibrium in the real economy from the perspective of overall size, the

equilibrium equation is: *Consumption* + *Investment* + *Net Exports (Exports −*
Imports) = *Consumption* + *Savings*; namely, total demand equals total supply.
Analysing the real economy from the perspective of structure, the corresponding equation requires a relative balance between social demand structures and
social supply structures, namely, balanced and coordinated proportions of
consumption, investment and imports and exports.

Analysing the real economy from the perspective of overall size, the money
supply must be determined according to total demand. Money, in its essence,
represents a type of credit relationship. It means that, without considering
capital markets, the money supply in the real economy comes from the loans
of commercial banks. 'When the commercial banks' assets (loans) rise, the
liabilities also rise, forming the growth cycle of loan→investment→income
→deposits→M_2' (Wang 2002: 49). Therefore, in the relationships between
money demand and supply formed only by residents, enterprises and commercial banks, newly released M_2 should equal the nominal GDP over a certain period of time. Ultimately, the central bank controls the money supply
by controlling the scale of the base money to deposit reserve ratio (influencing
the money creation multiplier) (Wang 2002).

In determining the money supply, which is a major tool of monetary
policy, we must not only prevent severe inflation caused by an overheated
economy, but also stimulate the real economy and prevent deflation during
economic depressions. Inflation is a particularly severe problem that must
be prevented and addressed by governments through their macroeconomic
policies. Although there are many opinions in current academic circles on the
interactive relationship between money supply and inflation, we believe that
progress in the reform of the financial field may have changed such factors
as the money multiplier effect, transmission mechanisms and the structure
of money, but the substantial effect of money supply on inflation has not
changed. China's macroeconomy experienced inflation from 1993 to 1996,
economic austerity from 1997 to 2001, and the dual pressure of domestic inflation and an economic downturn from the impact of international financial
turbulence, and the European debt crisis from 2009 to 2012, when domestic
and international economic imbalances simultaneously hindered the stability and growth of China's economy, bringing unprecedented challenges to
macro-regulation. Monetary policies should actively adjust to control inflation and hedge liquidity, and the growth of the money supply should serve the
development of the real economy.

From the perspective of structure, the money supply must serve the realistic
demands of economic growth. In the past decade, China's economic growth
has mainly been driven by investment and imports and exports. In many years,
investment rates were as high as 20 to 30 per cent. Imports and exports, despite
a sluggish period during the financial crisis, basically maintained a growth
rate of more than 20 per cent, with a peak of 37.2 per cent. In addition, the
consumption growth rate has basically been maintained within the range of
10 to 20 per cent, with less fluctuation (see Figure 5.3). However, there are still

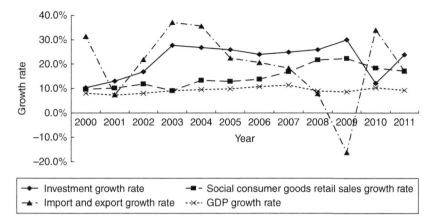

Figure 5.3 Growth rates: investment, social consumer goods retail sales, import and export and GDP
(Source: official website of the National Bureau of Statistics.)

large economic risks. We believe that a balance between the internal texture of the economy and various economic measures and indexes is a prerequisite for economic stability that can make an external impact. When an economy operates with unbalanced and uncoordinated economic measures and indexes, the economy is vulnerable, with lurking economic uncertainties and risks, and external factors can aggravate these uncertainties and risks into an economic crisis.

The economic risks lurking in an investment-driven economic growth pattern are manifested through the following processes. First, investment drives the overheating of the manufacturing industry, triggering inflation and causing future production surpluses. Second, the pattern intensifies the overuse and waste of resources, making it difficult for sustainable development to be maintained. Third, when high investment, high consumption and high pollution become an economic pattern, regulation and governance are difficult to execute, and the intensity and pace of policies become hard to grasp; thus, an economic slowdown occurs.

The economic risks lurking in an import- and export-driven economic growth pattern include the following. First, economic growth is mainly restricted by the trend of global economic growth; a general slowdown or depression in the world economy causes major domestic export companies to either shut down or overstock their inventories. For example, because of the financial crisis in the US and the subsequent European debt crisis triggered by the debt issues of Greece, Italy and Spain in the European Union (EU), the proportion of China's exports to the US, to its total exports dropped from 19.1 per cent in 2007 to 17 per cent in 2011, and the proportion of its exports to Europe to its total exports also dropped from 23.6 per cent in 2007 to

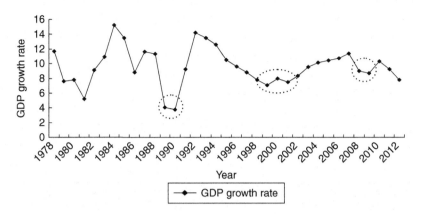

Figure 5.4 China's GDP growth from 1978 to 2012
(Source: official website of the National Bureau of Statistics.)

21.8 per cent in 2011. Second, China is restrained by the economic growth trends of the major world economies, so when those countries adjust their monetary policies, including interest rates and exchange rates, China must also passively adjust its economic policies or methods of regulation to prevent interest arbitrage by international capital organisations from striking a blow to its domestic economy. Third, unfavourable factors such as international politics, the global economy, natural disasters and public emergency events can easily influence domestic economic growth, consumer prices asset prices and exchange rates through transmission mechanisms, causing risks of underproduction or even the bankruptcy of enterprises and a high unemployment rate. Fourth, when a favourable surplus in the international balance of payments exists continuously, the central bank must release base money to pursue foreign exchange, causing risks of liquidity expansion and rising consumer and asset prices.

In examining China's economic growth during the 35 years from 1978 to 2012, there were three periods of large fluctuations, all caused by the impact of the external economic environment and all of which led to a sharp decline in China's imports and exports and a slowdown in economic growth. In 1989, economic growth hit a rock-bottom low when annual imports and exports increased by only 8.6 per cent, which was 15.8 percentage points lower than the previous year, and economic growth fell by 7.2 percentage points. From 1997 to 1999, China was affected by the Asian financial crisis, where imports and exports experienced a continuous decline and economic growth fell by 1.7 percentage points. In 2008, when China was affected by the global financial crisis, imports and exports declined by 5.7 percentage points compared with the previous year, and economic growth fell by 2.4 percentage points (see Figure 5.4). These three periods of economic slowdown were mainly triggered by external economic impacts; sustained and sound economic growth became increasingly vulnerable. Against this background, the issue of structural adjustment becomes especially important. In short, when the proportions of consumption, investment, imports and exports get out of balance, economic growth faces uncertainties, and risks (Xi 2008).

China experienced a period of serious inflation after the financial crisis, which was caused by the release of large amounts of money to stimulate investment and pursue foreign exchange. The inflation rate was as high as 8.7 per cent in 2008 and was maintained between 4 and 6 per cent for some time after. The negative effects of inflation continue to exist, and it has become an inevitable choice to prevent the underlying economic risks through controlling the money supply.

To cope with economic uncertainties and prevent systemic risks, China has established a quite complete legal system that calls for urgent implementation. Article II of the Law on PBOC states 'under the leadership of the State Council, the People's Bank of China (PBOC) formulates and implements monetary policies, prevents and mitigates financial risks and safeguards financial stability'. Article III of the Law on PBOC stipulates that 'the objective of monetary policy is to maintain the stability of currency value, so as to promote economic growth'. In other words, the Law on PBOC requires that the PBOC takes currency value stability as its goal, and it maintains economic stability and promotes economic growth through monetary policy tools, especially by controlling the money supply. These important institutional arrangements help prevent the uncertainties and risks in the real economy through laws and regulations.

5.3.2 *Money supply and the fictitious economy*

With the development of the market economy, the monetisation of China's economy has deepened. Especially given the background of global financial turbulence, the stability and safety of the fictitious economy cannot be ignored. Money supply and the fictitious economy are closely related, and the fictitious economy must be considered in determining the money supply.

The development of the fictitious economy and the real economy has been interdependent and mutually reinforcing. If the growth of the fictitious economy far exceeded that of the real economy, its overexpansion would cause a rapid increase in the price of long-term assets, such as stocks and real estate, forming a phenomenon of false prosperity in the entire economy and leading to the emergence of an economic bubble (Li and Yang 2000). For example, China's securities market is less sound than some other global markets in terms of stock index trends and total market value, and some periods have witnessed violent fluctuations of asset prices and obvious bubbles. Since 2006, the Shanghai Stock Exchange (SSE) Composite Index increased to 5,000 points in the second half of 2007 and hit a record high of 6,124 points on 16 October 2007. The Shenzhen Stock Exchange (SZSE) Component Index exceeded 10,000 points on 13 April 2007 and hit a record high of 19,531 points

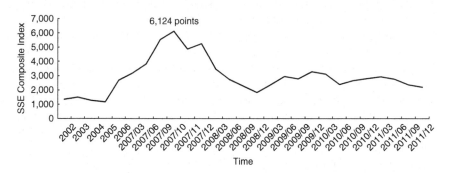

Figure 5.5 SSE Composite Index moving trend
(Source: official website of the China Securities Regulatory Commission.)

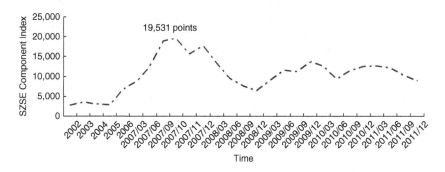

Figure 5.6 SZSE Component Index moving trend
(Source: official website of the China Securities Regulatory Commission.)

just half a year later on 31 October 2007, when the total market value of the two stock exchanges exceeded CNY32 trillion. After that point, however, the bubbles in the stock markets burst. The SSE Composite Index fell to 1800 points in December 2008 (a decline of 70 per cent) and lingers at approximately 2100–2300 today. The SZSE Component Index fell to 6485 points at the end of 2008 (a decline of 67 per cent) and it has fluctuated approximately 10,000 points since then (see Figure 5.5 and Figure 5.6). The bubbles in China's securities market formed very quickly, were maintained for a long period and fell very sharply; such wild fluctuations have rarely been observed throughout the history of world securities markets.

The price index for China's real estate market, however, basically remained stable in 2005 and has been on the rise since 2007. Using Beijing as an example, the average price of commodity houses in the four main urban districts was 14,000 CNY/m² in 2006, 18,000 CNY/m² in 2008 and increased to 55,000 CNY/m² in 2010, and has continued to rise. The prices in the real estate market seriously deviate from the actual income level of the residents. Thus, there are complicated relationships between the money supply, the stock market and the real estate market. The bubbles in the stock market burst, while the bubbles in the real estate market have become larger. Data from the National Bureau of Statistics show that in 2012 stock financing by domestic enterprises totalled CNY13.5 billion, which accounted for only 0.83 per cent of total social financing, while bank loans accounted for 28 per cent of total social financing. The total market value of the stock market was CNY23 trillion, which failed to reflect the general trend of macroeconomic growth. If the money supply remains unchanged or increases, the price of real estate will continue to increase. If China tightens its money supply to reduce investment in the real estate market or regulates the real estate market through other administrative measures, the bubbles will be pricked and prices will drop; as a result, the interests of banks, real estate developers and home buyers would be harmed. The question arises: how are we supposed to understand the bubble economy?

The bubble economy was certainly formed through the prerequisite of excess liquidity. The excess liquidity in China had the following causes. First, monetary resources were accumulated for a long period as the government implemented proactive fiscal and monetary policies. For example, in order to resist the impact of the financial crisis, the State Council released a CNY4 trillion investment package in November 2008. Second, because the favourable long-term trade surplus resulted in large amounts of foreign exchange, the PBOC had to release large amounts of base money to make foreign exchange purchases. This base money, except for the money used for exports, had no corresponding material objects. Third, asset securitisation enabled future income flows to be discounted as current asset stock, leading to an increase in the money supply. Fourth, a high rate of savings, inadequate effective demand and few and unsmooth investment channels resulted in too much liquidity (Xi 2009). Throughout history, financial crises have started from bubble economies, as observed from the evolution of the subprime crisis to the financial crisis in the US in 2008. Therefore, to prevent risks in the fictitious economy and especially to prevent a bubble economy formed from irrational expectations, excess liquidity is a primary concern.

Nevertheless, the fictitious economy has been characterised by high liquidity, instability, sensitivity and openness, and has sometimes displayed severe 'herd behaviour' because of information asymmetry. The fictitious economy's risky fluctuations have had a significant impact on economic development. Cheng has noted 'the fictitious economy is a double-edged sword, as it can promote the development of the real economy or can also damage it. Its greatest harm is that it may cause a financial crisis and may further trigger economic and political crisis, leading to social unrest' (Cheng 1999: 6). Therefore, it is an important goal of money supply policy to ensure the sound development of the fictitious economy.

It has reached a consensus in academic circles that a well-planned system of laws and regulations should be established to ensure the healthy development of the fictitious economy and the capital markets. From the perspective of methodology, Song emphasises that securities regulatory systems 'should not be a simple combination between economic systems and legal systems, and an in-depth study on this issue must rely on interactive complementation of multiple disciplines and multiple thinking perspectives' (Song 2009: 133). The design of regulatory systems should be guided by scientific methodologies. Chen has further clarified the objectives of regulatory reform, believing that China should retain its current pattern of separate regulation and legislation for different industries, while 'formulating financial service laws and financial consumer interest protection laws with the core issue being protecting the interests of financial consumers' (Chen 2011: 84). As for the trading of financial derivative products, Liu and Lou have proposed dividing the relevant legal issues into civil and commercial regulations of trading and attempting to make the basic legal logic as clear as possible because there is presently so little legislation on financial derivatives trading in China (Liu and Lou 2012). Liu takes a broad perspective and argues that 'financial laws are the core legal system for adjusting the fictitious economy' (Liu 2009: 79). To ensure the sound development of the capital markets, China has made efforts to improve the relevant laws, regulations and rules to construct a sound system of regulation. The Securities Law of the People's Republic of China, as the core of the guarantee system, specifies the norms for securities offerings and trading activities based on the principles of prudence and soundness. The Provisions on the Prohibition of Stock Market Access 2006, the Management Regulations on the Risk Control Indexes of Securities Companies 2008, the Regulations on the Risk Disposal of Securities Companies 2008 and other administrative laws, regulations and standardisation documents have also been released and implemented, providing institutional guarantees to standardise the operation of capital markets and prevent asset bubbles. However, due to many practical problems, the effect of the implementation of these laws and regulations did not achieve the desired degree (Xi 2011). Thus, there are still many issues that need to be discussed to further improve the legal guarantees and especially to strengthen the regulation of systemic risks in the capital markets according to the principle of prudence from macroeconomics.

5.3.3   *Money supply and the international economy*

The uncertainties and risks in both the real and the fictitious economy have become more complex since China began its transition and integration into the global economy. The global economic environment and the worldwide financial crisis have created increasingly unforeseeable difficulties in managing economic issues.

China's open economic environment has allowed it to become the world's second largest economy, with a GDP of CNY51.93 trillion and US$3866.76

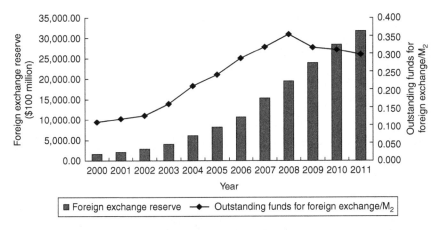

Figure 5.7 Foreign exchange reserve growth and the change of outstanding funds for foreign exchange/M$_2$
(Source: official websites of the National Bureau of Statistics and the People's Bank of China.)

billion of imports and exports in 2012. With such a large scale, China's economy is inevitably affected by fluctuations in international trade and the global economy. China's dependence on the external environment has especially intensified since its accession to the World Trade Organization (WTO), exceeding 50 per cent in 2002 and reaching 67 per cent in 2006. Meanwhile, China's trade surplus has also expanded, creating enormous foreign exchange reserves. PBOC data show that by the end of 2012, China's foreign exchange reserve surplus was US$3.31 trillion. The government holds a large amount of foreign exchange stock, which raises the questions of how to prevent a decrease in foreign exchange and how to effectively utilise investments. Due to restrictions on mandatory foreign exchange settlements, the PBOC purchases large amounts of foreign exchange, resulting in an expansion of base money and continuous increases in funds outstanding for foreign exchange. The index of outstanding funds/M$_2$ has long been maintained at approximately 30 per cent, and the index of M$_2$/GDP has been increasing, exceeding 180 per cent in 2011. The increasing M$_2$/GDP index has caused serious excess liquidity, creating questions about how to hedge liquidity and control the increase in both consumer prices and assert prices (see Figure 5.7). This transmission mechanism has aggravated the difficulties in economic regulation and has become an important cause of economic instability. Through this mechanism, the money supply is supposed to respond to the impact of the accumulation of foreign exchange, coordinate the unfavourable influence of exchange rate fluctuations, overcome the risk of excess liquidity as much as possible and ensure stable levels of domestic prices. Thus, the importance of a reasonable determination of money supply is quite obvious.

Under the current financial system, the relationship between foreign exchange reserves and money supply is in large part passive; in other words, the relationship between the funds outstanding for foreign exchange and liquidity is passive. Compared with the Regulations on Exchange Control of the People's Republic of China enacted in 1996, the newly amended Regulations on Exchange Control of the People's Republic of China of 2008 relaxed the stipulations regarding 'mandatory foreign exchange settlements' in the current account. Article XIII provides that 'foreign exchange income under current accounts may be retained according to relevant national regulations or sold to financial institutions that operate foreign exchange settlements and trading'. Currently, however, the central government has maintained strict control over capital accounts. Investments and relevant trading activities are subject to registration procedures, applications, and record filing with the foreign exchange administration authority of the State Council. Article XXVII establishes that the RMB exchange rate regime is a 'market-based and managed floating exchange rate regime'. Yu has stated that 'a country's exchange rate policies are largely dependent on the policy quota of the country's international balance of payments, which depends, in the final analysis, on the growth or development pattern of the country' (Yu 2010: 18). Over the long term, to address the issue of severe imported inflation caused by a passive release of base money from the large favourable surplus in the international balance of payments, efforts should be made in several respects. First, China should rely on the adjustment and transformation of the domestic economy and stimulate domestic demand to gradually reduce the country's dependence on the international economy, narrow the favourable surpluses in international trade and financial transactions, and maintain equilibrium and stability in the international balance of payments. Second, China should reform the relevant financial regulation mechanisms; adjust its institutional norms in the Regulations on Exchange Control of the People's Republic of China, and other laws, regulations and departmental rules, especially the foreign exchange administration system, and the RMB exchange rate regime; accelerate the process of RMB internationalisation; and construct solid 'buffer zones' to cope with the impact of international economic fluctuations on the domestic financial order.

5.3.4 Money supply and residents' deposits

Residents' deposits are the sources for credit loans from financial institutions and are an important link in the money supply mechanism. China's residents' deposits are mainly characterised by excessively high overall savings rates and weak signal mechanisms for interest rates.

Since the 1970s, China's national savings rate has consistently ranked among the highest in the world (see Figure 5.8), exceeding 50 per cent in 2006 and reaching 52.68 per cent in 2011. By the end of 2012, RMB deposits in China's financial institutions totalled nearly CNY92 trillion, 94.8 per cent

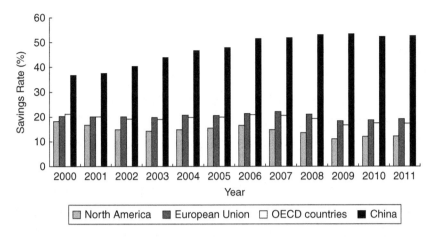

Figure 5.8 Comparison of savings rates (total savings to GDP) for major regions of the world
(Source: official website of the World Bank.)

of which were the savings of enterprises and residents. The high savings rate has an important influence on China's economic development that cannot be ignored.

China's savings rate has remained at a high level for many reasons. First, in an environment where the social security system has yet to be improved, residents save for a proverbial rainy day, especially to cover uncertain expenditures for nursing rooms and medical care. A high savings rate is manifested in the passive prevention of future uncertainties. Over the past decade, reform of China's social security system has seen slow progress. Due to restrictions on fiscal input, the household registration system and the development imbalance among regions, the Social Insurance Law of the People's Republic of China 2010 established the institutional setting for framework legislation, principled legislation and authorised legislation. The current urban and rural social security system provides a low level of social security that does not eliminate citizens' preventative psychology (Xi 2013). Second, because Chinese families must pay for many large-expenditure items, especially for housing rentals or purchases, people must save money for necessities. Third, the national fiscal investment in education represents a very small proportion of total fiscal expenditures. In 2012, China achieved its target of 4 per cent of GDP for fiscal investment in education for the first time, yet this amount is still lower than the world average, and many families must spend large amounts for their children's education. Fourth, China's social investment channels are relatively narrow, and fluctuations in the stock market, debt market and other investment fields are significant, making bank deposits, which feature relatively low risks, the first choice for investments by the public. In addition, compared with other countries and regions, East Asian countries are extensively influenced by the culture of Confucius that emphasises frugality and high rates of saving.

The overall high savings rate can provide funding support for economic development and raise investment capital, so as to create employment and help maintain rapid and steady economic growth. However, continued high savings rates could have a direct impact on the money supply, creating an interactive cyclical effect of 'more saving, more investment', which would curb domestic consumption and restrain the sustained steady growth of the national economy. It is necessary and urgent for China to seek a balanced level of savings.

The amount of savings is generally regulated through the interest rate. The interest rate is the price of funds in the credit market and is an import tool in regulating deposits and the money supply. In a mature market economy, interest rates would reflect the supply and demand for funds. The deposit and loan interest rates are the 'displayer' of the execution of monetary policies, which can fully reflect funds' supply–demand relationship in the financial market and the competitiveness of financial institutions. For a long time, China's interest-rate policies have been characterised by an unreasonable structure (as manifested in repeatedly observed actual negative interest rates and overly high deposit and loan rates set by the PBOC) (Xie and Yuan 2003). The supposed regulating efficiency of interest rates is distorted.

The benchmark interest rates for deposits in China's financial institutions are specified and adjusted uniformly by the PBOC. On 28 October 2004, the PBOC released the Notice on Adjustment of Deposit and Loan Rates in Financial Institutions (YF [2004] No. 251), which marked the beginning of the marketed-oriented reforms of deposit and loan rates. The notice specifies three main aspects of the reform efforts. The first step was to revise the original 'legal rate' to the 'benchmark rate', diluting the administrative colour of deposit and loan rates. Second, the loan rates for financial institutions (excluding urban and rural credit cooperatives) were given a lower limit of 0.9 times the benchmark interest rate and no upper limit, while deposit rates were given an upper limit of the benchmark interest rate and no lower limit. The third step was to require financial institutions to strictly execute the adjusted benchmark interest rate and floating range, strengthen the risk management of interest rates, reasonably determine deposit and loan rates according to their operational status, capital costs, and corporate risks. The PBOC specified the upper limit for deposit rates but did not establish a linkage mechanism between deposit rates and the inflation rate. Therefore, the PBOC does not actually adjust the interest rate between the central bank and financial institutions, but the deposit rate between financial institutions and depositors, which is, in essence, a fixed price between a buyer (the bank) and a seller (the depositor). As a result, deposit rates do not effectively reflect the supply and demand of funds in the market, and negative real interest rates are commonly observed. In the past decade, the PBOC has adjusted the RMB deposit rate

Table 5.1 Comparison between household deposit rates, the consumer price index over the same period and actual interest rates unit (%)

Time of interest-rate adjustment	One-year deposit rate	CPI value over the same period	Actual interest rate	Time of interest-rate adjustment	One-year deposit rate	CPI value over the same period	Actual interest rate
2002.02.21	1.98	0.00	1.98	2008.10.30	3.60	4.00	−0.40
2004.10.29	2.25	4.30	−2.05	2008.11.27	2.52	2.40	0.12
2006.08.19	2.52	1.30	1.22	2008.12.23	2.25	1.20	1.05
2007.03.18	2.79	3.30	−0.51	2010.10.20	2.50	4.40	−1.90
2007.05.19	3.06	3.40	−0.34	2010.12.26	2.75	4.60	−1.85
2007.07.21	3.33	5.60	−2.27	2011.02.09	3.00	4.90	−1.90
2007.08.22	3.60	6.50	−2.90	2011.04.06	3.25	5.30	−2.05
2007.09.15	3.87	6.20	−2.33	2011.07.07	3.50	6.50	−3.00
2007.12.21	4.14	6.50	−2.36	2012.06.08	3.25	2.20	1.05
2008.10.09	3.87	4.00	−0.13	2012.07.06	3.00	1.80	1.20

(Source: official websites of the National Bureau of Statistics and People's Bank of China.)

20 times, increasing it 13 times and decreasing it 7 times. However, most of the time, the one-year fixed deposit rates for financial institutions were lower than the consumer price index (CPI) during the same period, and the real negative interest rate was as high as −3 per cent (see Table 5.1). Therefore, passively saved household deposits designed to cope with future uncertainties and large expenditures have actually continuously depreciated. These large-scale and low-cost private savings are transformed into the assets of financial institutions in the form of loans that enter the fields of investment through the credit mechanism. In other words, long-term interest-rate control and the resulting phenomenon of negative interest rates have to some extent stimulated banks to expand their loan scale and intensify investments, thus influencing the money supply. Hence, to gradually strengthen the role of the interest rate as a price signal, market-oriented reforms of the interest rate should be accelerated and the Administrative Provisions on RMB Interest Rates should be revised to become important measures that will further deepen the reforms of the financial markets.

5.3.5 *Money supply and enterprises' loans*

China's macro-regulation is characterised by a combination of monetary policies, fiscal policies and industrial policies. Article XXXIV of the Law of the People's Republic of China on Commercial Banks 2003 stipulates that 'commercial banks operate loan businesses according to the demand of the national economy and social development and under the guidance of the state's industrial policies'. The Law of the People's Republic of China on Commercial Banks specifies the use and goal of commercial bank loans,

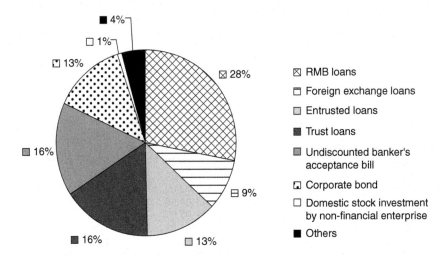

Figure 5.9 Weights of various financing approaches in total social financing in 2012
(Source: official website of the People's Bank of China.)

explicitly requiring that loan issuance by commercial banks must be in line
with the demand for economic and social development and the State's industrial policies. Monetary policies generate an impact on the industrial structure
through the credit loan transmission mechanism (Sun *et al.* 2012). Although
the PBOC has liberalised the upper limit and loan rate, and set the lower
limit at 0.9 times the benchmark interest rate, in adjusting the loan rate, the
PBOC actually adjusts the price between the supplier (the banks) and the
demander (the enterprises) in the supply and demand of capital. However,
whether enterprises actually borrow from the banks depends on a comparison
between corporate profit margins and the loan rate. As a result, China's interest-rate transmission mechanism is less influential, and the PBOC exerts control over the money supply through the banking system, which fully reflects
the effect of monetary policy.

The way enterprises apply to financial institutions for loans is the most
important indirect financing approach in China. However, with the increased
development of the economy and the construction of a multi-tier capital
market, the financing pattern for China's enterprises has transformed into a
diversified financing approach, with direct financing occupying a dominant
position. Nevertheless, by the end of 2012, PBOC data show that various
loans still account for 65.77 per cent of total social financing (see Figure 5.9);
hence, indirect financing still has an advantageous position in total social
financing.

When money flows from banks to enterprises, debt capital is transformed
into investment funds that directly participate in enterprise operations. Since
the social investment structure directly influences and determines the national

industrial structure, when Chinese enterprises seriously rely on bank credit for financing, the credit structure of financial institutions influences the national industrial structure, forming a transmission chain of 'bank credit structure → corporate investment structure → national industrial structure' (Wang and Guo 2011).

In 2009, the PBOC began to regularly release the *Statistical Report on the Direction of the Loan Investments of Financial Institutions*. The current data show that the growth of middle- and long-term loans for industry and infrastructure have gradually declined, loans for real estate development have violently fluctuated because of national macro-regulations, loans for small and medium-sized enterprises (SMEs) have featured high and stable growth, and loans for agriculture, rural areas and rural households have also witnessed rapid growth (see Table 5.2). The structural changes in the loan investment directions of financial institutions basically reflect the direction of China's industrial structure adjustments.

China's money supply is largely policy-dependent, and bank loans bear the weight of promoting industrial restructuring, which includes the following strategies. First, China wants to adjust the weights of agriculture, industry and the service sector in the national economy by steadily increasing agricultural modernisation and industrialisation and vigorously developing its service industry. Second, to transform the pattern of economic development, China must change its overdependence on investment and trade for economic growth, stimulate domestic demand and expand the domestic market while still maintaining reasonable growth in investments and exports. Third, to change the economic growth pattern of high-energy consumption and high pollution, China must encourage sustainable development and reduce the damage to resources and the environment during the process of economic development. Given the situation where bank credit remains society's main financing approach, China should employ funds to promote the sustainable upgrading of industry, and commercial bank credit can play an important role in this process. The National Development and Reform Commission amended the *Catalogue for Guidance on Industrial Structure Adjustment* in 2011. Under the guidance of the new edition of the *Catalogue*, commercial banks can divert credit funds to policy supported fields, such as modern agriculture, new technology industries and environmental protection industries and reduce or forbid investment in fields that feature high-energy consumption and high pollution to promote the adjustment, optimisation and upgrading of the industrial structure and improve and develop a modern industrial system.

The difficulty is that the PBOC's monetary policies are devoted to regulating total demand, while banks' credit policies reflect structural loan policies. The determination of whether an enterprise can apply for a loan depends on a comparison between the loan cost (interest rate) and the business' profit margin. As long as the profit margin is higher than the loan rate, enterprises can apply for loans; when the PBOC raises the deposit rate, banks increase

Table 5.2 Statistical statements of loan investment directions of financial institutions

Year		Mid- and long-term loans for industry			Mid- and long-term loans for infrastructure	Loans for real estate development	Loans for SMEs	Loans for agriculture, rural areas and rural households		
			Light industry	Heavy industry				Loans for rural areas	Loans for rural households	Loans for agriculture
2009	Accumulative new growth (100 million yuan)	10000	1524	7968	25000	5764	34000	—	—	—
	Year-over-year growth (%)	26.0	36.3	24.4	43	30.7	30.1	33.4	31.7	25.9
2010	Accumulative new growth (100 million yuan)	7990	2086	5904	16500	20200	—	—	—	—
	Year-over-year growth (%)	—	—	—	19.4	27.5	22.5	31.5	29.4	18.3
2011	Accumulative new growth (100 million yuan)	5171	147	5024	12300	12600	32700	22400	5017	2452
	Year-over-year growth (%)	—	—	—	9.0	13.9	18.6	24.7	19.1	11.2
2012	Accumulative new growth (100 million yuan)	2350	317	2033	9900	13500	—	23900	4999	3103
	Year-over-year growth (%)	3.8	5.1	3.7	7.1	12.8	—	19.7	15.9	11.6

(Source: official website of the People's Bank of China (portions of the data are calculated, and '—' represent data that have not yet been released).)

the quantity of loans. Under the indirect financing pattern, however, there are uncertainties regarding loan repayment between banks and enterprises. When these uncertainties are transformed into risks, it is possible that a crisis will hit the banks first, which is different from the case under a direct financing system where a crisis will first hit the investment banks. The solutions to these issues call for further study.

5.4 Conclusions

The determination of the money supply is the core issue of monetary policy. By regulating the money supply, central banks can maintain the proper balance between total social demand and supply and preserve overall price stability. By regulating the interest rate, central banks can influence the public's propensity to consume and save, and affect the cost and marginal efficiency of investment, thus regulating the proportion of consumption and savings in the national income and guiding the transition from savings to investment to realise a rational allocation of resources.

Empirical analysis shows that China's traditional quantitative money supply principles are no longer sufficient to reflect the reality of its money supply. China's money supply has become increasingly endogenous, and the role of the money supply in serving macroeconomic regulation and preventing economic risks is continuously strengthening.

This chapter proceeded from the monetary policy objectives of maintaining currency value stability and economic growth, as specified in the Law on PBOC, and used a risk-prevention perspective to propose that China should carefully manage the relationship between the money supply and the development of the real economy, the fictitious economy and the international economy. At the same time, China must balance the relationship between the money supply and important economic actors such as residents and enterprises, while considering the influence of such endogenous factors as commodity prices, asset prices, exchange rates, foreign exchange reserves, household deposit rates and enterprise loan rates. China should also strictly observe the Law of the People's Republic of China on Commercial Banks 2003, the Law of the People's Republic of China on Banking Regulation and Supervision 2006, Securities Law of the People's Republic of China 2013 and the Regulations on Exchange Control of the People's Republic of China 2008 to prevent such economic risks as inflation, asset bubbles and losses on exchanges, adjust the country's industrial structure, balance the relationship between investment, consumption and savings, and coordinate the balance between the domestic economy and the international economy.

We only presented an exploratory framework for analysis. Further research is needed regarding such issues as how to prevent systemic financial risks, how to maintain economic stability, financial stability and capital market stability, and how to manage the transmission mechanism between monetary policy variables and economic variables.

Notes

1 This chapter is sponsored by the National Social Sciences Project 'Countermeasure Studies on Maintaining China's Economic Stability, Financial Stability and Capital Market Stability' (Project No. 08AJY037) and the Beijing Municipal Key Interdisciplinary Project 'Law and Economics'.
2 For a detailed description see Xia and Liao (2001), Wang (2012a) or see Figure 5.1.
3 As discussed in this chapter, the real economy mainly refers to such production and service sectors as agriculture, industry, transportation and communication, commercial service and construction (see Liu (2009)).
4 The fictitious economy (or virtual economy) refers to the holding and trading of financial capital independent of the real economy (Cheng 1999; Liu 2009). In China, it mainly encompasses the trading activities in the financial market (stock market, futures market, options market, etc.) and real estate market (Li and Yang 2000).

References

Barr, M. S. (2012) 'The Financial Crisis and the Path of Reform', *Yale Journal on Regulation*, 24, 91–119.

Chen, J. (2011) 'Touzizhe Dao Jinrong Xiaofeizhe De Jiaodu Shanbian' (Role Transition from Investor to Financial Consumer), *Faxue Yanjiu (Chinese Journal of Law)*, 5, 84–95.

Chen, Z. (2005) 'Neisheng Huobi Gongji Lilun Shuping' (Commentary on Endogenous Money Supply Theories), *Jingji Pinglun (Economic Review)*, 4, 68–81.

Cheng, S. (1999) 'Xuni Jingji Yu Jinrong Weiji' (Virtual Economy and Financial Crisis), *Guanli Kexue Xuebao (Journal of Management Sciences in China)*, 3, 1–6.

Coffee, J. C. (2011) 'Systemic Risk after Dodd-Frank: Contingent Capital and the Need for Regulatory Strategies Beyond Oversight', *Columbia Law Review*, 111, 795–847.

Friedman, M. J. and Schwartz, A. J. (1963) *A Monetary History of the United States (1867–1960)*, Princeton: Princeton University Press.

Geng, Z. and Zeng, L. (2006) 'Hou Kai'ensi Xuepai De Neisheng Huobi Jiashuo: Zhongguo De Lizheng' (Post-Keynesian School's Endogenous Money Hypothesis: Empirical Evidence from China), *Guanli Kexue (Management Sciences in China)*, 4, 68–74.

Guo, T. (2006) 'Zichan Jiage, Tonghuo Pengzhang Yu Zhongguo Huobi Zhengce Tixi De Wanshang' (Asset Price, Inflation and the Improvement of China's Monetary Policy System), *Jinrong Yanjiu (Journal of Financial Research)*, 10, 23–35.

Keynes, J. M. (1971) *A Treatise on Money*, Cambridge: Cambridge University Press.

Lei, C. (1999) 'Zhongguo Huobi Xuqiu Guanxi De Shizheng Fenxi' (An Empirical Analysis of the Monetary Demand Relationship of China), *Zhongyang Caijing Daxue Xuebao (Journal of Central University of Finance & Economics)*, 9, 33–6.

Li, S. (2012) 'Hou Weiji Shidai "Taida Er Buneng Dao" Jinrong Jigou Jianguan Falv Wenti Yanjiu' (Review of Legal Issues relating to the Regulation of Post-crisis 'too big to fail' Financial Institutions), *Zhongguo Faxue (China Legal Science)*, 5, 88–102.

Li, X. and Yang, L. (2000) 'Xuni Jingji, Paomo Jingji Yu Shiti Jingji' (Fictitious Economy, Bubble Economy and Substantial Economy), *Caimao Jingji (Finance & Trade Economics)*, 6, 5–11.

Liu, J. and Sui, J. (2010) 'Zhongguo Huobi Zengzhang Buquedingxing Yu Jingji Zengzhang Guanxi Jianyan (1980–2008)' (A Test of the Relationship between Monetary Growth Uncertainty and Economic Growth in China: 1980–2008), *Zhongguo Shehui Kexue (Social Sciences in China)*, 4, 74–86.

Liu, S. (2009) 'Xuni Jingjifa De Lilun Sikao' (Theoretical Thoughts on Virtual Economy Law), *Zhongguo Zhengfa Daxue Xuebao (Journal of CUPL)*, CUPL, China 6, 73–86.

Liu, Y. and Lou, J. (2012) 'Jinrong Yansheng Jiaoyi De Falv Jieshi: Yi Hetong Wei Zhongxin' (Legal Explanation of Financial Derivatives: A Contractual Perspective), *Faxue Yanjiu (Chinese Journal of Law)*, 1, 58–76.

Lu, G. and Cao, L. (2007) 'Dangqian Woguo Huobi Gongji Neiwaishengxing Bianxi Ji Zhengce Qishi' (Analysis of the Exogeny and Endogeny of Contemporary Chinese Money Supply and Policy Advice), *Zhongyang Caijing Daxue Xuebao (Journal of Central University of Finance & Economics)*, 10, 32–7.

Luo, P. (2009) 'Meiguo Jinrong Jianguan De Falv Yu Zhengce Kunju Zhi Fansi' (Review of the Legal and Policy Dilemma of US Financial Regulation), *Zhongguo Faxue (China Legal Science)*, 3, 91–105.

Rose, P. and Walker, C. J. (2013) 'Dodd-Frank Regulators, Cost-Benefit Analysis, and Agency Capture', *Stanford Law Review*, 66, 9–16.

Schwarcz, S. L. (2008) 'Systemic Risk', *The Georgetown Law Journal*, 97, 193–249.

Song, X. (2009) 'Zhengquan Jianguan De Mubiao He Lujing' (The Purpose and Route of Security Regulation), *Faxue Yanjiu (Chinese Journal of Law)*, 6, 117–34.

Sun, Y., Wang, L. and Wang, L. (2012) 'Woguo Yanghang Huobi Gongji Dui Yinhang Xindai Yingxiang De Shizheng Yanjiu' (Empirical Study of the Impact of the Money Supply by China's Central Bank on Bank Credit). *Zhongyang Caijing Daxue Xuebao (Journal of Central University of Finance & Economics)*, 2, 34–40.

Wan, J. and Xu, T. (2001) 'Huobi Gongji De Neishengxing Yu Huobi Zhengce De Xiaolv: Jianping Woguo Dangqian Huobi Zhengce De Youxiaoxing' (Endogeneity of the Money Supply and the Efficiency of Monetary Policy: A Commentary on the Effectiveness of the Current Monetary Policy), *Jingji Yanjiu (Economic Research Journal)*, 3, 40–50.

Wang, C. (2002) 'Neisheng Huobi Chuangzao Guocheng: Lilun Chanshi Yu Shizheng Jianyan' (The Process of Endogenous Money Creation: Theoretical Statement and Empirical Examination), *Nankai Jingji Yanjiu (Nankai Economic Studies)*, 4, 49–54.

Wang, C. (2008) 'Neisheng Huobi Gongji Lilun De Yanjin Yu Zhanwang' (The Evolution of Endogenous Money Supply Theories), *Shanghai Jingji Yanjiu (Shanghai Economic Review)*, 5, 4–11.

Wang, G. (2012a) 'Zhongguo Huobi Zhengce Mubiao De Shixian Jili Fenxi: 2001–2010' (Realization Mechanism of China's Monetary Policy Targets: 2001–2010), *Jingji Yanjiu (Economic Research Journal)*, 12, 4–14.

Wang, G. (2012b) 'Zhongguo Huobi Zhengce Tiaokong Gongju De Caozuo Jili: 2001–2010' (The Operational Mechanisms of Monetary Policy Tools in China: 2001–2010), *Zhongguo Shehui Kexue (Social Sciences in China)*, 4, 62–82.

Wang, J. and Guo, X. (2011) 'Chanye Touzi Jiegou, Liudongxing Xiaoying He Zhongguo Huobi Zhengce' (Industrial Investment Structure, Liquidity Effect and Monetary Policy in China), *Jingji Yanjiu (Economic Research Journal)*, 2, 28–40.

Wang, S. (1992). 'Lun Huobi Gongji De Neishengxing Yu Waishengxing' (Endogenous and Exogenous Theories of Money Supply), *Zhongyang Caizheng Jinrong Xueyuan Xuebao (Journal of Central College of Finance & Economics)*, 1, 67–72.

Wu, Z. (2008) 'Hua'erjie Jinrong Weiji Zhong De Falv Wenti' (Legal Issues relating to the Wall Street Financial Crisis), *Faxue (Legal Science)*, 12, 29–35.

Xi, T. (2008) 'Jingji Zengzhang, Fengxian Fangfan He Zhidu Jianshe' (Economic Growth, Risk Safeguarding and Institution Building), *Zhongguo Renmin Daxue Xuebao (Journal of RUC)*, 6, 39–44.

Xi, T. (2009) 'Zhongguo Ruhe Yingdui Jinrong Weiji?' (China's Way of Dealing with the Financial Crisis), *Zhongguo Zhengfa Daxue Xuebao (Journal of CUPL)*, CUPL, China, 2, 87–96.

Xi, T. (2011) 'Falv, Jianguan Yu Shichang' (Law, Regulation and the Market), *Zhengfa Luntan (Tribune of Political Science and Law)*, 5, 63.

Xi, T. (2013) 'Lifa Pinggu: Pinggu Shenme He Ruhe Pinggu II' (Legislative Assessment: What to Assess and How to Assess II), *Zhengfa Luntan (Tribune of Political Science and Law)*, 1, 21–32.

Xia, B. and Liao, Q. (2001) 'Huobi Gongyingliang Yi Buyi Zuowei Dangqian Woguo Huobi Zhengce De Zhongjie Mubiao' (Money Supply not Suitable Anymore as an Intermediary Goal for Monetary Policy in China), *Jingji Yanjiu (Economic Research Journal)*, 8, 33–43.

Xie, P. and Yuan, Q. (2003) 'Woguo Jinnian Lilv Zhengce De Xiaoguo Fenxi' (Analysis of the Effect of Chinese Interest Rate Policy in Recent Years), *Jinrong Yanjiu (Journal of Financial Research)*, 5, 1–13.

Yu, Y. (2010) 'Jianzheng Shiheng: Shuangshuncha, Renminbi Huilv He Meiyuan Xianjing' (Witnessing Imbalances: Twin Surpluses, Renminbi Exchange Rate and the Dollar Trap), *Guoji Jingji Pinglun (International Economic Review)*, 3, 7–44.

Zhang, Y. (2010) 'Zhongguo Huobi Gongji Fenfxi Ji Huobi Zhengce Pingjia: 1986–2007' (Analysis of China's Money Supply and Assessment of China's Monetary Policy: 1986–2007), *Shuliang Jingji Jishu Jingji Yanjiu (The Journal of Quantitative & Technical Economics)*, 6, 47–55.

Zhao, J. and Gao, H. (2009) 'Zichan Jiage Bodong Dui Zhongguo Huobi Zhengce De Yingxiang: Jiyu 1994–2006 Nian Jidu Shuju De Shizheng Fenxi' (Impact of Asset Price Fluctuation on China's Monetary Policy: An Empirical Analysis Based on Quarterly Data from 1994–2006), *Zhongguo Shehui Kexue (Social Sciences in China)*, 2, 98–114.

Zhou, X. (2011) 'Jianli Fuhe Guoqing De Jinrong Hongguan Tiaokong Tixi' (Establishing a Financial Macro-Control System which is suitable for China), *Zhongguo Jinrong (China Finance)*, 13, 7–13.

Part II

The role of financial regulation

6 Recent developments in the regulation of auditors

An economic perspective

Niels Philipsen

6.1 Introduction

This chapter addresses recent developments in the regulation of auditors. Together with other gatekeepers in financial markets, such as underwriters, financial analysts and credit rating agencies, auditors play an important role by providing independent assurance to investors (shareholders and creditors alike) that a company's financial condition is portrayed correctly and fairly. The independence and integrity of auditors hence seem crucial for a proper functioning of financial markets. However, the many accounting scandals of recent decades (for example those involving Enron, Worldcom, Parmalat, AIG and many others) have raised serious questions about the independence and integrity of auditors and have already led to a wave of regulation worldwide. For example, the Sarbanes-Oxley Act of 2002 in the US and the Audit Directive of 2006 (Directive 2006/43/EC) in the European Union (EU) introduced stricter requirements on audit quality and auditors' independence, more regulatory oversight and mandatory rotation of auditors.

Chinese companies have been involved in various accounting scandals as well. According to recent publications in the financial media,[1] the US Securities and Exchange Commission (SEC) has been trying to obtain documents from Chinese audit firms (more particularly, the Chinese arms of the Big Four audit networks) for years, because the stocks of some of the Chinese companies involved in accounting scandals were listed in the US. Complying with the SEC's requests for handing over documents, however, would violate Chinese secrecy laws; hence, Chinese audit firms are caught in a difficult position, not being able to satisfy the requests of the SEC without breaching Chinese law and risking jail terms. Commentators have stated that the current 'international standoff [could] escalate and damage US–China economic relations', especially after a US SEC administrative law judge in January 2014 sanctioned the Chinese audit firms – a decision which was appealed by the firms involved.[2]

The above makes clear that regulation of auditors still is an important and heavily debated topic today. From the existing law and economics literature we know that regulation is considered efficient if it is directed at curing certain forms of market failure, i.e. if regulation serves the public interest rather than (predominantly) private interests. In the market for statutory audits, such market failure may result from:

- information asymmetry between auditors and audit clients, leading to deterioration of quality (*moral hazard* and *adverse selection*);
- negative and positive externalities of audit services on investors and on society at large; and
- a lack of competition in the market.

It is, however, not always necessary to find *regulatory* solutions to a market failure; sometimes liability rules or market-based instruments (like taxes and subsidies) are better or alternative solutions to cure a prevailing market failure.[3]

In order to solve problems of information asymmetry and externalities, various regulatory options are available, ranging from restrictions on false and misleading advertising and mandatory disclosure of information and certification, to licensing. Generally, all measures aimed at improving the quality of audit services, including auditing standards and rules of conduct, can be used to deal with information and externality problems. However, some forms of regulation clearly restrict competition much more than others. Licensing belongs to that category, as does for example price regulation and establishment restrictions.

It is not the aim of this chapter to consider all of these forms of regulation, as an abundant law and economics literature on this topic already exists.[4] Rather, the goal of this chapter is to analyse, from an economic perspective, recent developments concerning the regulation of auditors. More particularly, this chapter will deal with the proposals made to limit auditors' liability (Section 6.3) and to relax legal form and shareholding restrictions (Section 6.4), respectively. Both of these proposals have received much attention due to the fact that currently there is a lack of competition in the market for audits of large and quoted companies, an issue that will be discussed first in Section 6.2. Finally, Section 6.5 of this chapter provides some concluding remarks.

6.2   Background: a lack of competition

As pointed out above, competition in the auditing and accounting services sector for quoted and large companies is limited. Only four out of the former Big Eight accounting networks are left in the market: PricewaterhouseCoopers (PwC), Ernst & Young, Deloitte and KPMG. Moreover, an accounting firm cannot be both auditor and consultant for the same client, which further reduces the number of audit firms from which big audit clients can choose. One should also take into account that not all of the Big Four firms are equally specialized in certain sectors, for example the financial sector (London

Economics and Ewert 2006: 31–2). This, again, could further limit the number of options to choose from for audit clients.

The process of going from eight to five accounting networks took less than a decade and was caused by a series of mergers that began in 1989 and lasted until 1998.[5] The Big Five became a Big Four after the Enron scandal of 2001, which eventually resulted in the criminal prosecution and subsequent downfall of Arthur Andersen in 2002 (Philipsen 2009: 20–5). And although there are other accounting networks operating worldwide (for example BDO, Grant Thornton and Baker Tilly), studies by the US Government Accountability Office, London Economics (in a study for the European Commission) and the Organisation for Economic Co-operation and Development (OECD) have all concluded that these so-called 'mid-tier firms' are unwilling or unable to enter the market for audits of quoted and large companies (GAO 2003; GAO 2008; London Economics and Ewert 2006; Philipsen 2009). Reasons for the unwillingness of mid-tier firms to audit quoted and large companies include the high exposure to liability (in combination with problems in the insurance market) and market entry barriers related to reputation and capacity (Philipsen 2009: 27).

One of the main purposes of the above-mentioned studies was to find out whether the growth of the current middle-tier accounting firms could be encouraged, by taking away actual or perceived entry barriers to the market for audits of large and quoted companies. In that context, two possible solutions have been proposed in particular: (i) limiting auditors' liability, to be discussed in Section 6.3 of this chapter; and (ii) relaxing requirements relating to legal form and shareholding/membership, to be discussed in Section 6.4.

6.3   Regulation of auditors' liability[6]

Having witnessed the many accounting scandals that occurred in recent decades, accounting firms big and small fear the risk of being held liable in cases of fraud or mistakes by individual auditors. The risk of a 'mega' or 'catastrophic' claim can lead to insolvency problems even for the Big Four audit firms[7], which (considering the lack of competition described in this field in Section 6.2 above) would have dramatic consequences for companies, investors and capital markets. Therefore, reducing the risk of litigation could in the long run be beneficial for competition in the market for quoted and large companies, especially if it would lead also to lower premiums being charged by insurers or to an increase in the availability of insurance coverage for audit firms.

This argument motivated the European Commission to publish Recommendation (2008/473/EC), in which it recommended EU Member States to limit the civil liability of statutory auditors and audit firms arising from a breach of their professional duties. According to this Recommendation, Member States are allowed to choose between a liability cap,[8] a system of proportionate liability, and a form of contractual limitation, depending on which methods are most suitable for their respective civil liability systems (Article 5 of Recommendation 2008/473/EC). Preamble No. 3 of the Recommendation directly refers to the earlier mentioned link between competition problems and liability risks: 'Since unlimited joint and several liability may deter audit firms and networks from entering the international audit market for listed companies in the Community, there is little prospect of new audit networks emerging which are in a position to conduct statutory audits of such companies'.[9]

However, limiting auditors' liability, irrespective of whether it is aimed at solving problems related to competition and lack of insurance, may have some perverse effects. For example, a liability cap may reduce the incentives for auditors to conduct quality work (by negatively affecting the intensity of audit efforts) while it could also limit the ability of investors to recoup losses they incurred if an auditor was found to have committed fraud (GAO 2008: 56–7; Philipsen 2009: 28). In the following subsections the possible effects of a limitation of liability on, respectively, audit quality (6.3.1) and compensation of investors (6.3.2) will be further analysed. Section 6.3.3 provides some concluding comments.

6.3.1   *Limited liability and audit quality*

One could argue that *ex ante* quality regulation (such as the Sarbanes-Oxley Act in the US, the 2006 Audit Directive in the EU and the Law of China on Certified Public Accountants) and accounting standards (such as the International Financial Reporting Standards) are more direct instruments to guarantee a minimum quality of audit services than holding auditors liable *ex post*. Nevertheless, law and economics literature has shown repeatedly that liability rules can provide an important deterrent function, in that the threat of being held liable gives additional incentives to auditors to take care when performing a statutory audit.[10] A combination of regulation and liability rules would therefore be required in order to ensure an efficient level of care (meaning an efficient intensity of audit efforts) taken by auditors.[11] It should also be noted that quality regulation can *expand* liability in case the regulatory standards are violated. For example, the 2006 Audit Directive (2006/43/EC), with its stricter requirements regarding statutory audits and professional independence, may have increased the probability and scope of liability when auditors do not fulfil the higher regulatory standards imposed by this Directive.[12]

Having argued that liability rules provide some (additional but important) incentives to provide services of sufficient quality, we can look at the expected effects of limiting the exposure to liability. As a starting point, and as argued in the studies referred to above, it can be expected that capping the liability exposure of auditors or audit firms limits the deterrent effect of liability rules and may hence adversely affect audit quality, by negatively affecting the intensity of audit efforts.[13]

Bigus (2008) argued, however, that the potentially negative effects of liability caps for audit services are mitigated by some special characteristics that apply in case of auditors' liability. He argued that liability caps might even induce efficient levels of care taken by auditors, whereas unlimited liability might induce auditors to exert excessive care. The special characteristics of auditors' liability that he referred to include:

- the importance of reputation effects in the market for audits;
- auditors are liable only in cases of negligence (which gives them incentives to meet the due care standard);
- vaguely defined standards of due care (which provide additional incentives to exert care); and
- overcompensation as a result of liability for pure economic loss and wrong assessment of damages.

Reputation effects, the first characteristic of auditors' liability, can theoretically play an important role in mitigating information asymmetry problems. Information asymmetry between professionals and clients is considered as one of the most prominent market failures in professional services markets (Philipsen 2010: 205–6). An auditor's reputation for quality and independence has an impact on perceived audit quality, giving a signal to investors about the reliability of the financial statements of firms who are clients of that particular auditor. Obviously, reputation effects can also be negative, increasing the liability risk faced by audit firms. Arruñada (2004) states that the events following the Enron bankruptcy and the demise of Arthur Andersen have shown that the market is able to punish audit failures. Krishnamurthy *et al.* (2006), using a sample of former Arthur Andersen clients, show that reputation effects (following Andersen's criminal indictment in 2002) are significantly more negative when the market perceived also the auditor's *independence* to be threatened in addition to audit quality.

The second and third characteristics of auditors' liability have been central in several papers analysing either the effects of limited liability on auditors' level of care, or strategic interactions between auditors, investors and management.[14] It should be noted in this respect that, if negligence rules are already quite restrictive, particularly vis-à-vis third parties, then liability is unlikely to arise if auditors put in sufficient efforts and act in the public interest. This implies that one should not necessarily focus on limiting auditors' liability by capping amounts of compensation due; changing the norm, for example from negligence to gross negligence, can be an alternative way of limiting liability.

The fourth characteristic (overcompensation) was added by Bigus, who argued that the damage to investors who have suffered a loss from a wrong financial report usually considerably exceeds the *social* damage. Indeed, if an auditor has testified a wrongful report incorrectly 'there are some investors who might benefit because they may be able to sell their shares at a price which is too high, considering the true condition of the firm. Other investors may lose because they buy these shares at too high a price. Putting gains and losses together, the total loss of all shareholders is (significantly) lower than the loss suffered from the losers' (Bigus 2008: 10–11). However, this argument of possible overcompensation does not take into account distributional effects. It also does not take into account that there may be situations where private losses are *lower* than social losses, for example when a series of book-keeping scandals leads to an overall reduction of trust in auditors.

All of the above would suggest that the audit sector has special characteristics that mitigate some of the negative effects that can be expected from a limitation of liability. Moreover, it has been argued that a limitation of liability could even lead to increased efficiencies if audit firms could reduce the amount of time they spend protecting themselves against lawsuits (GAO 2008: 56).

6.3.2   *Limited liability and compensation*

The second concern raised above relates to compensation. In the studies by the US Government Accountability Office and the OECD (GAO 2008; Philipsen 2009) it was argued that investors need to be able to recoup losses they incurred if an auditor was found to have committed fraud. Because audit services are 'experience goods' or 'trust goods' (Nelson 1970; Darby and Karni 1973), investors need to rely on auditors, who act as gatekeepers. In addition, also a corporation's stakeholders – and, one might argue, financial markets – depend on the assurance work provided by auditors.[15] Fraud committed by auditors can hence have significant consequences, in the form of negative externalities imposed on stakeholders and society at large. Moreover, accounting scandals may lead to share price declines even if a company is not directly involved in the particular scandal, but its auditing network is (Autore *et al.* 2009).

In a majority of EU Member States, shareholders who are not bound by the contract between a company and its auditor can introduce claims against auditors under tort law. Liability caps would have a direct impact on the expected value of such claims (Commission Staff 2008: 31).[16] In other words, investors are less protected from fraudulent auditors, in the sense of not being able to recoup all of their losses. However, the primary solution to this problem, from a law and economics perspective, would be to minimize the risk of such moral hazard behaviour by auditors (or their audit clients) by focusing on audit quality. In other words, the solution should be found in creating the right mix of regulation and liability rules, which brings us back to the discussion in Section 6.3.1 and hence does not automatically exclude a limitation on liability.

6.3.3   *Evaluation*

In this section I discussed the argument (proposed in the literature) that a limitation of auditors' liability will reduce the liability risks associated with being active in the market for audits of large and quoted companies, which are mentioned by mid-tier accounting firms as a reason for not entering this market. Furthermore, limited liability would also have a positive impact on insurability. I showed, following the economic analysis of tort law, that generally one needs to be very careful in introducing limitations to liability. However, the audit sector has some unique characteristics that to some extent seem to mitigate the expected negative effects (on audit efforts and investor protection) of a liability limitation. These characteristics include the importance of reputational effects, the negligence standard that is applied and possible overcompensation of damages.

Obviously, limited liability cannot solve all competition problems. When introducing a liability cap or a system of contractual limitation, the liability limit would not only apply to the mid-tier firms, but also to the Big Four firms. Moreover, the question of how to deal with the alleged lack of reputation of the non-Big Four remains unanswered: even if these audit firms would now be (more) willing to enter the market for audits of large and quoted companies, their potential clients need to accept non-Big Four firms as their auditors. Nevertheless, recognizing the problem of lack of competition in the audit market and lack of insurability, a European-wide (or even world-wide solution) is warranted. Limiting liability can form part of that solution, next to already existing mechanisms such as quality regulation. With respect to auditors, *more* quality regulation (audit standards, mandatory rotation, educational requirements, regulatory oversight) has already been introduced, for example, in the US and EU. On the one hand, auditors that follow these stricter rules are less likely to be held liable in the sense of violating the due care standard. On the other hand, because more is required from auditors (in terms of audit quality and audit efforts), it can also be argued that their liability risks have expanded. This depends on the interpretation of due care standards by the relevant courts.

From an economic perspective,[17] an EU wide solution should take into account the existing differences between Member States in the field of tort law and contract law. The approach chosen by the European Commission, using a Recommendation rather than a Directive or Regulation, can therefore be applauded from this economic perspective, even if it may lack sufficient effect.

6.4   Legal form and shareholding requirements

The second possibility to increase competition in the audit market for large and quoted companies, as proposed in the literature, is to relax requirements relating to legal form and shareholding.[18] The US General Accounting Office concluded in 2003 that raising the capital to expand their existing infrastructure to compete with the Big Four is a challenge for the smaller accounting firms, in part because the partnership structure of most public accounting firms limits these firms' ability to raise outside capital: 'To expand their operations, accounting firms must look to other [difficult or unattractive] options, such as borrowing from financial institutions, merging with other accounting firms [...] or tapping the personal resources of their partners and employees'. (GAO 2003: 50–1). This finding was later confirmed by research for the European Commission (Oxera 2007) and in an OECD report (Philipsen 2009).

In professional services markets more generally, jurisdictions may apply rules that either prohibit the use of certain legal forms (e.g. a corporation) or prescribe a particular legal form (e.g. a partnership), usually with the aim to guarantee a high level of personal liability or with the aim to disallow external investment. Such legal form requirements apply particularly in relation to the legal professions. Furthermore, some jurisdictions have introduced rules that require (all or some) shareholders or managers in a professional services company to be members of that particular profession. Many jurisdictions also limit inter-professional cooperation, for example involving accountants and lawyers, by (totally or partially) banning multi-disciplinary partnerships (MDPs).[19]

Following the public interest approach to regulation,[20] legal form and shareholding/management restrictions are considered as one of the potential solutions to market failure, more particularly market failure in the form of information asymmetry (including problems of conflicts of interest) and negative externalities. However, a key question remains whether such restrictions are truly a proportional cure to information and externality problems, or whether other types of regulation (such as educational requirements, licensing and conduct regulation) would be better suited for this purpose.

With respect to auditors, Article 3 of the 2006 Audit Directive currently prescribes that in the EU auditors must hold a majority of the voting rights in an audit firm and that a majority of suitable qualified workers control the management board. A study by Oxera (2007: iii) found that all Member States have implemented these rules, and that some have even interpreted these specifications more strictly, by requiring 75 per cent or more of the owners of audit firms to be qualified auditors. Attempts by the European Commission to force EU Member States to further 'deregulate' existing legal form and shareholding restrictions are directed at services other than auditing. This includes 'general' accountancy services; however, these are already very liberal throughout the EU, particularly in relation to legal services (Maastricht University and Panteia 2014).[21]

In the US, certified public accountants must make up the majority ownership of all accounting firms, according to the American Institute of Certified Public Accountants. Other owners must be active participants in the firms (GAO 2008: 59). Also in Canada, a wide range of business restrictions exists in relation to its three recognized accounting designations, differing between the various provinces and territories. With respect to MDPs, incorporation is generally forbidden in Canada, although incorporation with comparable licensed professions is in some cases allowed (Competition Bureau 2007: 56–9).

The remainder of this section presents an overview of the theoretical (6.4.1) and empirical (6.4.2) literature that discusses the effects of restrictions on

ABSs and MDPs, with a particular focus on auditors. Section 6.4.3 evaluates this literature (6.4.3) and draws some conclusions.

6.4.1   Theory

6.4.1.1   Alternative business structures

Regulation that prohibits the formation of certain legal forms (more particularly, limited liability partnerships or corporations) is usually defended by the argument that unlimited liability has a strong disciplinary function towards the professionals in a partnership. If financial liability for harm or error could be limited or shared, it is feared that the professional's duty to the client might be compromised. If, in contrast, professionals in a partnership risk facing unlimited personal liability claims, this would give them incentives to monitor the quality of services provided by their partners (OECD 2000: 26; Van den Bergh 2007: 50). Whether this theory holds up in practice is doubtful, such as in the light of the many corporate and accounting scandals, e.g. the *Arthur Andersen/Enron* case.[22] According to Van den Bergh (2007: 50), a total ban on limited liability partnerships is unnecessary, as 'the interest of consumers may be adequately protected by imposing mandatory liability insurance or by measures which ensure an adequate capitalisation of the partnership'.

Restrictions to legal form have been discussed most extensively in relation to the legal professions. Many EU Member States restrict the ownership and management of law firms, by prohibiting law firms to be owned or managed by non-lawyers. Proponents of such rules argue that they are necessary to prevent that lawyers are pressured into acting in the commercial interests of the owners or investors rather than in the best interests of the client. However, it can easily be argued that lawyers themselves are also driven by profits and that at least minority participations held by other professionals should be considered (Van den Bergh 2007; Grout 2005).[23] Ownership restrictions limit the possibilities of achieving economies of scale and may serve as a barrier to expansion by limiting the possibilities to attract capital. Also, a prohibition on hiring non-lawyers as managers may inhibit innovation of more efficient methods to deliver legal services to consumers. Copenhagen Economics (2006: 15) mentions in that respect that outside owners might have better access to capital, or might be better at reducing costs or developing new business ideas. Such arguments can easily be transposed to other professions, including accountancy.

In an early study, the OECD argued that restrictions on organizational forms 'limit the creation of new and possibly more cost-efficient business structures. In considering whether to permit limited-liability corporate forms, it may be necessary to balance the risk of diluting those protections against the benefits of access to capital or management flexibility' (OECD 2000: 26–7). Similarly, Garoupa (2008: 483) argues that such restrictions are 'difficult to justify by reference to the public interest. If some aspects of professional services may favour partnerships over corporations, the market and not the professional body should be expected to solve this tendency'.[24] One should also take into account the many changes in the (international) legal services markets. If regulations in certain countries would allow only a limited number of organizational forms, this does not help the entry of foreign law firms, and partnerships. The latter argument is, of course, a crucial issue for the European Commission, with its focus on the internal market and the freedom of services and establishment, and explains why it recently commissioned another study on the topic of legal form and shareholding restrictions in services markets (Maastricht University and Panteia 2014).

The study by Copenhagen Economics, however, concluded with respect to the legal professions that there will only be small gains by opening up to other types of ownership. Because law firms are not heavily capital dependent, access to capital is probably not a real obstacle to law firms (Copenhagen Economics 2008: 49). As stated above, this is likely to be different for audit firms that are active in the market for large and quoted companies. Copenhagen Economics furthermore argued that outside ownership could damage the independence of lawyers and that 'there is a real risk that other types of owners (e.g. banks) would want to own their own law firms in order to increase the price towards their loyal clients'. Because lawyer independence and client confidentiality have to be observed at all times, and because this may conflict with the interests of non-lawyer owners, regulation that covers all owners should be designed, if outside ownership is to be allowed at all (Copenhagen Economics 2008: 15).

With regard to auditors, Oxera (2007: iii–iv) concluded that 'under the current rules, audit firms, as well as potential investors, might be restricted in their ability to choose the optimal corporate structure and the preferred financing structure. By giving firms at least the possibility of access to cheaper, outside capital, new entry opportunities may be created'. The authors also found, based on an analysis of decision-making processes in audit firms and their conclusions drawn from a series of interviews, that 'alternative ownership and management structures of audit firms, where the control over the audit firms is with external investors (non-auditors), are unlikely to significantly impair auditor independence in practice' (Oxera 2007: v). Despite these findings, Article 3 of the 2006 Audit Directive (introduced above) still applies today. In its 2009 report the OECD argued that:

> a solution [to the challenge of raising capital faced by smaller accounting networks] could perhaps be found in allowing both partnerships and unlimited liability joint stock companies (in which accountant partners were significant shareholders) to perform auditing and accountancy services. Gathering together the necessary resources for a new accounting firm would then be more feasible, because private investors could commit large funds to establishing the firm.
>
> (Philipsen 2009: 28)

Moreover, partners would be able to 'sell shares at market rates, and it would provide an assurance to large company clients about the validity of the accounting firms' (Philipsen 2009: 28). To make sure that auditors remain independent and provide high quality services, appropriate safeguards would need to be installed. In that respect we have to keep in mind the key question, which is whether or not conflicts of interest are exaggerated by the presence of external shareholders. The OECD argues that the problem of conflict of interests may be reduced if shareholders have unlimited liability, as is the case, for example with certain underwriting syndicates (Philipsen 2009: 27–8).

The US General Accounting Office in its 2008 report also discusses the proposal to allow outside ownership. It found, however, that market participants in the US generally thought that being able to raise capital from outside sources would have limited effect on their ability to expand their market share. Instead, these market participants highlighted a quite different problem, being a shortage of qualified accountants (GAO 2008: 59–60).

6.4.1.2 *Multi-disciplinary partnerships*

In a paper prepared for the OECD, Roger Van den Bergh (2007: 49–50) presents the arguments in favour of and against a ban on MDPs.

Arguments supporting a ban on MDPs include the following:

- guarding professional secrecy;
- preventing conflicts of interest;
- in relation to legal disciplinary partnerships (LDPs): barristers are more likely to give independent advice, if they remain separate from solicitors; and
- in relation to LDPs: prevention of mergers, which would result in further market concentration.

Arguments against a ban on MDPs include:

- consumers cannot profit from 'one-stop shopping';
- some economies of scope are not realized;
- there is no internal risk spreading;
- perhaps there will be less innovation: more difficult access to capital which may be needed to invest in equipment and infrastructure to improve consumer services; and
- in relation to LDPs: consumers will face a double mark-up on the services they receive, if barristers and solicitors are prevented from working together.

The arguments supporting a restriction on MDPs involving lawyers and accountants mainly come from the legal professions. First, it is argued that partnerships with other professionals threaten the lawyer–client relationship, if these professionals are not bound by a duty of professional secrecy (the US' 'attorney-client privilege'). Second, co-operation between lawyers and accountants may cause conflicts of interest that are detrimental for consumers. Mullerat (2000: 482–3) notes that 'both the accountant and the lawyer must be independent. But the accountant must also be impartial [...] while the lawyer in essence is partial (a defender of one party). The two of them working in association, becoming a single-adviser entity, could not carry out such conflicting functions'.

The main justifications for a ban on LDPs in common law countries, for example between barristers and solicitors, is that barristers should be able to give independent advice, and this ability would be compromised by a partnership with solicitors. In addition, LDPs would lead to mergers, with the effect that there will be fewer barristers that can provide services to smaller solicitor firms.[25] The latter two arguments (independence, fear of market concentration) have also been applied to MDPs consisting of lawyers and accountants.[26]

One of the early critics of MDPs in the US is the lawyer Lawrence J. Fox, who – before the Enron case even started – wrote an article attacking the big accounting firms, referring to all of the arguments mentioned above. Fox argued that the big accounting firms, by hiring thousands of lawyers, 'have mounted a frontal assault on the legal profession that threatens to destroy the foundation of professional independence, loyalty and confidentiality' (Fox 2000: 1097). He stated that these firms had violated the legal profession's rules on governing conflicts of interest and confidentiality, and rules prohibiting a limitation of lawyer liability and direct solicitation of clients. The shift in activities from (mainly) auditing to other services, such as consulting, data processing and legal services, thus not only threatens the independence of the accounting firms in conducting the auditing function, but also the independence of legal professionals. Furthermore, referring to empirical evidence of non-compliance with auditor independence rules by employees of these firms who were investing in audit clients, Fox did not believe in the 'firewalls [...] which separate those who work on an audit from those who want to invest in companies being audited' (Fox 2000: 1100–1).

In addition to the arguments put forward by the legal professions, also the economic literature provides a justification for restrictions on MDPs, based on 'agency costs'. It follows from Carr and Mathewson (1990) and Matthews (1991) that sole practitioners and professional partnerships are the most likely (i.e. least costly, in terms of providing the right incentives) form of organization, because effort in production and quality cannot be judged properly by non-professionals.[27]

The arguments against restrictions on MDPs follow predominantly from economic theory. The first argument presented by Van den Bergh is that MDPs would be able to offer 'full service' to consumers by bringing together the know-how of different professions. The second argument is related to economies of scope. A ban on MDPs would prohibit the exchange of information between different professionals on specific problems in a multi-disciplinary case. This is inefficient: allowing MDPs would save on transaction costs, because it would reduce the number of individual contacts between consumers and professionals (Van den Bergh 2007: 49). In relation to both ABSs and MDPs, Stephen and Love (2000) also refer to 'economies of specialization'. They note that:

> [i]n a multi-lawyer firm it is, perhaps, more likely that there will be a specialist within the firm who is the least-cost provider of the service function. The probability of this being so may increase the more lawyers there are in the firm. [...] the fewer the number of partners and the more specialized the service function required the more likely that the firm will not be the least-cost supplier. This may even be the more so if the firm is an MDP.
>
> (Stephen and Love 2000: 1005)

A similar point is made by Garoupa, who states that 'by banning other organisational forms [i.e. corporations, MDPs], the specialisation of professionals beyond particular aspects of their service (thus lowering the cost of providing services) and economies of scope (by providing a 'one-stop shop' service including lawyers, accountants, surveyors and tax advisers) are lost' (Garoupa 2008: 483). The third argument provided by Van den Bergh holds that different professions may face different business cycles and fluctuations in income. Not allowing MDPs would then take away the possibility to spread related risks among the partners. All of these benefits of MDPs can lead to lower prices for consumers. In addition, innovation may be promoted: if MDPs are allowed this may facilitate access to capital needed to invest in equipment and infrastructure to improve consumer services (Van den Bergh 2007: 49).

Looking at the list of economic arguments against a total ban on MDPs, the question is whether less restrictive means of regulation would be able to achieve the aims of guarding professional secrecy and preventing conflicts of interest. This seems a particularly relevant question in relation to MDPs involving accountants, because the tightened regulation introduced in many jurisdictions worldwide on auditors' independence, auditor rotation and the quality of accounting services (discussed briefly in Section 1 above) is aimed at solving the same agency problems. Van den Bergh answered the question in the affirmative, proposing various alternatives to a total ban on MDPs (Van den Bergh 2007: 49–50). He argued that least restrictive would be information remedies which simply require *informing the client* that the duty of confidentiality of one MDP member conflicts with the duty of disclosure of another MDP member. Alternatively, measures could be introduced that prevent certain information flows between different professions. One option would then be to introduce the so-called 'Chinese walls' that prevent information flows from professionals in the partnership who are bound by professional secrecy to other members in the partnership who are not. However, critics such as Mullerat (2000) and Scott and Konsta (1999) have argued that such 'Chinese walls' are difficult to apply in practice. Another option according to Van den Bergh would be to impose professional secrecy obligations on all partners in an MDP.[28]

6.4.2   Empirics

There is little empirical evidence that confirms any of the arguments presented in favour or against restrictions on MDPs, business form and outside ownership or management. Some of the arguments are indeed hard to test in practice. For example, one would need to be able to measure economies of scope generated by MDPs, or to measure adverse effects of MDPs on the duty to observe professional secrecy, or to analyse which (if any) new business models have been introduced as a result of outside ownership. On the other hand, it does not seem impossible to send out questionnaires to business clients in order to find out whether there is a demand for one-stop shopping, or what are their views and worries with respect to professional values of lawyers and auditors working for the same firm. However, so far I have not been able to find any empirical literature on these specific issues, apart from the research carried out for the *Clementi Report* in the UK, which suggested that indeed there appears to be some consumer interest in the convenience and accessibility of 'one-stop shopping' provided by MDPs (Clementi 2004: 133–4).

Some studies exist on different but related issues, outside the scope of auditing services. Stephen and Gillanders (1993) present evidence that mutual control within law firms in the UK mainly takes place through *ex ante* screening of prospective partners, rather than *ex post* through monitoring by professionals who are already in the partnership. This would undermine the main argument in favour of restrictions on limited liability partnerships (LLPs) (Stephen and Love 2000: 1009; Van den Bergh 2007: 50). Carr and Matthewson (1990) found that the average size of law firms in the US was larger in States where limited liability partnerships were allowed than in those where they were not, and considered this a possible indication of efficiency gains that can be obtained by forming LLPs. A similar conclusion was reached by Button and Fleming (1992), while analysing the architectural professions in the UK in the 1980s. According to Button and Fleming, the abolition of the rule preventing practice under limited liability led to a considerable growth in limited liability companies, almost entirely at the expense of 'sole principal' architectural practices.

In a US Federal Trade Commission study by Liang and Ogur (1973), the effects of MDPs between dentists and dental auxiliaries (i.e. hygienists and assistants) were investigated. In this study, States with and without a rule restricting the use of dental auxiliaries were compared. In the States without such a restriction, costs of individual treatments were 6 to 30 per cent lower, while the quality of services provided by auxiliaries (for the dental procedures studied) was found to be equal to that provided by dentists. This led the authors to conclude that 'relaxation of restrictions on the number of hygienists that a dentist may employ would benefit consumers by providing the same quality of service at a lower price' (Liang and Ogur 1987: 3).

Stephen (2002) found that in European jurisdictions where MDPs are permitted, commercial law is increasingly dominated by the legal branch of the major international accounting firms. The author provides an explanation of this in terms of the internal efficiency of law firms in various jurisdictions. As a result of EU legislation that aims for a Single European Market in legal services,[29] 'differences in efficiency of law firms arising from differences in competitive pressure across jurisdictions are likely to lead to cross-border mergers involving law firms from "efficient" and "inefficient" [i.e. those where competition is restricted, leading to higher fee levels] jurisdictions. Such mergers are likely to lead to pressure building up in the more regulated jurisdictions for further liberalisation of legal service markets' (Stephen 2002: 115). Therefore, so Stephen argues, EU legislation may indirectly increase efficiency, even though it does not directly reduce the power of national bar associations (Stephen 2002: 124).

For a case study on MDPs involving lawyers and other professions, I conducted a number of interviews myself in 2012 with representatives from (predominantly) Dutch organizations of notaries, tax advisers and accountants, and with the *Fédération des Experts Comptables Européens*.[30] The Netherlands was chosen because in that country, contrary to, for example, Belgium and Luxemburg, there is no prohibition on MDPs consisting of lawyers and notaries or tax advisers. MDPs between lawyers and accountants, however, are not permitted. Interviews with representatives from the Dutch associations of notaries and tax advisers, respectively, confirmed that Dutch professionals working in the big law firms sometimes encounter practical problems abroad. For example, Dutch MDPs consisting of notaries and lawyers are not allowed in (*inter alia*) Belgium and Luxembourg, while MDPs consisting of tax advisers and lawyers are not allowed in France and Slovakia. In these cases, in-house provision of services is not possible and external relationships with profession members in the Member States concerned need to be established. As a result, there are less opportunities to come up with creative solutions for clients (cf. the argument pro-MDPs from the economic literature, on innovation of consumer services) and, of course, this also prevents a one-stop shop from being created in those countries.[31] Moreover, it prevents risk spreading between professions from taking place. This is a lost opportunity in times of crisis given that, as it was suggested by some interviewees, the legal profession is, to a large extent, 'anti-cyclical' and the notary profession 'cyclical'. With respect to auditors, an interviewee from the Netherlands Association of Accountants stated that the arguments against MDPs generally put forward by lawyers (independence, conflicts of interest, legal privilege) are shared by a number of accountants (Panteia and Maastricht University 2012: confidential documents).

6.4.3   Evaluation

From the discussion of theoretical and empirical literature, we can conclude that there are many economic reasons to consider relaxing some legal form and shareholding restrictions and restrictions on MDPs. Arguments to support such restrictions seem to be based mostly on non-economic arguments (ethics, preventing conflicts of interest), which are important but often formulated in a very general way[32] and not supported by strong empirical evidence. Moreover, in an earlier study we conducted for the European Commission on free movement of lawyers (Panteia and Maastricht University 2012), we found that restrictions on ABSs and MDPs are not identified by stakeholders as one of the most important barriers to cross-border establishment or cross-border provision of legal services. Furthermore, one may wonder if business form restrictions are a proportional cure for the market failures of information asymmetry and externalities caused by low-quality services. After all, to a large extent these market failures can be addressed by more direct quality regulation (for example qualification requirements and licensing) also for auditors.

In a recent, but still unpublished, study conducted for the European Commission (Maastricht University and Panteia 2014), we found regarding accountants that there are currently no legal form requirements to be found in any EU Member State, while there are only limited restrictions on shareholding (or membership), voting rights and management in countries such as Belgium, France, Italy, Luxemburg, Malta and Romania. However, these findings apply only to accountants who are not auditors. Auditing services were not part of the study, the reason perhaps being that the discussion on the non-economic arguments mentioned above has not been resolved. The indices for legal form and shareholding requirements found in relation to other professions that were covered by the study, such as tax advisers and the legal professions (by far the most regulated), show that there are differences between the regulatory frameworks used in the various EU Member States, whereas the justifications provided for the existing rules are very similar. On the one hand, this can be considered evidence for the statement that some of the existing legal form and shareholding restrictions are not necessary or proportional. On the other hand, this can be considered as evidence for the statement that Member States rather than the European Commission should be able to decide, based on the national context and organization of the profession,[33] how to guarantee the proportionality of its regulations, provided, of course, that any restrictions are non-discriminatory. Moreover, if there is a demand for ABSs and MDPs, the market rather than EU regulation will lead Member States into re-assessing their rules on business structure.

Hence, unless there is strong empirical evidence showing the negative effects of restrictions on ABSs or MDPs on trade, sectoral productivity or GDP, no regulatory action at the European level seems warranted. Our recent statistical and economic analysis of the effects of legal form and shareholding restrictions (Maastricht University and Panteia 2014) did not find such evidence. Nevertheless, the 'values' of competition can be promoted by the European Commission (competition advocacy), so that Member States can act individually and to the extent possible. Alternatively, a Commission Recommendation, as in the case of auditor liability (Recommendation 2008/437/EC) could be an optional strategy for the European Commission.

6.5   Concluding remarks

Having addressed the proposals made (and actions taken) in the EU and US to deal with the lack of competition in the audit market for large and quoted companies, I now return to the question of whether these proposals can be supported from a law and economics perspective. Finally, I will discuss the implications of the analysis presented in this chapter for China.

From an economic perspective, the two main justifications for regulatory intervention in the audit market follow from information asymmetry between auditors and audit clients, which in an unregulated market are likely to result in low quality of services and moral hazard problems, and the possibility that low-quality services and fraud lead to negative externalities imposed on investors and society at large. Moreover, the current lack of competition in itself is also considered a market failure.

Regulation of audit quality and auditor independence can therefore be supported from a public interest (efficiency) perspective. However, the question remains how much regulation is needed, especially since the new and stricter rules in the EU and US may expand auditors' liability. Some of the recent rules on audit quality and auditors' independence are also difficult to enforce in practice due to the lack of competition: mandatory auditor rotation, for example, does not have much practical value if audit clients have only three or fewer audit firms to choose from, as I explained in Section 6.2.

Against this background – regulatory developments in the direction of more regulation of audit quality and independence – it is interesting to see that the European Commission is promoting *deregulation* in the related area of legal form and shareholding requirements in professional services sectors. The economic analysis presented in Section 6.4 above shows that there are many economic arguments that would support such deregulation, but that non-economic arguments and differences between (the organization of professions in) Member States seem to point at a more decentralized approach to this issue of allowing outside ownership and management. Such a 'bottom-up approach' to regulation would suggest that deregulation of legal form and shareholding requirements, if deemed necessary, needs to take place at the national level, following market demand for MDPs and ABSs (as in the UK), rather than through EU intervention in the form of a Directive. Although this relaxation of business form requirements seems to be in contrast with other recent regulatory developments in the EU, in practice this may not be the case; in the recent study we conducted for the European Commission on legal form and shareholding restrictions in professional services sectors (Maastricht University and Panteia 2014), the Commission requested to exclude auditing services from the analysis. Hence, changes in the regulation of business structures of audit firms are not expected soon, although it remains to be seen what action the EU will take. After all, allowing outside ownership has also been suggested by many as a solution to deal with the lack of competition problem, as I repeatedly pointed out above.

The other solution proposed to deal with competition problems, limiting auditors' liability, was discussed extensively in Section 6.3 of this chapter. I concluded that due to the special characteristics of auditors' liability, a limitation of liability is likely to have only limited adverse effects on deterrence, while having positive effects also for insurability. An important question remains *how* (cap, contractual limitation, proportional liability) and *how much* liability should be limited, which is an issue best dealt with at the national level, because of the many differences in tort law, contract law and organization of the accountancy profession. Leaving the choice to Member States, as provided in the EU Recommendation, can hence be supported from an economic perspective, although it may lack sufficient effect.

The implications for China can easily be distilled from the discussion above. If in China, like in many European countries and the US, there is a demand by clients of accounting services for alternative business structures, China could follow the examples of those Western countries where particular ABSs are already allowed. As shown in this chapter, economic theory provides several arguments in favour of allowing such ABSs and MDPs. And if China, in order to solve competition problems in its audit market (which are just as prevalent in China as they are in the EU and US) considers the option to limit auditors' liability, this would also be in line with developments in the EU and (to a large extent) with the economic analysis I presented in Section 6.3. It remains important, however, to guarantee the quality and independence of auditors, to prevent, to the extent possible, future accounting scandals and resulting losses for investors and financial markets. Moreover, despite their theoretical attractiveness the two proposals analysed in this chapter (limiting liability, allowing outside ownership) may not be able to take away all of the entry barriers (reputation, capacity) faced by mid-tier accounting networks.

Notes

1 'Big Four firms, China in talks over corporate audit impasse', *Reuters*, 24 January 2014, available at http://www.reuters.com/article/2014/01/24/us-china-audits-kpmg-usa-idUSBREA0N1AO20140124 (accessed 17 May 2014). 'Judge rules Chinese accounting affiliates of Big Four "willfully" violated U.S. law', *Washington Post*,

23 January 2014, http://www.washingtonpost.com/business/economy/judge-rules-chinese-accounting-affiliates-willfully-violated-us-law/2014/01/22/f9f48e6a-83af-11e3–8099–9181471f7aaf_story.html (accessed 17 May 2014).

2 Ibid.

3 There is an extensive literature on the need for regulation of professional services markets, including some of my own contributions. For more information, the reader is referred to this literature. See e.g. Shavell (1984); Stephen and Love (2000); Philipsen (2010, 2012).

4 Ibid. See more particularly the bibliography contained in Philipsen (2012).

5 GAO (2003: 12–15) presents a list of key factors that spurred consolidation in the audit market, which include: (1) the growing size and global reach of audit clients; (2) greater economies of scale; (3) the need for greater industry-specific and technical expertise; and (4) increasing or maintaining market share.

6 This section draws from a forthcoming publication in the *Geneva Papers on Risk and Insurance* (Philipsen 2014), where a more detailed exposé of limited liability for auditors is presented.

7 According to Levitt Jr. and Nicolaisen (2008: VII:27), a damage payout over US$500 million could result in the demise of such a firm. In 2008, US audit firms were defendants in 34 cases with damage claims in excess of US$1 billion, while in 2006 European audit firms were defendants in at least five cases of similar magnitude. See Levitt Jr. and Nicolaisen (2008: VII:25); London Economics and Ewert (2006); Koch and Schunk (2009: 3).

8 Caps can be introduced in various forms, such as a fixed monetary cap, a cap based on the size of the audited company (as measured by its market capitalization) and a cap based on a multiple of the audit fees charged by the auditor to its client. See also Doralt *et al.* (2008); Ojo (2009).

9 For further information see Philipsen (2014).

10 See more generally Shavell (1980); Dewees *et al.* (1996), and with respect to auditors Levitt Jr. and Nicolaisen (2008); Philipsen (2012). In addition, market instruments, such as reputational effects and repeat buying, may be relevant as well.

11 On the trade-off between liability rules and regulation, see Shavell (1984) and with respect to auditors, Philipsen (2014).

12 Similarly, in the US stricter requirements were introduced by the Sarbanes-Oxley Act 2002. I should note here that regulation can also *limit* liability, if regulatory standards are complied with and this is considered as proof of following the due care standard in a liability case (the regulatory compliance defence).

13 For example GAO (2003, 2008); London Economics and Ewert (2006); Levitt Jr. and Nicolaisen (2008); Koch and Schunk (2009).

14 See, for example, Schwartz (1997); Ewert (1999). See also Dye (1993).

15 On the principal-agent problems in corporate governance and the role of auditors more generally, see Kraakman *et al.* (2009).

16 In other EU Member States, such as the UK, claims against auditors (involved in statutory audits) can only be introduced by the company and not by the individual shareholders or third parties. Contractually arranged caps are a more feasible way of limiting auditors' liability in these jurisdictions.

17 More specifically, an 'economics of federalism' approach. Following Tiebout (1956), authors such as Van den Bergh (2000), Faure (2003) and Van Boom (2011) support a bottom-up approach to questions of harmonization. Moving to a higher level of regulation (e.g. transnational, federal, EU) is considered efficient only if the aim is to deal with transboundary externalities or a race to the bottom, or if economies of scale or transaction costs savings can be achieved.

18 These restrictions are also called business form and ownership restrictions.

19 Another possible type of business restriction, which however is less relevant as an entry barrier in accounting services markets, is a minimum capital requirement. This is a minimum investment threshold for access to the corporate form, which is rather common in EU Member States and in China, but much less so in the US. For an economic analysis of minimum capital requirements, see, for example Armour (2014) and Kraakman *et al.* (2009: 130–31).

20 See the introduction to this chapter.

21 See subsection 6.4.3.

22 For further details, see Philipsen (2009).

23 In this respect, Grout (2005) finds it difficult to understand the assumption that there is a distinction between the incentives of lawyers working together and their incentives when they are owned or majority managed by non-lawyers.

24 See also Hansmann (1990), on which Garoupa's argumentation is based.

25 For an extensive analysis of LDPs, see Clementi (2004: 108–28).

26 See, for example, the analysis by the European Court of Justice (ECJ) in the famous *Wouters* case (*Wouters* v. *Algemene Raad van de Nederlandse Orde van Advocaten*, C-309/99), where it was pointed out that the accountancy market is much more concentrated than the legal services market.

27 In addition, Carr and Mathewson (1990: 328) found that partnerships dominate sole practitioners when client cases are large and the detection of chiselling is low.

28 See also Deards (2002).

29 The author mentions the Establishment Directive (98/5/EC) and (to a lesser extent) the Mutual Recognition Directive (89/48/EEC), which applied at the time. Citizens of a Member State refused entry to the legal profession could qualify in another Member State and thereafter practice in the restrictive State, as long as the costs of this procedure are compensated by the gains from practising in the restrictive State. Any practice rules designed to restrict competition between lawyers in one jurisdiction, thereby raising fee levels, will attract lawyers from other jurisdictions where fees are lower, according to Stephen (2002: 118).

30 This case study was part of a wider study on free movement of lawyers: see Panteia and Maastricht University (2012). Unfortunately, most of the files are confidential, so concrete references cannot be provided.

31 It was noted furthermore (by notaries working in a large Dutch law firm) that lawyers in Luxemburg (and to a lesser extent in Belgium) operate almost like a cartel. They are not interested in cooperation with notaries.

32 See on this also Maastricht University and Panteia (2014).

33 Notably the legal, notary and tax advisory professions are regulated rather differently in each EU Member State, with different professional monopolies and exclusive tasks being assigned to the particular profession members.

References

Armour, J. (2006) 'Legal Capital: An Outdated Concept?', *European Business Organization Law Review*, 7, 5–27.

Arruñada, B. (2004) 'Audit Failure and the Crisis of Auditing', *European Business Organization Law Review*, 5, 635–43.

Autore, D. M., Billingsley, R. S. and Schneller, M. I. (2009) 'Information Uncertainty and Auditor Reputation', *Journal of Banking & Finance*, 33, 183–92.

Bigus, J. (2008) 'Does a Liability Cap Distort Auditors' Incentives to Take Care?', Munich: CESifo Group, 2008. Available online at: http://www.cesifo-group.de (accessed 17 May 2014).

Button, K. and M. Fleming (1992) 'The Effects of Regulatory Reform on the Architectural Profession in the United Kingdom', *International Review of Law and Economics*, 12, 95–112.

Carr, J. and Matthewson, F. (1990) 'The Economics of Law Firms: A Study in the Legal Organization of Firms', *Journal of Law and Economics*, 33, 307–30.

Commission Staff (2008) *Accompanying Document to the Commission Recommendation Concerning the Limitation of the Civil Liability of Statutory Auditors and Audit Firms – Impact Assessment (C(2008) 2274 final)*. European Commission: Brussels, Belgium, 5 June 2008.

Competition Bureau (2007) *Self-Regulated Professions: Balancing Competition and Regulation*, Gatineau QC, Canada.

Darby, M. R. and Karni, E. (1973) 'Free Competition and the Optimal Amount of Fraud', *Journal of Law and Economics*, 16, 67–88.

Deards, E. (2002) 'Closed Shop versus One Stop Shop: The Battle Goes On', *European Law Review*, 27, 618–27.

Dewees, D., Duff, D. and Trebilcock, M. (1996) *Exploring the Domain of Accident Law: Taking the Facts Seriously*, New York: Oxford University Press.

Doralt, W., Hellgardt, A., Hopt, K. J., Leyens, P. C., Roth, M. and Zimmermann, R. (2008) 'Auditors' Liability and its Impact on the European Financial Markets', *Cambridge Law Journal*, 67, 62–8.

Dye, R. (1993) 'Auditor Standards, Legal Liability, and Auditor Wealth', *Journal of Political Economy*, 101, 887–914.

Ewert, R. (1999) 'Auditor Liability and the Precision of Auditing Standards', *Journal of Institutional and Theoretical Economics*, 155, 181–206.

Faure, M. (2003), 'How Law and Economics may Contribute to the Harmonisation of Tort Law in Europe', in Zimmerman, R. (ed.), *Grundstrukturen des Europäischen Deliktsrechts*, Baden-Baden: Nomos, 31–82.

GAO (2003) *Public Accounting Firms: Mandated Study on Consolidation and Competition, GAO-03-864*, Report to the Senate Committee on Banking, Housing, and Urban Affairs and the House Committee on Financial Services, Washington, DC: United States General Accountability Office.

GAO (2008) *Audits of Public Companies: Continued Concentration in Audit Market for Large Public Companies Does Not Call for Immediate Action, GAO-08-163*, Report to Congressional Addressees, Washington, DC: United States Government Accountability Office.

Garoupa, N. (2008) 'Providing a Framework for Reforming the Legal Profession: Insights from the European Experience', *European Business Organization Law Review*, 9, 463–95.

Grout, P. A. (2005) 'The Clementi Report: Potential Risks of External Ownership and Regulatory Responses: A Report to the Department of Constitutional Affairs', *CPMO Working Paper Series no. 05/135*, University of Bristol, July 2005.

Hansmann, H. (1990) 'When Does Worker Ownership Work? ESOPs, Law Firms, Codetermination and Economic Democracy', *Yale Law Journal*, USA, 99, 1749–816.

Koch, C. W. and Schunk, D. (2009) 'Limiting Auditor Liability? – Experimental Evidence on Risk and Ambiguity Attitudes under Real Losses', June 2009. Available online at SSRN: http://ssrn.com/abstract=982027 (accessed 17 May 2014).

Kraakman, R., Armour, J., Davies, P., Enriques, L., Hansmann, H., Hertig, G., Hopt, K., Kanda, H. and Rock, E. (2009) *The Anatomy of Corporate Law: A Comparative and Functional Approach*, second edn, Oxford: Oxford University Press.

Krishnamurthy, S., Zhou, J. and Zhou, N. (2006) 'Auditor Reputation, Auditor Independence, and the Stock-Market Impact of Andersen's Indictment on Its Client Firms', *Contemporary Accounting Research*, 23, 465–90.

Levitt Jr., A. and Nicolaisen, D. T. (2008) *Final Report of the Advisory Committee on the Auditing Profession to the U.S. Department of the Treasury*, 6 October 2008.

Liang, J. N. and Ogur, J. (1987) *Restrictions on Dental Auxiliaries*, Washington, DC: Federal Trade Commission.

London Economics and Ewert, R. (2006) *Study on the Economic Impact of Auditors' Liability Regimes*, Final Report to EC-DG Internal Market and Services, London: London Economics, September 2006. Available online at: http://ec.europa.eu/internal_market/auditing/liability/index_en.htm (accessed 17 May 2014).

Maastricht University and Panteia (2014) *Inventory of Legal Form and Shareholding Requirements in the EU Services Sector and their Economic Assessment*, Report for European Commission/DG Internal Market and Services, Maastricht/Zoetermeer, 29 January 2014.

Matthews, R. C. O. (1991) 'The Economics of Professional Ethics: Should the Professions Be More Like Business?', *Economic Journal*, 101, 737–50.

Nelson, P. (1970) 'Information and Consumer Behavior', *Journal of Political Economy*, 78, 311–29.

OECD (2000) *Competition in Professional Services*, DAFFE/CLP/(2000)2, Paris: Directorate for Financial, Fiscal and Enterprise Affairs, Committee on Competition Law and Policy.

Ojo, M. (2009) 'Limiting audit firms' liability: A step in the right direction? (Proposals for a new audit liability regime in Europe revisited)', Munich Personal RePEc Archive, Paper no. 14878. Available online at: http://mpra.ub.uni-muenchen.de/14878 (accessed 17 May 2014).

Oxera (2007) *Ownership Rules of Audit Firms and their Consequences for Audit Market Concentration*, Final Report prepared for DG Internal Market and Services, Oxera Consulting Ltd, October 2007. Available online at: http://ec.europa.eu/internal_market/auditing/docs/market/oxera_report_en.pdf (accessed 17 May 2014).

Panteia and Maastricht University (2012) *Evaluation of the Legal Framework for the Free Movement of Lawyers*, Report for European Commission/DG Internal Market and Services, Zoetermeer – Maastricht, 18 December 2012.

Philipsen, N. J. (2009) *Competition and Regulation in Auditing and Related Professions*, DAF/COMP(2009)19, Paris: OECD, Directorate for Financial and Enterprise Affairs, Competition Committee. Available online at: http://www.oecd.org/dataoecd/8/8/44762253.pdf (accessed 17 May 2014).

Philipsen, N. J. (2010) 'Regulation and Competition in the Legal Profession: Developments in the EU and China', *Journal of Competition Law and Economics*, 6, 203–31.

Philipsen, N. J. (2012) 'Regulation of Accountants', in Van den Bergh, R. and Pacces, A. M., *Encyclopedia of Law and Economics: Regulation and Economics*, Cheltenham, UK: Edward Elgar, 715–42.

Philipsen, N. J. (2014) 'Limiting Auditors' Liability: The Case for (and against) EU Intervention', *Geneva Papers on Risk and Insurance*, forthcoming.

Schwartz, R. (1997) 'Auditors' Liability, Vague Due Care, and Auditing Standards', *Review of Quantitative Finance and Accounting*, 11, 183–207.

Shavell, S. (1980) 'Strict Liability versus Negligence', *Journal of Legal Studies*, 9, 1–25.

Shavell, S. (1984) 'Liability for Harm versus Regulation of Safety', *Journal of Legal Studies*, 13, 357–74.

Stephen, F. H. (2002) 'The European Single Market and the Regulation of the Legal Profession: An Economic Analysis', *Managerial and Decision Economics*, 23, 115–25.

Stephen, F. H. and Gillanders, D. D. (1993) 'Ex Post Monitoring versus Ex Ante Screening in the New Institutional Economics', *Journal of Institutional and Theoretical Economics*, 149, 725–30.

Stephen, F. H. and J. H. Love (2000) 'Regulation of the Legal Profession', in Bouckaert, B. and De Geest, G. (eds), *Encyclopedia of Law and Economics, Vol. III: The Regulation of Contracts*, Cheltenham, UK: Edward Elgar, 987–1017.

Tiebout, C. M. (1956) 'A Pure Theory of Local Expenditures', *Journal of Political Economy*, 56, 416–24.

Van Boom, W. (2011) 'Harmonizing Tort Law: A Comparative Tort Law and Economics Analysis', in Faure, M. (ed), *Tort Law and Economics, Encyclopedia of Law and Economics*, second edn, Cheltenham, UK, and Northampton, MA, USA: Edward Elgar Publishing, 435–49.

Van den Bergh, R. (2000) 'Towards an Institutional Legal Framework for Regulatory Competition in Europe', *Kyklos*, 53, 435–66.

Van den Bergh, R. (2007) 'Towards Better Regulation of the Legal Professions', in OECD, *Competitive Restrictions in Legal Professions*, DAF/COMP(2007)39, OECD: Directorate for Financial and Enterprise Affairs, Competition Committee, Paris, 17–71.

7 Controlling misrepresentation in securities markets

Is private enforcement trivial in China?

Tianshu Zhou[1]

7.1 Introduction

This chapter will evaluate the enforcement strategies on controlling public companies' misrepresentation in China's stock markets. Some research suggests that China has already implemented some legal rules in protecting investors (Howson 2008: 186; Shim 2005: 375). However, the enforcement of these legal rules is still problematic. Many argue that a considerable gap between the 'law on paper' and 'law in practice' exists in China's investor protection regime (Liu 2006: 311; Miles and He 2005: 279; Opper and Schwaag-Serger 2008: 245). This chapter therefore focuses on the enforcement of securities law.

The enforcement strategies in relation to securities law can be broadly divided into two categories. First, public enforcement is usually conducted by an administrative regulator. Second, private enforcement usually arises where private parties sue public companies or their executives. These strategies usually serve different functions. As summarized by Rose (2008):

> Commission enforcement operated primarily to deter securities fraud in order to promote society's collective interest in the integrity and efficiency of the capital markets; private enforcement, by contrast, operated primarily to compensate defrauded investors for their discrete losses – much like a common law claim for misrepresentation and deceit.
>
> (Rose 2008: 1310)

Some scholars have argued that private enforcement is trivial in China. For example, Pistor and Xu claim that private enforcement of investor rights has virtually been absent in China so far, not because of lack of demand for them, but because courts have restricted investor lawsuits (Xu and Pistor 2005: 184). Some US lawyers similarly argued that the public enforcement of which the China Securities Regulatory Commission (CSRC) takes charge should play a dominant role in regulating China's securities markets, because public enforcement under State administrative control is consistent with China's regulatory culture and social-political reality (Clarke 2008; Layton

2008). Liebman and Milhaupt also argue that 'civil liability' is not yet a 'major concern' for most listed companies (Liebman and Milhaupt 2008: 929). However, these arguments are usually based on an analysis of individual cases, but lack the support of systemic empirical evidence. Against this academic background, this chapter uses *misrepresentation* as a sample, to examine whether private enforcement of securities law is trivial in the Chinese context, as some scholars have argued. To answer this question, two types of evaluation will be performed in this chapter. First, private enforcement will be empirically compared with public enforcement in the Chinese context. Second, the data from private enforcement in China will be compared with that from the US, where private enforcement is far more prevalent. This chapter will be organized as follows. Section 7.2 introduces some basic information about China's securities markets, including the seriousness of misrepresentation and the deeper implications behind this phenomenon. Section 7.3 briefly introduces the research methodology of this chapter. Section 7.4 illustrates the data regarding private and public enforcement in China's securities markets. Section 7.5, by investigating the empirical data will substantially evaluate the private enforcement of China's securities law. Finally, a conclusion will be drawn and presented.

7.2 Some basics about China's securities markets

7.2.1 *Agency cost in China's securities markets and misrepresentation*

There is little doubt about the seriousness of insider misrepresentation in China's stock markets. In accordance with the interpretation of the Chinese Supreme Court, misrepresentation includes a major failure to disclose information, false statement, and a postponement/delay in disclosure, which are all breaches of the relevant rules of the securities law.[2] Empirical research shows that the vast majority of the CSRC's enforcement actions are against misrepresentation as defined by the Chinese Supreme Court. This particular type of misbehavior accounted for nearly 65 percent of all CSRC's enforcement actions during 1999 to 2003 (see Table 7.1).

The deeper implications behind misrepresentation in China's stock markets should be investigated. In its essence, misrepresentation is a result of information asymmetry between 'insiders' and 'outsiders'. The insiders' upper hand in access to corporate information usually triggers the problem of 'conflict of interest'. In economic terms, this is usually called the agency-problem or principal-agent problem. First, his part will introduce the general agency cost problems in China that give rise to misrepresentation will be presented. Second, it will introduce how public and private enforcement works in the Chinese context. On Chinese stock markets, listed companies can be divided into two groups based on their identity. One group are listed as State-owned enterprises (SOEs). The other group are private listed companies not

Table 7.1 Types of securities rules violations and number of enforcement actions (1999–2003)

Breakdown of enforcement actions	Number of occurrences	Percentage
Panel A:By violation type	6	2.16
Illegal share buyback	22	7.91
Inflated profit	7	2.52
Assets fabrication	10	3.60
Unauthorized fund use change	51	18.35
Postponement/delay in disclosure	51	18.35
False statement	7	2.52
Fund provision violation	78	28.06
Major failure to disclose information	7	2.52
Major shareholder embezzlement	39	14.03
Others	278	100.00
Total		

(Source: Huang (2010: 39).)

controlled by the State. As of the end of January 2013, there were 2,443 listed companies on China's stock markets. Of these, 953 were controlled by the State. These companies occupy nearly 51.4 percent of the total share value of all listed companies.[3]

Listed SOEs are still the major forces on the Chinese stock markets and their problems are therefore important and representative. Similar to Western companies, SOEs are formally incorporated. According to Xi, by corporatizing SOEs, the Chinese leadership intended to separate government administration from enterprise management, release the State from its unlimited responsibility for SOEs, raise funds to diversify SOE risks, and, consequently, improve enterprise efficiency (Xi 2005: 95). Separation between ownership and management nevertheless triggers an agency cost problem. This problem can be divided into two levels. First is the 'vertical agency problem' between corporate owners and managers. This problem arises where a manager, whilst being an agent, nevertheless pursues his or her own interest at the expense of the principal's interests. The second agency problem is the 'horizontal agency problem'. This is a problem between majority and minority shareholders. Here, majority shareholders may improperly use their overwhelming voting power to depress minority shareholders' interests by squeezing them out without fair compensation or misleading minority shareholders' investment by misrepresentation. Fortunately, although these two types of agency issues can coexist, they are usually mutually exclusive. Some studies indicate that the 'agency cost' between shareholders and executives is not a key issue in jurisdictions dominated by concentrated ownership (Cheffins 1999: 5; Cheffins 2000: 41). Majority shareholders hold the residual right to claim corporate property and the voting right to control the fundamental business decisions of the corporation. Therefore, they have both the incentive and ability to supervise the directors' performance (La

Porta *et al.*, 1999: 54). By contrast, in jurisdictions with dispersed owner-ship, not much focus is placed on the agency costs between majority share-holders and minority shareholders, as fewer powerful block-holders exist in this type of market.

Although ownership in most Chinese companies is concentrated, both types of agency problem are equally serious. In the course of Chinese economic reform and in seeking the autonomous management of SOEs, the govern-ment tends to delegate independent decision-making power to the executives of SOEs.[4] However, it has not developed an efficient system to supervise the conduct of those SOE managers (Xu *et al.* 2007: 93; Yang 2005: 8). Listed SOEs are usually supervised and controlled by their parent companies. In order to form a listed company, a promoter – usually a large SOE – has to contribute its essential operating assets (factories, workshops, or production lines) to the listed company. A listed company is a legally separate enterprise from its State-owned parent company, though; in reality it usually maintains a strong relationship with its parent company. Consequently, it is common for directors or managers in the listed company to also hold positions in the parent company (Liu 2006: 316). The main reason behind the weak super-vision of SOEs is the 'absent owner problem' (*Suoyou Zhe Quewei*). State-owned parent companies usually encounter incentive problems in supervising their listed subsidiaries. As the majority shareholder, the parent company has a residual claim to the profits made by a listed company. However, State-owned parent companies like State agencies are organized by individuals. The persons who are appointed to check and supervise listed SOEs do not have property rights in those companies. Rather, they are simply government offi-cials who earn a salary based on the governmental hierarchy, that is, around three times that of an unskilled worker. Wary of social unrest, the State does not want to pay SOE managers and also the supervisory officials in a man-ner that would make them too far detached from lower level workers (Tang and Wang 2007: 179). Arguably, promoting a listed SOE's decent market per-formance could be beneficial to an officials' political fortune. However, even this incentive is suspicious. As mentioned above, a listed SOE that takes over essential assets from its parent company is usually equipped with the best production line and the best-trained employees. More importantly, the parent company has to bear all sorts of burdens (e.g. debts, redundant personnel, etc.) that occurred before its separation from a listed subsidiary. These advan-tages guarantee listed SOEs strong productivity. Taking all these factors into consideration, majority shareholders may have little incentive in supervising executives' operation in listing SOEs. With this loose internal control system, executives can make considerable illegal profits by engaging in false disclosure and insider trading.

Another major concern regarding corporate governance in China is the fact that the board of directors sometimes merely 'rubber stamps' decisions and is controlled by a dominant shareholder, who may take advantage of this control to undermine minority shareholders' interests by self-dealing, manipulating share price and misrepresentation. Indeed, there has long been a serious issue with controlling shareholders engaging in 'tunnelling' activities. A number of cases in China have shown that the manipulation of a few insiders can trigger thousands of individual investors to suffer a loss of their investments.[5] According to a study of 173 listed companies in China, samples in which block-holders had illegally appropriated company assets constituted 37 percent of all samples (Zhang and Wu 2003: 24). For listed SOEs, their interdependence with their controlling shareholders gives rise to 'stealing' activities on a wide range of fronts. Officials who control the parent SOE may move the listed SOE's assets to the special purpose vehicle owned by a related party (e.g. friends or relatives). This type of related-party transaction naturally is closely connected with misrepresentation, as it cannot be properly disclosed to the general public. However, more commonly cases relating to 'tunnelling activities' do not involve appropriating a listed SOE's asset for personal benefit. As already highlighted, parent SOEs contribute their best-equipped facilities to subsidiaries in order to list them. However, maximizing profits is not the only demand made of an SOE by the government. The government usually expects SOEs to bring multiple benefits – for example stabilizing society by providing full employment, or providing strategic control of a particular industry where this cannot be achieved through proper regulation (Clarke 2006: 150). A parent SOE cannot fulfill all these tasks by itself. It may therefore sometimes need to strengthen other entities of the group by distributing the profits of its listed subsidiary between these entities. As some scholars point out "many SOEs are debt-ridden enterprises 'repackaged' for listing and continue to be controlled by their parent companies who having successfully seen to their IPO look towards them as cash cows for ready milking" (Tang and Wang 2007: 151). It seems that, in order to conceal improper profit distribution or corporate loans, misrepresentation to investors is inevitable.

For private listed companies, the horizontal agency problem is less complicated. Some leading Chinese entrepreneurs have shown a strong desire to expand their business empire by owning several listed companies and a number of other business entities. However, such a super-size business network does not always bring benefits and can, in fact, sometimes be a troublesome burden. According to statistics, from 2002 to 2005, the market regulator investigated nearly 40 corporate groups, relating to more than 200 listed companies. Most cases investigated involved illegal loans between members of a corporate group or undisclosed related party transactions (Cai 2005: 105). The main reason for these corporate scandals is that corporate groups are overloaded with a large number of business entities. Some corporate group owners have overestimated their capacity and recklessly became involved in several different business sectors. Business failure in one sector may easily trigger pressure from lenders or local government, which has granted a preference policy (e.g. a license authorizing a corporate group to use a certain kind of natural resource during a certain period). Therefore, related party transactions, illegal corporate guarantees, and false disclosure are usually employed to conceal the negative effects of business failure. In private listed companies, these manipulating strategies are employed in traditional tunnelling activities as well, which move companies' assets to majority shareholders' own pockets.

7.2.2 Public and private enforcement against misrepresentation in China

Both public enforcement and private enforcement can be applied in the context of regulating misrepresentation. In contrast, other types of misbehavior by market participants, such as manipulation of share price or insider trading, are mainly regulated by public authorities in China. Only a small number of private enforcement cases can be found (Zhou 2013). This is the main reason why this chapter takes misrepresentation to test these two enforcement strategies. The CSRC is the market regulator who takes charge of public enforcement in China's stock markets. In accordance with the Securities Law 2005,[6] the CSRC has an enforcement power against market participants. In accordance with Article 193, the CSRC is authorized to impose a fine on issuers and public companies, conducting misrepresentation (including disclosing misleading, false information or conducting a major omission in information disclosure). The range of this fine is between RMB300,000 (about EUR26,145) and RMB600,000 (about EUR72,289). The executives and any other person directly responsible for misrepresentation shall be given a warning and a fine ranging from RMB30,000 up to RMB300,000.

Private enforcement is the other key component of the enforcement strategy in controlling market participants' misrepresentation. During the period from 2002 to 2003, in order to ease the tension between aggrieved investors and State-owned listed companies, the Supreme Court issued a groundbreaking Notice[7] confirming that local intermediate courts are capable to hear securities litigations against misrepresentation. The Notice provided a workable legal regime for the private enforcement of securities law. In some respects, it was enacted in a plaintiff-friendly way. For example, it gives plaintiffs an autonomous position from which to choose which eligible parties they would like to sue. This means plaintiffs could pursue their interests by bringing litigation action against a 'deep pocket' defendant. Additionally, the provision applied a statute of limitations of two years to private securities litigations rather than the standard one-year special statute of limitations (Xi 2006: 495). Nonetheless, private enforcement is subject to administrative and criminal sanctions (public enforcement). In other words, aggrieved investors can only file a lawsuit against a party who has received an administrative fine from the CSRC or another administrative body like the Ministry of Finance on the basis of fraudulent disclosure, or parties convicted for misrepresentation by a court. The private enforcement regime has been integrated into the Securities Law 2005. However, the pre-trail condition is still not removed under the formal legislation.[8]

7.3   Research methodology

In order to collect empirical evidence, a fundamental question is how to evaluate public and private enforcement of securities law. Existing research provides several examples. The evaluation of law enforcement in stock markets can be divided into macro and micro levels. At the macro level, La Porta *et al.*'s research puts great emphasis on *disclosure requirements* and *liability rules*. Both of these are supposed to be essential elements that influence the enforcement of securities law. With respect to private enforcement, these scholars focus on the distribution of the *burden-of-proof* between plaintiff and defendant. With respect to public enforcement, they evaluate it by the following criteria: (i) supervisor's independence, (ii) investigative powers of the supervisor, (iii) administrative sanctions, (iv) criminal sanctions for violations of securities laws. These scholars build a positive relationship between enforcement of securities law, and stock market performance. Similar to their other research, the conclusion is that legal origin plays a major role in financial market development (La Porta *et al.* 2006: 1). Djankov *et al.* developed another formal index of public enforcement, based on whether the regulator can sanction a specified insider transaction via "(1) fine for the approving body; (2) jail sentences for the approving body; (3) fines for [principal wrongdoer]; and (4) jail sentence for the principal wrongdoer" (Djankov *et al.* 2008: 435). Another major contributor to this field, the World Bank, uses financial sector development indicators (FSDIs) to assess the institutional environment of financial markets. This research divides the institutional environment into three tiers. In the mid-tier level environment, it considers the investor environment. It is argued that private enforcement plays a more important role in prompting financial markets than public enforcement (World Bank 2006). In contrast, Jackson and Roe use a different index system to conduct similar research. In respect of public enforcement, they argue that evaluating enforcement ability by reviewing a regulator's power range is not a viable solution. The reason is that the regulator may be "captured", or due to other reasons, does not exercise its powers. These two scholars, in contrast, use two indicators to evaluate public enforcement, namely staffing levels of securities regulators and budgets. In respect of private enforcement, they use legal indices (a securities disclosure index, a liability index, and an anti-director rights index) and a judicial efficiency index to do their evaluation. Their conclusion is different from previous results. It finds that public enforcement rather than private enforcement is more important in correcting market failure in common law jurisdictions (Jackson and Roe 2009: 207).

However, as some lawyers argued, the results from these macro-level comparisons are not accurate. For example, authors may have ignored the functional equivalence rules in different jurisdictions during the comparison (Siems 2005: 531; Siems and Deakin, 2010: 120). Compared with these macro-level evaluations, a micro-level evaluation can generate more accurate results, although it may bear less theoretical implications. For example, some macro evaluations suggest that private enforcement plays a more active role in common law jurisdictions (La Porta *et al.* 2006: 1; Djankov *et al.* 2008: 435). However, comparative research by Armour *et al.* on private enforcement of securities law in the UK and the US shows that in the UK, private enforcement plays a limited role in enforcing securities law (Armour *et al.* 2009: 687; Armour 2010: 213).

This chapter constitutes a micro-level research project, focusing on the *ex post* enforcement of securities law. Although *ex ante* regulation is an important tool for the regulator to mitigate market failure, some research has indicated that extensive *ex ante* rule-making activities do not necessarily lead to extensive state involvement in rule enforcement. (Gadinis and Jackson 2007: 1239). As summarized by Coffee: "enforcement intensity seems inversely related to the intrusiveness of the government's *ex ante* involvement in the market. The closer the central government supervises *ex ante*, the less it relies on sanctions and penalties *ex post*" (Coffee 2007: 257). Given the complicated relationship between *ex ante* regulation and *ex post* enforcement, it is difficult to evaluate both mechanisms in one piece of research.

From a methodological perspective, this chapter employs several standards to evaluate the *ex post* enforcement strategies against misrepresentation. First, focus will be laid on the number of enforcement actions on misrepresentation under the Securities Law 2005 (from 2006 to 2012). This number can reflect the frequency of the enforcement actions against this particular misbehavior. Second, focus will be laid on the effect of the enforcement actions during the same period. For private enforcement, the total amount of compensation received by aggrieved shareholders from private litigation will be calculated. Further, the total amount of investors who received compensation through filing litigation before the People's Court will be calculated. For public enforcement, calculation of the total amount of administrative fines imposed by the administrative authority on the market participants based on misrepresentation will be given; also, the number of executives punished by the public regulatory body will be calculated.

7.4 Intensity of enforcement in controlling misrepresentation: rudimentary data

7.4.1 *Public enforcement*

7.4.1.1 *Search methodology*

First, I accessed all Administrative Punishment Decisions (Xingzheng Chufa Jueding, available online at http://www.csrc.gov.cn/pub/zjhpublic/ (accessed 4 June 2014)) in the CSRC's website database between 2006 and 2012. This generated 348 decisions, which I read to determine whether the decision could be included in my sample. Finally, 83 cases were found. Then, the following information was collected: (i) number of public enforcement actions in each year, (ii) amount of fine on public company, (iii) amount of fine on executives, and (iv) number of punished executives.[9]

7.4.1.2   Data

Table 7.2 Public enforcement of misrepresentation in China

Year	Number of punishments against misrepresentation	Punished executives	Fine on public companies (RMB)	Fine on executives (RMB)	Total administrative fine against misrepresentation (RMB)
2006	12	70	4,300,000	5,560,000	9,860,000
2007	11	60	3,800,000	3,200,000	7,000,000
2008	14	81	4,400,000	7,450,000	11,850,000
2009	10	70	2,800,000	3,540,000	6,340,000
2010	14	86	5,100,000	6,200,000	11,300,000
2011	9	71	3,800,000	6,250,000	10,050,000
2012	13	70	4,700,000	4,350,000	9,050,000

7.4.2   Private enforcement

7.4.2.1   Search methodology

The Chinese judiciary system does not provide an official database of judicial cases to the general public. Information about private enforcement is therefore mainly from second-hand material, such as news reports and journal articles.[10] The data has been collected by the following method: A keyword search was utilized, including the terms "company's name (company which has been punished by CSRC on the basis of misrepresentation)",[11] "misrepresentation" (*Xujia Chenshu*), and "private compensation" (*Minshi Peichang*) via Google Chinese website and Baidu (a Chinese search engine for websites, news, and journal articles). I found 38 cases from 2006 to 2012. All these cases are related to public punishment decisions on misrepresentation. One case is based on criminal punishment. Four cases are based on the punishment decisions issued by the Ministry of Finance. Of the cases, 33 are based on the CSRC's enforcement decisions. This means that about 39 percent of CSRC's public enforcement decisions are followed by private enforcement actions. This turnover rate is hardly impressive. Next, a summary was made of the following information on private enforcement during 2006 to 2012: (i) number of cases in each year, (ii) total compensation made by defendant to plaintiffs, and (iii) the number of plaintiffs.[12]

Nevertheless, some major omissions and inaccuracies still remain, even when a comprehensive search on the above data of each case has been made via the Internet and traditional media.[13] First, it is possible that some private litigation cases against misrepresentation were not captured by the data collection method used. This can be attributed to a lack of media attention given to cases where, e.g. the claimed compensation is minuscule, the number of plaintiffs is very small, or the media have been corrupted by the defendant. Second, the data collected might not always be complete in all cases. Particularly, this holds true when settlements between plaintiffs and defendants were reached due to confidentiality agreements underlying the settlements. The defendant sometimes requires the plaintiffs and their lawyers to sign a confidential agreement, which removes their right to disclose key information of the settlement to the general public. Third, while conducting cross-checks, ambiguity of data found in different sources may have contributed to the inaccuracy of the findings. Some cross-checks showed that different news reports told different figures. In cases of conflicting data in news reports the source with the higher reputation was given preference, e.g. newspapers or journals on securities markets were viewed as more reliable than Internet media. Another problem is that news reports and even some journal articles are not academic products: they widely used the terms including "approximately" (*Dayue*), "nearly" (*Jiangjin*), or "more than a certain number" (*Da yu mouyi shuzi*) in their description. As a result of the shortage of first-hand material, I keep these terms (which indicate the ambiguity of data) in this article. After having transparently addressed the problems encountered during data collection and evaluation, an objective presentation of the data is still viewed as viable based on the accessible materials. Yet, the data on the intensity of private enforcement might still be considered under-representative, considering the above-mentioned problems.

7.4.2.2 Data

Table 7.3 Private enforcement of misrepresentation in China

Year	Number of private enforcement cases against misrepresentation	Executives' compensation to investors	Number of compensated investors (approximate)	Total compensation made by public companies to investors (RMB, approximate)
2006	4	0	7	260,000
2007	7	0	250	189,452,337
2008	5	0	16	670,000
2009	7	0	294	23,855,224
2010	2	0	199	20,650,000
2011	5	0	6,842	45,389,265
2012	8	0	210	14,092,880

7.5 Implications

These sets of data provide a preliminary view on public and private enforcement. First, although the number of public enforcement cases is larger than the number of private enforcement cases, the conclusion can hardly be drawn that public enforcement is overwhelmingly advantageous for the enforcement of securities law, at least in misrepresentation cases (see Figure 7.1).

As mentioned, private enforcement against misrepresentation must be based on an administrative decision. Given that courts strictly apply this pretrail condition in each case, the number of private enforcement cases cannot exceed that of public enforcement cases. Furthermore, from a functional perspective, it seems that private enforcement is capable to fulfill its task, namely providing compensation to aggrieved shareholders (see Figure 7.2).

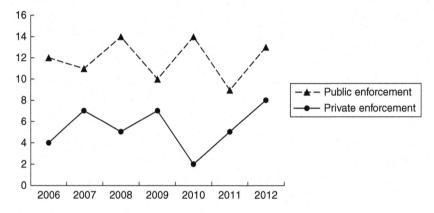

Figure 7.1 Frequency of public enforcement and private enforcement on the basis of misrepresentation 2006–12

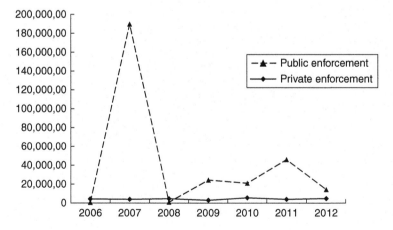

Figure 7.2 Economic burden on public companies on the basis of misrepresentation 2006–12

This function bears further implication. It seems that public and private enforcement can mitigate different levels of agency cost. The CSRC's *ex post* enforcement has considerable effect in controlling vertical agency costs between shareholders and executives. It consistently imposes fines on executives and even bans them from the market. From 2006 to 2012, 508 executives were punished by the CSRC in misrepresentation cases. The combined total fine on executives reached RMB36,550,000. In this respect, it has a considerable effect on reducing vertical agency costs. Nonetheless, public enforcement plays a less important role in punishing public companies and majority shareholders who are the major residual claimants. As already mentioned, the CSRC's power to impose fines on public companies is strictly controlled by the Securities Law 2005. Even when the CSRC imposes the maximum fine (RMB600,000) authorized by Article 193 of the Securities Law 2005 on public companies, this economic punishment hardly causes any substantial problem. The reason is the companies concerned are usually economically powerful. Private enforcement's major function is to offer compensation to aggrieved shareholders. For this purpose, it usually aims at the deep-pocket wrongdoer, i.e. public companies rather than their executives. Furthermore, compared with public enforcement, private enforcement damages are not capped at any limitation on the amount of compensation. The court can enforce any amount of justified compensation against public companies under the legal framework. Consequently, private enforcement imposes a much larger economic burden on public companies (see Figure 7.2). It also deeply influences majority shareholders' interest by reducing companies' distributable profits. It therefore can discourage majority shareholders to instruct their nominee director to engage in misrepresentation. It cures horizontal agency costs. It seems as if both public and private enforcement should be further enhanced under the current legal and institutional framework.

The second major finding from the empirical data is the diversification of location for the courts before which a securities litigation or securities litigations have been filed. In accordance with Article 9 of the Supreme Court's Note, private securities litigation should be filed before the local intermediate court located in the city in which the public company (defendant) is formally registered. The empirical data show that from 2006 to 2012, there were 17 local intermediate courts in different provinces in China fully engaged in hearing private securities litigations. More interestingly, nearly half of these courts only accepted one case, and no intermediate court accepted more than four cases during this period (see Table 7.4). Therefore, the geographical diversification of judiciary power leads to a lower intensity judiciary practice for each local court. Under these conditions, there is a major problem with this institutional arrangement. A long-standing argument casts doubt on the ability of judges to assess sophisticated market-oriented commercial activities or on their business judgment (Easterbrook and Fischel 1991: 98–9; Edward *et al.* 2001: 853). The diversification of location for these judiciary resources exacerbates the problem of a lack of expertise. It is hard to imagine that a local

Table 7.4 Chinese courts engaged in hearing securities litigation (2006–12)

Number of cases	Court location
4	City of Shanghai, Ningxia Province, Guangzhou Province, Zhejiang Province
3	Shangdong Province, City of Chongqing
2	Fujian Province, Henan Province, City of Beijing, Hubei Province
1	City of Tianjing, Hubei Province, Dongbei Province, Jiangsu Province, Shanxi Province, Yunan Province, Heinan Province, Sichuan Province

court, initially addressing complicated securities litigation, can successfully fulfill this task without struggling with the relevant law and evidence. The shortage of judicial expertise is therefore a potential problem that could lead to problematic and potentially unjust judicial decisions. Additionally, driving judges to contribute significant time and effort to learn the implications of complicated financial activities for only one particular case that emerges once every decade also wastes valuable local judicial resources. Furthermore, when the diversified allocation of judiciary resources is investigated using a comparative lens, it can be regarded as a disadvantage that weakens the role of private enforcement throughout entire institutional settings. Public enforcement by the CSRC, in contrast, is more centrally organized. Although the CSRC has some local branches, their enforcement power is strictly limited.[14] In other words, the power to impose substantial sanctions is accumulated in the hands of the CSRC's headquarters in Beijing. This hierarchical institutional arrangement enables the CSRC to enhance its relevant expertise through consistent enforcement activities. The local courts in widely diversified locations, although still under the loose control of the Supreme Court, have few opportunities to practice and upgrade their expertise in this particular field as compared with the CSRC. Therefore, the gap of expertise between the CSRC and the court system is compounded by an inefficient institutional structure. Under these conditions, a better arrangement would be to assign all private securities litigation cases to the Intermediate Courts in the cities of Shanghai and Shenzhen. The primary reason for this arrangement is not only that the judges in more economically developed regions appear to have more sophisticated expertise in commercial activities (Xu *et al.* 2013), but also that these courts have an obvious advantage in collecting relevant evidence for securities law cases, as they are located in the same cities as the stock exchanges.

After the comparison between public enforcement and private enforcement in China, this section compares the intensity of private enforcement between China and the US.[15] From this comparison, one can analyze whether private enforcement in China is far less intensive, as many assumed. In the US, there were 742 private litigation cases based on class actions involving companies listed at the New York Stock Exchange (NYSE) and

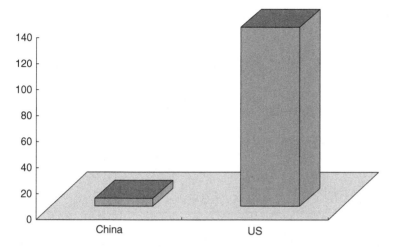

Figure 7.3 Private enforcement actions in China and the US (annual average 2008–12)

(Source: US data: Available online at: http://securities.stanford.edu/ (accessed 14 May 2014).)

the National Association of Securities Dealers Automated Quotations (NASDAQ) from 2008 to 2012.[16] In other words, on average 148 class action cases are heard by the Federal and State courts per year. According to statistics presented by Cornerstone Research, the percentage of misrepresentation cases reaches 92.8 on average in all class action cases within these five years.[17] Consequently, the average figure of misrepresentation cases within these five years is 137. In contrast, from 2008 to 2012 China's two stock exchanges, on average 5.4 cases were heard by the Chinese courts per year. These figures are not surprising. Private enforcement is far more intensive and frequent in the US than in China (see Figure 7.3). However, we should note that this outcome would be somewhat different, if one investigates it from a different perspective. A simple fact is that the market capitalization of NYSE and NASDAQ is about five times larger than that of China's two capital markets.[18] Accordingly, if one looks at the average score per trillion capitalizations, the advantage of the US private enforcement drops considerably (see Figure 7.4). In contrast, if one looks at the average score per thousand listed companies, the overwhelming superiority of the US will emerge again (see Figure 7.5).

Through the comparison of different aspects, a huge gap of private enforcement intensity between China and the US can be identified. This gap can be attributed to the considerable institutional differences. In China, the absence of class actions and lawyers' contingency fees in addition to the strict pre-trail condition diminishes the chance for the development of private enforcement. Despite these institutional disadvantages, a deeper difference related

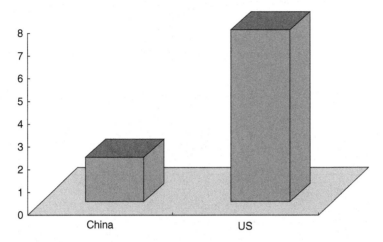

Figure 7.4 Private enforcement actions per trillion stock market capitalizations in China and the US (annual average 2008–12)

(Source: US data: Available online at: http://securities.stanford.edu/ (accessed 14 May 2014).)

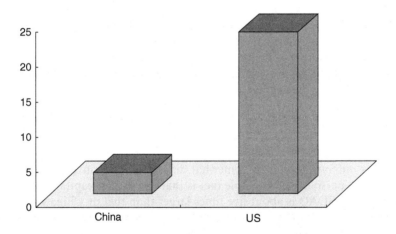

Figure 7.5 Private enforcement actions per thousand listed companies in China and the US (annual average 2008–12)

(Source: US data: Available online at: http://securities.stanford.edu/ (accessed 14 May 2014).)

to judiciary transparency and the media environment should not be ignored. Puchniak and Nakahigashi's recent research uses the concept of 'availability heuristic' to explain the dramatic increase of derivative actions in Japan. They first summarized that:

One of the most common mental heuristics that actors rely on when faced with complex decisions is the 'availability heuristic'. According to cognitive research, the availability heuristic commonly causes actors to overestimate the relevance of salient, or memorable events. Instead of making their decisions based on the actual probability of an event occurring, they base their decisions upon the probability of the event occurring according to their memory. Such a mental shortcut can often lead to sub-optimal decisions, as events that are vivid or well publicized leave the actor with the impression that the event is more likely to occur than actual statistical probability would suggest.

(Puchniak and Nakahigashi 2012: 59)

These authors then provide some solid evidence to illustrate that media hype is effective in triggering the 'availability heuristic' of market participants. Many over-optimistic, misguiding news reports and the enormous academic fervor surrounding one or two landmark judiciary decisions can lead to the "overconfidence bias problem": market participants take a simplified decision-making strategy (commonly referred to as 'mental heuristics'[19]) without carefully weighing the costs and benefits, when filing a derivative action (Puchniak and Nakahigashi 2012: 59–61).

This behavioral law and economics theory also offers an explanation to China's shortage of private enforcement. In China, the media environment of legal or financial affairs is opposite to that of Japan. In the process of searching for private enforcement cases, a considerable phenomenon cannot be ignored. News reports usually use passive terms, such as "time-consuming" (*Shijian Rongchang*), "beset with difficulties" (*Kunnan Chongchong*), and "deadlock litigation" (*Susong Kunjing*) to describe private enforcement of securities law.[20] These news reports may constitute an availability heuristic oriented by a negative impression of private enforcement among investors. Furthermore, despite a few landmark cases, financial news reports are reluctant to disclose substantial information on private enforcement, especially the total amount of compensation paid by the public company to investors and the number of investors who successfully obtained compensation. In many cases, they merely inform the public that a specified case has been filed before a court, but they do not follow up on the progress of a case in trial stage. Accurate data related to these topics are difficult to identify and obtain. Although some securities lawyers occasionally disclose this information on their personal websites, no non-governmental organization (NGO) or educational institution collects and discloses the relevant data to the general public systemically.

In respect of the passive terms and descriptions of the news reports, one explanation is that by this method, financial media try to force policymakers to improve the current institutional regime of private enforcement, e.g. through eliminating the pre-trail condition and formulating a workable class action system. However, it is difficult to explain the shortage of news reports that disclose key information on private litigation. There may be a shortage because the accessibility of the judiciary decision is limited even for the media, or maybe because the media are captured by listed companies. No matter what the reason is, the media environment in fact discourages investors' attempts to pursue private litigation by formulating a general impression that private action of securities law in China is troublesome, time-consuming, and unpredictable. In contrast, the transparency and accessibility of judiciary data is far more sophisticated in the US. Educational institutions and consulting companies take advantage of their expertise, academic and market resources to collect accurate information about securities class actions.[21] These entities also provide professional and scientific analyses of the relevant data. This trajectory enables individual investors to overcome the availability heuristic, and to rationally evaluate the costs and benefits of class action. Consequently, improving private enforcement is not only a task aimed at reforming the institutional setting, but also a task aimed at fostering a wide-range of market forces.

7.6   Conclusion

This chapter resulted in three key findings about public enforcement and private enforcement of securities law in China. First, based on empirical evidence, public enforcement and private enforcement of securities law serve different functions. The former cures vertical agency costs and the latter cures horizontal agency costs. Both public and private enforcement strategies should be further promoted. Consequently, even in a transitional economy such as China, private enforcement should not be regarded as a trivial instrument for controlling securities market problems. Although these findings are not powerful enough to provide theoretical feedback on the 'private versus public enforcement' debate between La Porta *et al.* and Jackson and Roe, it still provides an important insight for understanding enforcement strategies in China. Second, the inefficiency of private enforcement in China can be partly attributed to the diversified allocation of judiciary resources, which exacerbates the courts' disadvantage stemming from a lack of expertise, especially compared with the centrally organized public regulator. Third, the comparison between private enforcement in China and the US proves once more the standard argument on China's private enforcement of securities law. It illustrates that private enforcement in China is under-developed. Providing more investor-friendly legal institutions is an important step in order to improve private enforcement. However, as Clarke has already pointed out, civil society institutions are also important for China's corporate governance and securities law enforcement (Clarke 2008). As a result, fostering a more balanced financial media environment and enhancing the accessibility of data on judiciary decisions is equally important in prompting private enforcement in China.

Notes

1 I am grateful to Prof. Michael Faure, Prof. Guangdong Xu, Prof. Mathias Siems and Prof. Niels Philipsen for their insightful comments. This research is supported by the Program for Young Innovative Research Team, and Young Lecturer's Supporting Program at the China University of Political Science and Law (CUPL).

2 Zuigao Renmin Fayuan Guanyu Shouli Zhengquan Shichang Yin Sujia Chengshu Yinfa De Minshi Qinquan Jiufen Anjian Youguan Wenti De Tongzhi (The Notice on Relevant Issues Concerning Accepting Civil Tort Dispute Cases Caused by Misrepresentation on Securities and Several Provisions on Hearing Civil Compensation Caused by Misrepresentation on the Securities Markets) issued by China's Supreme Court on 15 January 2002, Article 17, which states that misrepresentation involves the market participating in a breach of "relevant law and regulation during their IPO or securities transactions in the secondary market by disclosing false information, misleading information, omitting material information, or not appropriately disclosing information."

3 A report made by the State-owned Asset Supervision and Administration Commission, for details see 'Gouyou Konggu Shangshi Gongsi Zhan A Gu Zongshizhi 51.4%' (Listed SOEs occupied 51.4 percent of Market Capitalization) Yicai Network, full text available at: http://www.yicai.com/news/2013/01/2404678. html (accessed 17 May 2014).

4 According to Articles 7 and 10 of Interim Measures for the Supervision and Administration of State-Owned Assets of the Enterprises, the business decision should be independent from the administrative influence and a clear separation between ownership and control should be established. It means in principle that the governmental agencies will adopt a 'hands-off' approach on the daily business of the State-owned corporations, and all State-owned corporations should make the "management decision by their own and take full responsibility for their profits and losses", e.g. see Shipani and Liu (2002).

5 See Shanghai Zhengquan Jiaoyi Suo (Shanghai Stock Exchange),'Guanyu Dui Shanghai Lengguang Shiye Gufen Youxian Gongsi Gongkai Qianze de Gonggao' (Notice on Public Criticism on Shanghai Lengguang Shiye plc) 11 June 1999, available at: http://static.sse.com.cn/sseportal/ps/zhs/ (accessed 29 May 2014) Shenzhen Zhengquan Jiaoyi Suo (SZSE), 'Guanyu dui Beijing Zhongguancun Keji Fazhan (Konggu) Gufen Youxian Gongsi Yuyi Gongkai Qianze de Gonggao' (Notice on Public Criticism on Beijing Zhongguancun Keji Fazhan plc) 28 September 2001. Available online at: http://www.szse.cn/ (accessed 17 May 2014); see also (Jiang *et al.* 2005).

6 China first passed a Securities Law in 1998. See Zhonghua Renmin Gongheguo Zhengquan Fa (Securities Law of the People's Republic of China), adopted by the Ninth Session of the Standing Committee of the Sixth National People's Congress, 29 December 1998, effective 1 July 1999 (hereinafter, Securities Law 1999). The Securities Law of People's Public of China 2005, (Zhonghua Renmin Gongheguo Zhengquanfa 2005) was adopted by the 18th Meeting of the Standing Committee of Tenth National People's Congress, 27 October 2005, effective 1 January 2006 (hereinafter, Securities Law 2005).

7 See *supra* note 2.

8 Article 69 of the Securities Law 2005 states: "Where the prospectus ... issuing corporate bonds, financial statement, listing report, annual report, midterm report, temporary report or any information as disclosed that has been announced by an issuer or a listed company has any false record, misleading statement or major omission, and thus incurs losses to investors in the process of securities trading, the issuer or the listed company shall be subject to the liabilities of compensation."

9 From a methodological perspective, 'data transparency' is essential in numerical comparative law. For this point, see Siems (2005). In order to enhance data transparency, a file including more detailed empirical information of both private and public enforcement has been uploaded on the Internet. Available online at: http://pan.baidu.com/s/1ottA3 (accessed 17 May 2014). The updated file provides more detailed information, including: (i) each case's docket number, (ii) the company's name, (iii) quantity of the punishment on public company in each case, and (iv) quantity of punishment on each executive in each case.

10 Alternative approaches that provide first-hand materials were sought. While using the largest case law system organized by Peking University, i.e. the *Beida Fabao* system, unfortunately, only two cases about private enforcement against misrepresentation were found. One is the *Daqing Lianyi* case, the other is the *Huawen Keji* case.

11 As mentioned above, there is a pre-trial condition stating that shareholders can only sue a public company after an administrative or criminal party is punished by the regulatory authorities, or a court verdict has been administered. Therefore, searching for the name of companies which have been punished by the CSRC using terms such as "misrepresentation" *(Xujia Chenshu)* and "private compensation" (*Minshi Peichang*) on the Internet is a reasonable, and maybe the only, method to search for these types of cases.

12 The uploaded file provides more detailed information, including: (i) the name of the defendant (a public company) in each case, (ii) the public enforcement basis of the litigation, (iii) the result of each case (settlement, claim upheld, or claim dismissed), (iv) the quantity of compensation made by public company in each case (if applicable), (v) the quantity of investors who get the compensation in each case (if applicable), (vi) the location of the court which hears the litigation, and (vii) the source of the information.

13 Many lawyers find that the accessibility of judiciary data is quite limited in China, e.g. see Clarke (1996: 201). However, something we should bear in mind is that this kind of inaccuracy of data is not a 'Chinese problem'. Instead, it usually occurs in empirical research on enforcement actions at a micro level. Even in a jurisdiction with a much higher level of administrative and judiciary transparency, this kind of research still suffers from the problems of 'under-representation of data' and 'incompleteness of data'. Sometimes, estimated data based on the accessible materials is inevitable, e.g. see Armour (2010; see Table 4 and Table 6 in the article) and also see Armour *et al.* (2009: 608 and 705).

14 Up to 2013, the CSRC only granted limited law enforcement powers to three branches, located in Shanghai, Guangdong, and Shenzhen. The CSRC reserves its power to review the enforcement by these local authorities in order to prevent the problem of 'local protectionism'. For relevant information, see a report by Founder Securities, available at: http://www.foundersc.com/zqyw/13/10/12/5K26403574FS.shtml (accessed 17 May 2014).

15 For public enforcement in China and the US, a similar comparative research has been done; see Huang (2010a).

16 Source: Stanford Law School Securities Class Action Cleaning House, in cooperation with Cornerstone Research, available at: http://securities.stanford.edu/index.html (accessed 17 May 2014).

17 See Cornerstone Research (2012: 6), available at: http://securities.stanford.edu/clearinghouse_research.html (accessed 17 May 2014).

18 There are about 2,800 listed companies, with a global market capitalization of about US$18 trillion in NYSE (data from NYSE's website). There are about listed 3,700 companies, with market capitalization of about US$1.9 trillion in NASDAQ (data from NASDAQ website). As of the end of January 2013, the capitalization

of China's two capital markets was US$4.1 trillion. The total number of listed companies is 2,443. (See *supra* note 2.)

19 Although simplified decision-making strategies may result in sub-optimal decisions, they are commonly used because actors lack the time, cognitive ability, or information to conduct a more thorough analysis (i.e. the actors have a 'bounded rationality'). See Puchniak and Nakahigashi (2012: 59–61).

20 For some examples of the new reports that use passive descriptions, see 'Hangxiao Ganggou An Dui Gumin Fayuan Doushi Xinketi' (Hangxiao Ganggou Case: A New Lesson for Investors and Court), *Xinhua Meiri Dianxun* (Xinhua Daily Telegraph), full text available at: http://news.xinhuanet.com/mrdx/2007–11/27/content_7154961.htm, (accessed 17 May 2014). 'Gumin Weiquan Lajuzhan', (Seesaw Battle of Investors' Protection) *Chutian Dushi Bao* (*Chutian City News*) second edn, September 2010. 'Minshi Susong Lianbai Gumin Weiquan Jubu Weijian' (A Series of Private Litigation Loss: Protecting Investors' Right is Beset with Difficulties) 21CN Caijing (21cn Finance), full text available at: http://finance.21cn.com/newsdoc/zx/a/2013/0713/03/22747421.shtml (accessed 17 May 2014) and also see Yang Yanyan, 'Quanti Anjian de Susong Xingshi jiqi Jiazhi Quxiang' (Group Litigation: Practical Form and Value Orientation) 2011(5) Qinghua Faxue (*Tsinghua Law Journal*) 167–76. This article elaborately records how Chinese lawyers and media negatively appraise securities litigation cases in which investors get their compensation successfully.

21 See e.g. Stanford Law School Securities Class Action Cleaning House in cooperation with Cornerstone Research, and RAND Corporation, a report about public and private enforcement in the US, available at: http://www.rand.org/pubs/rgs_dissertations/RGSD224.html (accessed 17 May 2014).

References

Armour, J. (2010) 'Enforcement Strategies in UK Corporate Governance: A Roadmap and Empirical Assessment', in Pacces, A. (ed), *The Law and Economics of Corporate Governance: Changing Perspectives*, Chelthenham, UK: Edward Elgar Publishing, 213–59.

Armour, J., Black, B., Cheffins, B. and Nolan, R. (2009) 'Private Enforcement of Corporate Law: An Empirical Comparison of the United Kingdom and the United States', *Journal of Empirical Legal Studies*, 13, 687–722.

Cai, R. (2005) 'You ShangshiGongsiZaoxiYundongYinfa De Sikao (Some Thoughts Concerning Listed Company's Profit Making System)', *Shenyang NongyeDaxueXuebao, Journal of Shenyang Agricultural University*, 2, 98–101.

Cheffins, B. (1999) 'Current Trends in Corporate Governance: Going from London to Milan via Toronto', *Duke Journal of Comparative and International Law*, 10, 5–42.

Cheffins, B. (2000) 'Minority Shareholder and Corporate Governance', *Company Lawyer*, 21(2), 41–2.

Clarke, D. (1996) 'Methodologies for Research in Chinese Law', *University of British Columbia Law Review*, 30, 201–9.

Clarke, D. (2006) 'The Independent Director in Chinese Corporate Governance', *Delaware Journal of Corporate Law*, 31, 125–228.

Clarke, D. (2008) 'The Ecology of Corporate Governance in China', *GWU Legal Studies Research Paper, no. 433*. Available at: http://ssrn.com/abstract=1245803 (accessed 20 February 2013).

Coffee, J. (2007) 'Law and the Market: The Impact of Enforcement', *University of Pennsylvania Law Review*, 156, 229–308.

Cornerstone Research (2012), '2012 Securities Class Action Filings: A Year In Review'. Available at: http://securities.stanford.edu/clearinghouse_research.html (accessed 17 May 2014).

Djankov, S., La Porta, R., Lopez–de–Silanes, F., Shleifer, A. (2008), 'The Law and Economics of Self–dealing', *Journal of Financial Economics*, 88, 430–65.

Easterbrook, H., and Fischel, D. (1991) *The Economic Structure of Corporate Law*, Cambridge, MA: Harvard University Press.

Edward, G., Johnson, S. and Shleifer, A. (2001) 'Coase v. Coasians', *Quarterly Journal of Economics*, 116, 853–99.

Gadinis, S. and Jackson, H. (2007) 'Markets As Regulators: A Survey', *Southern California Law Review*, 80, 1239–1382.

Howson, N. (2008) 'Article 148 of China's 2005 Company Law: Precocious Convergence in the Chinese Court', in B. S. Wang (ed), *Shi JianZhong De GongsiFa (Company Law in Practice)*, ZhongguoShehuiKexueChuban She (China Social Science Academic Press), 186–99.

Huang, X. (2010a) 'In Defence of China's Public Enforcement in Equity Market', *International Company and Commercial Law Review*, 21(10), 327–37.

Huang, X. (2010b) 'Modernizing the Chinese Capital Market: Old Problems and New Legal Response', *International Company and Commercial Law Review*, 21(1), 26–39.

Jackson, H. and Roe, M. (2009) 'Public and Private Enforcement of Securities Laws: Resource-Based Evidence', *Journal of Financial Economics*, 93, 207–38.

Jiang, G. H., Lee, C. M. and Yue, H. (2005) 'Tunneling in China: The Surprisingly Pervasive Use of Corporate Loan to Extract Funds from Chinese Listed Companies', *Johnson School Research Paper Series* 31–06. Available at: http://papers.ssrn.com/sol3/papers.cfm?abstract_id=861445 (accessed 17 May 2014).

La Porta, R., Lopez-De-Silanes, F., Shleifer, A. and Vishny, R. (1999) 'Corporate Ownership around the World', *Journal of Finance*, 54, 417–516.

La Porta, R., Lopez-de-Silanes, F., Shleifer, A. (2006) 'What Works in Securities Laws?', *Journal of Finance*, 61, 1–32.

Layton, M. (2008) 'Is Private Securities Litigation Essential for the Development of China's Stock Market', *New York University Law Review*, 83, 1948–78.

Liebman, B. and Milhaupt, C. (2008) 'Reputational Sanction in China's Security Market', *Columbia Law Review*, 108, 929–83.

Liu, J. Q. (2006) 'Corporate Governance in China: From the Protection of Minority Shareholders Perspective', *Corporate Governance Law Review*, 2, 311–41.

Miles, L. and He, M. (2005) 'Protecting the Rights and Interests of Minorities Shareholders in Listed Companies in China: Challenge for the Future', *International Company and Commercial Law Review*, 16, 275–90.

Opper, S. and Schwaag-Serger, S. (2008) 'Institutional Analysis of Legal Change: The Case of Corporate Governance in China', *Journal of Law and Policy*, 26, 245–69.

Puchniak, D. and Nakahigashi, M. (2012) 'Japan's Love for Derivative Actions: Irrational Behaviour and Non-Economic Motives as Rational Explanations for Shareholder Litigation', *Vanderbilt Journal of Transnational Law*, 45, 1–82.

Rose, A. (2008) 'Reforming Securities Litigation Reform: Restructuring the Relationship Between Public and Private Enforcement of the Rule 10B-5', *Columbia Law Review*, 80, 1301–64.

Shim, S. (2005) 'Corporate Governance Reform in China', *Company Lawyer*, 57, 375–78.

Shipani C. and Liu, J. H. (2002) 'Corporate Governance in China, Then and Now', *Columbia Business Law Review*, 2000, 1–69.

Siems, M. (2005) 'Numerical Comparative Law: Do We Need Statistical Evidence in Law in Order to Reduce Complexity', *Cardozo Journal of International and Comparative Law*, 13, 521–40.

Siems, M and Deakin, S. (2010) 'Comparative Law and Finance: Past, Present and Future Research', *Journal of Institutional and Theoretical Economics*, 166, 120–40.

Tang, L. H. and Wang, J. W. (2007) 'Modeling an Effective Corporate Governance System for China's Listed State-Owned Enterprises: Issues and Challenges in a Transitional Economy', *Journal of Corporate Law Studies*, 7, 143–83.

World Bank (2006), Institutional foundations for financial markets. Available at http://siteresources.worldbank.org/inttopaccfinser/Resources/Institutional.pdf.

Xi, C. (2005) 'Transforming Chinese Enterprise: Ideology, Efficiency and Instrumentalism in the Process of Reform', in Gillespie, J. and Nicholson, P. (eds), *Asian Socialism A Legal Change*, Australian National University Press, 91–114.

Xi, C. (2006) 'Case Note: Private Enforcement of Securities Law in China: DaqingLianyi co v. ZHONG Weida and Others HeiLongjiang High Court', *Journal of Comparative Law*, 2, 492–96.

Xu, C. G. and Pistor, K. (2005) 'Governing Stock Markets in Transition Economies: Lessons from China', *American Law and Economics Review*, vol. 184–210.

Xu, D. L., Zhao, G. D. and Li, G. H. (2007) 'GuoyouGongsiZhili Moshi De Yanjiu' (The Study on the Corporate Governance Mode for State-owned Enterprise), *JingjiPinglun* (*The Review of Economy*), 4, 93–7.

Xu, G. D., Zhou, T. S., Shi, J. and Zeng, B. (2013) 'Fiduciary Duties in China', *European Business Organization Law Review*, 14, 57–95.

Yang, J. Z. (2005) 'Comparative Corporate Governance: Reforming Chinese Corporate Governance', *International Company and Commercial Law Review*, 16, 8–17.

Zhang, H. and Wu, Z. D. (2003) 'WoguoShangshiGongsiZijinZhanyong de Xianzhuan Ji TezhengYanjiu' (*The Characteristics of Appropriation of Public Companies' assets in China*), ShangshiGongsi (*Journal of Public Companies*), 5, 17–26

Zhou, T. S. (2013) 'Legal Regulation of China's Securities Markets: Recent Improvements and Competing Advantages', in Faure, M. and Xu, G. D. (eds), *Economics and Regulation in China*, Routledge, 64–84.

8 Monitoring shadow banking

The case of China

Wenjing Li

8.1 Introduction

Since the financial crisis hit the US in 2007, the term 'shadow banking' has been mentioned repeatedly in newspapers, TV and Internet media, as it is regarded as one of the major reasons for the crisis.[1] It is commonly believed that the collapse of major broker-dealers such as Bear Stearns and Lehman Brothers severely damaged the entire financial system and posed a systemic risk to it (Bernanke 2009, 2010, 2012). Although most countries now have established a rigid oversight on the traditional banking system, the monitoring and regulation of the shadow banking system is still rather weak. The behavior and risks in which Lehman Brothers were involved have been ignored or underestimated for a long time, but these risks existing in the so-called shadow banking system triggered the crisis and damaged the whole financial system.

The shadow banking system comprises a very important element of the worldwide financial system, and monitoring the shadow banking system became a pressing need on the international agenda after the crisis. The Financial Stability Board (FSB) has been extremely concerned about the shadow banking systems in different countries and issued annual reports on this issue starting from 2011.[2] Furthermore, some countries like the US and international organizations like the FSB put in place several important regulations and institutions in order to coordinate and protect the financial system – especially from the risks caused by shadow banking.[3]

One remarkable trend is that the shadow banking system expanded more rapidly in emerging countries, and it also played a very important role in the financial system of China. According to the FSB, the shadow banking system expanded many times over the last decades (FSB 2012). This holds particularly true in China, since the Chinese government adopted a package of stimulus policy measures in order to alleviate the impact of the worldwide financial crisis in 2009. A huge sum of liquidity was created and flowed into the Chinese financial market in 2009. A considerable proportion of this liquidity flowed into the shadow banking system. Now more and more scholars are concerned about the risks the shadow banking system in China poses;

some scholars even suspect that Chinese shadow banking may result in a next subprime crisis (Zhang 2013).

This chapter aims to analyze the Chinese shadow banking system and compare it with other countries. The chapter is divided into six sections: Section 8.2 defines and illustrates the shadow banking system; Section 8.3 analyzes the shadow banking system and considers whether it should be regulated; Section 8.4 describes shadow banking in China; Section 8.5 deals with how to monitor such a system; and Section 8.6 concludes.

8.2   What is shadow banking?

8.2.1   Definition

"While the term 'shadow banking' is used widely in the news media and in policy discussions, there is as yet no clear commonly-agreed definition" (FSB 2012). In fact, it is commonly regarded that this term was introduced by Paul McCulley in 2007 and many scholars and organizations tried to define it later, especially after the financial crisis.[4] Below, several popular and influential definitions about this term are discussed.

As mentioned above, Paul McCulley first referred to it as: "non-banking investment conduits, vehicles, and structures."[5] According to his definition, shadow banking is distinct from the traditional banking system. However, there are various 'non-banking financial institutions', such as securities, trusts and insurers, that provide different financial services as well. Thus, it is not so clear whether we should regard all such non-banking financial institutions as shadow banking.

The Federal Reserve economist Zoltan Pozsar regarded shadow banking as "financial intermediaries that conduct maturity, credit and liquidity transformation without explicit access to central bank liquidity or public sector credit guarantees" (Pozsar *et al.* 2010, revised in 2012: 1). According to Pozsar, such intermediaries include "finance companies, asset-backed commercial paper (ABCP) conduits, structured investment vehicles (SIVs), credit hedge funds, money mutual funds, securities lenders, limited-purpose finance companies (LPFCs) and government-sponsored enterprises (GSEs)" (Pozsar *et al.* 2010, revised in 2012: 1). Moreover, the shadow banking system has three sub-systems, namely the government-sponsored shadow banking sub-system, the 'internal' shadow banking sub-system and the 'external' shadow banking sub-system. The government-sponsored shadow banking sub-system refers to credit intermediation activities funded through the sale of agency debt and mortgage-backed securities (MBS), which mainly includes conforming residential, and commercial mortgages such as Fannie Mae and Freddie Mac in the US. The 'internal' shadow banking subsystem refers to the credit intermediation process of a global network of banks, finance companies, broker-dealers and asset managers and their on- and off-balance sheet activities – all under the umbrella of the financial holding companies. The 'internal' shadow banking sub-system is extremely active and important in China, which will be explored in the third section of this chapter. Finally, the 'external' shadow banking sub-system refers to the credit intermediation process of diversified broker-dealers and to a global network of independent, non-bank financial specialists that include captive and standalone finance companies, limited purpose finance companies and asset managers. The 'external' sub-system seems to be quite important in the US, as famous broker-dealers, such as Lehman Brothers and Bear Stearns triggered the financial crisis in 2007. In his report, Pozsar also pointed out that those intermediaries could be regarded as part of the market-based financial system, as on the one hand they can increase the efficiency of credit intermediation by providing credit transformation, maturity transformation and liquidity transformation; on the other hand, since they are under-regulated, less transparent and interconnected with the traditional banking system, they could be a vital factor in triggering the systemic risk to the whole financial system (Pozsar *et al.* 2010, revised in 2012).

Gorton *et al.* also devoted a very important paper to this topic. In their paper the authors pointed out that the shadow banking system "performs the same functions as traditional banking, but the names of the players are different and the regulatory structure is light or nonexistent" (Gorton *et al.* 2010: 261). Gorton *et al.* documented the rise of shadow banking and analyzed the advantages of such a system. Moreover, they found that, like the safe harbor rule in US bankruptcy law, some institutions provided incentives for the rise of the shadow banking system. Finally, they proposed some future regulatory regimes for the shadow banking system. Concretely, they proposed the use of insurance for money market mutual funds (MMMFs), combined with strict guidelines on collateral for both securitization and repurchase agreements (repos), with regulatory control established by chartering new forms of narrow banks for MMMFs and securitization, and using the bankruptcy safe harbor to incentivize the compliance on repos. However, Shleifer expressed his suspicion of whether the proposal of narrow banks for MMMFs and securitization could be practical or not (Gorton *et al.* 2010).[6]

As the governor of the Federal Reserve, Bernanke also held several important speeches regarding the issue of shadow banking. Bernanke argued that shadow banking, as usually defined, comprises a diverse set of institutions and markets that, collectively, carry out traditional banking functions – but do so outside, or in ways only loosely linked to, the traditional system of regulated depository institutions (Bernanke 2012: 3).

Schwarcz also observed the emergence of shadow banking, and pointed out that shadow banking means: "not only the provision of financial products and services by shadow banks, but also the financial markets used to provide those products and services" (Schwarcz 2012: 622). Furthermore, Schwarcz expressed his interests in the rapidly developing shadow banking in China.

The FSB is now extremely concerned about the monitoring of shadow banking. Since 2011, it regularly issues annual reports on shadow banking in different jurisdictions. The FSB described the shadow banking system as credit intermediation involving entities and activities outside the regular banking system (FSB 2011, 2012 and 2013).

Although the term has been defined differently by various scholars and organizations there appear to be some common facts in their definitions. From the above-mentioned definitions it can be concluded that shadow banking encompasses (i) providing credit intermediation (which was regarded as the function of traditional banks), (ii) via non-traditional banks. Such a system includes several intermediaries, e.g. MMMFs, repos, asset-backed securities (ABSs), collateralized debt obligations (CDOs) and ABCPs. Moreover, it is commonly agreed that the regulation of such systems is still quite weak.[7]

However, the above-mentioned definitions still beg the question whether the term 'non-banking' needs to be interpreted in relation to non-banking *entities* or non-banking *activities*.

Pursuant to Schwarcz, the term "shadow banking" should be defined broadly. It should include not only the provision of financial products and services by shadow banking, but also the financial markets used to provide those products and services (Schwarcz 2012), since only a broader definition will be flexible enough to encompass the inevitable evolution of financial products and services over time. Therefore, he proposed to use the term 'shadow banks' to refer to the entities but to use the term 'shadow banking' in relation to both entities *and activities*. The term shadow banking should be understood in a broader way, because traditional banks can also provide wealth management and securitization services to their clients.[8] Accordingly, this is also classified as an 'internal' shadow banking sub-system by Pozsar (Pozsar *et al.* 2010, revised in 2012). In Section 8.4 I will explain that the traditional banking system now plays a vital role in providing shadow banking services in China.

8.2.2 *A snapshot of shadow banking*

The shadow banking system emerged in the late 1960s in the US due to the interest-rate ceilings on demand deposits provided by Regulation Q and has expanded dramatically in the past decades.[9] It is commonly agreed upon that the development of the shadow banking system could be regarded as a market-based evolution of the financial system along with private innovation and regulatory changes (Gorton *et al.* 2010; Pozsar *et al.* 2010, revised in 2012). After the emergence and expansion of the shadow banking system, more and more pressure to its competitors, the commercial banks, was created. Thus, the traditional banks went into decline, when shadow banking emerged (Gorton *et al.* 2010).

The FSB has issued data and reports regarding shadow banking annually since 2011. According to its reports, the other financial intermediaries (OFIs[10]) grew rapidly before the crisis, rising from US$26 trillion in 2002 to

US$62 trillion in 2007, then declined slightly in 2008 but increased subsequently to reach US$67 trillion in 2011, equivalent to 111 per cent of the aggregated gross domestic product (GDP) of all jurisdictions (*FSB Report 2012*). In 2012, non-bank financial intermediation grew by US$5 trillion and reached US$71 trillion. It represents on average about 24 per cent of total financial assets, about half of the banking system assets, and 117 per cent of the GDP (*FSB Report 2013* 2013). The *FSB Reports 2012–13* also presented several interesting facts about the worldwide shadow banking system.

First, the advanced economies still own the largest non-bank financial systems: the US has the largest shadow banking system, with assets of US$23 trillion in 2011, followed by the Euro area (US$22 trillion) and the UK (US$9 trillion).

Second, the growth of OFIs in the whole world (8.1 per cent) was considerably higher than GDP growth. Furthermore, the developments in emerging countries are quite remarkable (around 20 per cent), while OFIs grew most in China in 2012 (42 per cent). However, even though the growth rate is quite remarkable, the scale of OFIs is still smaller in the emerging economies. Furthermore, the shadow banking system must contribute to a financial deepening in these jurisdictions, especially when the financial repression in these jurisdictions is considered. Therefore, the FSB is quite cautious to monitor whether there is any increase in risk factors that may be caused by maturity transformation or leverage due to the rapid expansion of credits provided by shadow banking.

Third, the *FSB Report 2013* (2013) showed that the most rapid growth in 2012 was in real estate investment trusts (REITs) and funds (30 per cent). This trend also holds true in China. Because of the housing price boom, the Chinese government adopted harsh restrictions to limit loans from banks to developers. However, REITs became a vital channel for developers to collect funds from the market. Considering that the housing prices increased dramatically in China over last year, the Chinese government is seeking to provide more restrictions on REITs in order to alleviate the oversupply of liquidity into housing market and the price bubbles.

Summarizing the above, in a broad way, shadow banking could be regarded as credit intermediation provided by the non-banking system. It expanded in the last decades and increased the vulnerability of the financial system, especially during the crisis. Moreover, compared with the traditional banking system, the regulatory regime provided only weak regulation before the crisis.

8.3 Do we need to regulate shadow banking?

8.3.1 *Shadow banking could increase efficiency*

Just like a coin, there are two sides to shadow banking as well. First of all, shadow banking can potentially increase economic efficiency while also increasing risk to the financial system (Schwarcz 2012).

As Gorton *et al.* point out, shadow banking emerged in order to alleviate the distortion from the Regulation Q and eventually changed the regulatory regime (Gorton *et al.* 2010). Moreover, Pozsar and Schwarcz also regarded it as a market-based instrument, as shadow banks can demonstrate the market power and demand of the private parties, especially when the traditional financial market was over-regulated and distorted (Pozsar *et al.* 2010, revised in 2012; Schwarcz 2012). For example, financial repression could be quite common in emerging countries like China (Xu 2013) and the traditional banking system may be distorted there, yet the shadow banking system can partially alleviate such distortion via a more flexible arrangement, as is visible in the emergence of wealth management services after 2009 (Zhang 2013). Moreover, shadow banking systems can create more liquidity by a higher leverage (Wray 2010), which has become a booster for the real economy in the last decades.

8.3.2   Shadow banking could aggregate risks

The shortcomings of shadow banking systems were mentioned quite often by scholars of law and economics after the financial crisis, as shadow banking was also the source of some key vulnerabilities during the crisis (Bernanke 2010).

As pointed out by Bernanke, most shadow banking entities and activities were not subject to consistent and effective regulatory oversight. For example, there is no prudential regulation for special purpose vehicles (SPVs), ABCPs, hedge funds or financial companies. There is not a single restriction on the leverage of such entities, while the regulatory standards on the quality of their risk management or the prudence of their risk-taking are quite weak. Therefore, the lack of regulation may amplify the following vulnerabilities of the shadow banking system (Bernanke 2009).

The shadow banking system is more dependent on unstable short-term wholesale funding and, unlike traditional commercial banks, there is no deposit insurance system that can cover shadow banking. Thus investors may 'run away' if any rumour arises, which may cause difficulties for the whole system due to investors' lack of sufficient information needed to determine the financial conditions of firms. Therefore, the vulnerability related to short-term funding brings more uncertainty to the system, which is also regarded as a structural weakness of the system (Bernanke 2010). The maturity mismatch and the potential fear of a runaway can severely damage the shadow banking system when the market is down or rumours arise.

As the regulatory regime on the shadow banking system is weak, especially before the financial crisis, financial firms managed risks by themselves. However, self-management of risk inherent to the shadow banking system was deficient. For example, the underwriting standards were very low for mortgages to subprime borrowers. Furthermore, many risks could not be tracked in the balance sheets of traditional banks, so these risks were not exposed. These shortcomings caused risks that were not diversified by the different financial firms but heavily concentrated in the shadow banking system. Hence, the risks to the whole system could be triggered by some unforeseeable incidents, such as the collapse of Lehman Brothers.

The shadow banking intermediaries often utilize much higher leverages than traditional banks. The excessive leverages enable investors to obtain higher profits in good times, but in bad times, losses will be greater. Therefore the risk was enlarged and the quality of capital declined. Dudley (2009) argued that the crisis shows the failure of regulators and market participants alike to fully understand and appreciate the strength of the amplifying mechanisms, particularly those of the shadow banking system that exacerbated the business and financial cycles in the financial system at the time of the Crisis.

Gorton *et al.* stated that the risks which caused the financial crisis were gathered in several types of short-term debts (repos, ABCPs, MMMFs shares) that were initially perceived as safe and 'money-like' but later found to be imperfectly collateralized. They argued that the core problem in the financial crisis was "a run on repos ... [i]n the crisis, withdrawals in the form of increased repo haircuts causing deleveraging and spreading the subprime crisis to other asset classes" (Gorton *et al.* 2010: 280). In this way the crisis amounted to a banking panic, structurally similar to many of the previous panics involving money-like instruments such as bank notes and demand deposits but with the 'banks' taking a new form.

The FSB (2011) also regarded that non-bank financial institutions (NBFIs) are the major source of systemic risks to the financial system via providing liquidity to the economy and the connection with the traditional bank system. Furthermore, the FSB pointed out that the interconnectedness between banks and shadow banking entities (FSB 2012) could cause a systemic risk. First, banks and shadow banking entities are highly connected, especially in China. Banks are often part of the shadow banking credit intermediation chain or provide (explicit or implicit) support (for example in the form of guarantees) to the shadow banking entities to enable cheap financing and maturity/liquidity transformation. Second, banks and shadow banking entities provide funds to each other through loans and investments in financial products. Third, banks may be owners or investors of shadow banking entities, e.g. finance companies or broker-dealers. Therefore, the interconnectedness between the two systems can create systemic risks as a distress in a shadow banking entity (or a bank) may easily spill over to a bank (or a shadow banking entity). Furthermore, this interconnectedness may aggregate the leverage and thus increase the risks of asset price bubbles, especially when entities of both systems invest in the same (or correlated) assets, for example infrastructure investments in China. Systemic risks can also build up when banks and shadow banking entities have common exposures to certain sectors or financial instruments. Moreover, interconnectedness can amplify market reactions when the market liquidity is scarce in financial markets – indeed such reactions can themselves intensify the loss of liquidity. The case of the credit crunch in China in 2013 could be a very important case.[11] Banks are thus likely to be significantly affected by developments in the shadow banking system and vice versa.

Although shadow banking can increase the efficiency by market-oriented intermediaries, the risks in the shadow banking system cannot be ignored, as its regulation is weak, the risk management is deficient, the leverage ratio is excessive and it is funded mainly by short-term debt. Therefore, many scholars cited the shadow banking system as the primary contributor to the financial crisis, because the vulnerabilities it caused could ripple throughout the entire financial system, and form a systemic risk due to the interconnectedness between banks and shadow banking entities (Schwarcz 2008). Therefore, considering the risks in the shadow banking system and the interconnectedness between shadow banking and traditional banking, the systemic risk caused by the shadow banking system could be a major risk to the traditional banking system; the risks in shadow banking shall be monitored.

8.4 An application to China

8.4.1 Shadow banking in China

As pointed out by the FSB, the booming of shadow banking can be regarded as the most remarkable event in the Chinese financial system. The size of shadow banking has expanded dramatically since 2009 due to the stimulus policy of the Chinese government (FSB 2012).

The development of shadow banking in China can be traced back to the beginning of this century, especially after 2004, the year when China started to liberalize its financial market and increase the discretion for banks to set the floating space of the interest rate (Yi 2009). The circulation of the banks' wealth management products increased from RMB0.04 trillion in 2004 to RMB16.99 trillion in 2011,[12] as they provided a very popular alternative for the banks to avoid the rigid requirements in the traditional credit services. At the same time, clients can obtain a higher return than traditional deposits, although the risks are also increased (Yin and Wang 2013).

The annual increase rate of the assets of NBFIs was over 20 per cent in the past five years due to the expansion of the liquidity and the cooperation from banks (PBOC 2014). The size of shadow banking in China was estimated as large as over RMB26 trillion in China, comprising of three sectors: (i) off-sheet financing of banks (RMB10.3 trillion), (ii) NBIs (RMB10.3 trillion), and (iii) informal finance (private loan) (RMB5.8 trillion) (Wei *et al.* 2013).[13]

The most remarkable character of the Chinese shadow banking system is the dominant role of the banks' off-sheet financing and the cooperation between banks and NBIs. Therefore, Chinese banks played a vital role in the shadow banking activities (Yin and Wang 2013; Wei *et al.* 2013).

8.4.2   The rise of Chinese shadow banking

Similar to the US, the rise of the shadow banking system could also be regarded as a market-based response to the banking regulation in China, especially to interest and credit regulation. It is commonly agreed that there is a severe distortion of the Chinese financial market because of China's interest-rate regulation, which is also referred to by many scholars as a major form of financial repression (Che 2011; Lu and Yao 2004). The over-regulation has distorted the financial system in China and is regarded as an important reason contributing to the expansion of Chinese shadow banking (Lu and Yao 2004; Wei *et al.* 2013).

8.4.2.1   Interest-rate regulation

The regulation on the interest rate in China was adopted as early as the 1950s, since the government started the economic restoration in order to accumulate capital and utilize capital with lower costs. The Chinese government set the cap for the deposit and loans for Chinese banks. Such a cap is often much lower than the market level, which could be estimated by the level of the informal credit (private loan) market (Lu and Yao 2004). In the last decades, the underestimated interest rate subsidized investors and producers in China (Xu 2013). Particularly, the inflation rate became rather high in the last decade; more and more depositors realized that they would be suffering losses if they kept savings in the banks. Therefore, more and more Chinese depositors preferred to accept wealth management products from the banks as an alternative (Yin and Wang 2013).

Credit rationing, or credit discrimination, is also quite common in China. The State-owned banks (SOBs) prefer to provide loans for the State-owned enterprises (SOEs) or their related enterprises, so it is quite hard for the private sector in China to obtain a loan via the formal bank system (Lu and Yao 2004). However, the private sector is usually more efficient and more active in China, thus requiring the financial support from non-banking institutions such as the shadow banking system (Xu 2013).

Besides financial regulation, economic policy also affected the flow of credit, as the SOBs could reduce loans for the industries disliked by the government. As housing prices rose dramatically in 2009 (see Figure 8.1), causing housing to be more and more unaffordable for ordinary citizens, the Chinese government was under pressure to regulate housing prices. One instrument adopted to control the housing price was a restriction of the loans to the real estate industry in order to avoid over-investment. However, the demand for capital in the real estate industry reached RMB 8.6 trillion in 2013.[14] Therefore, on the one hand, many developers were offered a very high interest for funds, while on the other hand, many banks preferred to provide capital for the developers via the cooperation from trust and security companies (such as REITs).

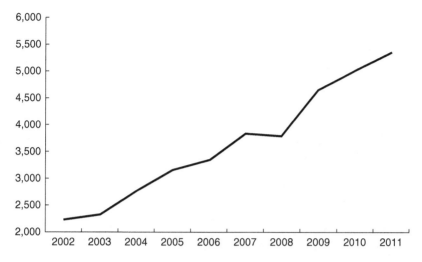

Figure 8.1 Average housing sales price (RMB/m^2)
(Source: NBS.)
Note: the National Bureau of Statistics (NBS) changed its statistical approach in 2011, thus data after 2011 cannot be equally compared to earlier data.

Therefore, the unbalanced economic structure and the harsh regulation on banks could be regarded as a very important factor for the development of Chinese shadow banking. Furthermore, the increased liquidity that flowed into the Chinese financial markets during the past five years must also be regarded as an important factor in the rapid expansion of shadow banking in China. The fast increase in liquidity in China is also connected to the boom of shadow banking. According to data from the People's Bank of China (PBOC), M2 supply increased from RMB49.6 trillion to RMB107 trillion since 2009, namely, the M2 increased more than 115 per cent in the last five years in China (see Figure 8.2).[15]

There are several factors to explain the increased liquidity. First, since 2009 the Chinese government adopted a huge package of economic stimulus to avoid the stagnation due to the financial crisis in the US. The central government claimed to invest RMB4 trillion to stimulate the economy, however the central government planned to invest RMB1.18 trillion while the local governments were also required to invest the remaining RMB2.82 trillion. In order to collect funds the local governments explored the urban development investment vehicle (UDIV) loans; the local government debt reached RMB 10.7 trillion, which increased around 60 per cent in 2009 due to the expenditure from the economic stimulus.[16]

The financial sector developed rapidly due to the stimulation policies, as demonstrated by the data of China Banking Regulation Commission

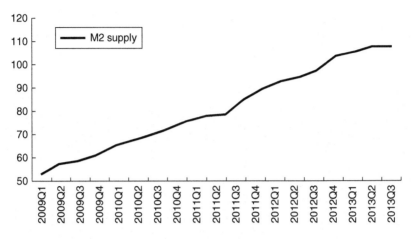

Figure 8.2 M2 supply in China (RMB trillion)

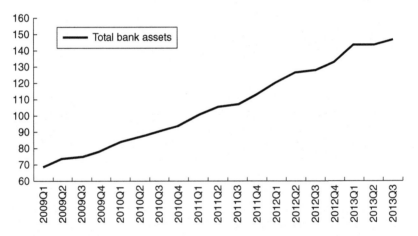

Figure 8.3 Total bank assets of China 2009–13 (RMB trillion)
(Source: CBRC.)

(CBRC). Since 2009 the bank assets have increased almost 111 per cent due to the stimulus (see Figure 8.3).

The liquidity in China could also be connected to the influx of capital from abroad. The exchange rate of the RMB became a debated issue, because some other countries accused China of manipulating the exchange rate in order to undervalue the RMB and maintaining the competitiveness of Chinese products and services. Foreign currency reserves increased from US$1.91 trillion to US$3.66 trillion since 2009 (see Figure 8.4); because the quantitative easing (QE) policy of the Federal Reserve created plenty of liquidity in the US,

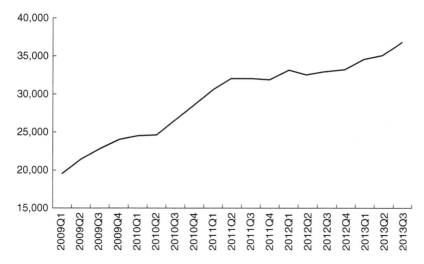

Figure 8.4 Foreign currency reserve 2009–13 (US$100 million)
(Source: PBOC.)

a huge sum of "hot money" from the US flowed into China "in order to earn a short-term profit on interest rate differences and/or anticipated exchange rate shifts" (Martin and Morrison 2008: 1) via the undervalued RMB, higher interest rate and booming property price in China.[17]

Although it is quite obvious that there is excessive liquidity in China due to the monetary policy and influx of capital, it is doubtful whether this money flowed into the real economy. Because of the distorted financial system, SOBs are closely connected to the local government and SOEs. Most loans have been provided to the local government and SOEs and a large proportion of the funds have been invested into infrastructure, which is a policy favored by the local governments.[18] Many of the actual new loans made available by the banks have been directed only at politically favoured projects, mostly infrastructure projects, as well as real estate companies.[19] Moreover, the traditional banking system preferred off-balance-sheet financing to move funds for a higher return and avoid the harsh regulation. In the meantime, many private enterprises are unable to satisfy their capital needs from the formal banking sector; many of these companies have been increasingly turning toward the informal market for private loans, which also increased the demand for shadow banking.[20]

Shadow banking caused more concerns in China due to the credit crunch in the middle of 2013, as it hit the Chinese financial market in June 2013. Because of the shortage of funds, banks increased the interbank rate and overnight the interbank loan rate reached 13.7 per cent on 17 June 2013 (see Figure 8.5), which shocked the PBOC and clearly showed us that although there may be an excess liquidity, a large proportion of this liquidity is coming from outside

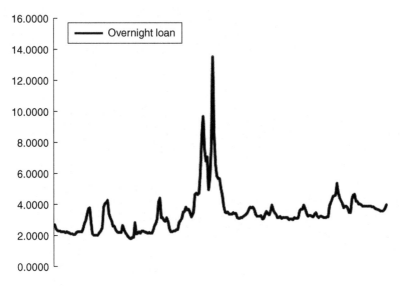

Figure 8.5 Interest rate of overnight interbank loan
(Source: Shibor.)

of the traditional banking system. Furthermore, the credit crunch also demonstrated that the mismatch of the Chinese credit market is quite severe, as Chinese banks and shadow banking are dependent on short-term funding, but the investments funded by them are often long term, such as infrastructure. As reminded by Bernanke, the mismatch was a factor that triggered the financial crisis, such as the insolvency of Bear Stearns (Bernanke 2009).

To sum up, I believe that the boom of shadow banking in China could be attributed to over-regulation and to the existence of excess liquidity. The existence of the shadow banking system in China must be viewed from two sides: on the one hand it satisfies the demand from many private enterprises and investors via the financial deepening process in China, but on the other hand it also aggregates risks outside the supervision of the regulators.

8.5   Monitoring the shadow banking system

8.5.1   *The international experiences*

It is commonly agreed that the shadow banking system was weakly regulated before the financial crisis, therefore efforts were made in order to monitor, and regulate such systems (Bernanke 2009, 2010, 2012; Gorton *et al.* 2010; Schwarcz 2012). Since the public regulators were under criticism for failing to oversee the risks in the shadow banking system after the crisis, they started to reform after the crisis in order to enable the regulatory regimes to be capable of monitoring shadow banking.

As a result of the crisis, the US drafted the Dodd-Frank Act in order to protect financial consumers, which entered into force in 2010.[21] Dodd-Frank is mentioned as the most important reform of the financial regulatory regime after the depression era. The core reforms adopted by the US after the Act can be summarized as follows: the consolidation of regulatory agencies, the elimination of the national thrift charter and a new oversight council to evaluate systemic risks, comprehensive regulation of financial markets including increased transparency of derivatives (bringing them onto exchanges), consumer protection reforms including a new consumer protection agency and uniform standards for 'plain vanilla' products (as well as a strengthened investor protection),[22] tools for financial crises (including a 'resolution regime' complementing the existing Federal Deposit Insurance Corporation (FDIC) authority to allow for orderly winding down of bankrupted firms and including a proposal that the Federal Reserve receive authorization from the Treasury for extensions of credit in "unusual and exigent circumstances"), various measures aimed at increasing international standards and cooperation (including proposals related to improved accounting and tightened regulation of credit rating agencies). Furthermore, a new regulator, the Financial Stability Oversight Council (FSOC), was also created by the Act in order to enforce it.[23]

As the impact of the crisis was felt worldwide and the risk caused by shadow banking is beyond the boundaries of countries, an international framework to monitor the risk was also required. The Basel III Accord was drafted and several rules on monitoring shadow banking were provided in that Accord. Therefore, the G20 required a new organ of the FSB to be created in order to monitor the (systemic) risk worldwide; a special Standing Committee on the Assessment of Vulnerabilities (SCAV) was also established in order to evaluate the risk.

8.5.2 The regulatory regime and practice in China

Shadow banking is also developing rapidly in China and therefore there is a need to oversee it. However, the regulatory regime in China consists of an institutional approach that was challenged by the problems arising from shadow banking.[24]

Under the present framework of the Chinese regulatory regime, the regulators carry out their tasks according to the functions they are assigned, although most jurisdictions have reformed in order to move toward an integrated approach or a twin peaks approach in the last decades (Group of Thirty 2008).[25]

Before the early 1990s, all financial supervision was carried out by the PBOC. Through several reforms in the last 20 years, China has moved to an institutional approach as the banking, securities and insurances sectors are supervised by different agencies. While most jurisdictions that have implemented reforms in the past 25 years have tended to move toward an integrated approach or a twin peaks approach, China did not. Under the previous regulatory structure, all financial supervision was consolidated within the PBOC, China's central bank. Through a series of reforms over the past 25 years, China has moved to an institutional approach, where the banking, securities and insurance sectors are supervised by separate agencies. In 1998, the China Securities Regulatory Commission (CSRC) has been formed as the agency to regulate the securities and futures sector. In the same year, the China Insurance Regulatory Commission (CIRC) was established to oversee the insurance industry. In 2003, the China Banking Regulatory Commission (CBRC) was founded and it has been conferred the power, most of which was transferred from the PBOC, to supervise the banking sector under the present framework. Banks, financial asset management companies, trusts, investment companies and other depository financial institutions are regulated by the CBRC. In the meantime, the PBOC is concentrating on formulating and implementing monetary policies and ensuring current financial stability. Under the present regime, although the CBRC is responsible for regulating the banking sector, there are still some entities in the informal financial sector, such as pawn shops, financing guarantee institutions, micro-finance companies, etc., which need approval by local governments and these unregulated entities (informal banks) are occasionally surveyed or investigated by the PBOC (Group of Thirty 2008).

In the past five years, due to the rapidly developing financial market, the institutional approach has been facing a challenge as it is rigid and fragmentary when the financial services are more and more integrated and previous boundaries between traditional banking, securities and insurances have become blurred. Banks and other institutions are providing services outside their traditional area via certain forms. The independent regulators confronted more difficulties, because a complicated financial activity can involve many firms from different financial departments, and a firm may provide different types of financial services, such as credit, insurance, trust, securities, etc. Such conditions increased the pressure on supervisors to coordinate before acting.

The regulation of shadow banking is posing a typical challenge for the institutional approach. The regulatory policies applied to shadow banking and the responsibilities of the regulators need to be clarified. Interagency coordination – backed by memoranda of understanding for information sharing – needs to be strengthened to prevent episodes of building up systemic risks via cross-market financial products or activities.

Under the present regime, the CBRC is regarded as the major authority that must regulate shadow banking in China and since 2009 the CBRC has published several directives in order to strengthen the monitoring of shadow banking in China, concentrating on the off-sheet financing and the wealth management products of Chinese banks.[26] However, it is difficult to assess whether such regulations have achieved a positive outcome, because the shadow banking activities are quite flexible and the enforcement regime of the regulators has always been fairly weak in China. Moreover, the current regulation by the CBRC does not provide any special framework to protect the investors of the shadow banking activities; such an arrangement will leave the Chinese investors in an unfavorable position.

In summary, striving for an effective oversight of shadow banking is a global goal, but the regulatory regime in China is confronted with increasing difficulties in monitoring its shadow banking system. Although the CBRC issued several directives to enhance the supervision on shadow banking, details on the enforcement of these directives have not been disclosed. However, the enforcement of law (law in action) is more important than law on the books (Pistor 2000). Moreover, the investor protection rules are still weak under the present regime, as the judicial remedies for the Chinese investors are ranked among the worst in the world (Brockman and Chung 2003).

8.6 Conclusions

Shadow banking must be regarded as a coin with two sides: it can increase the efficiency of the financial system and boost economic development, but at the same time it also aggregates risks to the financial system; and these risks caused by shadow banking are often overlooked. The principle for regulating shadow banking shall be maximizing economic efficiency and minimizing systemic risks (Schwarcz 2012). Considering the repressed financial system and distorted economy in China (Xu 2013), I believe that the boom of shadow banking must be regarded as a market response to the financial repression and unbalanced economic structure and it can alleviate the financial repression by providing more market-oriented services. A recent example is that of an Alipay MMMF called Yu'E Bao, which is comparable to the PayPal MMMF in the US. It grew from 0 to more than US$40 billion in a period of only eight months (from June 2013 to February 2014), because the annualized return of the Alipay MMMF is around 6 per cent. This annualized return rate is much higher than the interest rate fixed by the Chinese government; therefore about 81 million people have invested their money into Yu'e Bao.[27] The emergence of Yu'E Bao illustrates how shadow banking (for example in the form of MMMFs) can provide an alternative for investors seeking high market returns from their investment. Gary Gorton (2010) also pointed out that MMMFs expanded quite rapidly when the Regulation Q was enforced in the US, and Gorton believes that MMMFs must be regarded as a market power that forced the US government to abolish interest regulation.

However, shadow banking also increased the risks in the presently distorted financial system by, for example, giving the local government the ability to obtain excessive loans. Moreover, Gennaioli *et al.* (2013) found that the shadow banking system could be extremely fragile as the securitization facilitates risk-taking levels. Therefore, the shadow banking system must be supervised in order to oversee the risks, to increase transparency of the shadow banking system, and to provide better investor protection, which are all vital for the regulation of shadow banking.

Notes

1 Bernanke (2009, 2010, 2012), Gorton (2010) and Schwarzc (2012) explain the connection between shadow banking and the crisis.
2 The FSB was founded in response to the global financial crisis 2008. In 2009 the Group of Twenty (G20) Finance Ministers and Central Bank Governors created the FSB as a successor to the Financial Stability Forum (FSF). More information on the FSB is available at: https://www.financialstabilityboard.org/ (accessed 18 May 2014).
3 President Obama signed the Dodd-Frank Act in 2010, and the FSB established the SCAV in order to assess financial risks, especially in the shadow banking system.
4 Paul McCulley "coined the term 'shadow banking system' in August 2007 at the Fed's Annual Symposium in Jackson Hole". See McCulley, *The Shadow Banking System and Hyman Minsky's Economic Journey*, available at: http://media.pimco.com/Documents/GCB%20Focus%20May%2009.pdf (accessed 18 May 2014).
5 Paul McCulley, 'Comments Before the Money Marketeers Club: Playing Solitaire with a Deck of 51, with Number 52 on Offer', available at: http://web.archive.org/web/20100206185224/http://www.pimco.com/LeftNav/Featured+Market+Commentary/FF/2009/Global+Central+Bank+Focus+April+2009+Money+Marketeers+Solitaire+McCulley.htm (accessed 18 May 2014).
6 See Shleifer's comments, in the section of his paper entitled 'Comment and discussion'.
7 Bernanke (2009, 2010, 2012), Gorton (2010) and Schwarzc (2012) all argue that the regulation of shadow banking is weak.
8 Wealth management services offered by Chinese commercial banks have expanded a lot over the last decade. These services are different from the traditional deposit and loan services provided by these banks.
9 Regulation Q was introduced in the 1960s, and imposed an interest-rate ceiling on commercial banks. It was attacked by many economic scholars as it distorted the loan market. See Friedman (1975).
10 The OFI data were used as a proxy to evaluate the size of shadow banking by the FSB (although the size of shadow banking shall be narrower than OFI).
11 There were plenty of reports on this issue, see: 'What Caused China's Cash Crunch?', available at: http://www.economist.com/blogs/economist-explains/2013/07/economist-explains-2 (accessed 18 May 2014); 'The Chinese Cash Crunch Is No Surprise', available at: http://online.wsj.com/news/articles/SB10001424127887324637504578562892161598164 (accessed 18 May 2014); 'China Gambles That A Credit Crunch Can Rein In Shadow Banking', available at: http://www.forbes.com/sites/afontevecchia/2013/06/24/china-is-right-to-use-liquidity-crunch-to-target-shadow-banking-but-leverage-raises-risks/ (accessed 18 May 2014).
12 Data is available at: http://roll.sohu.com/20121121/n358243265.shtml (accessed 18 May 2014).
13 Estimated by CSC, see Wei *et al.* (2013).
14 Data source: National Bureau of Statistics of the PRC, available at: http://data.stats.gov.cn/normalpg?src=/lastestpub/quickSearch/m/mgd09.html&h=800 (accessed 18 May 2014).
15 According to the World Bank, "money and quasi money comprise the sum of currency outside banks, demand deposits other than those of the central government, and the time, savings, and foreign currency deposits of resident sectors other than the central government. This definition of money supply is frequently called M2", available at: http://data.worldbank.org/indicator/FM.LBL.MQMY.CN (accessed 18 May 2014).
16 Available at: http://www.audit.gov.cn/n1992130/n1992150/n1992500/2752208.html (accessed 18 May 2014).

17 According to GFI, since 2006 over US$400 billion has poured into China outside the official channels, with inflows in the first quarter of 2013 alone topping US$50 billion. See http://www.economist.com/news/finance-and-economics/21594345-despite-strict-currency-controls-money-finding-its-way-china-hot-and (accessed 18 May 2014).

18 Capital Group, *Shadow Banking in China 2013*, available at: https://server.capgroup.com/capgroup/action/getContent/file/GIG/North_America/Market_Insights/Capitals_Views/II_07_2013_Shadow_Banking_in_China.pdf (accessed 18 May 2014).

19 *The Rising Mismatch In Chinese Credit Markets*, available at: http://www.businessinsider.com/the-rising-mismatch-in-chinese-credit-markets-2011-8 (accessed 18 May 2014).

20 Ibid.

21 The text of the Dodd-Frank Act is available at: http://www.cftc.gov/ucm/groups/public/@swaps/documents/file/hr4173_enrolledbill.pdf (accessed 18 May 2014).

22 'Plain vanilla' refers to the basic standard form of a financial instrument, as the US Department of the Treasury appealed that they "propose that the regulator be authorized to define standards for 'plain vanilla' products that are simpler and have straightforward pricing."

23 *Financial Regulatory Reform*, available at: http://www.treasury.gov/initiatives/Documents/FinalReport_web.pdf (accessed 18 May 2014).

24 An 'institutional approach' to financial regulation implies that the rules and regulators are established separately according to the institutional type, for example the CSRC is the regulator for securities, the CBRC is the regulator for banks, the CIRC is the regulator for insurance.

25 An 'integrated approach' of financial regulation implies that all financial regulation is concentrated in a single agency. The 'twin peaks' approach was adopted in the UK in 2012, and means that deposit takers, insurers and major investment firms will have two groups of supervisors, one focusing on prudential regulation (the Prudential Regulatory Authority (PRA)) and one focusing on conduct regulation (the Financial Conduct Authority (FCA)). More details of the twin peaks approach can be found in: *Twin-Peaks Regulation: Key Changes and Challenges* (KPMG 2012), available at: http://www.kpmg.com/UK/en/IssuesAndInsights/ArticlesPublications/Documents/PDF/Advisory/twin-peaks-brochure.pdf (accessed 18 May 2014).

26 The most important directive by the CBRC on the regulation of shadow banking is the Notification of the China Banking Regulatory Commission on Relevant Issues concerning Regulating the Investment Operation of Wealth Management Business of Commercial Banks, which was issued in March 2013. It sets restrictions on the range of assets in which wealth management products can invest, and put limits on the cooperation between banks and securities companies as well. The text of the Notification (in Chinese only) is available at: http://www.cbrc.gov.cn/govView_2B22741AFBC446CF890636DACAB71166.html (accessed 18 May 2014).

27 Available at: http://www.nytimes.com/2014/03/03/business/international/web-banks-offering-high-interest-rates-rise-in-china.html?hpw&rref=business&_r=0 (accessed 18 May 2014).

References

Bernanke, B. S. (2009) 'Reflections on a Year of Crisis'. Available at: http://www.federalreserve.gov/newsevents/speech/bernanke20090821a.htm (accessed 18 May 2014).

Bernanke, B. S. (2010) 'Causes of the Recent Financial and Economic Crisis', Testimony before the Financial Crisis Inquiry Commission, Washington, DC, 2 September 2010. Available at: http://www.federalreserve.gov/newsevents/testimony/bernanke20100902a.htm (accessed 18 May 2014).

Bernanke, B. S. (2012) 'Some Reflections on the Crisis and the Policy Response'. Available at: http://www.federalreserve.gov/newsevents/speech/bernanke20120413a.pdf (accessed 18 May 2014).

Brockman, P. and Chung, D. Y. (2003) 'Investor Protection and Firm Liquidity', *The Journal of Finance*, 58(2), 921–37.

Che, D. (2011) 'The Cause and Inefficiency of Financial Regulation', *Economic Research Journal (Jing ji Yan jiu)*, 2, 41–50.

Dudley, W. C. (2009) 'Proceedings from the Center for Economic Policy Studies (CEPS) Symposium 2009: More lessons from the crisis'. Available at: http://www.bis.org/review/r091117a.pdf (accessed 18 May 2014).

Financial Stability Board (2011) 'Shadow Banking: Strengthening Oversight and Regulation 2011'. Available at: https://www.financialstabilityboard.org/publications/r_111027a.pdf (accessed 18 May 2014).

Financial Stability Board (2012) 'Global Shadow Banking Monitoring Report 2012'. Available at: https://www.financialstabilityboard.org/publications/r_121118c.pdf (accessed 18 May 2014).

Financial Stability Board (2013) 'Global Shadow Banking Monitoring Report 2013', Available at: https://www.financialstabilityboard.org/publications/r_131114.pdf (accessed 18 May 2014).

Friedman, B. M. (1975) 'Regulation Q and the Commercial Loan Market in the 1960s', *Journal of Money, Credit and Banking*, 7 (3), 277–96.

Gennaioli, N., Shleifer, A. and Vishny, R. W. (2013) 'A Model of Shadow Banking', *The Journal of Finance*, 58(4), 1331–63.

Gorton, G., Metrick, A., Shleifer, A. and Tarullo, D. K. (2010) 'Regulating the Shadow Banking System', (with comments and discussion), *Brookings Papers on Economic Activity*, 261–312.

Group of Thirty (2008) 'The Structure of Financial Supervision: Approaches and Challenges in a Global Marketplace'. Available at: http://www.group30.org/images/PDF/The%20Structure%20of%20Financial%20Supervision.pdf (accessed 18 May 2014).

Lu, F. and Yao, Y. (2004) 'Legality, Financial Development and Economic Growth under Financial Repression', *Social Science in China*, 1, 42–55.

Martin, M. F. and Morrison, W. M. (2008) 'China's "Hot Money" Problems', *CRS Report for Congress*. Available at: http://www.fas.org/sgp/crs/row/RS22921.pdf (accessed 18 May 2014).

McCulley, P. (2009) 'The Shadow Banking System and Hyman Minsky's Economic Journey'. Available at: http://media.pimco.com/Documents/GCB%20Focus%20May%2009.pdf (accessed 18 May 2014).

Pistor, K., Raiser, M. and Gelfer, S. (2000) 'Law and Finance in Transition Economies', *Economies in Transition*, 8(2), 325–68.

Pozsar, Z., Adrian, T., Ashcraft, A. and Boesky, H. (2010, revised in 2012) 'Shadow Banking', *Federal Reserve Bank of New York Staff Report*. Available at: http://www.newyorkfed.org/research/staff_reports/sr458.pdf (accessed 18 May 2014).

Schwarcz, S. L. (2008) 'Systemic Risk', *The Georgetown Law Journal*, 97, 193–249.

Schwarcz, S. L. (2012) 'Regulating Shadow Banking', *Review of Banking & Financial Law*, 31, 619–42.

Schwarcz, S. L. (2012) 'China 2012 Lecture: Shadow Banking and Financial Regulation'. Available at: http://papers.ssrn.com/sol3/papers.cfm?abstract_id=2182601 (accessed 18 May 2014).

United States Department of the Treasury (2009) 'Financial Regulatory Reform: A New Formation'. Available at: http://www.treasury.gov/initiatives/Documents/FinalReport_web.pdf (accessed 18 May 2014).

Wei, T., Liu, Y., Yang, R., Zeng, Y. and Wang, J. (2013) 'Debate: Chinese Shadow Banking and Financial Reform', *Financial Development Review* (Jin Rong Fa Zhan Ping Lun), 2, 1–51.

Wray, L. R. (2010) 'What Do Banks Do? What Should Banks Do?', *Working Paper no. 612 of Levy Economics Institute of Bard College*. Available at: http://www.levyinstitute.org/pubs/wp_612.pdf (accessed 18 May 2014).

Xu, G. (2013) 'Financial Repression, Economic Distortion, and China's Growth Miracle', in Faure, M. and Xu, G. (eds), *Economics and Regulation in China*, Abingdon, Oxon and New York: Routledge, 11–47.

Yi, G. (2009), 'The Liberalization Proceeding of the Interest Rate during China's Thirty Years Open and Reform', *Journal of Financial Research*, 1, 1–14.

Yin, J. and Wang, Z. (2013) *Shadow Banking and Bank's Shadow*, Beijing: Social Sciences Academic Press.

Zhang, J. (2013) *Inside China's Shadow Banking: The Next Subprime Crisis?*, Honolulu, HI: Enrich Professional Publishing Inc.

Part III

Design of financial instruments

9 Cartel enforcement in China

Monetary or criminal sanctions?

Michael Faure and Jingyuan Ma

9.1 Introduction

In recent years, criminalizing business conduct has attracted the attention of policy makers around the world. 'Economic crime' is, however, not a new concept; dating back to 1890, the Sherman Act in the US has already defined illegal cartel conduct as a crime. From an economic perspective, criminalization of anti-competitive behavior can reach the goal of deterring future infringers. This chapter investigates whether criminalization could be a solution to improve the enforcement of antitrust law in China. The Anti-Monopoly Law (AML) in China entered into force in August 2008 and since then a major issue being debated among public policy makers (Zhao 2008) and academic scholars (Van den Bergh and Faure 2011) is how this law could be better implemented and enforced. This chapter aims at contributing to this debate and discusses whether and to what extent criminalization could be applied to the enforcement of cartel agreements under the Chinese AML.

The starting point of this analysis is the classic model developed by Gary Becker. The Becker criteria indicate that an effective enforcement of law would induce the potential infringer to fully internalize the social harm that is caused by the crime (Becker 1968). This chapter discusses the economic justifications for applying monetary or criminal sanctions to cartel agreements. The analysis focuses on the assumptions, circumstances and the limitations of the economic analysis of antitrust criminalization, by incorporating the insights from law and economics literature, as well as the recent findings from behavioral law and economics studies. At the end of this chapter, it provides alternative mechanisms to increase the probability of detection, as well as the level of sanctions when the assumptions of the Becker model, for instance, judicial independence and enforcers pursuing public interest, are not fully satisfied in China. The general conclusion of this chapter is that it may be not the right time for China to criminalize antitrust law. The experience in the EU and the US has shown that in order to improve the enforcement of the AML, other mechanisms can be implemented to increase the 'price' of the antitrust law infringement.

The structure of this chapter is as follows. After this introduction, the second section presents an overview of the current enforcement mechanisms in the AML in China. The third section discusses the economic theory of criminalization and focuses on the economic criteria, being the costs and benefits of criminalizing antitrust infringements. It also provides a few refinements to the traditional economic model of criminalization by discussing the relevance of recent literature applying behavioral law and economics to crime and looking at criminalization from a public choice perspective. Those refinements may also have an influence on the desirability to criminalize antitrust. The fourth section provides a brief comparison between the development of antitrust criminalization in the US and the EU. Finally, in the fifth section we discuss the central question of this chapter, whether based on economic theory and the experiences in the US and EU, criminalization of antitrust in China would be indicated. Attention is more particularly paid to alternatives to criminal enforcement, such as administrative sanctions (which are to some extent already currently available in China). The last section concludes.

9.2   Legal liabilities and penalties under the AML

In Chapter 7 of the AML, legal liabilities and penalties are briefly discussed. Article 46 stipulates that when a monopoly agreement is reached and performed, a fine of between 1 per cent up to a maximum of 10 per cent of the sales revenue in the previous year shall be imposed. If the monopoly agreement has not been implemented, a fine of less than RMB500,000 shall be imposed. This punishment, however, can be mitigated or exempted if the business operator voluntarily reports the conditions on reaching the monopoly agreement and provides important evidence to the anti-monopoly authority. Article 47 stipulates that the penalty for the abuse of the dominant position is also an administrative fine of between 1 per cent up to a maximum of 10 per cent of the sales revenue in the previous year. Article 48 imposes penalties on concentrations. That is, the anti-monopoly authority will "order it to cease doing so, to dispose of shares or assets, transfer the business or take other necessary measures to restore the market situation before the concentration within a time limit, and may impose a fine of less than RMB500,000."[1]

Criminal liabilities specifically targeting antitrust violations are not found in the AML (Wei 2013: 131). Articles 52 and 54 have mentioned criminal sanctions for parties who do not provide proper evidence during the investigation, as well as for investigators who abuse their power during the investigation. Article 52 stipulates the penalty for providing fraudulent information. If during the process of antitrust inspection and investigation, "business operators refuse to provide related materials and information, provide fraudulent materials or information, conceal, destroy or remove evidence, or refuse or obstruct the investigation in other ways, the anti-monopoly authority shall order them to make rectification," a fine will be imposed on individuals of less than RMB20,000, less than RMB200,000 on entities. In serious situations, the anti-monopoly authority may impose a fine of RMB20,000 up to RMB100,000 on individuals, and a fine of RMB200,000 up to RMB1,000,000 on entities. Moreover, where a crime is committed, the relevant business operators shall assume criminal liability. However, the Article concerned does not precisely define what is exactly meant by a 'crime'. The use for the word crime in this context is remarkable since the violations of the AML are not criminalized but only subject to administrative fines. Hence it remains mysterious what the legislator precisely meant with the notion of 'crime'.

9.3   The economic theory of criminalization

9.3.1   *The economic model of crime*

Nobel Prize Winner Gary Becker has identified a cost minimization model of law enforcement (Becker 1968). Although Becker's model was created in the context of criminal law, it can also be applied to violations of antitrust law, even though the sanctions that are imposed in that context are not formally considered crimes. The starting point for Becker's model is that a person will only commit a crime when the expected utility exceeds the costs.

Potential criminal activities are altered when the costs of the consequences are increased by law enforcement. Becker defined the optimal amount of enforcement as dependent on three resources: the cost of apprehending and convicting the offenders, the nature of the punishment, and the responses of the offenders to the changes in enforcement. The Becker model shows that the decision on sanction mechanisms depends on the information on the gain to the offender as well as the probability of detection (Van den Bergh and Faure 2011. 64). The expected punishment cost, which is equal to the expected social cost of the crime, is calculated as the probability that the sanction will be imposed on the criminal multiplied with the magnitude of the punishment.[2]

Hence, the prospective criminal's decision on whether or not to commit a crime could depend on:

$$U > p \times S$$

where:

U = utility of the offender derived from committing the crime
p = probability of being apprehended and sanction being imposed
S = the magnitude of the sanction that is imposed

Becker identified the trade-offs involved in minimizing the costs in law enforcement and one of the most important trade-offs is the probability of being punished (p), as contrasted with the severity of the sanctioning (S).

The potential offender makes a calculation *ex ante*, considering the probability of being apprehended and the level of punishment and compares this to the utility that could be derived from committing the crime (Schwartz 1979: 1076). Consequently, the magnitude of the sanctions multiplied by the probability that the sanction will be applied equals the 'price' of engaging in activities that violate the law (Schwartz 1979: 1079). This price must be set at an efficient level. If the price is too low, there will be an excessive amount of harmful activities. Conversely, if the price is set too high, the process and punishment costs involved in law enforcement would be too high and the social cost of punishing offenders will exceed the social benefit. Shavell argues that to achieve the goal of deterring socially undesirable acts, the criminal sanction should increase when the probability of conviction falls (Shavell 2004: 551).

From an economic perspective, the goal of the criminal law is not to eliminate all crime, but to reduce the level of crime to a level where the social loss is minimized (King 2010: 15). In that respect an optimal balance has to be found between the probability of detection (p) and the sanction (S). Hence, when the probability of being apprehended is low, the severity of sanctions should be set high, to offset the decreased expected price, in order to reach the expected optimal level of deterrence. Therefore, the enforcement structure will be desirable when the price is efficiently established, in which situation the process and punishment costs must be justified by the benefits that are generated from deterring harmful conduct (Schwartz 1979: 1079–80). Easterbrook argues that the optimal price is to be set equal to the externalities caused by the harm, divided by the probability of prosecution (Easterbrook 1983: 292). When the cost of allocating resources to reach this level of the optimal price is too high, this price might be reduced until the marginal benefit of the crime is equal to the marginal cost in crime control (Easterbrook 1983: 292). This is an application of Stigler's idea that society should not strive for a reduction of all crime at all costs, but rather for an optimum enforcement of laws, taking into account the costs of crime control (Stigler 1970: 526).

9.3.2 Administrative fines or criminal sanctions: the economic criteria

As we have just shown, economic theory perceives deterrence as the main goal of criminal law.[3] This to some extent contrasts with the legal theory where criminal law is viewed as aiming at punishing morally unacceptable acts, and the goals of criminal law include retribution, rehabilitation, incapacitation and education (Dau-Schmidt 1984: 87). However, from an economic perspective the question arises whether the economic goal of deterrence can only be reached via the criminal law. The answer to that question largely depends on which type of sanction is needed.

The economic justification for the use of sanctions and punishment is to make law infringers internalize the social costs. The level of penalty should be set equal to the social cost of the crime (Posner 1980a: 73). There are basically two types of penalties: monetary and non-monetary (which usually refers to imprisonment). From a legal perspective, monetary sanctions can either be administrative fines or take the form of criminal fines.

Economists have long advocated that when deterrence could be achieved in the same way through those types of sanctions, fines would be preferred to imprisonment penalties (Posner 1980b; Polinsky and Shavell 1979; 1991; 1993). The straightforward economic reason is that a prison sanction leads to substantial costs for society, whereas fines can shift funds from the perpetrator to society. The question, however, arises whether the fine should necessarily be collected via a criminal procedure. The costs of an administrative procedure, through which fines are imposed, are substantially lower than the imposition of fines by means of criminal procedure (Faure 2009: 324). It can hence be concluded that in principle, administrative law is more desirable when the monetary sanctions (including the administrative fines) will be effective (Polinsky and Shavell 1979; Shavell 1985). The second issue is that in most legal systems the criminal proceedings are more accurate. The reason for this is that the investigations are conducted by professional lawyers (Faure 2009: 325) and the sanction is imposed by an impartial judge (Van den Bergh and Faure 2011: 65). The criminal procedure may thus have higher accuracy and better reduced error costs (Faure *et al.* 2009: 173–6). Administrative proceedings are less costly, but the error costs can be higher. Therefore, administrative fines should be applied to cases where the deterrence goal can be achieved by relatively modest sanctions (Faure 2009: 326). However, imprisonment, which would obviously lead to much higher error costs, should not be imposed through an administrative procedure.

From an economic point of view, the reason why criminal sanctions are needed is to reach the goal of deterrence (Shavell 1985; Coffee 1980). To effectively deter future violations, the level of sanctions must be higher than the damage caused. The compensation that victims receive under civil law is often not sufficient to deter offences. By imposing criminal sanctions, offenders are not allowed to conduct certain behavior that is prohibited by the criminal law, even if they are willing to compensate the victims (Faure 2000; Bowles *et al.* 2008: 402–3). In particular, the sanction of imprisonment should be imposed when monetary sanctions such as fines are not sufficient to reach the deterrence goal. This refers to the situation where the probability of detection is low and the risk of defendants being judgment-proof is high (Bowles *et al.* 2008: 405). However, criminal sanctions also suffer a few drawbacks to achieve the deterrence goal (Shavell 1993: 275). In most cases, the possibility of apprehending law infringers is not high enough. Given the large benefits of the infringement, in order to reach the deterrence goal, the sanction level should be set very high (Shavell 1993: 275) to offset the low probability of detection. However, this will make the crime more risky, which imposes additional costs on those who are risk averse (Easterbrook 1983: 293).

9.3.3   *Towards criminalization of antitrust law*

Applying the Becker framework, which is largely based on the idea of deterrence, to competition law is widely accepted by policy makers. In 2005, a survey conducted by the International Competition Network (ICN) among 19 antitrust authorities has concluded that the deterrence goal is the principle objective of anti-cartel enforcement (ICN 2005: 53; Connor 2008b: 39). In the view of the US Department of Justice (DOJ) Antitrust Division, price fixing is a rational economic crime and such behavior should be deterred.[4]

Following the analysis we just presented, the deterrence of antitrust can be achieved by imposing a fine which reflects the social harm caused by the violation multiplied with the probability of detection. If deterrence could hence be achieved through (high) fines, prison sanctions (and thus criminal law) would not be needed and deterrence could be achieved via monetary sanctions that, as we argued above, could also be imposed as administrative fines. The social harm created through cartels, however, is significantly high. Studies on the estimation of cartel harm generally shows that most cartels could raise profits by at least 10 per cent, and the annual cartel harm could exceed billions of dollars (Clarke 2012: 79; Scott 2008). Moreover, the optimal fine in cartel cases would presumably have to be quite high in order to outweigh the low probability of detection. The estimation of the probability of detection of cartels varies between 10 and 17 per cent in the US[5] (Connor and Lande 2005: 519; Bryant and Eckhard 1991: 531) and between 16 and 30 per cent in Europe (Wils 2001: 13; Connor 2010: 3).[6] Seeing the significant cartel harm and the relatively low probability of detection, the choice between the forms of legal sanctions is dependent on the extent to which the law deters undesirable acts (Coffee 1992: 1876). Some claimed that contrary to Stigler's view, with respect to hardcore cartels the enforcement goal is 'total deterrence'. Werden and Simon claimed that the sanction of imprisonment should be used in all hardcore cartel cases, and cartel conduct should be eliminated (or deterred to the maximum level) rather than taxed[7] (Werden and Simon 1987: 933). They argued that the harm caused by cartels can be so high that the optimal fine according to the Becker model would be in excess of the financial capacity of most corporations (Werden and Simon 1987: 927). At the same time, others have argued that the sanctions should remain at a desirable level to avoid the risks of over deterrence, in which situation the corporation may over invest in corporate monitoring and compliance, and these costs may ultimately be passed on to consumers (Ginsburg and Wright 2010: 5).

Another problem in cartel cases is that in most antitrust cases the infringers are corporations. Since the harm generated by a cartel is significant, and the detection rate is relatively low, the Becker criteria show that in order to guarantee an effective deterrence the level of fines imposed on corporations involved in a cartel infringement should be remarkably high. Moreover, the deterrence effects on corporations are often reflected by the effectiveness of sanctions on the real persons who make decisions on behalf of the corporation (Blair 1985: 436). Hence, the question arises whether criminal sanctions should be imposed on individuals. Posner argued that individuals should not be punished by criminal sanctions as the company has a superior advantage in preventing their employees from committing anticompetitive acts (Posner 1976: 226). To the contrary, many others have advocated criminal sanctions for the reason that imposing fines on cartel participants is far from sufficient to deter future infringements, as fines are often indemnified (Werden and Simon 1987: 931; Stone 1980: 47–56). Wils argued that adding individual criminal penalties provides an effective solution in situations where charging fines is impossible. Moreover, it also solves the internal management problems within the firm that may lead to antitrust violations (Wils 2001: 23–4). Although there is rather little empirical evidence on the deterrence effect of criminal sanctions on individuals,[8] this view has been accepted and supported by prosecutors in the US (Hammond 2002). As Scott Hammond, the Deputy Assistant Attorney General of the DOJ once claimed: "Individual accountability through the imposition of jail sentences is the single greatest deterrent to cartels" (Hammond 2005b: 3). In 2006, Thomas O. Barnett, the Assistant Attorney General at the Antitrust Division of the DOJ, claimed "[t]he ultimate goal of cartel enforcement is deterrence, and deterrence only works when consequences are real. To effectively deter cartels, antitrust enforcers must aggressively and predictably prosecute cartelists and use the full range of weapons in the enforcement arsenal, from fines to jail time to restrictions on international movement" (Barnett 2006). Criminal sanctions on cartel offenses have also been applied in other jurisdictions, such as Austria, Canada, France, Germany, Greece, Ireland, Israel, Japan, Norway, the Slovak Republic, South Korea and Switzerland (Hammond 2002: 575; Baker 2001: 696; Wagner-von Papp 2010).

Nevertheless, it is crucial to mention that to reach the goal of effective deterrence, the antitrust policy set must be transparent, certain and predictable to ensure business operators clearly understand the differences between compliance and violation, as well as the consequences of their behavior (Baker 2001: 697). This requires not only a clear design of the anti-cartel rules, but also sufficient financial and intellectual support for the enforcement of these rules, to ensure that the potential infringers are threatened by a severe penalty and that in this way anti-competitive conduct is effectively deterred. Therefore, relying on antitrust criminalization to achieve the deterrence goal is nevertheless a costly solution, if the given jurisdiction is not well equipped with an efficient antitrust enforcement system.

9.3.4　Refinements of the economic model of crime: a behavioral law and economics perspective

The Becker model is developed based on the rationality assumption. Several limitations of applying the rational choice theory in the implementation of legal rules have been mentioned by behavioral law and economics scholars (Korobkin and Ulen 2000: 1067; McAdams and Ulen 2009). The findings of the behavioral law and economics literature have also been applied to criminal law. For example, it is held that the criminals are in a specific group with extreme risk preferences, and people in different groups may perceive the severity of punishment differently (Robinson and Darley 2004: 193; Baron and Kennedy 1998). It is also held that as a consequence of a number of heuristics and biases, in reality the severity of punishment is often weakened (McAdams and Ulen 2009). Behavioral theory has also been applied to antitrust (Reeves and Stucke 2011; Stucke 2007), although it is also debated and some have argued that behavioral antitrust is "not ready for the main stage" (Van den Bergh 2013).

Some of the findings of the behavioral literature may have some relevance for the enforcement of antitrust law. To some extent, it is argued that firms may not always act as rational offenders according to the Becker model; arguments are also made that behavioral biases may affect the deterrent effect of criminal law and that those biases may also influence the behavior of law enforcers and judges. It is interesting to briefly analyze to what extent these findings can refine the traditional economic analysis of crime, more particularly when applied to antitrust. However, we immediately have to add that some issues that are now presented as the results of behavioral literature (e.g. the fact that firms may not always base their decision on violation on a rational calculation of costs and benefits) are of course not new to behavioral theory. Many scholars familiar with compliance theory have often held that violations may be the result of a variety of processes whereby, more likely than not, a lack of information and a resulting unintentional violation will often be the cause of corporate crime rather than a rational cost-benefit analysis (Hawkins 1984).

9.3.4.1   Behavioral perspectives on criminals

The behavioral economics theory indicates that due to the high cost of processing information, as well as the cognitive limitations of human beings, actors often do not conduct complex cost-benefit analysis when they make decisions. Instead, people engage in a process of 'satisficing', meaning that in their decisions people do not choose the option that maximizes their utility, but rather choose one that satisfies their aspiration (Simon 1979: 503). This is also defined by Herbert A. Simon as 'bounded rationality' (Simon 1956; Korobkin and Ulen 2000: 1069). According to Korobkin and Ulen, bounded rationality in decision making is justified by two reasons. The first reason is that such decisions are made to specially meet aspiration (Korobkin and Ulen 2000: 1075). The decision that makes the actor feel satisfied may be different from the decision that maximizes the actor's utility. The second reason is the use of heuristics (Korobkin and Ulen 2000: 1076), which makes the assumption of maximizing expected utility fail.

Under the Becker model, to increase the 'price' of law infringement, either the severity of punishment or the probability of detection should be enhanced in order to offset the potential benefit for the criminals. It is generally argued by economists that increasing the level of punishment is cheaper than increasing the probability of detection, which requires the efforts from police, prosecutors and judges (Korobkin and Ulen 2000: 1089). However, this probability of detection is the perceived probability, that is, potential infringers have to make a prediction on how likely they will be convicted, and they might under or overestimate this frequency (Stucke 2006: 485; Wils 2001: 8). Therefore, it is important to convey the information to the criminals with regard to the severity of the punishment, as well as the likelihood of being detected. Of course, it is well known (and again, not new to behavioral law and economics) that potential infringers may not have accurate information on probabilities or sanctions. A comment from one Federal District judge has proven that executives may not even know the sentencing guidelines (*Federal Sentencing Guidelines Manual*) which state the criminal liabilities for antitrust violations (Stucke 2006: 485).

In addition to the difficulty of discovering the perceived probability, criminals also suffer from 'overconfidence bias', as they may not believe that bad things will happen to them. In antitrust cases, executives may believe, given their skills and expertise, that they are more likely to avoid detection (Stucke 2012). In this case, antitrust authorities should set a higher level of sanction, such as the penalty of imprisonment, to overcome such bias. However, when this information is processed to managers, executives may also suffer from the availability heuristic, overestimating the probability of detection (Stucke 2012: 16); hence, managers (in particular, those who are risk averse) might conduct conservative decisions to avoid potential risks, which would have a negative impact on the business transactions. In this respect, criminalization generates side effects on business activities.

The implication of behavioral law and economics on antitrust should remain modest, however, when the potential criminal is a firm, rather than an individual. Firms are more capable to combat cognitive biases than individual consumers (Van den Bergh 2013: 211). Under the pressure of competition, the 'irrational' firms who made bad decisions will be driven out of the market. In a repeated game, firms are incentivized by the market mechanism to make profit-maximizing decisions (Van den Bergh 2013: 211). The rationality of the firm can be discussed by the following three separate issues. The first issue concerns the different behavior of people as individuals and in a group setting (Reeves and Stucke 2011: 1540). There is also evidence in criminal law and economics literature showing that the potential infringers as a group have a higher risk preference, and think less about the consequences of their conduct (Robinson and Darley 2004: 179). In particular, the empirical evidence on the decision-making process within the firm is still far from sufficient (Stucke 2007: 532–6), as Coase described the *intra* firm behavior is as a "black box" (Coase 1992: 714).

The second issue is whether the manager of the firm makes profit-maximizing decisions. The chief executive officer (CEO) of the firm may suffer overconfidence bias as well, just as the individual actor in the market does.

Armstrong and Huck argued that CEOs and entrepreneurs may tend to be "disproportionately over optimistic" because such behavior is encouraged by the internal promotion procedures (Armstrong and Huck 2010: 25). The third is the variations between firms. Given the differences on structure, identity, cultural norms, regulatory environment, size and purpose of firms, a large variation in the degree of firms' heuristic biases has been observed. In reality, business executives are engaging in competition to make better decisions, and if all firms are rational, such competitive advantage would not be expected to exist (Reeves and Stucke 2011: 1543; Stucke 2007: 534).

9.3.4.2 Behavioral perspectives on deterrence effects

According to economic theory, the main goal of criminalizing antitrust law is to better deter future infringers. The deterrence goal should be discussed first by separating the targets into two groups: one is the group of potential infringers who have not been confronted with a criminal conviction yet (general deterrence); and the second group considers the recidivists (specific deterrence). In practice, the deterrence effect of criminal law is influenced by a much larger range of factors than the probability of detection and the severity of punishment, as indicated by Becker. Robinson and Darley pointed out that imposing the most serious penalty on the crime of rape will simply incentivize every rapist to kill the victim – the strategy that maximizes the private gain of the criminal (Robinson and Darley 2004: 186). In practice, the extent to which criminal law achieves the goal of deterrence depends on how accurate and sufficient the punishment is conducted (Robinson and Darley 2004: 186). For example, behavioral scientists have provided evidence showing that after being affected by a positive or negative event, people are able to adapt to new circumstances (Robinson and Darley 2004: 187). This adaptation effect is named by Brickman and Campbell as the 'Hedonic treadmill' (Brickman and Campbell 1971: 287). The prisoner might be able to adapt to the environment of the prison after experiencing it for some time (Robinson and Darley 2004: 188). Moreover, Daniel Kahneman's research shows that the duration of the negative experience does not have a significant impact on the remembered pain of such experience (Kahneman 1999: 4; Redelmeier and Kahneman 1996: 3). This result indicates that what matters most in setting the severity of the punishment is not the duration of prison term; instead, it is the intensity of the negative experience.[9] These findings provide valuable insights for the design of punishment especially for the recidivists.

9.3.4.3 Behavioral perspectives on the antitrust enforcers and judges

Behavioral law and economics does not only affect potential perpetrators and the deterrent effect of the criminal sanction, but may equally influence antitrust enforcers as well as the judiciary. Empirical tests conducted by Guthrie, Rachlinski and Wistrich showed that the decision-making process of the judges was influenced by five cognitive biases: anchoring,[10] framing effects,[11] hindsight bias,[12] representativeness[13] and egocentric bias[14] (Guthrie *et al.* 2001: 784). Their study shows that judges are unaware of their cognitive illusions and make decisions by relying on heuristics, which results in systematic errors in their judgments (Guthrie *et al.* 2001: 784). The research by Englich, Mussweiler and Strack confirms the anchoring effects in judicial decisions and shows that the sentencing decisions of legal experts are heavily influenced by sentencing anchors (Englich *et al.* 2006). Selective optimism may also play an important role with other stakeholders in the litigation system, more particularly with lawyers. Self-serving bias can play a role in the analysis of the chances of winning a lawsuit by lawyers. As a result, lawyers systematically anticipate their trial prospects as being better than they objectively are (Korobkin and Ulen 2000: 1093). This may be one of the explanations why many more cases than one would expect go to trial instead of being settled. Those biases could obviously play a role as well in antitrust litigation.

9.3.5 Refinement of the economic model: a public choice perspective

The Becker model is developed under several assumptions. One of these assumptions is obviously that agencies examining potential violations and prosecutors bringing cases to court work in the public interest in order to serve the goal of optimal deterrence. Wils further argues that there are also several conditions that will have to be met in order to make the specific sanction of imprisonment an effective instrument to deter hardcore cartels (Wils 2005: 39). The first condition is that sanctions are imposed through a system with a dedicated investigator and prosecutor. The second condition is that the investigation process must be provided with sufficient power. The third condition is that judges or juries are willing to convict, and the fourth condition is that the opinion that cartels deserve severe (criminal) punishment must be supported both publicly and politically (Wils 2005: 39).

These general conditions underlying the Becker model and specifically the criminalization of antitrust law will in some cases be difficult to meet. This is more particularly the case when, as public choice theory predicts, bureaucrats do not serve the public interest, but rather their private interest. This may also be problematic in cases where there is no independent judiciary, but where the judiciary is equally serving particular political goals. As we will argue below, these types of public choice issues may well affect the effectiveness of antitrust enforcement, and more particularly the potential criminalization of antitrust violations in China.

9.3.6 Other reasons why criminalization of antitrust may fail

According to Clarke (Clarke 2012: 77), there are other reasons why antitrust criminalization may fail. One of the most important factors that should be taken into account considering criminalization of cartel conduct is whether it has been supported by public opinion (Clarke 2012: 77; Stucke 2006; Parker 2006: 598). Compared with traditional crimes, the 'economic harm' caused by cartel conduct, normally attracts a less emotional and moral response from the public (Clarke 2012: 77), especially in jurisdictions that do not have a well-established competition culture. Clarke points out that the lack of public awareness of the serious harm caused by cartel conduct leads to a weak political will to make the change towards antitrust criminalization (Clarke 2012: 78). However, the recent trend of criminalizing cartel agreements in many jurisdictions is seen as a 'top-down' approach, that is, imposing criminal sanctions is more driven by the pressure from transnational cartel enforcement, rather than the 'bottom-up' process that is led by widespread public opinion (Harding 2006). There are other circumstances when the public perception on criminalizing cartel conducts is led by the opinions from legal experts (Harding 2006).[15] Therefore, if the process of criminalizing the AML in China is driven by the transnational enforcement interests, the success of antitrust criminalization depends on the extent to which the professional opinion is aligned with such interests from abroad.

9.4   Criminalization of the antitrust law in the US and the EU

9.4.1   *Criminalization of the antitrust law in the US*

Antitrust criminalization is labeled as an 'American approach', as criminalization is commonly used for 'hardcore'[16] cartels in North America, especially the US (Harding 2002: 393). In the US, although under the Sherman Act in 1890[17] all types of restrictive agreements and unilateral monopolistic conducts were considered illegal, in practice the enforcement of criminal provisions is mainly limited to hardcore cartels (Wils 2006; Harding 2006: 2). During the first several decades after the enactment of the Sherman Act, antitrust violations were not considered as a serious crime; hence, the criminal sanctions on enterprises and individual infringers were rarely used by the judges (Calkins 1997: 428; Baker 2001: 694–5). In 1974, antitrust violations were made felonies by Congress, and the Antitrust Procedures and Penalties Act 1974 increased the maximum imprisonment days for individuals from one year to three years, and the maximum corporate fine was increased from US$50,000 to US$1 million[18] (Baker 2001: 695). In particular, the budgets for antitrust enforcement were significantly increased (Baker 2001: 695). Since the 1980s, the number of criminal cases enforced by the DOJ has increased dramatically and during the period 1980 to 1984, the criminal prosecutions reached a peak with 404 cases (Gallo *et al.* 1994: 36). Meanwhile, an increase in the criminal prosecution of individuals involved in cartel cases has been observed. This phenomenon is supported by both an increase in frequency of imprisonment and an increase in the severity of punishment. In 1990, the maximum corporate fine was increased to US$10 million[19] and in 1991 the *Sentencing Guidelines* were implemented, resulting in a more uniform enforcement in criminalizing antitrust violations (Baker 2001: 696). From 1990 to 1994, the proportion of defendants in antitrust cases that were sentenced to jail was 25 per cent, and this number increased to 31 per cent during the period of 1995 to 1999, to 46 per cent from 2000 to 2004 and reached 54 per cent from 2005 to 2007 (Connor 2008b: 34). Parallel with the increase in frequency, the severity of prison sentences has also been increased. From 1990 to 1999, the total prison days sentenced were 3,313 days on average, and this number increased to 12,722 for the period of 2000 to 2009 and reached 23,398 from 2010 to 2012.[20] The number of imprisonment days per person imposed has doubled from 238 days during the period 1990 to 1994, to 623 days from 1995 to 2007 (Connor 2008b: 35).

9.4.2 *Criminalization of competition law in the EU*

In Europe, the enforcement of antitrust law relies more on administrative control. Unlike the US antitrust law (which pays attention to the behavior of business) EU competition law (both at a European and at national level) examines cartel behavior by taking a regulatory administrative approach, with a special focus on the market outcome, rather than a moral judgment (Harding 2002: 408). However, during the last two decades, a debate on antitrust criminalization in Europe could be observed (Harding 2002: 393). The trend of criminalizing hardcore cartels is mainly driven by the efforts of EU Member States, due to the reason that within the institutional framework of the EU, imposing criminal sanctions by an EU institution requires a transfer of power from Member States to the European level. With respect to the criminal law at that time (2003) this requirement was probably beyond the competences of the European legislator (Kunzlik 2003: 331). Regulation No 1/2003 grants EU Member States the power to enforce their national competition laws and to impose criminal sanctions (Wils 2005: 17). Article 5 of Regulation No 1/2003 empowers the Member States to enforce national competition laws by imposing administrative or criminal fines on individuals or companies (Wils 2005: 18). In recent years the fine on cartels has increased dramatically, even to a level that is 'quasi-criminal' – as the EU Advocate-Generals called it (Shaffer and Nesbitt 2011: 7).[21] Meanwhile, there are considerations with respect to the criminal nature of the fines imposed by the Commission, under the framework of Article 6(1) of the European Convention for the Protection of Human Rights and Fundamental Freedoms (ECHR). In particular there are debates regarding the tension between the fundamental rights of private parties and the role of the Commission "as investigator, prosecutor and adjudicator." However, under Article 23(5) of Regulation No 1/2003, it has been stated that fines imposed by the Commission "shall not be of a criminal law nature." This may change since the entry into force of the Treaty on the Functioning of the European Union (TFEU) which allows under Article 83(2) TFEU *inter alia* the adoption of common " 'minimum rules' with regards to the definition of criminal offences and sanctions if the approximation of criminal laws and regulations of the Member States proves essential to ensure the effective implementation of a Union policy in an area which has been subject to a harmonization measure." On this basis, the Commission already issued a communication "towards an EU criminal policy: ensuring the effective implementation of EU policies through criminal law".[22] This communication intends to provide, *inter alia*, guidance with respect to the interpretation of Article 83(2) of the TFEU. This communication clearly holds that the new article provides the possibility for EU institutions to determine which EU policies require the use of criminal law as an additional enforcement tool. Hence, it should be stressed that since the entry into force of the Lisbon Treaty (within particular conditions) it has become easier for EU institutions to force Member States to use criminal sanctions. This obviously is still a different issue than the application of criminal law by the EU institutions itself, but given the recent trend towards an increasing use of the criminal law, it cannot be excluded that that issue may come on the political agenda as well.

9.5   Towards criminalization of antitrust law in China?

We will now draw some conclusions from the refinements of the economic model of crime with respect to antitrust enforcement which we have just presented and ask the question how some of these refinements apply to the specific case of China, more particularly in relation to the question of whether a criminalization of antitrust would be indicated. We will first argue that for particular reasons private litigation in China may today be underused and that hence an improvement of private enforcement of antitrust may be more preferred than a criminalization (9.5.1). Next, we will argue that, given the particular situation of government agencies and the judiciary in China, a shift of powers to the judiciary (which would be the consequence of criminalization) may at this moment not be indicated (9.5.2). Then we will argue that, rather than moving to criminalization, there are possibilities to improve the functioning of the six-year-old AML within the current administrative law enforcement. We will argue that there are ways to do this by improving the two main factors that are crucial in the Becker model (p and S) and hence to examine possibilities to increase the price of antitrust violations (9.5.3).

9.5.1   Improving private enforcement of antitrust

One lesson for improving the functioning of antitrust enforcement can be drawn from the behavioral biases that we have discussed above.[23] We indicated *inter alia* an overconfidence bias with individuals. This may have an important influence on the enforcement of antitrust law as well.

Weinstein has argued that individuals are more likely to tend to be overconfident when the event is 'controllable' than in case the event is 'uncontrollable' (Weinstein 1980: 808). This finding may provide explanations on the private litigation of antitrust cases in China. Rational choice theory indicates that lawsuits will be settled except when plaintiffs and defendants perceive the results of the trial substantially different (Korobkin and Ulen 2000: 1093; Babcock *et al.* 1995: 1337). This theory indicates that if the plaintiffs and defendants are both well informed and have similar estimations on the trial results, they would prefer to settle out of the court. In contrast, if the rationality assumption does not hold, it is more likely that the plaintiffs perceive the antitrust trial prospects in China as an 'uncontrollable' event; therefore, they are more likely to be less confident than the defendants. Consequently, it is 'rational' for these plaintiffs to give up the efforts of bringing lawsuits to the court, which leads to a rather weak private enforcement of the AML. Given the evidence of self-serving bias provided by the US legal studies, if both plaintiffs and defendants are over-confident, they will anticipate the trial results in two distinct directions: both will anticipate results that are favorable to their side, therefore, there should be more trials than there would be under the rational choice model (Korobkin and Ulen 2000: 1094). However, in China, the antitrust cases brought by private parties are still very limited. Following this analysis, instead of quickly jumping to the conclusion of imposing criminal sanctions on antitrust infringers, it is more important for the antitrust authorities in China to take efforts to incentivize private parties to litigate, and improve legal institutions which can give the plaintiffs of antitrust cases the right 'confidence'.

9.5.2 *Problems with bureaucracy and the judiciary in China*

When addressing the public choice perspective[24] we mentioned that an important assumption is that enforcing agencies and the judiciary are all working together in the public interest to deter antitrust violations. If the judges are willing to serve public interest, the choice between criminalizing antitrust law and imposing administrative fines depends on whether the judges or the administrative regulators have more specialized expertise in dealing with antitrust cases. Generally speaking, judges are more trusted given the fact that they are more independent and obtain superior information on the cases. In contrast, the public choice analysis becomes more relevant if there is evidence showing that judges are rather pursuing their private interests, or judicial decisions are influenced by legislatures at a superior level and by external political pressures. In this case, the level of transparency and accuracy of court opinions and decisions remains low.

Attention should be drawn to the differences between the legal tradition in China and in Western countries. According to Winston, in contrast to the rule of law, the Chinese legal tradition follows the rule by law,[25] and law is perceived as amoral, and the function of the law is to strengthen state control (Winston 2005: 313). This understanding empowers the ruler to interpret the law, which results in the situation that the ruler enjoys the status 'above-the-law' (Li 2011: 6; Winston 2005: 314). For example, it has been argued that in many East Asian countries economic development is the most important political goal, and the concern of facilitating economic reform even overrides individual rights (Tay 2007; Killion 2004: 511). Another issue is whether the judges are qualified to deal with complicated antitrust cases. It has been argued that the courts in China are relatively weak and judges are not qualified enough to handle complex cases (Clarke 2003: 108). This situation has been dramatically improved after the State judicial examination in 2002 and the enactment of the Civil Servant Law in 2005 (Michelson and Li 2012: 4). However, it remains a challenging task to train judges to deal with antitrust criminal cases.

Of course, the problem with the enforcement of antitrust law in China is that there are today problems with political influence both at a level of the administration as well as, at a level of the judiciary. However, one should realize that when China would move to the criminalization of antitrust, this would also imply the introduction of prison sanctions,[26] in which case error costs would, as we have argued above,[27] strongly increase. Given the specific influence of the political elite and potential interest groups on the judiciary in China, one can argue that criminalization may lead to potentially high error costs which should give raise to some caution when pleading for criminalization of antitrust violations. Given those problems, it may be more appropriate to look at the possibilities to increase the expected sanctions within the current administrative law framework.

9.5.3   *Increasing the sanction*

As we have argued above[28] the expected sanction for a potential violator consists of the probability (p) of being apprehended and convicted and then a sanction (S) imposed. Hence, the expected sanction for the potential offender consists of the outcome of the sanction multiplied with the probability. We argue that there are substantial possibilities to increase both the p and the S within the current Chinese model of administrative enforcement of antitrust law.

9.5.3.1   *Increasing fines*

The first factor is to improve the level of sanctions. Compared with the corporate and individual fine that is charged by the antitrust authorities in the US and the EU, the sanction set by the Chinese antitrust authority is rather low. In the US, between 1990 and 2004, the maximum corporate fine was limited to US$10 million.[29] In 2004, this statutory limit was increased to US$100 million by the Antitrust Criminal Penalty Enhancement and Reform Act, which came into force 2004, signed by President George W. Bush, and the maximum individual fine was increased from US$350, 000 to US$1 million (Clarke 2012: 82; Hammond 2005a: 1). Since then, the average fines imposed on corporate cartels has increased dramatically. The average annual cartel fines rose from US$297 million between the fiscal years 1995 and 1999; to US$558 million in fiscal years 2005 to 2007. Since 1995, the major source of these cartel fines is from non-US firms (Connor 2008a: 104). The amount of cartel fines set by the Antitrust Division in the US, however, is not the highest worldwide. Between 2000 and 2004, the fines set by the EU were 200 per cent higher than the cartel fines by the Antitrust Division (Connor 2008a: 106). The cartel fines by all EU authorities amounted to US$11.6 billion in 2005, accounting for 77 per cent of the cartel fines that are charged by all antitrust authorities around the globe. In 2008, the EU Commission imposed EUR1.38 billion in total – the highest fine in the history of antitrust enforcement worldwide – on companies participating in a car glass cartel (Anderson and Cuff 2011: 402).[30] In particular, the fine for Saint Gobain which amounted to EUR896 million was at the time the highest cartel fine ever imposed on a single company (Anderson and Cuff 2011: 402). After Regulation No 1/2003 came into force, the violation of Article 101 of the TFEU can be charged fines up to 10 per cent of the undertakings or association of undertakings' global turnover in the preceding business year.[31] Since 2006, for the recidivist of hardcore cartel cases this fine can be charged from 30 per cent of relevant sales, up to 100 per cent.[32]

A closer look at the amount of fines on global cartel cases, however, indicates that the amount of fines imposed by the EU and US are at a comparable level.[33] In the *Lysine* case, the fine imposed by the US antitrust authority was US$92.5 million, whereas in Europe this amount was US$97.9 million. In the *Citric Acid* case, the US authority charged US$110.4 million and the European antitrust authority charged US$120.4 million. Similarly, in the *Vitamins* case, the company was fined US$906.5 million and in Europe it was fined US$756.9 million (Buccirossi and Spagnolo 2005: 10).

In contrast, the fine imposed on cartels according to the AML is relatively low. Article 46 of the AML states: "Where business operators reach a monopoly agreement and perform it in violation of this law, the anti-monopoly authority shall order them to cease doing so, and shall confiscate the illegal gains and impose a fine of 1 up to 10 per cent of the sales revenue in the previous year [...] In the instance where the monopoly agreement has yet to be implemented: a fine of less than 500,000 Yuan shall be imposed." In 2010, the National Development and Reform Commission (NDRC)[34] office at Guangxi Province reported a cartel case. The cartel was organized by manager Que Zhihe, from Nanning Xian Yi Ge Food Plant, in November 2009 and 18 producers joined this cartel and jointly raised the price of rice noodles in Nanning. In January 2010, this cartel was extended to Liuzhou and another 15 rice noodle producers participated, resulting in an approximately 26 per cent increase of wholesale rice noodle prices and an average 14 per cent increase of retail prices.[35] The penalty that was imposed by the NDRC on the cartel participants was an administrative fine. The three major organizers received a RMB100,000 fine (approximately US$14,700) and 18 other participants received fines ranging from RMB30,000 (approximately US$4,400) to RMB80,000 (approximately US$11,700) and the remaining 12 producers who cooperated with the investigation only received administrative warnings.[36] It is not clear whether this sanction was imposed according to Article 46 of the

AML or Article 15 of the Regulations on Administrative Sanctions for Price-related Illegal Conduct and the Law of Administrative Sanctions or Article 40 of the Price Law[37] (Wei 2013: 131).

The *Green Mung Bean Cartel* was the second case that was brought by the NDRC after the *Rice Noodle Cartel* case.[38] On 17 October 2009, over 100 distributors in Jilin Province attended a meeting to increase the price of green mung beans. This meeting led to a price increase of 220 per cent of green mung beans in May 2010 across the country. The organizer of this cartel, Jilin Corn Center Exchange (JCCE), received a fine of RMB1 million from the NDRC and this amount was the highest fine that the NDRC imposed after the promulgation of the AML.[39] Three other companies were charged fines ranging from RMB300,000 to RMB500,000. Other participants, however, only received administrative warnings.[40]

On 26 January 2011, the State Administration of Industry and Commerce (SAIC), another antitrust authority in China, imposed a fine of RMB200,000 on the Committee for Concrete for the anticompetitive conduct of dividing the concrete market.[41] This Committee belongs to the Lianyungang City Construction Material and Machinery Association. The investigation started by receiving information from the whistleblower and was conducted by a special team from the SAIC Jiangsu Province branch. These cases showed a positive movement in the enforcement of cartel rules in China. Compared with the fines imposed by antitrust authorities in the EU and the US, the fine that cartel members received in China is still modest, and one factor that explains this situation could be the fact that the AML in China is still relatively young and the rules towards cartel agreements still need to be clarified.[42]

9.5.3.2   *Increasing the probability*

The second factor is to increase the probability of detection. Under the current structure, the detection of potential antitrust infringers mainly relies on public powers. To increase the probability of detection, the participation of private parties should be enhanced. One way is to incentivize private parties to report to the antitrust authority and the other way is to promote a leniency program. In the US, since 1997, over US$2.5 billion fines have been charged for antitrust crimes and over 90 per cent of this was conducted through investigations supported by leniency applicants (Hammond 2004: 1). In the US, under the Antitrust Criminal Penalty Enhancement and Reform Act, which came into force in 2004, the benefits of the leniency program include granting single damages, instead of treble damages (Wils 2006: 15). However, only one company can benefit from full immunity from fines (Hammond 2004: 5). In Europe, according to the Leniency Notice issued by the European Commission in 2006,[43] the first undertaking who cooperates with the investigation will receive a reduction on the fine ranging from 30 to 50 per cent, and the second will receive a 20 to 30 per cent reduction, and the third will receive a reduction of up to 20 per cent (Wils 2006: 10).

Wils argued that a leniency program has the strong advantage of obtaining information from the participants (both individuals and companies) who are involved in the cartel (Wils 2006: 21). More importantly, the information collected through leniency programs is generally reliable, as reporting false information will be at the risk of losing the immunity from punishment (Wils 2006: 21). Nevertheless, to effectively implement the leniency programs requires several prerequisites that the current enforcement agency of the AML in China may not fully satisfy. These preconditions include that the participants of the cartel must be provided with a threat of severe sanctions,[44] while exposed to a high risk of detection; moreover, the cartel enforcement policy must to a large extent be transparent and predicable.[45] It is more likely to observe that a leniency program would function better when antitrust law is criminalized, as the sanction level will be significantly increased. However, when other presumptions that are mentioned above are not met, criminalizing cartel conduct will only impose challenges and uncertainties on future antitrust enforcement. At this stage, it is more important for the antitrust enforcers in China to improve the transparency, predictability and credibility of its competition policy, and to pave the way for the introduction of leniency programmes as well as criminal sanctions in the near future.[46]

9.6 Concluding remarks

During the last six years, the enforcement of the Anti-Monopoly Law (AML) in China has been highly reliant on public enforcement and the sanctions imposed on antitrust violators are mainly administrative fines. By taking a law and economics perspective, this chapter draws attention to the possibility of imposing criminal sanctions on cartelistic behavior in China. The economic analysis of optimal legal sanctions developed by Gary Becker shows that offenders should fully internalize the social costs, and criminal sanctions may have to be imposed in order to sufficiently deter future infringements. Following the Becker model, the economic theory on criminalization was further developed by Posner, Shavell, Polinsky, Landes and others during the 1980s. In recent years, these models were reinvestigated by utilizing insights offered by behavioral law and economics, and scholars examine the situation in particular when the assumption of rationality does not hold. After presenting the discussions on the economic theories of antitrust criminalization, this chapter asked the question to what extent criminalizing cartel conduct could improve the enforcement of the AML in China. It should be emphasized that some of the conditions for applying the criminal law mentioned in traditional economic models – for example, that judicial decisions are transparent and independent – may be difficult to apply to the specific case of China. Therefore, criminalization may not be the best solution. Instead, other alternatives should be carefully reconsidered to increase the 'price' for antitrust violation in China, for example the administrative fines should be significantly increased, and the probability of detection should be enhanced by improving the mechanisms to collect information from private parties.

The economic analysis presented in this chapter did not have the normative goal of providing the final answer to the question of whether criminalization of antitrust violations in China was indicated. The goal of the analysis presented here was to show the conditions under which criminalization may work as they follow from the economic literature. The behavioral law and economics literature as well as the public choice analysis further provide valuable refinements of traditional models especially as far as the behavior of offenders and regulators is concerned. The policy maker in China may benefit from these findings from economic theory in order to further improve both the substance and the enforcement of its antitrust law.

Notes

1 In this chapter, the English translation of the AML is taken from http://english. peopledaily.com.cn/90001/90776/90785/6466813.html (accessed 4 February 2014).
2 According to Posner (1980a: 72–7), the theory of economic analysis to punishment was firstly developed by Jeremy Bentham in the eighteenth century. See Bentham (1789).
3 The deterrence argument is rooted in the utilitarian theory, which indicates the goal of imposing punishment as a form of suffering which reduces the utility of individuals is to prevent future crime. See Beccaria (1767) and Bentham (1789).
4 Antitrust Division Memorandum on Guidelines for Sentencing Recommendations in Felony Cases under the Sherman Act, 24 February 1977. See Blair (1985: 440).
5 In 1986, according to the estimation by Douglas Ginsburg, the Assistant Attorney General for Antitrust, the probability of cartels being detected was only around 10 per cent. See Sentencing Options Hearing before the United States Sentencing Commission, in *United States Sentencing Commission: Unpublished Public Hearings*, 15 July 1986. There are concerns about whether this estimation is valid. See Connor and Lande (2005: 519). Bryant and Eckard estimated that in the sample period from January 1961 to December 1987, this probability in the US in a given year was around 13 to 17 per cent. Bryant and Eckhard (1991: 531).
6 Wils argues that in Europe, 16 per cent is already an optimistic estimate. See Wils (2001: 13). Combe, Monnier and Legal's model published in 2008 shows that the probability of detecting cartels in the EU is between 12.9 per cent and 13.3 per cent annually. See Combe *et al.* (2008). In 2010, Connor concluded that: "most scholars believe that it (the probability of being apprehended) averages less than 30 per cent." See Connor (2010: 3).
7 According to Cooter, the differences between taxing ('prices') and sanctioning is that by imposing a tax, the actor will internalize the social harm of her conduct, and the level of this 'price' depends on the amount of external harm; in contrast, the goal of sanctions is to deter, and the level of sanctions depends on the need for deterrence, which indicates the expected cost of the conduct is high enough to prohibit such conduct. When there is clear standard in the community regarding what conduct should be prohibited, but the level of external harm is unclear, sanctions should be used. For the opposite situation, prices should be used. See Cooter (1984).

8 According to the report by the Organisation for Economic Co-operation and Development (OECD) "[t]here is no systematic evidence proving the deterring effects of sanctions on individuals and/or assessing whether such sanctions can be justified." See OECD (2005).

9 In particular, it is important to increase the maximum intensity and the end intensity of the painful experience. However, the punishment with high intensity, short duration and with the most intensive, painful punishment at the end is usually defined as 'torture'. Robinson and Darley (2004: 190–1).

10 Anchoring effects refer to a randomly chosen starting point that will influence the estimates. Anchoring will, e.g. be very important in the behavior of judges in relation to the sanction that has been claimed by the prosecutor and that will hence function as an 'anchor' from which it may become difficult to deviate.

11 Framing effect refers to decisions that are influenced by how gains and losses are framed (Tversky and Kahneman 1981: 453–8).

12 Hindsight bias refers to overestimating the likelihood of an event after learning it did occur (Korobkin and Ulen 2000: 1095–100).

13 Representative effects refer to ignoring the actual statistical information and making a biased judgment between the reality and its appearance.

14 Egocentric bias refers to overestimating one's own abilities. This is also referred to as selective optimism and overconfidence. Unrealistic optimism may lead to underestimation of the probability that unpleasant events will happen to one self. See *inter alia* Jolls (1998: 1658–63) and Sunstein (1997: 1182–4).

15 To better understand cartel conduct, as a crime indeed requires certain economic and legal expertise. As Stucke held "it may be that few people in society, if asked about price-fixing, would graph in their minds a triangle representing the deadweight welfare loss" (Stucke 2006: 495).

16 Hardcore cartel is a commonly used term since the late 1990s. The definition of hardcore cartels provided by the OECD entails "an anti-competitive agreement, anti-competitive concerted practice or anti-competitive arrangement by competitors to fix prices, make rigged bids (collusive tenders) establish output restrictions or quotas, or share or divide markets by allocating customers, suppliers, territories, or lines of commerce." See OECD, Department of Trade and Industry (2001). See also Recommendation of the Council Concerning Effective Action against Hard Core Cartels, issued by OECD 1998. See Clarke (2012: 81). David King argues that compared with hardcore cartels, softcore cartels are the behaviors that competitors intent to secure profits (such as by fixed prices) which may not lead to deadweight losses. In many jurisdictions, hardcore cartels are prohibited *per se*, whereas softcore cartels are subject to public interest or rule of reason tests (King 2010: 6).

17 Section 1 of the Sherman Act reads: "Every contract, combination in the form of trust or otherwise, or conspiracy, in restraint of trade or commerce among the several States, or with foreign nations, is hereby declared to be illegal" (Sherman Act 1890, Ch. 647, §§ 1–2, 26 Stat. 209).

18 Antitrust Procedures and Penalties Act 1974, Pub L. No. 93–528, § 3, 88 Stat. 1706, 1708.

19 Antitrust Amendments Act 1990, Pub. L. No. 101–588, § 4, 104 Stat. 2879, 2880.

20 Criminal Enforcement: Fine and Jail Charts, US Department of Justice, available at: www.justice.gov/atr/public/criminal/264101.html#c (accessed 4 February 2014).

21 Opinion of Advocate General Kokott, Case C-97/08, *Akzo Nobel NV and Others* v. *Commission of the European Communities* (39, 2009 E.C.R. I-8237).

22 COM (2011) 573 of 20 September 2011.

23 See subsection 9.3.4.1.

24 See subsection 9.3.5.

25 According to Winston, this way of legal thinking has been elaborated by an ancient legal scholar Han Feizi (*ca.* 280–233 BC), Winston (2005). For a discussion of the distinction between the rule of law, and the rule by law, see E. W. Orts (2001).

26 Otherwise, there would be no point in criminalization since monetary fines can also be imposed via the current system of administrative law.

27 See subsection 9.3.3.

28 See subsection 9.3.1.

29 Antitrust Amendments Act of 1990, Pub. L. No. 101–588, 104 Stat. 2879 (Codified at 15 U.S.C. § 1, (2000)). See Ginsburg and Wright (2010: 4).

30 Commission Decision Summary No. COMP/39125 (*Car Glass*), 2009 OJC173/13.

31 Article 23 of Council Regulation No 1/2003, 2003 OJ (L1) 1 EC. This turnover is calculated as the sum of the total turnover of all members in the given market.

32 *Guidelines on the Method of Setting Fines*, Official Journal C 210, 1 September 2006. See Ginsburg and Wright (2010: 4).

33 Note that the fines imposed by the European Commission have increased dramatically during the last 15 years, see *European Commission, Cartels: Overview* available at: http://ec.europa.eu/competition/cartels/overview/index_en.html (accessed 4 February 2014).

34 The NDRC is one of the antitrust enforcement agencies in China.

35 'First Price Cartel Cases under the Chinese AML', Cleary Gottlieb Steen & Hamilton LLP, 21 May 2010.

36 According to Article 46 of the AML "where any business operator voluntarily reports the conditions on reading the monopoly agreement and provides important evidence to the anti-monopoly authority, it may impose a mitigated punishment or exemption from punishment as the case may be [...]." However, at that time, leniency policy had not been officially proposed by the NDRC. This decision may be issued according to Article 15 of the Regulations on Administrative Sanctions for Price-related Illegal Conduct and the Law of Administrative Sanctions, Article 27. See *First Price Cartel Cases Under the Chinese AML*, Cleary Gottlieb Steen & Hamilton LLP, 21 May 2010.

37 According to Article 40 of the Price Law if there are illegal gains, the violator might be fined up to five times the value of the illegal gains; if there are no illegal gains, a fine from RMB100,000 up to RMB1,000,000 will be imposed.

38 See China Fines Agricultural Companies for Agreeing to Raise the Price of Their Products, Eversheds, LLP. 16 July 2010, available at: http://www.eversheds.com/global/en/what/articles/index.page?ArticleID=en/China_Focus/China_fines_agricultural_companies_for_agreeing_to_raise_the_price_of_their_products(accessed 4 February 2014).

39 This NDRC decision was issued according to the Price Law, and the Provisions on Administrative Penalty against Unlawful Price-Related Practices. See *China Fines Agricultural Companies for Agreeing to Raise the Price of Their Products*, Eversheds, LLP.

40 It is not clear whether the NDRC has applied the leniency policies in this case. In addition to the decision from the NDRC, there was another distributor that was fined RMB20,000 by the Guangdong Provincial Price Bureau.

41 'First Cartel Fines in China Following New Regulations', McDermott Will & Emery, 25 February 2011, available at: http://www.mwe.com/publications/uniEntity.aspx?xpST=PublicationDetail&pub=5902&PublicationTypes=d9093adb-e95d-4f19–819a-f0bb5170ab6d (accessed 4 February 2014).

42 Ibid.

43 Wils (2006: 10). See also Commission Notice on Immunity from Fines and Reduction of Fines in Cartel Cases, [2006] OJ C 298/17.

44 It refers to the threat of criminal liabilities, according to Hammond, if this sanction is financial penalty, the level must be set severely punitive. See Hammond (2004: 7).

45 According to Hammond, "severe sanctions, heightened fear of detection, and transparency in enforcement policies" are the three major elements to ensure the effectiveness of leniency programs. See Hammond (2004: 5).
46 For a comprehensive discussion on implementing leniency programs in China, see Oded (2013).

References

Anderson, D. and Cuff, R. (2011) 'Cartels in the European Union: Procedural Fairness for Defendants and Claimants', *Fordham International Law Journal*, 34, 385–430.

Armstrong, M. and Huck, S. (2010) 'Behavioral Economics as Applied to Firms: A Primer', *CESifo Working Paper no. 2937.*

Babcock, L., Loewenstein, G., Issacharoff S. and Camerer C. (1995) 'Biased Judgments of Fairness in Bargaining', *American Economic Review*, 85, 1337–43.

Baker, D. I. (2001) 'The Use of Criminal Law Remedies to Deter and Punish Cartels and Bid-Rigging', *The George Washington Law Review*, 69, 693–714.

Barnett, T. O. (2006) 'Seven Steps to Better Cartel Enforcement', 11th Annual Competition Law and Policy Workshop, European Union Institute, Italy, 2 June 2006. Available at: http://www.justice.gov/atr/public/speeches/216453.htm (accessed 3 February 2014).

Baron, S. and Kennedy, L. W. (1998) 'Deterrence and Homeless Male Street Youths', *Canadian Journal of Criminology*, 40(1), 27–60.

Becker, G. S. (1968) 'Crime and Punishment: An Economic Approach', *Journal of Political Economy*, 76(2), 169–217.

Bentham, J. (1789) *An Introduction to the Principles of Morals and Legislation*, Oxford: Claredon Press.

Blair, R. D. (1985) 'A Suggestion for Improved Antitrust Enforcement', *The Antitrust Bulletin*, 30, 433–56.

Bowles, R., Faure, M. G. and Garoupa, N. (2008) 'The Scope of Criminal Law and Criminal Sanctions: An Economic View and Policy Implications', *Journal of Law and Society*, 35(3), 389–416.

Brickman, P. and Campbell, D. (1971) 'Hedonic Relativism and Planning the Good Society', in Appley, M. H. (ed), *Adaptation-level Theory: A Symposium*, 287–302.

Bryant, P. G. and Eckhard, E. W. (1991) 'Price Fixing: The Probability of Getting Caught', *Review of Economics and Statistics*, 531–6.

Buccirossi, P. and Spagnolo, G. (2005) 'Optimal Fines in the Era of Whistleblowers, Should Price Fixers still go to Prison?', *Lear Research Paper* 05–01.

Calkins, S. (1997) 'An Enforcement Official's Reflections on Antitrust Class Actions', *Arizona Law Review*, 39, 413–52.

Clarke, D. C. (2003) 'China's Legal System and the WTO: Prospects for Compliance', *Washington University Global Studies Law Review*, 2, 97–120.

Clarke, J. (2012) 'The Increasing Criminalization of Economic Law – A Competition Law Perspective', *Journal of Financial Crime*, 19(1), 76–98.

Coase, R. H. (1992) 'The Institutional Structure of Production', *American Economic Review*, 82(4), 713–19.

Coffee, J. C. (1980) 'Corporate Crime and Punishment: A Non-Chicago View of the Economics of Criminal Sanctions', *American Criminal Law Review*, 419–76.

Coffee, J. C. (1992) 'Paradigms Lost: The Blurring of the Criminal and Civil Law Models – and What Can Be Done About it', *Yale Law Journal*, 101, 1875–94.

Combe, E., Monnier, C. and Legal, R. (2008) 'Cartels: The Probability of Getting Caught in the European Union', *Bruges European Economic Research Papers no. 12.*

Connor, J. M. (2008a) 'Anti-Cartel Enforcement by the DOJ: An Appraisal', *The Competition Law Review*, 5(1), 89–121.

Connor, J. M. (2008b) 'The United States Department of Justice Antitrust Division's Cartel Enforcement: Appraisal and Proposals', *The American Antitrust Institute Working Paper* no. 08–02.

Connor, J. M. (2010) 'Recidivism Revealed: Private International Cartels 1990–2009'. Available at: http://papers.ssrn.com/sol3/papers.cfm?abstract_id=1688508 (accessed 7 February 2014).

Connor, J. M. and Lande, R. H. (2005) 'How High Do Cartels Raise Prices? Implications for Optimal Cartel Fines', *Tulane Law Review*, 80, 513–70.

Cooter, R. (1984) 'Prices and Sanctions', *Columbia Law Review*, 84, 1523–60.

Dau-Schmidt, K. G. (1984) 'Sentencing Antitrust Offenders: Reconciling Economic Theory with Legal Theory', *William Mitchell Law Review*, 9(1), 75–100.

Easterbrook, F. H. (1983) 'Criminal Procedure as a Market System', *The Journal of Legal Studies*, 12(2), 289–332.

Englich, B., Mussweiler, T. and Strack, F. (2006) 'Playing Dice with Criminal Sentences: The Influence of Irrelevant Anchors on Experts Judicial Decision Making', *Personality and Social Psychology Bulletin*, 32, 188–200.

Faure, M. G. (2000) 'Compensation of Non-Pecuniary Loss: An Economic Perspective', in Magnus, U. and Spier, J. (eds), *European Tort Law*, Liber Amicorum for Helmut Koziol, Frankfurt am Main: Peter Lang, 143–59.

Faure, M. G. (2009) 'Environmental Crimes', in Garoupa, N. (ed) *Criminal Law and Economics*, 3, Cheltenham: Edward Elgar.

Faure, M. G., Ogus, A. and Philipsen, N. (2009) 'Curbing consumer financial losses: the economics of regulatory enforcement', *Law and Policy*, 31(2), 161–91.

Gallo, J. C., Dau-Schmidt, K. G., Craycraft, J. C. and Parker, C. J. (1994) 'Criminal Penalties under the Sherman Act: A Study of Law and Economics', *Research in Law and Economics*, 16, 25–71.

Ginsburg, D. H. and Wright, J. D. (2010) 'Antitrust Sanctions', *Competition Policy International*, 6(2), 3–39.

Guthrie, C., Rachlinski, J. J. and Wistrich, A. J. (2001) 'Inside the Judicial Mind', *Cornell Law Review*, 86, 777–830.

Hammond, S. D. (2002) 'From Hollywood to Hong Kong – Criminal Antitrust Enforcement is Coming to a City near You', *Loyola Consumer Law Review*, 14, 567–76.

Hammond, S. D. (2004) 'Cornerstones of an Effective Leniency Program', Speech at the ICN Workshop on Leniency Programs, Sydney, Australia, 22–23 November 2004.

Hammond, S. D. (2005a) 'An Overview of Recent Developments in the Antitrust Division's Criminal Enforcement Program', speech to the American Bar Association, Kona, HI, 10 January 2005.

Hammond, S. D. (2005b) 'Ten Strategies for Winning the Fight Against Hardcore Cartels', Deputy Assistant Attorney General, US Department of Justice, Antitrust Division, Address at the No. 3 Prosecutor's Program, 18 October 2005.

Harding, C. (2002) 'Business Cartels as a Criminal Activity: Reconciling North American and European Models of Regulation', *Maastricht Journal of European and Competition Law*, 9, 393–419.

Harding, C. (2006) 'Business Collusion as a Criminological Phenomenon: Exploring the Global Criminalization of Business Cartels', *Critical Criminology*, 181–205.

Hawkins, K. (1984) *Environment and Enforcement Regulation and Social Definition of Pollution*, Oxford: Clarendon Press.

International Competition Network (ICN) (2005) 'Defining Hard Core Cartel Conduct, Effective Institutions, Effective Penalties', vol.1, Report Prepared by the ICN Working Group on Cartels, Bonn, Germany. Available at: http://www.internationalcompetitionnetwork.org/uploads/library/doc346.pdf (accessed 3 February 2014).

Jolls, C. (1998) 'Behavioural Economic Analysis of Redistributive Legal Rules', *Vanderbilt Law Review*, 51, 1653–77.

Kahneman, D. (1999) 'Objective Happiness', in Kahneman, D., Deiner, E. and Schwartz, N. (eds), *Well-Being: The Foundations of Hedonic Psychology*, New York: Russell Sage Foundation.

Killion, M. U. (2004) 'Post-WTO China and Independent Judicial Review', *Houston Journal of International Law*, 26, 507–60.

King, D. (2010) 'Criminalization of Cartel Behavior', *Ministry of Economic Development Occasional Paper 10/01*.

Korobkin, R. B. and Ulen, T. S. (2000) 'Law and Behavioural Science: Removing the Rationality Assumption from Law and Economics', *California Law Review*, 88(4), 1051–144.

Kunzlik, P. F. (2003) 'Globalization and hybridization in antitrust enforcement: European "borrowing" from the US approach', *The Antitrust Bulletin*, 48, 319–54.

Li, L. (2011) 'The "Production" of Corruption in China's Courts – the Politics of Judicial Decision-Making and Its Consequences in a One-Party State', *US-Asia Law Institute NYU Working Paper Series 2011*.

McAdams, R. H. and Ulen, T. S. (2009) 'Behavioural Criminal Law and Economics', in Garoupa, N. (ed), *Criminal Law and Economics*, Cheltenham: Edward Elgar; reprinted in De Geest, G. (ed), *Encyclopedia of Law and Economics*, XI, Cheltenham: Edward Elgar.

Michelson, E. and Li, K. (2012) 'Judicial Performance without Independence: The Delivery of Justice and Political Legitimacy in Rural China', presented at workshop on 'Work-in-Progress on Chinese Law', Center for Chinese Legal Studies, Columbia Law School, 9 May 2012.

Oded, S. (2013) 'Leniency and Compliance: Towards an Effective Leniency Policy in the Chinese Anti-Monopoly Law', in Faure, M. G. and Zhang, X. (eds), *The Chinese Anti-Monopoly Law, New Developments and Empirical Evidence*, Cheltenham: Edward Elgar, 142–64.

OECD (2005) Policy Roundtables, Cartel Sanctions against Individuals. Available at: http://www.oecd.org/competition/cartels/34306028.pdf (accessed 4 February 2014).

Orts, E. W. (2001) 'Rule of Law in China', *Vanderbilt Journal of Transnational Law*, 34, 43–116.

Parker, C. (2006) 'The "Compliance" Trap: the Moral Message in Responsive Regulatory Enforcement', *Law and Society Review*, 40(3), 591–622.

Polinsky, A. M. and Shavell, S. (1979) 'The Optimal Trade Off between the Probability and the Magnitude of Fines', *American Economic Review*, 880–91.

Polinsky, A. M. and Shavell, S. (1991) 'A Note on Optimal Fines When Wealth Varies among Individuals', *American Economic Review*, 81, 618–21.

Polinsky, A. M. and Shavell, S. (1993) 'Should Employees be Subject to Fines and Imprisonment Given the Existence of Corporate Liability?', *International Review of Law and Economics*, 13, 239–57.

Posner, R. A. (1976) *Antitrust Law: An Economic Perspective*, Chicago: The University of Chicago Press.

Posner, R. A. (1980a) 'Retribution and Related Concepts of Punishment', *The Journal of Legal Studies*, 9(1), 71–92.

Posner, R. A. (1980b) 'Optimal Sentences for White Collar Criminals', *American Criminal Law Review*, 400–18.

Redelmeier, D. and Kahneman, D. (1996) 'Patients' Memories of Painful Medical Treatments: Real Time and Retrospective Evaluations of Two Minimally Invasive Procedures', *Pain*, 116, 3–8.

Reeves, A. P. and Stucke, M. E. (2011) 'Behavioral Antitrust', *Indiana Law Journal*, 86, 1527–86.

Robinson, P. H. and Darley, J. M. (2004) 'Does Criminal Law Deter? A Behavioral Science Investigation', *Oxford Journal of Legal Studies*, 24(2), 173–205.

Schwartz, W. F. (1979) 'An Overview of the Economics of Antitrust Enforcement', *Georgetown Law Journal*, 68, 1075–102.

Scott, P. (2008) 'Go Directly to Jail', *Global Competition Review*, 11(10), 6–8.

Shaffer, G. C. and Nesbitt, N. H. (2011) 'Criminalizing Cartels: A Global Trend?', *University of Minnesota Legal Studies Research Paper Series no. 11–26*.

Shavell, S. (1985) 'Criminal Law and the Optimal Use of Non-monetary Sanctions as a Deterrent', *Columbia Law Review*, 85, 1232–62.

Shavell, S. (1993) 'The Optimal Structure of Law Enforcement', *The Journal of Law and Economics*, 36, 255–88.

Shavell, S. (2004) *Foundations of Economic Analysis of Law*, Cambridge: Harvard University Press.

Simon, H. A. (1956) 'Rational Choice and the Structure of the Environment', *Psychological Review*, 63(2), 129–38.

Simon, H. A. (1979) 'Rational Decision-making in Business Organizations', *The American Economic Review*, 69(4), 493–513.

Stigler, G. J. (1970) 'The Optimum Enforcement of Laws', *Journal of Political Economy*, 78(3), 526–36.

Stone, C. D. (1980) 'The Place of Enterprise Liability in the Control of Corporate Conduct', *Yale Law Journal*, 90(1), 1–77.

Stucke, M. E. (2006) 'Morality and Antitrust', *Columbia Business Law Review*, 3, 443–547.

Stucke, M. E. (2007) 'Behavioral Economists at the Gate: Antitrust in the 21st Century', *The University of Tennessee Legal Studies Research Papers Series no. 12*.

Stucke, M. E. (2012) 'The Implications of Behavioral Antitrust', *University of Tennessee Legal Studies Research Paper no. 192*.

Sunstein, C. R. (1997) 'Behavioral Analysis of Law', *The University of Chicago Law Review*, 64, 1175–95.

Tay, A. E. (2007) '"Asian Values" and the Rule of Law', in P. Costa and D. Zolo (eds), *The Rule of Law: History, Theory and Criticism*, Berlin: Springer, 565–86. Available at: http://www.juragentium.org/topics/rol/en/tay.htm (accessed 3 February 2014).

Van den Bergh, R. (2013) 'Behavioral Antitrust: Not Ready for the Main Stage', *Journal of Competition Law and Economics*, 9(1), 203–29.

Van den Bergh, R. and Faure, M. G. (2011) 'Critical Issues in the Enforcement of the Anti-Monopoly Law in China: A Law and Economics Perspective', in Faure, M. and Zhang, X. (eds), *Competition Policy and Regulation*, Cheltenham: Edward Elgar, 54–75.

Wagner-von Papp, F. (2010) 'What if All Bid-Riggers Went to Prison and Nobody Noticed? Criminal Antitrust Law Enforcement in Germany', in Beatonwells, C. and Ezrachi, A. (eds), *Criminalising Cartels: Critical Studies of an Interdisciplinary Regulatory Movement*, Oxford: Hart Publishing.

Wei, D. (2013) 'Antitrust in China: An Overview of Recent Implementation of Anti-monopoly Law', *European Business Organization Law Review*, 14(1), 119–39.

Weinstein, N. D. (1980) 'Unrealistic Optimism about Future Life Events', *Journal of Personality and Social Psychology*, 39(5), 806–20.

Werden, G. J. and Simon, M. J. (1987) 'Why Price Fixers Should Go to Prison?', *The Antitrust Bulletin*, 32, 917–38.

Winston, K. (2005) 'The Internal Morality of Chinese Legalism', *Singapore Journal of Legal Studies*, 313–47.

Wils, W. P. J. (2001) 'Does the Effective Enforcement of Article 81 and 82 EC Require not only Fines on Undertakings but also Individual Penalties, in Particular Imprisonment?', European University Institute, Robert Schuman Center for Advanced Studies, 2001 EU Competition Law and Policy Workshop/Proceedings, reprinted in Ehlermann, C. D. and Atanasiu, I. (eds) *European Competition Law Annual 2001: Effective Private Enforcement of EC Antitrust Law*, Oxford/Portland OR: Hart Publishing.

Wils, W. P. J. (2005) 'Is Criminalization of EU Competition Law the Answer?', in Cseres, K. J., Schinkel, M. P. and Vogelaar, F. O. W. (eds), *Remedies and Sanctions in Competition Policy: Economic and Legal Implications of the Tendency to Criminalize Antitrust Enforcement in the EU Member States*, Cheltenham: Edward Elgar.

Wils, W. P. J. (2006) 'Leniency in Antitrust Enforcement: Theory and Practice'. Available at: http://papers.ssrn.com/sol3/papers.cfm?abstract_id=939399 (accessed 7 February 2014).

Zhao, X. (2008) 'The Features, the Functions, the Characteristics and the Main Institutional Concepts of the AML' (original in Chinese: 反垄断法的性质、地位、特征及其主要制度理念). Available at: http://jjs.ndrc.gov.cn/gzdt/t20080829_233729.htm (accessed 3 February 2014).

10 Climate change and financial instruments to cover disasters

What role for insurance?

Qihao He[1]

10.1 Introduction

Although not all scientists agree that climate change is responsible for recent extreme weather trends, most scientists believe that climate change is probably more responsible than not for increased catastrophes caused by extreme weather (Intergovernmental Panel on Climate Change 2007; Oreskes 2007; Hecht 2008; US Government Accountability Office 2007).[2] A 2006 report by the United Nations Framework Convention on Climate Change (UNFCCC) argued that by 2040 it is likely that the damage resulting from climate change might be as high as $1 trillion annually (United Nations Environment Programme Finance Initiative Climate Change Working Group 2006; Faure 2007).[3] American International Group (AIG), Swiss Re, Lloyd's of London, and other leading insurers all identify climate change as a major threat for global risk management (AIG 2009; Swiss Re 2008).

Data shows that the frequency of and losses caused by natural catastrophes have mounted. We can see this from the marked increase in the number of natural catastrophe events from 1970 to 2012.

There has also been a marked increase in the amount of insured natural catastrophe losses in the world from 1970 to 2012.

Due to both climate change and an increasing concentration of the world's population in vulnerable areas (Mani *et al.* 2003), it is reasonable to predict that natural catastrophe disasters will become more frequent, more intense and more costly in the coming years. Looking at the world map, the US, China and many European countries are all vulnerable to natural catastrophes and the risk of loss is increasing significantly (US Government Accountability Office 2002; US Government Accountability Office 2005; Department of Civil Affairs of People's Republic of China 2009). In the last decade, Hurricane Katrina in 2005 killed 1,300 people and caused estimated insured losses of US$48.1 billion, and Hurricane Ike in 2008 caused an estimated insured loss of US$17.6 billion (Kunreuther and Michel-Kerjan 2010: 118). In China, direct economic losses caused by catastrophes are around US$25 billion almost every year and the number will be considerably larger if indirect economic losses such as disaster relief are taken into consideration (Department of

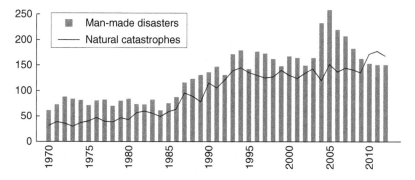

Figure 10.1 Number of events from 1970 to 2012
(Source: Sigma 2013a.)

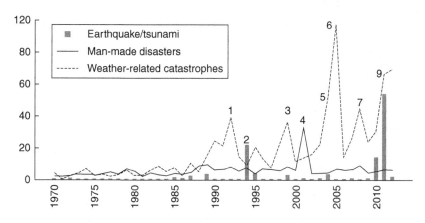

1   1995: Hurricane Andrew
2   1994: Northridge earthquake
3   1999: Winter Storm Lother
4   2001: 9/11 attacks
5   2004: Hurricanes Ivan, Charley, Frances
6   2005: Hurricanes Katrina, Rita, Wilma
7   2008: Hurricanes Ike, Gustav
8   2010: Chile, New Zealand earthquakes
9   2011: Japan, New Zealand earthquakes
        Thailand flood

Figure 10.2 Insured catastrophe losses from 1970 to 2012
(Source: Sigma 2013a.)

Civil Affairs of People's Republic of China 2009). For example, the Pearl River Delta is a densely populated metropolitan area comprised of Hong Kong, Guangzhou and Shenzhen situated in one of the world's most disaster-prone regions; floods and typhoons put more people at risk there than in any other metropolitan area in the world (Swiss Re 2013). Similar catastrophes and losses threaten the EU as well (US Government Accountability Office 2005).

Global climate change has caused many weather-related catastrophes in the world, and the losses have been increasing dramatically during the past years. Various legal and business mechanisms and tools can be used to manage catastrophe risks and cover catastrophe losses, such as insurance, government subsidies and risk securitization. In theory, private insurance can be an efficient financial instrument to cover disasters, as will be explained in Section 10.2. In practice, private insurance plays an important role in developed countries such as the US. Based on the above background and discussion, this chapter addresses the following question: taking into account China's transition economy and specific socialist system, what is the role of private insurance to cover disasters and how does it distribute catastrophe risks sustainably? Furthermore, I will propose that mandatory multi-year insurance may be a possible solution to be considered.

10.2   The mechanism of insurance to cover disasters

10.2.1   *Introduction*

Natural catastrophes, such as hurricanes, floods, typhoons and snowstorms, are classified as 'fundamental risks' rather than 'particular risks', and they often cause much more severe losses than particular risks (Kulp 1956: 3–4).[4] Bruggeman (2010: 7) defines a catastrophe as a rapid onset single-event disaster that causes a substantial amount of damage and/or that involves numerous victims. Banks (2005: 5) has expanded the definition from the traditional view of a single event that causes sudden changes to include instances of a gradual accumulation of many small incidents, perhaps precipitated by the same catalyst, leading to the same scale of damages/losses; such events may not actually be recognized as catastrophes until a long period of time has passed and many losses have accumulated. From a government perspective, for example, the Centre of Research on the Epidemiology of Disasters (CRED) treats a catastrophe risk as "a situation or event, which overwhelms local capacity, necessitating a request to national or international level for external assistance; an unforeseen and often sudden event that causes great damage, destruction and human suffering" (The Em-Dat Glossary 2012). According to the Federal Emergency Management Agency (FEMA) of the US, an event where related federal costs reach or exceed US\$500 million is deemed as 'catastrophe' (US Government Accountability Office 2009). In this chapter, I focus on climate change that affects the incidence of weather-related catastrophes. Hence, I would like to define natural catastrophes for the purpose of this chapter as a weather-related event that occurs infrequently, but causes very significant human and financial losses (He and Chen 2013).

Risk and uncertainty are closely connected concepts, but they should be properly separated from each other. Almost 100 years ago, Frank Knight in his book *Risk, Uncertainty and Profit* carefully distinguished between risk and uncertainty. Risk refers to a *measurable* exposure and uncertainty refers to *unmeasurable* exposure. The uncertainty of an exposure cannot be quantified or put into a number value. This difference is relevant to insuring major catastrophes, because when there is 'too much' unpredictability, there is additionally too much uncertainty to quantify an exposure to loss (Knight 1971: 233).[5] In subsection 10.3.1 below, I will describe the challenges of dealing with uncertainty in catastrophe management.

Traditionally, the role of the insurance industry is to distribute risks. The risk management process is based on three pillars: risk assessment (or risk analysis), risk control and risk financing. Among these, insurance is an important way of risk financing to transfer risk (Outreville 1998: 45–64; Thoyts 2010: 286–95).

Many law and economics scholars favor insurance as a private market mechanism for distributing catastrophe risk, especially when compared with government-provided compensation (Faure and Heine 2011). For example, Kunreuther (1968), Epstein (1996), Priest (1996) and Kaplow (1991) argue that insurance is better equipped to deal with catastrophe risks due to its advantages of lower transaction costs, lower adverse selection and more efficiency as a result of competitive markets.

10.2.2   The mechanism of insurance to cover disasters

Insurance is regarded as an important tool to cover losses caused by disasters because of its specific characteristics. Emmett and Therese Vaughan give definitions of insurance from two different viewpoints. From the viewpoint of individuals, insurance is a device to transfer risk, whereas from the viewpoint of society, insurance is a device to reduce risks through pooling (Vaughan and Vaughan 2007: 34–44). 'Risk transfer' refers to a process by which an individual substitutes a small certain cost which is called the premium for a large uncertain financial loss which is the contingency insured against; meanwhile, 'risk pooling' is the process of combing a sufficient number of homogeneous exposures into a group to make the losses statistically predictable for the group as a whole (Vaughan and Vaughan 2007: 34–44). When insurance contributes to risk transfer and risk pooling, Figure 10.3 depicts the process of insuring disasters.

10.2.3   Risk aversion

In insurance economics, 'risk aversion' is commonly used to describe individuals' attitude to risk (Seog 2010: 18–33). A person is said to be risk-averse "if she considers the utility of a certain prospect of money income to be higher than the expected utility of an uncertain prospect of equal expected monetary value" (Cooter and Ulen 2008: 50).

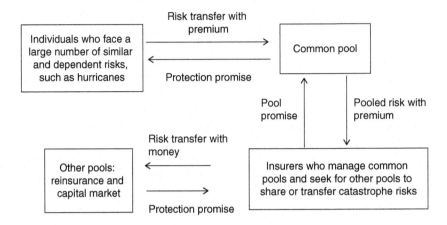

Figure 10.3 The mechanism of insurance to cover disasters

The concept of risk aversion can explain the use of insurance to cover disasters. People who are risk-averse want to transfer risk. Then the question is who would like to take this transferred risk? When a risk is relatively small (it depends on an individual's attitude, and people's attitudes to risk are different), a risk-averse individual may become risk-neutral. The relatively risk-neutral person may play the role of insurer by taking others' risk. This mechanism is efficient if no one suffers damage and someone becomes happier by transferring the risk, satisfying the conditions for 'Pareto Optimality' (Seog 2010: 35–9).[6]

Assuming, however, that all individuals are strictly risk-averse, then no one would like to take someone else's risk. Under such circumstance, a possible alternative is risk pooling. By risk pooling, each individual relies on the pool and all members of the pool become relatively risk neutral when they face a larger risk (Borch 1962: 424–44). If individuals' risks are independent from each other, this risk pooling mechanism also conforms to the law of large numbers by which the future risk is more certain in larger groups. This may make the risk easier to underwrite in the aggregate than for any particular individual because it reduces uncertainty (Kunreuther and Roth 1998: 24–6; Baker and Logue 2013: 3–4; Bruggeman 2010: 59–60).[7]

10.2.4 *The current state of the catastrophe insurance market*

Over the last few decades, the number of natural catastrophes has risen (Sigma 2012). During this time, insurers who underwrote these exposures would face more insured losses. In the US in 1992, Hurricane Andrew struck Florida and cost insurers US$21.6 billion (Florida Office of Insurance 2006). In 2005 Hurricane Katrina caused about US$48 billion in catastrophe-related insured losses – a historic record in US (Kunreuther and Michel-Kerjan 2010:

Table 10.1 The most costly insured catastrophes worldwide from 2003 to 2008

(Source: Swiss Re 2009 and the Insurance Information Institute in New York.)

$ billion insured loss	Event	Victims (dead or missing)	Year	Area of primary damage
17.6	Hurricane Ike	348	2008	US, Caribbean, *et al.*
5.0	Hurricane Gustav	153	2008	US, Caribbean, *et al.*
6.3	Winter Storm Kyrill	54	2007	Germany, UK, NL, France
48.1	Hurricane Katrina	1,836	2005	US, Gulf of Mexico, *et al.*
13.8	Hurricane Wilma	35	2005	US, Gulf of Mexico, *et al.*
11.1	Hurricane Rita	34	2005	US, Gulf of Mexico, *et al.*
14.6	Hurricane Ivan	124	2004	US, Caribbean, *et al.*
9.1	Hurricane Charley	24	2004	US, Caribbean, *et al.*
5.8	Hurricane Frances	38	2004	US, Bahamas
4.4	Hurricane Jeanne	3,034	2004	US, Caribbean, *et al.*
4.0	Typhoon Songda	45	2004	Japan, South Korea
3.7	Storms	45	2003	US

(Source: Adapted from Kunreuther and Michel-Kerjan 2009.)

Notes: dollar amounts are indexed to 2008.

119–20). In 2009, Swiss Re and the Insurance Information Institute issued the report *Twenty-Five Most Costly Insured Catastrophes Worldwide, 1970–2008* (Kunreuther and Michel-Kerjan 2009a). From 2003 to 2008, the number of insured catastrophes is almost half of the whole 38 years. The details of the insured catastrophes from 2003 to 2008 are shown in Table 10.1.

The total cost of catastrophes in 2012 was US$186 billion worldwide, of which US$77 billion was covered by insurers (Sigma 2013a). Therefore, the gap between insured and non-insured losses was US$109 billion (Sigma 2013a). Even in the US, the biggest private insurance market in the world, catastrophe insurance also faces many challenges. After Hurricane Katrina in 2005, a lot of insurance firms cut back their coverage in coastal areas. As of 2012, many catastrophe losses have remained uninsured. In 2007, Florida responded to non-insured catastrophe risks by setting up its own government-backed insurance company, the Citizens Property Insurance Corporation. Due to the subsidized price of coverage, by 2010 this company had become the largest catastrophe insurance underwriter (Kunreuther *et al.* 2013: 11–12). In the US, the free market has always been honored, and it is regarded as an integral part of its culture (Swartz 2002). However, insurers have withdrawn from the catastrophe insurance market, causing government to intervene. In the next section, I use a supply–demand framework to analyze the specific actors and anomalies of the catastrophe insurance market.

10.3   A supply–demand framework analysis of catastrophe insurance in covering disasters

From the above analysis, we can learn that the insurance mechanism is generally efficient through risk transfer and risk pooling. However, insurers have done relatively little to address catastrophe risks, and even cut back coverage in exposure to losses. Flood insurance in flood-prone areas of the US is a typical example (Kunreuther and Roth 1998: 40).[8] This quandary raises the question of which barriers prevent insurers from underwriting catastrophe insurance policies. As a matter of fact, barriers exist on both the supply side and the demand side (Hecht 2008). This section attempts to explore the supply–demand dynamics.

10.3.1   Supply of catastrophe insurance

On the supply side, classic economic theory assumes that insurance companies are maximizing their long-run expected profits in a competitive insurance market (Kunreuther *et al.* 2013: 18). However, in the real world, the insurer's behavior often differs from the classical theory as I will discuss.

10.3.1.1   Insurability restriction of catastrophe risk

In theory, catastrophe risks might make good business for insurers because bearing risks for money is the business of insurers. However, insurers will decide whether or not to cover a catastrophe risk based on whether that risk is insurable. A risk is considered insurable if it satisfies at least two requirements: first, the insurer must have the ability to identify, quantify and estimate the chances of disasters and the resulting losses; and second, the insurer must have the ability to set and collect appropriate premiums for catastrophe risks (Kunreuther and Michel-Kerjan 2007; Kunreuther and Roth 1998: 27–38).

10.3.1.1.1   PREDICTABILITY

Many insurable risks, such as house fires or automobile accidents, occur on a regular basis. It is possible to identify and quantify such risks and to estimate losses of such accidents by using historical data. For catastrophes, however, identifying and quantifying risks is more difficult due to the low probability of these disasters and thus limited historical data. Furthermore, the uncertainty of catastrophes increases the difficulty of estimating the frequency and damages of disasters (Cummins and Lewis 2003). These obstacles make it almost impossible for catastrophe risks to satisfy the first requirement of insurability. However, new developments in scientific information technology, especially big data,[9] may make it easier to identify and quantify a catastrophe risk (Mayer-Schoenberger and Cukier 2013).

10.3.1.1.2 PRICING

Price setting is the other challenge for catastrophe risks. Setting premiums is influenced by both *intrinsic factors*, such as the ambiguity of risks, the degree of correlated risks, and asymmetric information about the risk, plus the *extrinsic factors*, such as rate regulation and capital market requirements. In this part I will only analyze intrinsic factors, and examine extrinsic factors in subsection 10.3.1.3.

Insurance pricing theory makes a distinction between risk and uncertainty. Uncertainty refers to *un-measurable* exposure. The uncertainty of an exposure cannot be quantified or assigned a number value. The value of the *un-measurable* exposure is 'unknowable', therefore making it impossible to rationally calculate a rational charge for taking the exposure. In other words, uncertainty leads to unreliable insurance premiums.

Asymmetric information about the risk often includes moral hazard and adverse selection.[10] Moral hazard occurs when the insured has an informational advantage from better knowing his risk and expected losses. The insured will then have a tendency to take risks since the insurers will bear most of the loss, and thus the possibility of a loss will increase after the insured purchases the insurance (Bruggeman 2010: 61–4). For example, when an individual purchases a hurricane insurance policy, the individual may have no interest to perform mitigation work on the house such as making it storm proof. When a hurricane occurs, the possibility of the house being damaged increases. Adverse selection means that those with the highest risk are most likely to buy the insurance (Bruggeman 2010: 64–6). For example, people who live in flood-prone areas are most likely to purchase flood insurance, while others are not. This will lead to a flood insurance pool that is full of high risks.

The avoidance of correlated risks is a very important prerequisite for a large risk pool. The law of large numbers as the basic principle of insurance depends on independent events so the insurer can spread the risk over a large risk pool (Priest 1996). Looking at catastrophe risks, each catastrophe may cause thousands of concentrated losses. For example, the Hurricane Katrina in 2005 struck thousands of houses in the city of New Orleans. The exposed properties are classified as a highly correlated risk, which has a bad effect on the evaluation of the insurability of catastrophe risks and makes pricing premiums unreliable.

10.3.1.2 Capacity restriction of insurers

Due to the highly correlated nature and potential aggregation of losses from catastrophes, the capacity of the insurance market may not be sufficient to absorb those losses. The potential losses from catastrophe risks are severe and uncertain. As discussed above, Hurricane Andrew caused about US$25 billion in losses in Florida. Insurers paid over US$21.6 billion in claims related to Hurricane Andrew. Moreover, annual losses are highly variable, and may require a large sum of money to cover high losses in some years. Big losses such as Hurricane Andrew led 11 property-casualty insurance companies to become insolvent (US Government Accountability Office 2002). Hurricane Andrew revealed that Florida faced a 'capacity gap', which is the difference between the amount of the available insurance industry capital and the demand for catastrophe coverage (King 2005). As a matter of fact, insurers and financial market experts knew that outside capital was needed to supplement the industry's capacity after Hurricane Andrew (King 2005). In 2005 Hurricane Katrina also showed that the insurance industry may not have sufficient capital to cover every mega-catastrophe. Total damages associated with Hurricane Katrina are expected to exceed US$200 billion. The federal government expected to spend over US$100 billion for response and recovery efforts associated with Hurricane Katrina (King 2005).

10.3.1.3   *Profitability condition of catastrophe insurance*

Based on the classic economic theory,[11] insurers supply insurance in order to maximize their long-run expected profits. In some circumstances, even when the risk is insurable and the insurer has the capacity to cover the risk, underwriting some risks may not be economically profitable due to other obstacles.

The first such obstacle is rate regulation. In the US, insurance is mainly regulated at state level. The 'rate' refers to the premium of the policy, which sometimes is regulated. Due to consumer protection concerns, insurance commissioners may require catastrophe insurance policy premiums to be 'affordable', which may prevent insurers from pricing policies to accurately reflect risk (Hecht 2008). Insurers who have to supply catastrophe insurance at such affordable prices will not be able to make profits.

The second is the short-run profit horizon of insurers. Many insurance companies are public-owned corporations in which there is a separation of ownership and management control. Even if the owners/investors are risk-neutral and prefer to underwrite a catastrophe risk to maximize long-run expected profits, managers may follow a safety-first rule as a result of risk aversion and fail to underwrite that risk (Kunreuther *et al.* 2013: 146–54).[12] According to a McKinsey and Company report from 2005 "shortsighted behavior is widespread" among managers and their myopic behavior shows their disfavor to developing products for long-run profits (Dobbs *et al.* 2005). Insurance company managers are not immune from this myopia.

The third obstacle is the 'appetite' of insurers.[13] As with food, appetite varies with experience, preferences and 'digestive capacity'. Even if a catastrophe risk is insurable, if insurers have no appetite for it, they will decline to write policies. As noted by Trevor Maynard of Lloyd's, insurers "cannot insure our way out of the problem" because "[r]einsurers and alternative capital market providers will not accept risk on terms that are not commercially viable" (Maynard 2008).

10.3.1.4   *A short summary of the supply of catastrophe insurance*

From the above discussion, we can see that obstacles are ahead for insurers to underwrite catastrophe insurance policies. Considering the nature of catastrophe risks, it is difficult to fulfill all insurability requirements. Due to the high potential losses of catastrophe exposures, insurers' capacity and appetite to cover such losses is not sufficient. Furthermore, there are still some obstacles for insurers to make profits. In sum, the supply of catastrophe insurance is limited and volatile.

10.3.2   *Demand for catastrophe insurance*

On the demand side, classic economic theory posits that individuals will make decisions under uncertainty according to the *expected utility theory of choice* (Kunreuther *et al.* 2013: 8).[14] According to Nobel Prize winner Kenneth J. Arrow, individuals purchase insurance because they are willing to pay a certain small premium to protect against an uncertain large loss (Arrow 1971: 199–200).

In other words, a potential rational victim residing in a hazard-prone area will voluntarily purchase catastrophe insurance if they perceive the premium to be sufficiently low in comparison to the risks.

However, many people fail to purchase insurance offered even at subsidized prices against low-probability but high-consequence disasters (Kunreuther *et al.* 2013: 113). Flood insurance offered by the National Flood Insurance Program (NFIP), whose rates and terms are set by Congress, is an example of this anomaly. During the NFIP's first four years, fewer than 3,000 out of 21,000 flood-prone communities entered into the subsidized flood insurance program; by 1992, a conservative estimate of coverage suggests that less than 20 per cent of homes located in the flood-prone areas bought flood insurance; in 1997, the Federal Insurance Administration estimated that only about 27 per cent of households living in high-risk flood areas were insured (Kunreuther and Roth 1998: 55). The reasons why demand for catastrophe insurance coverage is so low are as follows.

10.3.2.1   *Intuitive thinking v. deliberative thinking*

In Daniel Kahneman's book *Thinking, Fast and Slow*, the author adopted terms of thinking originally proposed by the psychologists Keith Stanovich and Richard West, which he labels System 1 and System 2, as follows:

- *System 1*: operates automatically and quickly, with little or no effort and no sense of voluntary control. This is often described as *intuitive thinking*.

- *System 2*: allocates attention to effortful and intentional mental activities including simple or complex computations or formal logic. The operations are often associated with the subjective experience of agency, choice and concentration. This is often described as *deliberative thinking.*

(Kahneman 2011: 20–1)

When people are identified with System 2, they make choices and decide what to think about and what to do with consciousness and reasoning (Kahneman 2011: 15). Classic economic theory assumes that consumers' behavior will follow expected utility theory, which requires consumers (the decision maker) to follow System 2 to make deliberative choices. In reality, much human behavior conforms to the more automatic and less analytic System 1, which results in many biases and simplified anomalies. When consumers face catastrophic disasters, however, System 1 (intuitive thinking) does not work well and results in many anomalies in demand of catastrophe insurance, such as failing to buy insurance maximizing to consumers' expected utility.

10.3.2.2 *Prospect theory*

Prospect theory, which was developed by Daniel Kahneman and Amos Tversky, is a descriptive choice model that predicts actual behavior better than expected utility theory (Kahneman and Tversky 1979). This model is helpful in explaining consumer anomalies in purchasing catastrophe insurance.

The value function of prospect theory, which separates losses from gains, states that the pain from a certain loss will be viewed as larger than the positive feeling from an uncertain gain (Kunreuther *et al.* 2013: 96–8).[15] In other words, people tend to be loss averse. For example, when a consumer confronts a 20 per cent chance of losing US$100 versus the certainty of losing US$20, he/she will avoid the certain loss of US$20 and take the risk of losing US$100. According to the value function of prospect theory as applied to insurance, consumers are more willing to take an uncertain risk than suffer a certain loss in the form of a premium payment (Kunreuther *et al.* 2013: 115). This tendency to treat a certain loss as more painful than the pleasure of uncertain gains is also termed as "myopic loss aversion" (Benartzi and Thaleer 1995). It makes even actuarially fair insurance unattractive, let alone low-probability and high-consequences catastrophe insurance, where it is difficult to charge accurate premiums. Due to loss-aversion, consumers tend to choose not to buy catastrophe insurance. For extreme catastrophe risks, consumers will just ignore the risk. Prior to a disaster, they contend it will not happen to them. As a result, they will not spend money to invest in protective measures, such as catastrophe insurance (Kunreuther and Michel-Kerjan 2010: 126–30). However, when the disaster truly happens, they may feel remorse that they did not buy insurance.

10.3.2.3   *The goal-based model of choice*

The goal-based model of choice developed by David H. Krantz and Howard Kunreuther is another theory of decision making based on preset goals rather than on maximizing expected utility (Krantz and Kunreuther 2007). In the area of insurance, these goals are categorized as:

* financial protection by risk sharing
* getting benefits from investment
* emotion-related goals
* satisfying legal or other official requirements
* satisfying social and/or cognitive norms (Krantz and Kunreuther 2007).

The goal-based model also shows that consumers do not always maximize their expected utility (Hecht 2008). For example, consider flood insurance: before a flood strikes, residents seldom buy flood insurance to protect themselves. At this stage, there are concerns that buying flooding insurance is not a good investment in view of the anticipated benefits. But after suffering flood damage, they will purchase insurance to satisfy emotional goals. Following flood damage, anxiety is high and reducing it by purchasing insurance is a salient goal (Kunreuther *et al.* 2013: 103). When several consecutive years pass with no flood, however, many people cancel their flood policies (Michel-Kerjan *et al.* 2011). Avoiding anxiety is not that important and reducing burdensome premiums becomes more important.

10.3.2.4   *Relying on government bailouts*

Another reason why some people do not buy catastrophe insurance is because they believe that if they suffer catastrophic damages, the government should and will bail them out (Faure and Bruggeman 2008; Hecht 2008; Kunreuther *et al.* 2013: 114–15). Due to government compensation, individual incentives to buy insurance are diminishing. For example, in the US, the federal government normally provides public disaster relief if a state declares emergency following a natural disaster (Kunreuther *et al.* 2013: 114–15). If the government's response falls short after natural disasters, it will face heavy political pressure. Criticism of the former President Bush Administration's response to Hurricane Katrina is an example.[16] This reason for people's reduced demand of insurance is not really anomalous but based on rational behavior.

However, relying on the government leads to problems. A government's bailout may lead to a 'natural disaster syndrome' in which people fail to voluntarily adopt cost-effective loss-reduction measures (Kunreuther 1996). This will lead to a quandary called the 'Samaritan's Dilemma', which describes the ethical challenges of helping to provide relief that will in fact further reduce residents' incentives to invest in protection measures, such as buying insurance and mitigation (Faure and Bruggeman 2008).

10.3.2.5 *A short summary of demand for catastrophe insurance*

Consumer behavior when purchasing catastrophe insurance deviates from classic economic theory. Scholars create models from the viewpoint of behavioral economics to explain such anomalies. These models include intuitive and deliberative thinking, prospect theory and the goal-based model of choice. Additionally, due to repeated government bailouts, consumers' choice of not buying catastrophe insurance appears quasi-rational.

10.3.3 *A short conclusion: feasibility of catastrophe insurance*

From the above supply–demand framework analysis, we learn that underwriting catastrophe insurance faces both supply-side and demand-side barriers. On the supply side, problems with insurability and capacity hamper the underwriting process. Meanwhile, on the demand side, consumers buy insufficient catastrophe insurance due to behavioral anomalies.

In the next section, I will apply this supply–demand framework to analyze China's catastrophe insurance market, and explain why no catastrophe insurance system has been instituted even since the Great Sichuan Earthquake of 2008 (Zhou 2008).[17] And then, I propose some solutions for the feasibility of catastrophe insurance in China in order to optimize the role of private insurance in covering disasters.

10.4 Catastrophe insurance in China: how does insurance play a role in covering disasters?

10.4.1 *Natural disasters and catastrophe insurance in China*

China suffers some of the most severe national catastrophes in the world. Floods affect the eastern part of China almost every year. In 1998, the Yangtze River flood affected almost half of China and caused direct economic losses of US$40 billion. In the southeast, typhoons affect the coastal areas just like hurricanes affect the southeast of the US. Earthquakes occur in the western and northern areas of China. Beijing was significantly affected by the Tangshan Earthquake in 1976. In 2008, the Great Sichuan Earthquake struck the southwest and caused losses exceeding US$100 billion. Catastrophes cause direct economic losses of around US$25 billion in China every year and the amount would be considerably larger if indirect economic losses such as disaster relief were included (Department of Civil Affairs of the PRC 2009).

The losses from natural catastrophes are severe, and the social and economic harm to millions of people needs to be carefully considered and managed. Unfortunately, national catastrophe risk management is far from well established. At present, the government plays the major role in compensating victims in China (Zhou 2008). However, catastrophe compensation imposed a considerable fiscal strain on the government budget, while being far from enough for the victims. Since 1990, government catastrophe compensation averaged only around US$1 billion every year, which is just a drop in the ocean compared with the average US$25 billion in direct economic losses from catastrophes (Department of Civil Affairs of the PRC 2009). It follows that encouraging and attracting market forces, especially the insurance industry, to participate in catastrophe risk management is important and urgent.

Natural disaster insurance started only recently in China (Shi *et al.* 2007). Catastrophe insurance is still not formally available in China, although there are some natural disaster insurance policies underwritten by the People's Insurance Company of China (PICC).[18] This partly explains why insurance compensation is so low after catastrophes in China. For example, after the Yangtze River floods of 1998, insurance covered only about 1.25 per cent of economic losses, that is, US$500 million coverage out of a total loss of US$40 billion. The same thing happened after the Great Sichuan Earthquake where only US$300 million of the losses were covered by insurance companies, only 0.3 per cent of the total losses incurred (*China Youth Daily 2011*). As a consequence, there is a strong desire to establish catastrophe insurance. The Great Sichuan Earthquake has proven to be a very important catastrophe for accelerating catastrophe insurance, which the Fourth National Finance Working Conference confirmed in 2012.[19]

However, China is creating the legal infrastructure for agricultural natural disaster insurance. A Regulation on Agriculture Insurance has been promulgated and became effective in March 2013.[20] Article 8 and Article 17 both prescribe agricultural catastrophe insurance: Article 8 provides that the central government has the duty to establish subsidized agricultural catastrophe insurance and encourages local government to follow this step; Article 17 prescribes that any insurance company which wants to insure agriculture should have catastrophe insurance arrangements. The development of agricultural disaster insurance will lay a foundation for the establishment of catastrophe insurance.

10.4.2 Why catastrophe insurance has not been quickly established since the Great Sichuan earthquake

In this section, I apply the supply–demand framework presented in Section 10.3 above to offer an explanation for catastrophe insurance not having been quickly established since the Great Sichuan Earthquake.

10.4.2.1 Supply restrictions

10.4.2.1.1 LACK OF CATASTROPHE DATA

Lack of catastrophe data makes it difficult for insurers wishing to identify, quantify and estimate the chance of disasters and to set premiums for catastrophe risks. Up to now the acquisition of such data has not been completed in China. The effort of collecting data is continuing. For example, from 1998 to 2002 the Swiss Reinsurance Company cooperated with Beijing Normal University to complete the 'Digital Map of China Catastrophe Events' (Zhongguo Juxing Dianzi Zainan Ditu) that includes historic data, geographic data, weather data and other types of data since the twelfth century (Guo and Wei 2005). This digital map will be very helpful in the pricing of catastrophe insurance. In 2009, the China Insurance Regulation Commission (CIRC) promulgated the Catastrophe Insurance Data Acquisition Regulation (JR/T0054–2009), which specified the standard for the acquisition of catastrophe insurance data.[21] Meanwhile, the catastrophe risk evaluating and standardizing target accumulations (CRESTA) is developing a new catastrophe risk division system for China.[22] This new system demarcates the existing 60 partitions into 2,472 partitions that substantially improve the data's accuracy and transparency.[23] However, this effort is still underway and needs more work (Tian and Luo 2012).

10.4.2.1.2   RELATIVELY LOW CAPACITY OF CHINA'S INSURANCE INDUSTRY

Along with the rapid growth of China's economy, the growth of the Chinese insurance industry has been impressive. However, China's primary insurance industry still has much less capacity to deal with catastrophe risks than its leading western companies, although it has been growing fast since 1979. Comparing with advanced markets, the data presented in Table 10.2 show China's lower insurance penetration and insurance density.

Similarly, the total capital of China's property insurance companies is much lower than the total amount of losses caused by natural disasters. Table 10.3 shows the existence of this big gap.

Reinsurance is an important potential complement for expanding the capacity of underwriting risks. However, reinsurance currently does not supply strong support for the catastrophe insurance in China. At present, the China Reinsurance (Group) Corporation (China Re) is the only State-owned reinsurance group in China, with capital of US$6.068 billion. China Re is in a monopoly position and occupies about 80 per cent of the whole reinsurance market in China. Although China's reinsurance market has become open to foreign reinsurance companies after China's entry into the World Trade Organization (WTO), only a few reinsurance companies, such as Swiss Re and Munich Re, have established business operations in China and they are only at an initial step to reinsure risks.

10.4.2.1.3   REGULATORY OBSTACLES

Insurance is strictly regulated in China, especially through rate regulation, solvency regulation, and form regulation. These regulations create additional

Table 10.2 Insurance penetration and density of selected countries

	China	US	Japan	Netherlands
Insurance penetration: premiums as in per cent of the GDP in 2012	2.96	8.18	11.44	12.99
Insurance density: premiums per capita in USD in 2012	178.9	4047.3	5167.5	5984.9

(Source: Sigma 2013b.)

Table 10.3 Capital of main Chinese property insurers compared with natural disaster losses (US$ billion)

	2007	2008	2009	2010
Net capital of main insurers	5.5	5.1	6.9	9.0
Natural disaster losses	38.1	189.5	40.1	86.1

(Source: *Yearbook of China Insurance 2008–11.*)

obstacles to the provision of catastrophe insurance. For example, consider earthquake insurance. If insurers want to underwrite earthquake risks in enterprise property policies, they must submit the policies to the CIRC for approval (CIRC 2001). This rule retarded the emergence of earthquake catastrophe insurance. It existed for a long time and the CIRC has not promulgated any new rules on earthquake insurance (Tian and Luo 2012).

10.4.2.2 Demand restrictions

10.4.2.2.1 IRRATIONAL BEHAVIOR BY CONSUMERS

Insurance had a late start in China. In 1979, the central government announced the 'Notice on Restoration of the Domestic Insurance Business and Strengthen the Insurance Agency' (*Guanyu Huifu Guonei Baoxian Yewu He Jiaqiang Baoxian Jigou De Tongzhi*).[24] Private insurance agencies resumed their businesses in China.[25] The insurance market and products are not well developed. As a result, Chinese consumers have weak incentives to purchase insurance products. For catastrophe disasters, due to their low-probability nature, consumer awareness and demand are even weaker (Yue *et al.* 2013). Consumers do not always behave rationally and maximize their expected utility to protect themselves from catastrophe losses by buying insurance. Myopic loss-aversion can also explain this anomalous behavior. Prior to a disaster, consumers believe that natural disasters will not happen to them. In addition, they regard the premium as a certain loss that is more painful than the possible future gains.[26]

Before the Great Sichuan Earthquake, few people and enterprises bought earthquake insurance even though they lived in earthquake-prone areas. However, after that earthquake's severe destruction, the sale of property insurance products including earthquake coverage increased dramatically (Tian and Luo 2012). According to the goal-based model of choice (10.3.2.3), avoiding anxiety over earthquakes became the overriding goal following the Great Sichuan Earthquake.

10.4.2.2.2   RELYING ON A GOVERNMENT BAILOUT

Consumer demand for catastrophe insurance in China has also been blunted by expectations of a government bailout. Historically speaking, China is a country where the government paid a lot of attention to preventing and distributing catastrophe losses. Taking the Qing Dynasty, for example, *Records of Laws and Systems of Qing Dynasty* (*Da Qing Hui Dian Shi Li*) listed 12 articles on "Disaster Defence and Reduction Policies" (Chen 2004).[27] To date, the government still plays a major role in distributing catastrophe risk and compensating victims (Zhou 2008). Qinghua Xian and Xiaolan Ye use public crisis management theory (Putra 2009[28]) to analyze the Chinese government's experience in distributing catastrophe risk (Xian and Ye 2009). For example, after the Great Sichuan Earthquake in 2008, the central and local governments played a key role in combining and allocating the resources of society in disaster relief, and earned a good reputation (Qin and Chen 2009). Counterpart Aid between local governments is also a widely used method to distribute catastrophe risk (Lan 2011; Zhao and Jiang 2009).[29]

Because of reliance on government compensation, however, individuals' incentives to buy catastrophe insurance are diminishing. According to an empirical study of catastrophe insurance in five Chinese provinces, there is a negative correlation between government relief and insurers' property and causality premium income (Tian and Zhang 2013). Offering 'free' government relief will cause a heavy and unpredictable burden for the government's financial budget. Furthermore, it also leads to the 'Samaritan's Dilemma',[30] which will further reduce consumers' incentives to invest in protection measures, such as buying catastrophe insurance and mitigation.

10.4.3   *'Mandatory multi-year insurance' as a possible solution for insuring catastrophes*

Faced with the 'Samaritan's Dilemma', the Chinese government is encouraging the establishment of a private catastrophe insurance system where insurers play a more important role. After years of deliberation, especially after the Great Sichuan Earthquake in 2008, China accelerated the promotion of catastrophe insurance. Establishing a catastrophe insurance system has gradually become a national priority (Zhou 2008). After the Regulation on Agriculture Insurance, which includes stipulations on catastrophic natural disaster insurance, took effect in March 2013, the CIRC is now drafting the Regulation on Catastrophe Insurance.[31] CIRC has also approved two catastrophe insurance pilot programs, the Shenzhen City Program and the Yunnan Province Program (Dong 2013). CIRC's Shenzhen Bureau will disclose its "Catastrophe Insurance Project in Shenzhen City" in the near future (*Financial Times* (China) 2013).

As the above analysis has shown, the insurance market faces both supply-side and demand-side obstacles. How to play insurance's role becomes an important question. Howard Kunreuther and other professors have proposed multi-year insurance contracts to overcome the obstacles (Kunreuther *et al.* 2013: 228–43; Kunreuther and Michel-Kerjan 2010: 115–40; Kunreuther and Michel-Kerjan 2009a: 333–50; Kunreuther and Michel-Kerjan 2009b). Kunreuther already proposed mandatory insurance several decades ago (Kunreuther 1968). Michael Faure and Véronique Bruggeman also suggest that mandatory/compulsory insurance could solve the lack of demand and/ or supply (Faure 2007; Faure and Bruggeman 2008; Faure and Bruggeman 2013). Furthermore, this suggestion is supported by Anastasia Telesetsky, who treats mandatory catastrophe insurance as a risk-sharing mechanism serving the goals of both corrective and distributive justice (Telesetsky 2010).

10.4.3.1 Multi-year insurance

Multi-year insurance refers to an insurance in which policies are sold for consecutive years rather than only for one year, tied to the property as opposed to the property owner, as in the traditional annual policy (Kunreuther and Michel-Kerjan 2009b; Kunreuther *et al.* 2013: 228–43). Multi-year insurance can satisfy two fundamental objectives better than annual policies: controlling actual losses and providing financial protection against catastrophic losses (Kunreuther *et al.* 2013: 228–32). Thus it can be a strong tool to solve both the supply-side and demand-side challenges to the provision of catastrophe insurance.

On the supply side, multi-year insurance enlarges insurers' capacity by extending the term of the insurance policy. When a catastrophe occurs, multi-year insurance can distribute aggregated losses over different years. Moreover, multi-year insurance can reduce transaction costs, for both insurers and consumers. For example, consumers' search cost of renewing policies and insurers' marketing cost of underwriting policies can be significantly reduced compared with annual insurance policies (Kunreuther *et al.* 2013: 233).

On the demand side, consumers generally like to purchase insurance after suffering catastrophe damage such as floods to reduce anxiety. When several consecutive years pass without any flood, however, many people cancel their flood policies. Multi-year insurance has the potential to deal with this problem while annual policies do not, because under the annual policies, an insured party can cancel the next year's coverage easily. Multi-year insurance would also encourage consumers to invest in cost-effective loss-reduction mitigation measures in exchange for premium reductions or another bonus (Kunreuther *et al.* 2013: 233–38).

However, multi-year insurance can pose some challenges. Consumers who buy a multi-year policy will be more concerned about insurers' financial insolvency over a long period (Kunreuther *et al.* 2013: 236). In addition, it does not solve consumers' reliance on a government bailout. These problems may be solved by mandating catastrophe insurance as discussed in the next section.

10.4.3.2   *Mandatory insurance*

Mandatory disaster coverage is often discussed as a tool to solve the above supply and demand anomalies. Supporters list some benefits. Telesetsky (2010: 710) proposes that "the most important reason for mandating catastrophe risk insurance is to compel industry actors to take action under the supervision of the profit motivated insurance industry." Faure (2007) argues that mandatory insurance can improve efficiency, correct market failure, promote distributive justice, price accurately and regulate more efficiently. A well-known mandatory insurance example is the French property damage insurance, which requires property owners to pay a supplementary premium for mandatory natural disaster coverage (Faure and Bruggeman 2008).

Nevertheless, mandatory insurance may pose some challenges. It may lead to paternalism, risk advertising as an alternative, overgeneralization, anticompetition, no available insurance market, etc. (Faure 2007).[32]

10.4.3.3   *Mandatory multi-year insurance*

From the discussion on multi-year insurance and mandatory insurance, it follows that we may combine these two tools to wed their merits while diminishing their drawbacks. For example, multi-year insurance does not address consumers' reliance on government bailouts. According to the empirical study of catastrophe insurance in five Chinese provinces, mentioned in subsection 10.4.2.2.2 above, due to biases and misunderstanding, few residents will voluntarily purchase catastrophe insurance (Tian and Zhang 2013). Mandatory insurance removes that moral hazard by requiring almost everyone to purchase catastrophe insurance and thus decrease reliance on government compensation dramatically. In contrast, mandatory insurance may not function well in an insurance market without competition. However, multi-year insurance has the potential to allow insurers to underwrite the policy reflecting real risk, and different insurers may compete with each other to attract consumers.

As mentioned above, China suffers some of the most severe national catastrophes in the world. If mandatory multi-year insurance existed, it would reduce the financial burden on governments to compensate disaster victims (Faure and Bruggeman 2008). If premiums of mandatory multi-year insurance sufficiently reflect risks, the insurance industry can play an important role in covering catastrophe risks.

10.5 Conclusion

Climate change, its implications for catastrophes and the question of how losses caused by natural disasters can be covered are hot topics that will attract more and more attention in coming years. Accordingly, how to sustainably distribute catastrophe risks is of pressing concern, especially for those countries and regions that have many natural disasters, for example the US, China and the EU.

Insurance is one of mankind's greatest inventions, an extraordinarily useful tool to reduce risk (Kunreuther *et al.* 2013: 13). Insurance is a good device to transfer risk for individuals. They can substitute a small certain cost which is called the premium for a large uncertain financial loss. Compared with government intervention, insurance is better equipped to deal with catastrophe risks due to its advantages of lower transaction costs, lower adverse selection and more efficiency as a result of competitive markets. Furthermore, when facing catastrophe risks, mandatory multi-year insurance, which weds the merits of mandatory insurance and multi-year insurance while diminishing their drawbacks, deserves more attention.

There is no doubt that insurance could and should play an important role in covering catastrophic disasters, especially in China where private insurance still plays a limited role in distributing catastrophe risks.[33] Taking into account that China suffers some of the most severe national catastrophes in the world, a mandatory multi-year insurance in which premiums sufficiently reflect risks may be a good choice.

Notes

1 SJD Candidate, LLM (Honors) in Insurance Law, University of Connecticut School of Law. I would like to thank Prof. Michael Faure, Dr. N. J. Philipsen, Prof. Guangdong Xu and other participants in the China–EU Symposium: "Law and Finance: The Role of Law and Regulations in Sustaining Financial Markets", May 2013, Beijing. I am grateful to Prof. Patricia A. McCoy and lecturer Douglas Simpson at the University of Connecticut School of Law for their very helpful comments. I acknowledge the financial support from the China Scholarship Council (File No: 201306640015) for my studies in the US.
2 Global climate change is occurring on a significant scale, as has been well documented in the scientific literature.
3 "It seems very likely that the [sic] there will be a 'peak' year that will record costs over 1 trillion USD before 2040."
4 The distinction between fundamental and particular risks is based on the discussion of hazard by Kulp. Fundamental risks are those caused by conditions more or less beyond the control of the individuals and involve losses that affect a large number of populations, see Kulp (1956).

5 This book was originally written in 1921.
6 "Pareto optimality" (also called "Pareto efficiency") is a state of allocation of resources in which it is impossible to make any one individual better off without making at least one individual worse off, see Seog (2010).
7 The law of large numbers is the mathematical theorem which says that for a series of independent and identically distributed random variables, the variance of the average amount of a claim payment decreases as the number of claims increases.
8 Flood insurance was first offered by private insurers in the late 1890s. However, the loss for insurers was so large that they left the market. In 1968, the Congress created the NFIP as an alternative means to offer coverage subsidized by the federal government, see Kunreuther and Roth (1998).
9 There is no rigorous definition of big data. Initially the idea was that the volume of information had grown so large that the quantity being examined no longer fit into the memory that computers use for processing, so engineers needed to revamp the tools they used for analyzing it all. One way to think about the issue today is that big data refers to things one can do at a large scale that cannot be done at a smaller one, to extract new insights or create new forms of value, in ways that change markets, organizations, the relationship between citizens and governments and more. Big data is not about trying to 'teach' a computer to 'think' like humans, instead, it's about applying mathematics to huge quantities of data in order to infer probabilities. See Mayer-Schoenberger and Cukier (2013).
10 Asymmetric information exists in the situation where one party has more or better information than the other in the transaction.
11 The defining features of classical economics are based on: "[A]ll human behavior can be viewed as involving participants who (1) maximize their utility (2) from a stable set of preferences and (3) accumulate an optimal amount of information and other inputs in a variety of markets." In other words, the classical economics literature starts from the assumption that human beings make their decisions based upon rational analysis, such as an objective weighing of costs and benefits. See Becker (1976) and Bruggeman (2010).
12 The safety-first rule (or safety-first model) is a model of insurer pricing that reflects the insurer's threshold probability that losses for a specific event will not exceed a pre-specified value. See Kunreuther *et al.* (2013).
13 Appetite is a subjective criterion of profitable restriction, which generally refers to the willingness of insurers to underwrite policies. Inspired by lecturer Douglas Simpson.
14 This theory assumes that individuals with accurate information about risks decide on insurance purchases by making explicit trade-offs between the expected benefits and the costs of different policies, see Kunreuther *et al.* (2013).
15 Value function is the term borrowed from mathematics. In the coordinate system, the x-axis depicts the magnitude of the gain or loss, and the $v(x)$ and $v(-x)$ represent the value associated with a gain (x) or loss $(-x)$. The value function is steeper in the loss domain than in the gain domain. This is shown in the coordinate system, where the curve of $y(-x)$ is steeper than the curve of $y(x)$.
16 'Katrinagate' fury spreads to US media (2005), available at: http://tvnz.co.nz/view/page/425822/609550 (accessed 21 May 2014).
17 Generally speaking, catastrophe insurance systems may be established one or two years after a catastrophe struck a region. However, five years passed away, catastrophe insurance has still not been established in China. See Zhou (2008). Also see 'CIRC Is Promoting Regulations of Catastrophe Insurance, and Two Places Are on the Experiment Project', available at: http://www.iic.org.cn/D_newsDT/newsDT_read.php?id=106741 (accessed 21 May 2014).

18 According to the latest news from CIRC 'Shenzhen City Catastrophe Insurance Framework' was officially adopted by the municipal government on 30 December 2013. This catastrophe insurance framework includes three different parts: the first part is the government catastrophe assistance insurance which is bought by the Shenzhen municipal government to supply the basic assistance for all residents, the second part is catastrophe fund and third part is private catastrophe insurance, available at: http://www.circ.gov.cn/web/site0/tab5168/info3900215.htm (accessed 21 May 2014).

19 The National Finance Working Conference is the supreme finance conference in China and it decided the most important finance issues such as establishing the China Securities Regulation Commission (CSRC) and the CIRC at the first conference, establishing the China Banking Regulation Commission (CBRC) and decided that the three major State-owned commercial banks (China Banks, China Construction Bank and China Commerce Bank) should start an initial public offering (IPO) at the second conference, and establishing the China Investment Corporation at the third conference. The Conference is held almost every five years in Beijing. Available at: http://finance.ce.cn/sub/2011/jrgzhy (accessed 21 May 2014).

20 No. 61 Decree of the State Council of the People's Republic of China, available at: http://www.gov.cn/zwgk/2012–11/16/content_2268392.htm (accessed 21 May 2014).

21 CIRC Order 52 (2009).

22 The CRESTA organization was established by the insurance and reinsurance industry in 1977 as an independent body for the technical management of natural hazard coverage. CRESTA's main goal is to establish a uniform and global system to transfer electronically aggregated exposure data for accumulation risk control and modeling among insurers and reinsurers. Available at: https://www.cresta.org (accessed 21 May 2014).

23 Swiss Re Beijing Branch, available at: http://eol.yzu.edu.cn/eol/common/script/onlinepreview.jsp?countadd=1&lid=2912&resid=234015 (accessed 21 May 2014)

24 Available at: http://www.china.com.cn/aboutchina/txt/2009–11/25/content_1895 1984.htm (accessed 21 May 2014).

25 On 20 October 1949, the People's Insurance Company of China (PICC) was established. However, in the socialist planned economy framework, there is no need for business insurance. From 1958 to 1978, the insurance business virtually disappeared. It was not until 1979, after the Third Plenary Session of the Eleventh Chinese Communist Party (CPC) Central Committee, and the process of institutional transformation towards a market economy began, that the State Council gave its approval for the Conference of the Branch Heads of the People's Bank of China (PBC) to gradually revive domestic insurance operation.

26 For a more detailed discussion, see Section 10.3.2.2 on prospect theory.

27 The measures include, but are not limited to, the following: food supply, river control and levee building, eradication of locusts, information dissemination, and so on. Also See Chen (2004).

28 In summary, there are four main criteria to measure the performance of public sector crisis management. First, the question is whether or not the government has a crisis management system within its organization. Second is the question as to the sensitivity of the government to multi-identities (including ethnic, class, age and gender) while rescuing the victims. The criterion is related to the decision-making strategy in a crisis situation. Fourth is the question of how successfully the government can adjust its bureaucratic norms with emergent norms in the crisis situation. See Putra (2009).

29 Counterpart Aid is a support model full of Chinese characteristics. Following the central government's requirement, some local governments who have strong economic power, assist and support the reconstruction of disaster-affected areas. For example, after the Great Sichuan Earthquake, the Shandong Province was responsible and helped the reconstruction of the BeiChuan County – an earthquake-struck area. See Lan (2011) and Zhao and Jiang (2009).
30 See Section 10.3.2.4 relying on government's bailouts.
31 Available at: http://www.iic.org.cn/D_newsDT/newsDT_read.php?id=106741 (accessed 21 May 2014).
32 Paternalism happens when the legislature in fact forces potential victims to purchase an insurance policy even if there would be no demand. Risk advertising as an alternative applies if the lack of information would be the reason for a duty to insure, and one could hold that regulation aiming at providing information might to some extent be a less interventionist remedy than mandatory insurance. Overgeneralization occurs when a generalized duty to purchase flooding coverage, for example, creates the risk that the duty is also imposed on those who constitute no risk at all, such as the owner of an apartment on the tenth floor. Anti-competition problems happen when a so-called tie-in agreement forces a consumer to buy a specific service or product together with another product, which may restrict competition. No available insurance market mainly refers to catastrophic losses suffered in developing countries where a large part of these losses is not covered under insurance at all. Where insurance markets are not available to a large part of the population, requiring mandatory disaster insurance will of course not be the miracle solution. See Faure (2007).
33 The catastrophe disaster loss covered by insurance is less than 5 per cent in China. It is far and away less than the international normal loss ratio of 36 per cent. See *Economic Observer* (2013).

References

AIG (2009), 'AIG's Policy and Programs on Environment and Climate Change'. Available at: http://www.naic.org/documents/committees_Ex_climate_survey_sample_responses_AIG.pdf (accessed 21 May 2014).

Arrow, K. J. (1971) *Essays in the Theory of Risk-Bearing*, Chicago: Markham Publisher Corporation.

Baker, T. and Logue, K. (2013) *Insurance Law and Policy: Cases and Materials*, Wolters Kluwer Law & Business.

Banks, E. (2005) *Catastrophe Risk, Analysis and Management*, Chichester: Wiley.

Becker, G. (1976) *The Economic Approach to Human Behavior*, Chicago: University of Chicago Press.

Benartzi, S. and Thaleer, R. (1995) 'Myopic Loss Aversion and the Equity Premium Puzzle', *Quarterly Journal of Economics*, 110, 73–92.

Borch, K. H. (1962), 'Equilibrium in a reinsurance market', *Econometrica 30*, 424–44.

Bruggeman, V. (2010) *Compensating Catastrophe Victims: A Comparative Law and Economics Approach*, Alphen aan den Rijn: Kluwer Law International.

Chen, H. (2004) 'Qingdai fangzai Jianzai De Zhengce Yue Cuoshi' (Disaster Defense and Reduction Policies in the Qing Dynasty), *Qingshi Yanjiu* (*Studies in Qing History*), 3, 41–52.

China Youth Daily (2011) 'Establishing Catastrophe Insurance System faces acceleration', 14 March 2011.

CIRC (2001) 'The Notice of Regulating Approving Procedure of Extended Earthquake Insurance in Enterprise Property Insurance Policy'. Available at: http://www.circ. gov.cn/tabid/106/infoIID/18742/frtid/3871/Default.aspx (accessed 21 May 2014).

Cooter, R. and Ulen, T. (2008) *Law & Economics*, Addison-Wesley.

Cummins, J. D. and Lewis, C. M. (2003) 'Catastrophe Events, Parameter Uncertainty and the Breakdown of Implicit Long Term Contracting: The Case of Terrorism Insurance', *Journal of Risk and Uncertainty*, 26(2–3), 153–78.

Department of Civil Affairs of People's Republic of China (2009) 'Minzheng Shiye Fazhan Tongji Baogao (1990–2008)', (Statistic Report on Civil Affair Development (1990–2008)).

Dobbs, R., Leslie, K. and Mendonca, L. T. (2005) 'Building the Healthy Corporation', *McKinsey Quarterly*, 63.

Dong, B. (Vice Director of CIRC Property Insurance Department) (2013) 'ZhuBu Jianli Fuhe Zhongguo Guoqing De Juzai Baoxian Zhidu' (Gradually Establishing Catastrophe Insurance Program which conforms to China's Specific National Condition), speech at 23rd FAIR Conference in September 2013. Available at: http:// www.sinoins.com/zt/2013–09/18/content_74763.htm (accessed 21 May 2014).

Economic Observer (2013) 'CIRC is Promoting to Stimulate Regulation on Catastrophe Insurance', *Economic Observer*, October 2013. Available at: http://www.iic.org. cn/D_newsDT/newsDT_read.php?id=106741 (accessed 21 May 2014).

Epstein, R. A. (1996) 'Catastrophe Responses to Catastrophe Risks', *Journal of Risk and Uncertainty*, 12, 287–308.

Faure, M. G. (2007) 'Insurability of Damage Caused by Climate Change: A Commentary', *University of Pennsylvania Law Review*, 155, 1875–99.

Faure, M. G. and Bruggeman, V. (2008) 'Catastrophic Risks and First-Party Insurance', *Connecticut Insurance Law Journal*, 15, 1–52.

Faure, M. G., and Bruggeman, V. (2013) 'Green Paper on the insurance of natural and man-made disasters (COM (2013) 213 final): Reaction of the Malta FORUM of Legal Experts on Climate Change Adaptation'.

Faure, M. G. and Heine, K. (2011) 'Insurance Against Financial Crises?', *New York University Journal of Law and Business*, 8, 117–50

Financial Times (China) (2013), 'Jianli Juzai Baoxian Zhidu Buke Yidaoqie', (Establishing Catastrophe Insurance System Should Allow Flexibility), *Financial Times (China)*, 13 November 2013.

Florida Office of Insurance (2006) 'Task Force on Long-Term Solutions for Florida's Hurricane Insurance Market'. Available at: http://www.floir.com/siteDocuments/ lts_2006.pdf (accessed 21 May 2014).

Guo, X. and Wei, X. (2005) 'Woguo Faxing Juzai Zhaiquan de Nandian yu Duice' (The Difficulties and Solutions for Issuing Catastrophe bonds in China), *China Insurance*, 6, 23–7.

He, Q. H. and Chen, R. H. (2013) 'Securitization of Catastrophe Insurance Risk and Catastrophe Bonds: Experiences and Lessons to Learn', *Frontiers of Laws in China*, 8(2), 523–58.

Hecht, S. B. (2008) 'Climate Change and the Transformation of Risk: Insurance Matters', *UCLA Law Review*, 55, 1559–620.

Intergovernmental Panel on Climate Change (2007) 'Climate Change 2007: The Physical Science Basis'. Available at: http://www.ipcc.ch/ipccreports/ar4-wg1.htm (accessed 21 May 2014).

Kahneman, D. (2011) *Thinking, Fast and Slow*, New York: Farrar, Straus and Giroux.

Kahneman, D. and Tversky, A. (1979) 'Prospect Theory: An Analysis of Decision under Risk', *Econometrica*, 47(2), 263–92.

Kaplow, L. (1991) 'Incentives and Government Relief for Risk', *Journal of Risk and Uncertainty*, 4, 167–75.

King, R. (2005) '*Hurricanes and Disaster Risk Financing Through Insurance: Challenges and Policy Options*', Cong. Research Serv., R132825.

Knight, F. (1971) *Risk, Uncertainty and Profit*, Beverly Hills: Phoenix Books.

Krantz, D. and Kunreuther, H. (2007) 'Goals and Plans in Decision Making', *Judgment and Decision Making*, 2(3), 137–68.

Kulp, C. A. (1956) *Casualty Insurance*, New York: Ronald Press.

Kunreuther, H. (1968) 'The Case for Comprehensive Disaster Insurance', *Journal of Law and Economics*, 11(1), 133–63.

Kunreuther, H. (1996) 'Mitigating Disaster Losses through Insurance', *Journal of Risk and Uncertainty*, 12, 171–87.

Kunreuther, H. and Roth, R. J. Sr. (1998) *Paying the Price: the Status and Role of Insurance against Natural Disasters in the United States*, Washington, DC: Joseph Henry Press.

Kunreuther, H. and Michel-Kerjan, E. O. (2007) 'Climate Change, Insurability of Large-Scale Disasters, and the Emerging Liability Challenge', *University of Pennsylvania Law Review*, 155, 1797–842.

Kunreuther, H. and Michel-Kerjan, E. O. (2009a) *At War with the Weather: Managing Large-scale Risks in a New Era of Catastrophes*, Cambridge, MA: MIT Press.

Kunreuther, H. and Michel-Kerjan, E. O. (2009b) 'Encouraging Adaptation to Climate Change: Long-Term Flood Insurance', *Resources for the Future*, Issue Brief 09–13.

Kunreuther, H. and Michel-Kerjan, E. O. (2010) 'Market and Government Failure in Insuring and Mitigating Natural Catastrophes: How Long-Term Contracts Can Help', in Brown, J. R. (ed), *Public Insurance and Private Markets*, Washington, DC: AEI Press, 115–43.

Kunreuther, H., Pauly, M. V. and McMorrow, S. (2013) *Insurance and Behavioral Economics: Improving Decisions in the Most Misunderstood Industry*, Cambridge: Cambridge University Press.

Lan, Y. (2011) 'Duikou Zhiyuan: Zhongguo Tese De Difang Zhengfu Jian Hezuo Moshi Yanjiu' (A Study on the Counterpart Aid: A Cooperation Pattern between Local Governments with Chinese Characteristics), XiBei Shifan Daxue Shuoshi Xuewei Lunwen (Thesis of the College of Political and Law of Northwest Normal University).

Mani, M., Keen, M. and Freeman, P. K. (2003) 'Dealing with Increased Risk of Natural Disasters: Challenges and Options', *IMF Working Paper*, Fiscal Affairs Department.

Mayer-Schoenberger, V. and Cukier, K. (2013) *Big Data: A Revolution That Will Transform How We Live, Work, and Think*, New York: Houghton Mifflin Harcourt.

Maynard, T. (2008) 'Climate Change: Impacts on Insurers and How They Can Help With Adaptation and Mitigation', *The Geneva Papers on Risk and Insurance*, 33(1), 140–6.

Michel-Kerjan, E., Forges, S. and Kunreuther, H. (2011) 'Policy Tenure under the U.S. National Flood Insurance Program', *Risk Analysis*, 32(4), 644–58.

Oreskes, N. (2007) 'The Scientific Consensus on Climate Change: How Do We Know We're Not Wrong in Climate Change', in DiMento, J. and Doughman, P. (eds),

Climate Change: What It Means for You, Your Children, and Your Grandchildren, Cambridge, MA: MIT Press, 65–99.

Outreville, F. (1998) *Theory and Practice of Insurance*, Dordrecht: Kluwer Academic Publishers.

Priest, G. L. (1996) 'The Government, the Market, and the Problem of Catastrophe Loss', *Journal of Risk and Uncertainty*, 12, 219–37.

Putra, F. (2009) 'Crisis Management in Public Administration', *Planning Forum*, 13/14, 152–77.

Qin, Z. and Chen, L. Q. (2009) 'Mode of managing catastrophic risk in China', *Journal of Wuhan University of Science and Technology (Social Science Edition)*, 11(2), 33–41.

Seog, S. H. (2010) *The Economics of Risk and Insurance*, Chichester: Wiley-Blackwell.

Shi, P. J., Tang, D., Liu J., Chen, B. and Zhou, M. (2007) 'Natural Disaster Insurance Issue and Strategy of China', 1st International Conference on Asian Catastrophe Insurance.

Sigma (2012) 'Swiss Re's Latest Sigma Study on Natural Catastrophes and Man-made Disasters in 2011', Swiss Reinsurance Company.

Sigma (2013a) 'Natural Catastrophes and Man-made Disasters in 2012: A Year of Extreme Weather Events in the US', Swiss Reinsurance Company.

Sigma (2013b) 'World Insurance in 2012 Progressing on the Long and Winding Road to Recovery', Swiss Reinsurance Company.

Swartz, K. (2002) 'Justifying Government as the Backstop in Health Insurance Markets', *Yale Journal of Health Policy, Law, and Ethics*, 2(1), 89–108.

Swiss Re (2008) 'Financial Solutions for Weather Risks'.

Swiss Re (2013) 'Mind the risk: cities under threat from natural disasters'.

Telesetsky, A. (2010) 'Insurance as a Mitigation Mechanism: Managing International Greenhouse Gas Emissions through Nationwide Mandatory Climate Change Catastrophe Insurance', *Pace Environmental Law Review*, 27(3), 691–734.

The Em-Dat Glossary (3 March 2012), 'The International Disaster Database'.

Thoyts, R. (2010) *Insurance Theory and Practice*, Oxford: Routledge.

Tian, L. and Luo, J. (2012) 'Gong Xu Shuang Yue Shu Xia Zhong Guo Ju Zai Bao Xian Zhi Du De Xuan Ze – Chang Qi Ju Zai Bao Xian De Ke Xing Xing Yan Jiu' (The Choice of China Catastrophe Insurance Institution Based on the Restrictions of Supply and Demand – the Feasibility Study of Long Term Catastrophe Insurance), *Wuhan Daxue Xuebao (Zhexue Shehui Kexue Ban)* (Wuhan University Journal (Philosophy & Social Sciences)), 65(5), 111–18.

Tian, L. and Zhang, Y. (2013) 'Woguo Juzai Baoxian Xuqiu Yingxiang Yinsu Shizheng Yanjiu: Jiyu Wusheng Bufen Baofei Shouru Mianban Yanjiu' (Influence Factors of Catastrophe Insurance Demand in China – Panel Analysis in a Case of Insurance Premium Income of Five Provinces), *Wuhan Ligong Daxue Xuebao (Shehui Kexue Ban)* (Wuhan University of Technology (Social Science Edition)), 26(2), 175–9.

United Nations Environment Programme Finance Initiative Climate Change Working Group (2006) 'Adaptation and Vulnerability to Climate Change: The Role of the Finance Sector', 14. Available at: http://www.unepfi.org/fileadmin/documents/CEO_briefing_adaptation_vulnerability_2006.pdf (accessed 21 May 2014).

US Government Accountability Office (2002) 'Catastrophe insurance risk: the role of risk-linked securities and factors affecting their use', GAO-02-941.

US Government Accountability Office (2005) 'Catastrophe risk: U.S. and European Approaches to Insure National Catastrophe and Terrorism Risks', GAO-05–199.

US Government Accountability Office (2007) 'Climate Change: Financial Risks to Federal and Private Insurers in Coming Decades Are Potentially Significant', GAO-07–285.

US Government Accountability Office (2009) 'Experiences from Past Disasters Offer Insights for Effective Collaboration after Catastrophe Events', at 2, note 4, GAO-09–811.

Vaughan, E. J. and Vaughan, T. M. (2007) *Fundamentals of Risk and Insurance*, New York: John Wiley and Sons.

Xian, Q. H. and Ye, X. L. (2009) 'The Practices of Chinese Government Catastrophe Risk Management and Its Role Definition', *Journal of Insurance Professional College*, 23, 43–8.

Yue, T., Ning, J. H. and Fan, M. Y. (2013) 'Wo Guo Ju Zai Bao Xian Zai Bao Xian Ti Xi De Gou Jian Yan Jiu' (The Research on the Establishment of Chinese Catastrophe Insurance and Reinsurance System), *ZhongGuo Waizi* (Foreign Investment in China), 16, 255–8.

Zhao, L. and Jiang, Y. J. (2009) 'Difang Zhengfu Duikou Zhiyuan Moshi Fenxi' (Analysis of Local Government Coordinated Assistance Modes), *ChengDu Daxue Xuebao (Sheke Ban)* (*Journal of ChengDu University* (Social Science Edition)), 2, 4–7, 25.

Zhou, Y. L. (Vice President of CIRC) (2008) '*Quan Shehui Diyu Fengxian Nengli Buduan Tigao*' (The Ability of Defensing Catastrophe Risk is Improving for the Whole Society), International Catastrophe Insurance Fund Management Symposium. Available at: http://insurance.hexun.com/2008–10–23/110361174.html (accessed 21 May 2014).

11 Project finance contracts, essential components, and basic strategic advantages

Federico Wesselhoefft[1]

11.1 Introduction

Project finance contracts (PFCs) have gradually become key tools for the financing of exceptionally large and costly projects[2] serving both the private as well as the public sectors.[3] These are very sophisticated organizations that require high transaction costs for their implementation.[4]

During the last years, the extraordinary organizational complexity and the growing popularity of PFCs have generated a proliferation of industry-oriented as well as interdisciplinary academic literature on the matter. However, academic literature dealing with specific agency conflicts in PFCs is still scarce. This dispersion may well result from the diversity of theoretical stances studying agency conflicts in the literature of corporate law and corporate finance as well as from the complexity and structural varieties adopted by PFCs in practice. Despite theoretical and practical difficulties, based on their essential elements, some literature comparing agency relationships in corporate transactions and in PFCs has already been produced.[5]

This chapter highlights the results of the first of three components of ongoing research on the law and economics of PFCs. Three distinct pillars have been identified in this study in progress: the first pillar explores the agency conflicts generated by large projects in corporate transactions and how these conflicts are avoided by PFCs; the second pillar analyzes the agency conflicts within PFCs; and the third pillar explores possible legal implications from those agency conflicts in project finance.

As derived from the first pillar, this chapter describes the classic agency conflicts among stakeholders in corporate finance structures that are exacerbated in the presence of exceptionally large projects, and how these agency costs are not present in PFCs. In other words, from a descriptive stance, this chapter reviews the classic agency costs of corporate finance that are not present in PFCs when dealing with very large projects. Consequently, what remains beyond the scope of this particular analysis is a study of agency conflicts that take place within PFCs as well as the derivative considerations on the circumstances under which parties would opt for corporate or for project finance.[6]

After this introduction, Section 11.2 considers the essential components, features and individual strategies of parties in PFCs. Section 11.3 describes the costs and feasibility aspects of PFCs. Section 11.4 focuses on the conflicts between shareholders and creditors as a class: the distress costs of debt, the debt overhang problem, the asset substitution, the debt dilution and asset dilution strategies are considered in particular. Section 11.5 explores the same conflict between shareholders and creditors, but focuses on strategies implemented within individual contractual interactions: this section first explores the conflicts between companies and individual input providers, and between companies and banks. In Section 11.6 conflicts between ownership and managers stemming from the free cash-flow problem as well as from managerial risk-aversion. Prior to the conclusions, the last section analyzes the conflicts between controlling shareholders and dispersed investors – these are essentially the adverse selection problems in equity and to a minor extent also in debt.

11.2   The essential components of project finance contracts

11.2.1   A concept

Also known as non-recourse or limited recourse operations, PFCs are both investing and financing operations in which a capital intensive project[7] and a loan financing it are legally allocated under the property of a dedicated legal entity. This project company, a bankruptcy remote special purpose vehicle (SPV), is owned and fully controlled by sponsors who are the originators and usually also key input providers to the project.[8] In PFCs, a coordinated group of banks – usually a syndicate (hereinafter indistinctively: the lenders, or the financing party) – provide the larger part (often about 70 per cent) of total capital requirements for the project in the form of senior debt, whereas the remainder is contributed by sponsors in the form of equity of the SPV, 100 per cent of which remains in the hands of sponsors. As equity holders, sponsors are residual claimants to variable profits from the contract; as key input providers to the project, sponsors habitually also subordinate parts of their contractual remunerations to the claims of the financing party. Even though during the different phases of projects sponsors may provide limited and exceptional collaterals in favor of the SPV, it is an essential feature of PFCs that, for the servicing of the financing debt, the financing party relies mainly on the cash flow generated by the SPV during operation and after completion of the project (Finnerty 2007: 1; Fabozzi and De Nahlik 2012: 1). The fact that sponsors agree on liquidated damages clauses and other protections against the consequences of their individual breaching of the SPV or to the lenders does not interfere with the non-recourse nature of PFCs which relates to an obligation of the SPV.

11.2.2   Basic features and common strategies

Two particular characteristics of PFCs are to be considered for the understanding of the common and individual strategies of stakeholders. These are:

first, the non-recourse nature of its financing debt; and second, the singularity of a project to be completed under the property of a dedicated bankruptcy remote legal entity. A consideration of these two attributes serves to put light in the logic behind the risk-allocation strategies and key contractual mechanisms observed in these operations.

The non-recourse nature of PFCs implies that lenders cannot direct their claims against third parties in the case that the SPV does not generate sufficient proceeds to serve its financing debt. This condition has an important strategic-related implication. From the stance of these uncollateralized lenders, for a project to be bankable without collaterals, in principle it would be necessary that the responsibilities for the fulfilling of all tasks and the prevention of all foreseeable eventualities that are necessary for the completion of a project are allocated to identifiable parties via individually enforceable mechanisms, so that, as much as possible, no components or possible risks to the project are left unattended (Dewar 2011: 81; Vinter *et al.* 2013: 155). The implementation of this strategy, which would usually appear as a problematic endeavor if information costs are considered, is greatly facilitated by the fact that in PFCs, a single limited-life project can be evaluated on its own merits, without the positive or negative influences of other business units coexisting under the same corporate umbrella.

Consistent with this, during the design stage, i.e. before completion and operation phases,[9] sponsors approach the financing party with a business proposal which includes specific enforceable provisions governing all key variables of projects. These provisions not only cover the sequence under which input providers will deliver all contributions needed for the project, including management and operation, but also describe the ways in which all foreseeable contingencies, including costs overruns, should be solved during the life of the project. Typically, these terms will also specify marketing studies or the existing agreements with parties or State agencies purchasing the proceeds from the project (hereinafter, the off-taker), concession agreements, insurance policies dealing with all exogenous risks and any pertinent authorization to pursue particular activities, etc. For best enforcement of risk-allocating mechanisms (i.e. for the observability of performances) it is a common strategy to leave the SPV in charge of administrative issues and to outsource to sponsors all tasks required for the completion of the projects (i.e. leaving without actual involvement in the project beyond holding its property and the contractual organization). Ideally, as the design stage of the project advances and the interaction with lenders progresses, project finance operation should begin to appear in documents as a fully predictable future scenario.

A virtue of PFCs is that they generate an environment of high-interest alignment among all parties involved. The fact that in project finance key providers subordinate substantial parts of their expectations to the completion of a common single project which depends materially on the unanimous contributions of all stakeholders creates incentives for parties to spend extra efforts not only in delivering their material inputs but also in reciprocally monitoring their actions and managing the project better. Authors refer to this as the "community of interest" in project finance (Howcroft and Fadhley 1998).

Finally, project financing can best be thought of as a form of asset-based financial engineering (Finnerty 2007: 398). Unlike corporate businesses, where reinvestment opportunities are variable and multiple, and in a sense also unforeseeable with a vocation to perpetuity, project finance transactions are one-time, fully self-contained, individually financed events with a definitive life cycle where most of the fundamental components of projects are pre-arranged by sponsors prior to seeking debt from the financing party (Gatti *et al.* 2013).

11.2.3   *The structuring of project finance contracts*

Project finance agreements may be structured by a variety of individual contractual links among stakeholders. These arrangements greatly depend on the characteristics of each of the projects. There are, however, certain instruments that can be mentioned as being typical in these organizations. Perhaps with the exception of shareholder agreements among sponsors, in general, key contractual mechanisms are oriented to protecting the interests of lenders as the main risks-takers.

Beyond the loan agreement and covenants between the financing party and the SPV, and besides the provision contracts between the SPV and sponsors, in PFCs some instruments relate the financing party directly with sponsors, and some others also link the financing party with the SPV, sponsors and the off-taker via direct agreements (Hoffman 2009: 113; Vinter *et al.* 2013: 307). Typically, via negative and positive covenants, representations and conditions precedents, the financing party will make sure that sponsors comply with certain obligations that are of key value to the project. These obligations often relate to the provision of information, to the maintenance of insurance protections, perhaps to some exclusivity rights to the SPV (so that sponsors do not diverge their efforts to serving other clients) and so on. Lenders regularly request liquidated damages and collaterals to ensure the effective enforcement of sponsors' obligations of different types with the SPV. These contractual mechanisms habitually include the capacity of the financing party to execute loan accelerations as well as other penalties after a breaching of a sponsor or of other key input providers with the SPV has been detected (i.e. a cross-default provision).

For the purpose of this analysis, it is worth mentioning certain types of clauses that are relevant for risk-allocating purposes in PFCs. These are the financial ratios and control accounts, the cascade or cash waterfall schemes and step-in rights mechanisms implemented by lenders via direct agreements. Financial ratios reflect several variables that can be monitored for risk prevention and also for the enforcement of disciplining measures. These clauses may capture the relationship between expected revenues and outstanding debt, or between debt and equity to be kept by sponsors as further cash is injected from lenders (Gatti 2013: 284; Vinter *et al.* 2013: 225). The cash waterfall schemes, or cascade agreements, describe the sequence and specific conditions under which banks will deliver and receive funds as the project progresses. Via direct multiparty agreements among the lenders, sponsors, the SPV and the off-takers, lenders insure that under critical circumstances they have the legal capacity to take control over certain components or even over the property of the SPV. These are called step-in rights, in virtue of which the financing party might take over some of the contractual commitments of the SPV so that they are assigned to new contractors under its supervision[10] (Gatti 2013: 305; Yescombe 2014: 194). Furthermore, in virtue of these step-in rights, lenders may enforce securities on the shares of the SPV and eventually take ownership of its share capital.

Back-to-back and pass-through mechanisms are also commonly used in PFCs. In this context, a back-to-back provision may stipulate that the products that are delivered by input providers should comply with the identical quality standards that the SPV is expected to deliver to an off-taker, especially if these are modified *ex post* (Vinter *et al.* 2013: 93). A pass-through provision, also in this context, usually implies that the extra costs and possible penalties assumed by the SPV as a consequence of the underperformance of an input provider should be dealt with by the latter (Vinter *et al.* 2013: 91).

11.2.4 The special purpose vehicle and its dynamics

Special purpose vehicles function as the nexus of contracts in the core of PFCs. These project companies may be arranged under different legal types: they can, e.g. be set up as a corporation, limited liability partnership, limited liability company or a trust. Even though it could be argued that, following tax incentives, some project finance operations are in fact structured around unincorporated joint venture agreements or unlimited liability companies, it is typically the case that project companies are legal entities that provide limited liability protections (Finnerty 2007: 131; Yescombe 2014: 40). Under non-limited liability companies or around joint venture agreements, sponsors often reconstruct the non-recourse condition of PFCs by providing in the loan agreements that lenders will have no access to other collaterals beyond certain business units or of individual assets – in the case of security interests.

Remote incorporation and asset partitioning are however features of fundamental value to lenders.[11] To the financing party, it is of great importance that the project's asset and cash flows are not mixed with those of other business units where they may be used for other purposes. Also of critical importance to the financing party is that the project is protected from being dismantled and sold to serve the claims of other creditors in case an insolvency procedure is opened against a debtor under corporate financing structures (i.e. entity shielding).

On the side of sponsors, limited liability is a highly appreciated feature against risk contamination from the large project being completed. When unlimited partnerships or joint ventures are used, a frequently used strategy for limiting potential liabilities consists of setting up a buffer line of limited liability SPVs between the actual sponsoring companies and the project company managing the project.[12] It is not uncommon to see PFCs with more than one SPV, or having shell companies used for particular purposes in the different industrial sectors. Besides, more than one SPV are often used in leasing operations or when securitization phases are implemented (Fabozzi and De Nahlik 2012: 168). For simplicity, in the rest of the chapter, projects will be considered as having a single SPV.

The applicable legal norms as well as the characteristics of contractual instruments that regulate the life of SPVs are also influenced by the fact that, under PFCs, only a single and limited-life and highly idiosyncratic project is to be completed. In PFCs, the SPV is an instrumental component of a larger contractual system designed to nest the SPV itself, a particular project and a non-recourse loan agreement financing it. Consistent with this, it is generally the case that most of the contractual elements and variables that are the objects of default statutory rules (which have been designed by legislators to be applied in different environments) are replaced by the specific contractual arrangements implemented during the design phase of the project. In PFCs, specific provisions tend to substitute the application of default statutory rules far more than in other contractual environments. Furthermore, in PFCs, key aspects that are regularly the sources of conflicts among stakeholders (e.g. the investment, the financing and the dividend and distribution policies) are fully detailed before any risks are incurred.

First, on the investment dimension, the SPV can only invest in a particular project as its single growth option and under the conditions that have been accepted by the financing party. Second, on the financing side, all funding sources are also well arranged in advance. In PFCs lenders agree on a schedule for the use of lent funds which is synchronized with the progress and completion of substages of the project. The financing party also request that sponsors and input providers make funds available in the form of equity, or of subordinated loans in case unforeseen events arise.[13] Third, in relation to the dividend distribution and reinvestment policies, in PFCs, reinvestment is not possible with a single project to be completed, whereas dividends are invariably subordinated to the service of the financing debt.

What is more, in PFCs, stakeholders themselves have different characteristics compared with those in corporate finance settings. These individual aspects help to eliminate or mitigate conflicts in project finance settings. In PFCs there are no minority or disperse shareholders that may be expropriated by insiders. Instead, there may be passive sponsors who are highly qualified institutional investors. On the side of creditors, financing sources come from a single syndicate of lenders that are capable of enforcing most of the relevant aspects of the project. Bonds are commonly used in PFCs but they are issued with the intervention of qualified intermediaries under the supervision of the financing party. In fact, project finances contracts – so as to avoid any chance of debt dilution – are the lenders (i.e. creditors) who habitually also control the access of the SPV to alternative sources of financing.

Besides, in PFCs, a low number of parties dealing with a single project allows that important decisions are more swiftly taken by operating committees acting under simplified procedures involving lenders and possibly representatives from public agencies (Yescombe 2014: 86 and 136). Resulting from this, managerial discretion may be limited to the administration of less transcendental matters, thus mitigating the common conflicts between ownership and control of corporate structures.

Finally, the high risks at stake and the low number of parties make alternative means of dispute resolutions involving highly specialized arbitrators and mediators a less costly option that is frequently used in PFCs (Yescombe 2014: 161 and 174).

11.3   The contractual feasibility and the costs of project finance contracts

From a strictly contractual stance, PFCs have two feasibility boundaries. The first relates to the difficulties that the financing party faces when finding information on the project; the second relates to the challenge of determining the most efficient risk-allocating strategy (Dewar 2011: 81).

These two boundaries are transaction costs related and they are by no means exclusive of PFCs only. Generally speaking, transaction costs (i.e. the costs of revealing information, of bargaining on contractual terms and of enforcing stipulations) are key variables to the successful implementation of all contractual settings. In PFCs, however, as mentioned above, these difficulties become critical due to the fact that the financing party shapes its prospects from the expected enforcement of side arrangements dealing with all the needs of a project. The availability of information is therefore of crucial relevance for the feasibility of PFCs, more so than for most of the other collateralized financing alternatives.

In relation to the cost of finding information, even though PFCs are structured around a single project, due to the complexity of contracts, the identification of risks and contingencies may still be a challenging endeavor to the financing party as the main risk-taker. Despite the fact that they may be experts in the particular sectors, neither the financing party nor its advisors are designers or providers of material inputs involved in the material completion of projects. Therefore they are not the best information providers. Information finding efforts of lenders may be also jeopardized by information rent seeking strategies of highly asymmetric sponsors.

These difficulties in finding information have important implications over the second challenge of determining the most efficient risk-allocating strategy. A simplistic risk distribution strategy that is frequently used as an effective solution against uncertainties consists of recurring to fixed-price, date-certain (i.e. 'turnkey') arrangements covering entire areas of a project (Yescombe 2014: 218). Consider a typical engineering, procurement, construction and management (EPCM) scheme as the ones often used for the provision of nuclear power facilities (Vinter *et al.* 2013: 504). Ideally, under this common strategy, parties may specify fixed rewards and expected outcomes for those four general components of the project and let each of the sponsors deal with their individual contingencies after insuring the SPV only against the risks affecting the project as a whole (i.e. sovereign credit risk, currency rate fluctuations, *force majeure* at the SPV levels, etc.). However, if used in purity without flexible provisions (as is never the case), this solution may be effective but highly inefficient and also very costly to sponsors.

These strict provisions may be difficult to accept by sponsors for two reasons. First, the magnitude of possible damages resulting from individual defaults, the uncertainties over possible variation on individual costs, and the lack of readjustment possibilities would imply that premiums and contingency provisions to be assumed by sponsors would be high. Second, the incompleteness of contracts and the material complexity and asymmetries of information may allow the implementation of opportunistic strategies among sponsors.

These are efficiency trade-offs and feasibility boundaries from information costs and bounded rationality problems that are common to all contractual arrangements and that have a particular impact in non-recourse financing of specific assets. Dewar (2011: 81) illustrates the critical need for parties to find and specify information by mentioning a figure of 30,000 as being an average number of the pages used for the documenting of typical power plants projects.

A remark should be made here: although inefficient due to the implied high premiums and contingency provisions, the use of strict fixed-price date certain non-adjustable contracts may effectively make project's outcomes more predictable, ultimately improving the willingness of lenders to provide financing.

Fundamentally, due to the non-recourse for project finance structures to be implemented, most foreseeable risks and contingencies must have been *ex ante* forecasted and effectively prevented as a prerequisite for its bankability so that a single project may progress smoothly towards completion without conflicts among stakeholders. The feasibility of PFCs greatly depends on the costs that parties must incur to reveal information on the project and also to distribute risks and efforts among sponsors via enforceable mechanisms. This consideration is commonplace in managerial literature referring to the amount of transaction costs incurred by stakeholders in PFCs.[14]

11.4   Conflicts between shareholders and creditors as a class

The first agency conflict to be analyzed relates to the sources of agency costs between shareholders and creditors as a class that are not feasible in PFCs. In this section, the asset substitution overinvestment problem, the debt overhang underinvestment problem, the debt dilution incentives and the asset dilution strategies will be described. Next, distress costs as a motivating factor for parties to recur to PFCs will be addressed (Esty 2003). Finally, in an additional section, the opportunistic strategies from shareholders against individual contractors (i.e. input providers and banks) will be considered.

11.4.1 *Project finance contracts, large projects and distress costs in corporate structures*

One of the most relevant merits of the structural features of PFCs is that they mitigate the financial distress costs that are generated by very large projects when they are financed by companies using debt. This subsection includes: first, a brief consideration of the sources and nature of distress costs in general; second, a description of how distress costs are generated in corporate finance transactions by the levels of debt in capital structures; and third, a reference of how distress costs are produced by the material features of projects and by the double-way risk contamination hazards. The subsection will be concluded by a description of how distress costs from large and specific projects are highly mitigated in PFCs.

11.4.1.1 *The nature and the sources of distress costs*

The definition of the concept of distress costs has changed in academic literature during the last decades. Initially, the scope of the definition of distress costs only covered losses from liquidating a defaulting organization. In more recent literature, the concept of distress costs is usually understood as including a wide array of costly items also covering externalities from corporate defaults to society as a whole.[15] Today, it is commonly accepted in the literature that, in addition to the (direct) costs of bankruptcy statutory reorganizations or liquidations, the concept of distress costs also includes the types of (indirect) costs, both financial and economic, that companies and contracting parties experience in the vicinity of insolvency.[16] Much of the indirect distress costs arise in the form of contractual, formal or relational, precautions incurred by claimholders as soon as default gradually appears as a likelier outcome. As Cornaggia observes: "Indeed, distress is not best considered a binary state but rather a continuum of financial health. Many firms take actions that have wealth implications for employees, customers, suppliers, creditors, and shareholders long before default or bankruptcy" (Cornaggia 2011: 358). As explained by Myers (1977), the costs of financial distress are incurred when the firm comes under the threat of bankruptcy, even if bankruptcy is ultimately avoided.

Examples of distress costs include the losses generated by workers withholding personal investments, by clients seeking alternative sources of supplies, by input providers bargaining for shorter terms, by creditors requesting security interests or collaterals from third parties, by the losses of reputation affecting market shares and in general, etc. Bargaining and other transaction costs incurred by prospective creditors in designing protective covenants against agency conflicts are to be listed among these indirect distress costs too. Agency costs are components of indirect distress costs that grow with volatility and with higher expected losses from a more likely default (Malitz 1986). Extensively, distress costs also include the opportunity costs of the restrictiveness of debt covenants accepted by the company so as to preserve its access to debt financing sources.

In relation to the financing of large projects, two key factors can be identified as determinants of the significance of financial distress costs: first, the magnitude of the expected losses from default, and second, the probability of default. Whereas the magnitude of foreseeable losses from liquidation or reorganization essentially depends on project specifics, the probability of default largely depends on the volatility of corporate cash flows. In the financing of large projects, volatility is itself determined or affected by many factors which can be grouped as relating to first, capital structure (debt to equity ratio); and second, to the material composition of assets and projects (e.g. the size of projects within other business units under the same company, the liquidity of its assets or how much of the project's costs are fixed or variable).[17]

More broadly, distress costs and their impact over the strategies of parties and over agency costs are items of central importance at the time of selecting an optimum composition of financing sources, and as such, they lie in the core of modern capital structure doctrines.[18] Distress costs have been widely considered by empirical studies in the field of insolvency law and economics.[19]

Before analyzing how PFCs mitigate the distress costs generated, the sources of distress costs and how distress costs are originated and affected by the presence of large projects under corporate structures must be considered.

11.4.1.2   *Capital structure and volatility induced distress costs*

Very large projects that are capital intensive regularly require companies to seek financing in the form of debt.[20] This section analyses how in corporate finance settings, volatility and its consequential distress costs may be generated by the sole presence of debt (i.e. debt to equity ratios) in capital structures.[21]

A way to explain how debt itself leads to volatility is to consider how the company changes its capacity to absorb the impact of exogenous factors without defaulting on its contractual obligations by simply varying the presence of debt on its capital structure.[22] Consider a company financed largely with equity and with a rather insignificant amount of debt: this company, with very little enforceable commitments would be very unlikely to default on its senior obligations, as a little generated welfare would suffice to satisfy its creditors. Consequently, most of the generated funds (even if they were small but as long as they would surpass those minor needs) could be either reinvested, or distributed as dividends. In practical terms of likelihood of default, such a company would be fairly insensitive to exogenous risks affecting the performance of its particular projects. On the other hand, a company financed mainly with debt will need to consistently produce a certain basic amount of wealth to serve its outstanding obligations. Subsequently, as debt grows, gradually smaller variations in generated welfare may leave the company closer to its insolvency, hence, this company would be highly sensitive to influences of exogenous factors affecting its projects. Accordingly, to shareholders, higher debt over equity means expanded distributable benefits during days of prosperity, and also a sooner and more likely insolvency during days of hardship (i.e. higher volatility of cash flows).

Modigliani and Miller (1958; 1963) showed that in theory, i.e. under strong assumptions, namely the absence of bargaining frictions and other distortive incentives, including taxes, creditors could sharply internalize the expected losses from volatility in the prices or the interest charged for the risky debt financing they provide. In real life, however, there are uncertainties about the future, asymmetries, moral hazards as well as tax incentives that deprive Modigliani and Miller's irrelevance propositions from realistically holding. These frictions incentivize creditors to spend efforts in costly precautions that ultimately expand indirect distress costs. The costs of these precautions have an impact over the price of debt ultimately affecting the debt capacity of companies.

11.4.1.3 *Material aspects of very large projects: Coinsurance versus risk contamination and distress costs*

So far, the impact of debt over volatility and its consequential distress costs has been described; now, attention will be given to the distress costs generated by the relative size and by the material characteristics of the assets of exceptionally large projects.

It is well known that in corporate finance investments, the bundling of a multiplicity of organizationally independent projects under a corporate umbrella serves as an efficient coinsurance device. A certain number of independent projects reacting differently to exogenous factors allow companies to absorb some of the impacts from unexpected events over particular business units (Leland 2007). Large projects may generate a stable free cash flow that may help to reduce the aggregated volatility of the company cash flow, thus lowering distress costs and ultimately allowing for an increase of its debt capacity. These are some of the benefits of coinsurance from integration which are strictly financial, i.e. independent from positive or negative operational synergies at the industrial level (Froot *et al.* 1993).

However, the integration of the financing of exceptionally large projects with other business units may not always be efficient: under certain circumstances, coinsurance benefits from integration may be dominated by the costs that large, specific and risky projects might externalize to other business units. In corporate finance contracts, the relative size of projects, the correlations of volatilities between projects and companies, and finally, the degrees of specificities involved (redeployability or reversibility of investments as referred to in Pindyck (1991)) are factors that determine the sign of financial synergies from integrating projects and companies. In the extreme, under corporate financing structures, a risky project may drag an otherwise healthy investing firm into default in the same manner that a mismanaged company may bring healthy business units to their liquidation (Esty 2003). This phenomenon, called risk-contamination, has been considered in models by Lewellen (1971) and more recently by Leland (2007). Risk contamination problems have also been mentioned as one of the motivations for using PFCs by Esty (2003) and empirically by Alam (2010).

Additionally, low liquidities and high specificities (and low redeployabilities) of assets from very large projects affect companies in other aspects associated to the distress levels and to its costs. Low liquidity from large projects reduces the capacity of companies to access the cash that they need for coinsurance via cross-subsiding, or hedging, in the words of Froot *et al.* (1993), and for avoiding exhausting internal sources of finance, that are essential for preventing distress costs. This is due to the fact that real and financial flexibilities are substitutes, as modeled by Mauer and Triantis (1994) and empirically confirmed by MacKay (2003).[23] Consistent to this, from an empirical stance, Titman and Wessels (1988) described how debt levels are negatively related to the 'uniqueness' of a firm's line of business. Distress costs may also induce companies to sell assets under time constraints (Brown *et al.* 1994). Also, distress costs have been shown to affect the bargaining power of companies when dealing with specific providers (Sarig 1998).

11.4.1.4   *Mitigation of the costs of financial distress*

By allocating all financing contracts in a separate legal entity without recourse to sponsors, PFCs remove the financing debt from the balance sheets of sponsors, thus avoiding volatility induced distress costs from debt to equity ratios.

Besides, by keeping large projects beyond the property of sponsors, PFCs avoid distress costs from internal risk contamination hazards that are exacerbated by the size of projects, by the volatilities of their cash flows, capital intensiveness, and by the expected losses from their specific and barely redeployable assets (Leland 2007).

As mentioned in the first section, the financing of projects under the property of a legally remote corporate entity allows investors to evaluate projects and risks on their own merits without the risky interference of other business units (Alam 2010; Esty 2004: 6). More precisely, in PFCs the only residual distress costs perceived on the side of sponsors would be determined by their equity investments on the SPV, as well as by the possible losses from the contractual obligations defaulted by the SPV against sponsors as input providers.

11.4.2   Project finance contracts avoid asset substitution and risk-shifting problems

In this section I will show how PFCs lack the structural features that in corporate finance structures allow the asset substitution and overinvestment problems. First, a description of the nature of the asset substitution problem will be given. Second, the section will make a reference to the impact of exceptionally large projects over the asset substitution incentives and to the costs of some of the contractual solutions available under corporate finance settings. Third, the infeasibility of asset substitution strategies under corporate finance contracts will be briefly mentioned.

11.4.2.1   The essentials of the asset substitution problem in corporate structures

Jensen and Meckling (1976) and Galai and Masulis (1976) referred to the asset substitution problem as an investment distortion and also as a form of abusive risk shifting against creditors, under which shareholders extract wealth from debt holders by directing the company towards projects that are riskier than optimal, often having negative net present value (NPV). The intuition behind this strategy is rather simple: under a limited liability shelter, shareholders harvest the benefits from successful operations while externalizing most of the costs of business failures to creditors. As a consequence of the limited liability protection, the volatility of cash flows has a different value to shareholders, to the company as a whole and to creditors. As a general rule, as fix benefit claimants, creditors prefer that the company pursue less risky projects, which may be also less profitable to the company and to shareholders. As variable profit seekers, shareholders, in contrary, prefer riskier and more rewarding business opportunities, even if this means lower value to the company and naturally also to creditors. In the words of Kraakman *et al.* (2005: 186–9) "shareholders may prefer a large slice of a smaller pie." Broadly speaking, it can be safely said that asset substitution, as risk-shifting incentives in general, do grow with debt.[24]

Without considering contractual arrangements targeting the particular asset substitution issues, generally speaking, two limitations to the asset substitution strategies may be mentioned; one legal, and the second one of material nature. The legal limitations to the types of projects that a company might attempt to capture may come from the provisions in corporate charters (the articles of incorporation) specifying the scope of their business activities. From the material point of view, risk shifting may be limited by the production flexibility of assets in place (MacKay 2003). Both limitations are however somewhat ineffective. First, in most jurisdictions charters may be modified without the consent of creditors (Kraakman *et al.* 2005: 186–9). Second, even though low redeployability of assets may preclude the use of such goods for other riskier projects, such low redeployability may however not impede that cash flows generated by the efficient use of those assets are invested in other too risky businesses (i.e. cross-subsiding).

11.4.2.2　*Very large projects and the costs of asset substitution strategies*

Significant effort has been devoted to analyzing the factors affecting the asset substitution problem. Some of these studies describe the role of aspects that are commonly seen in the financing of exceptionally large and costly projects (i.e. the degree of financial leverage, the long-term maturities, the volatilities from leverage, the uncertainties from large investments, and financial distress).

First, the use of debt for funding exceptionally costly projects increases the degree of financial leverage of investing companies with its consequential increases in volatility of cash flows and in the value of the limited liability shelter (Leland 2007). Consistent with this, Green and Talmor (1986) modelled a positive correlation between financial leverage and risk-shifting incentives. Second, for the financing of costly projects, companies may choose long-term debt so as to avoid the agency costs associated with short term.[25] Using numerical simulations, Parrino and Weisbach (1999) have related the incentives to overinvest in risky projects to the duration of financing debt in a firm's capital structures. Third, other authors have also studied the relationships between volatility (in the case of large projects, from risk contamination possibilities), expected values of projects, and (over)investment incentives. Eisdorfer (2008) provided empirical evidence on the positive correlation between volatility, distress levels (from leverage), and risk-shifting incentives.

In order to prevent companies from pursuing growth options that may be riskier than optimal, a variety of contractual alternatives have been considered besides the basic imposition of direct restrictions over investment policies.

With the general purpose of dealing with both underinvestment and overinvestment incentives and agency costs, among other solutions, Myers (1977) proposed the use of short-term debt maturing prior to the investment needs. Jensen and Meckling (1976), Barnea *et al.* (1980) and Barnea *et al.* (1981) explored the impact of callable debt, stock options and convertible securities; Stulz and Johnson (1985) proposed the used of secured debt. Malitz (1986) suggested to avoid risk-shifting incentives by simply limiting the use of debt; Haugen and Senbet (1981) proposed the use of stock options; and Green (1984) recommended the use of warrants to moderate investment incentives related to the presence of debt. Smith and Warner (1979) made one of the earliest empirical observations on the ways in which covenants where used to mitigate these types of agency conflicts.[26]

Even though they may mitigate asset substitution problems, all these strategies entail their own trade-offs. Gertner and Scharfstein (1991) show that the use of short-term bonds may raise the market value of debt, leading to debt overhang. Besides, empirical evidence shows that covenants and collateral pledges are, in any case, less effective in mitigating the asset substitution problem from production flexibility (MacKay 2003). Furthermore, in most of the cases covenants include financial flexibility restrictions that jeopardize the access of companies to shorter terms of debt which mitigates underinvestmen and overinvestment incentives, as described by Childs *et al.* (2005). Similarly, Hennessy and Tserlukevich (2008) have shown how some of these instruments, particularly convertible debt, cannot solve the asset substitution problem in dynamic settings. Finally, after having analyzed the effects of seniority rules over investment incentives, Berkovitch and Kim (1990) showed how most financial mechanisms "indirectly specify the relative seniority for the claims of existing debt holders *vis-a-vis* present and future security holders" eventually leading to further over investment and/or underinvestment results. Distortions over seniority of claims also exacerbate agency conflicts among creditors in the vicinity of insolvency.[27]

More recently, in a paper exclusively targeting the asset substitution problem, Vanden (2009) considered a specific type of financial instrument with dynamically variable face values correlated to the value of the company with an elasticity higher than 1.[28] In theory, such an instrument should allow for close to optimal investment incentives. This contractual solution does, however, have its implementation feasibility drawbacks in a context of high asymmetries. Interestingly, analogous mechanisms are observed in PFCs where penalties and rewards (based on proxies for risk, as certificates of advances and financial ratios) are regularly implemented by cash waterfall clauses. In PFCs these mechanisms are feasible under the lowered costs of information permitted by the allocation of a single project under a special purpose company with a dedicated accounting system.

11.4.2.3 Asset substitution strategies are not feasible in project finance contracts

Several features of PFCs eliminate all legal and material possibilities of asset substitution strategies (Esty 2003). These characteristics relate, first, to the fact that, in PFCs, the assets are being funded, owned and operated by a dedicated and independent legal entity, and second, to the types of assets involved in the project which are usually valuable for particular purposes only.

Completing and operating projects under the property and control of a separate company impedes asset substitution strategies in three ways: first, in the legal dimension, the special purpose company has a single business objective or activity which had been approved by the financing party before assets were put in place in PFCs; there are precedent conditions, covenants, direct agreements underwritten by the SPV as well as by individual sponsors which as technical defaults and cross defaults events, allow the financing party to accelerate the loan agreement – and to request liquidated damages – in case the SPV pursues different objectives than those precisely predefined. In PFCs, subtle ways of asset substitution could hypothetically include a renegotiation with an off-taker in relation to specific conditions of original projects the terms and conditions set up under off-taker contracts are key variables of fundamental importance for the risk distribution and bankability of projects, which are invariably examined and regulated with full attention *ex ante* by lenders. Second, the fact that PFCs comprise the completion of projects under a dedicated company allows assets to be managed under the qualified surveillance of both sponsors and lenders. Third, as part of the common strategy of all parties, in PFCs most tasks and contributions are in fact contracted out to key input providers (Yescombe 2014: 40). Consequently, in PFCs most of the hardware remains under the property of input providers, while the SPV commonly keeps only a few productive components under its control.

In relation to the types of assets, non-recourse financing structures are typically used for the funding of projects that include highly specific assets. Consider the case of a large motor highway, a hospital or a satellite communication system: these assets may not be easily redeployed for other purposes.

11.4.3   *Project finance contracts reduce the debt overhang underinvestment problem*

By preserving the debt capacity of sponsors, PFCs prevent the debt overhang problem. In this section, first, the generalities of the debt overhang problem will be presented; second, a description of how corporate finance-based solutions fail to mitigate the debt overhang problem as a source of underinvestment will be given; finally, it will be mentioned how the structural features of PFCs avoid the debt overhang problem from its roots.

11.4.3.1   *The generalities of the debt overhang underinvestment problem*

In his seminal article, Myers (1977) presented the debt overhang problem as the reluctance of rational equity holders to provide further contributions to a project after they anticipate that a significant part of the welfare to be generated from their investments will be captured by existing debt holders. Under this classic framework, as the costs of debt growths, the seniority of debt leaves lower returns to equity holders as residual claimants of variable benefits. Low return values deter shareholders from providing further equity investments. The debt overhang problem is known in financial literature as one of the agency costs of debt and results in companies skipping projects with positive NPV in later stages.

However, the debt overhang problem does not result exclusively from the price of debt or from the degree of financial leverage. Shareholders' incentives to provide extra equity depend on its return value, i.e. on the capacity of companies to distribute dividends. Generally, the debt overhang problem stems also from costs indirectly related to the levels of debt. As one example, we may consider the impact of restrictive covenants (i.e. as in Borgonovo and Gatti 2013) which may have been designed for other purposes as preventing debt dilution (Kraakman *et al.* 2005: 117; Schwartz 1989); these contractual precautions may deprive the company of its financial flexibility and result in an increase in the costs of debt, ultimately reducing the distributable benefits to junior equity.

There is a body of literature considering the actual impact of the debt over-hang problem as a source of underinvestment (Parrino and Weisbach 1999; Titman and Tsyplakov 2007; Mao 2003). Specifically related to the case of companies funding exceptionally large, long-term projects, Diamond and He (2012) has modelled the association among maturity, value of assets in place, volatility, profitability of investments, and the debt overhang problem.[29]

11.4.3.2   *The debt overhang problem and the costly solutions under corporate finance transactions*

Besides the variety of financial arrangements described above, which pre-vent asset substitution strategies and that have been considered for mitigat-ing both overinvestment and underinvestment incentives, other contractual alternatives have been studied to mitigate the particular debt overhang prob-lem. One of the earliest specific solutions applicable to the debt overhang problem came from Myers (1977), who originally proposed short-term debt to mitigate the debt overhang underinvestment. Other authors suggested the implementation of restrictions to cash distributions to induce companies to increase their investment levels (Smith and Warner 1979; Malitz 1986); fur-ther solutions that have been proposed comprised the use of sophisticated financing contracts, such as convertible debt (Green 1984), or simply renego-tiating existing debt before new projects are financed (Fama 1980). Kalay (1982) offered empirical evidence on the effects of dividends and other cash distribution restrictions that, by forcing firms to retain funds, also induced them to undertake investment projects, thus mitigating the debt overhang problem.

In corporate finance transactions, however, most of these solutions imply costly compromises. Short-term debt, as proposed by Myers (1977), may involve an increase on the volatility of equity, which may lead to more over-hang (Diamond and He 2012). Additionally, as much as companies do not have access to alternative sources of financing, short-term debt may also per-mit liquidation threats from short-term creditors (Gertner and Scharfstein 1991). Furthermore, restricting cash contributions as proposed by Smith and Warner (1979) and observed empirically by Kalay (1982) may also be costly: as shown by Berkovitch and Kim (1990: 33), depending on other fac-tors, including asymmetries of information, delaying dividends may also gen-erate overinvestment incentives. In general, all contractual preventions, that instead of inducing companies to increase investment levels are directed to mitigate individual losses from default, will also affect seniority hierarchies among creditors, with their consequential distortions described in the previ-ous section.

11.4.3.3   *Project finance contracts and the debt overhang problem*

In PFCs, sponsors allocate all debt financing contracts on a project dedicated legal entity (Esty 2004: 7). By doing so, PFCs avoid the debt overhang problem at the sponsor level. At the level of the SPV, all sources of financing, either in the form of debt or equity are prearranged to be delivered either by the financing party or by sponsors as the project progresses. PFCs allow for typical contractual arrangements specifically used for these purposes, including the waterfall schemes (Vinter *et al.* 2013: 236), the debt to equity ratios, and other particular coverage and control accounts (Vinter *et al.* 2013: 225). At the sponsor level, debt may only be needed to finance their up-front contributions as input providers to the project or to finance their equity investments in the SPV.

11.4.4   *Debt dilution strategies and creditor hierarchy conflicts*

Debt dilution is the opportunistic strategy under which shareholders acquire further debt to the detriment of existing bondholders of the company (Schwartz 1989; 1997). As a result from debt dilution strategies, unprotected debtors may subsidize debt financed new investments. Moreover, the access to extra debt at a lower cost (subsidized by old claimants who failed to internalize debt dilution hazards in the prices they charged for their financing) may imply that the company undertakes projects that, under other circumstances, it would have efficiently declined to fund (Kraakman *et al.* 2005: 117).

Kalay (1982) offered empirical evidence on how companies use dividend and other cash distributions restrictions to force firms to retain funds in prevention of debt dilution incentives. Broadly speaking, however, and besides recurring to short-term debt, debt dilution strategies may be prevented by either restricting companies from acquiring further debt or by allowing creditors seniority privileges that might protect them from the exposure of collateral dilution. Seniority privileges may be implemented via sophisticated financial instruments. However, these solutions are costly, and the analysis made in relation to costs stemming from the contractual solutions available against overinvestment and underinvestment problems applies here as well.

Structural features of PFCs avoid debt dilution possibilities, as well as inter-creditor conflicts, and also their consequential investment distortions. In PFCs, debt dilution strategies are not feasible because they are designed and implemented for the funding of a single limited-life transaction. Inter-creditor conflicts are also not conceivable in PFCs having a single financing party monopolizing the provision of debt to the SPV that is also arranged before funding needs become a reality.

11.4.5   *Project finance contracts avoid asset diluting strategies*

Another manifestation of the conflicts between shareholders and creditors that are exacerbated in corporate transactions by the informational asymmetries of very large and materially complex projects are the asset dilution strategies.

By asset dilution strategies, corporate finance and legal literature describe a group of opportunistic actions under which controlling shareholders may extract wealth directly from the company, thus reducing the collateral value of the organization to the detriment of creditors (Smith and Warner 1979; Kraakman *et al.* 2005: 116; De Jong and Van Dijk 2007). Asset dilution strategies may be implemented directly by shareholders acting as de facto managers or performed by *de jure* managers acting on the behalf of owners; asset dilution strategies may transfer wealth to shareholders as a class, for instance, by allowing illegal (informal) dividends, or instead by granting benefits to only some of the shareholders usually in control of the company. A distinctive feature of asset dilution strategies is that they are often implemented in contravention of legal norms in protection of the integrity of collaterals.

Asset dilution may take many forms. Shareholders may siphon benefits from the company by commingling personal and company assets. They may also extract benefits from the legal entity by not reporting self-dealing transactions below market conditions. Furthermore, by manipulating accounting information, shareholders may acquire goods and services from the company at undervalued prices. They may also disguise losses and proceed to the distribution of dividends "as usual" and in violation of charters or of applicable insolvency regulations. Asset dilution encompasses all illegitimate ways under which wealth may be transferred from the company to shareholders.

Besides, in exceptionally large projects, asymmetries of information before completion, and the abundance of cash flow during the operation, lead to a moral hazard problem which is analogous to that originally described by Jensen (1986) in relation to managerial indiscipline: internal sources allow controlling shareholders to camouflage asset diluting strategies of a project's assets as well as within other business units via cross-subsiding, so that expropriations may pass undetected by monitoring and accounting systems.

As a direct expropriation of a corporation's assets, asset dilution strategies affect the interests of creditors only indirectly by increasing both the likelihood and the expected losses from default. Before affecting creditors, however, the spoliation of corporate organizational value also harms minority equity holders in their expected profits. Asset dilution strategies are nevertheless associated or studied as an agency problem between ownership and creditors; this is because, first, as owners expecting variable dividends from the business, minority shareholders have access to legal disciplining mechanisms that can be triggered pre-emptively during the life of businesses (i.e. not only in the vicinity of insolvency or after default has been verified, as is the case of creditors).[30] Second, shareholders of publicly traded companies also have the option to sell their shares defensively (Kraakman *et al.* 2005: 40). Creditors, in contrast, bargain with their eyes focused on the collateral value of corporate assets that are now under opportunistic threats.

By allowing the completion of a single transaction by a separate organization, structural features of PFCs help mitigate asset dilution incentives in both informational and material dimensions. On the informational dimension, the allocation of assets under the property of a SPV allows for the design of accounting and monitoring systems that are bespoke and dedicated exclusively to project assets. A dedicated informational system allows creditors to identify key issues and to request information regarding managerial control which can be produced free of the influences from exogenous factors affecting other business units. On the material dimension, the allocation of project assets under the remote command of a SPV, which itself is in many ways operated in a cooperative effort of sponsors, obstructs the material access of controlling shareholders to project assets with exclusivity or beyond the sight of other sponsors.

11.5   Project finance contracts avoid the costs of conflicts between companies and individually related parties

So far, I have described the agency conflicts and the strategies implemented by shareholders against creditors as a class. In corporate financed structures, certain aspects of exceptionally large projects also exacerbate conflicts between companies and individual contracting parties. In this section, the conflicts between companies and input providers as well as between companies and individual creditors will be considered. Project finance contractual structures reduce the return value of opportunistic actions from both input providers and from important debt financing suppliers.

11.5.1   *Very large projects and opportunistic incentives from input providers*

In corporate finance settings, the material characteristics of large and long-term development projects have important effects over the feasibility of opportunistic strategies from input providers. Material complexities affect the costs of information and often imply high degrees of specificities around projects that leave companies vulnerable to expropriations.

In contracts in general, *ex ante*, the lack of accurate information on future contingencies affects the capacity of parties acting under bounded rationality constraints to write comprehensive contracts that *ex post* exacerbates the holdup problem (Williamson 1985; Tirole 1986). *Ex post*, material complexity also affects the observability of efforts and outcomes allowing for moral hazard problems (Alchian and Demsetz 1972; Holmstrom 1979; Shavell 1979).

One distinctive feature of corporate transactions is that they complete projects that are built and operated with their cash flows commingled with those of other business units under the same corporate umbrella. This particular characteristic of corporate financing not only allows for coinsurance benefits and risk contamination hazards (Leland 2007; MacKay 2003) but also has substantial implications for the ways in which companies interact with their individual contracting parties. These implications relate to the sharing of risks to the monitoring incentives and to readjustment costs.

In relation to the internal risk sharing features and the opportunistic incentives in corporate finance transactions: first, coinsurance benefits might exacerbate opportunistic incentives by expanding the amounts of welfare that might be extracted from particular projects without significantly affecting corporate default risks and consequential return values of their own claims; second, the commingling of risks and cash flows under the property of the same debtor implies that the assets of a particular project may serve to cross-subsidize opportunistic strategies from contractors related to other business units of the same company.

These cross-subsiding hazards also bring consequences over the monitoring and contractual precautions strategies: as much as contracting parties anticipate risk contamination possibilities, they may also be incentivized to reorient their efforts from the material monitoring of individual projects to the seeking of contractual safeties from the investing companies owning individual projects. This redirection of efforts from the now less relevant material monitoring of projects towards the bargaining for contractual safeties, brings about two consequences: first, the investing company, as a whole, may perceive the costly impact of the restrictive protective covenants implemented by the individual creditors; second, the decrease in material monitoring of particular projects may leave those business units more vulnerable to the hidden actions from other key input providers.

11.5.2 *Very large projects and opportunistic strategies from concentrated debt holders*

The concentration of debt provision contracts in the hands of a few sources has several benefits that have been studied in academic literature. These benefits are mostly derived from the costs and quality of the externalized information. First, before lending, the concentration of debt in fewer hands implies higher risks and higher incentives for banks to both better scrutinize projects and companies, and also, to better monitor borrower's businesses as they progress (Chemmanur and Fulghieri 1994). Second, the availability of information, and in general the lower transaction costs, allows for low-cost readjustments that positively affect the ways in which banks and borrowers interact (i.e. relational banking). Fewer creditors can more easily readjust conditions in case of need, and also they can more easily renegotiate after an insolvency procedure has been opened (Manove *et al.* 2001; Bolton and Scharfstein 1996; Couwenberg and De Jong 2006).

The concentration of long-term debt does, however, have its costs to both borrowers and lenders. In order to avoid high-risk exposures, providers of long-term debt financing regularly request the implementation of several types of contractual precautions; these precautions often allow for privileges that may be enforced by lenders under their own discretion. This discretion may allow for opportunistic strategies from banks.

Abusive strategies may take two basic forms depending on whether or not they include a renegotiation stage: first, without renegotiating, lenders may exercise their privileges for their own benefit (i.e. beyond its original purposes and regardless of the borrower's interest); and second, lenders may use the discretionary enforcement of provisions to build bargaining power to extract concessions in holdup situations. Examples of the first strategy include the possibilities that a lender "strategically release industry-specific information to better its own interests at the expense of the firm" (Agarwal and Elston 2001: 227). In application of debt covenants, banks may be also allowed to participate actively in board meetings or in the governance systems of borrowers; by utilising these types of privileges, banks may extract benefits by persuading debtors to seek more costly and less risky financing from equity sources against their interests (Kroszner and Strahan 2001: 420). In relation to the second strategy, possible threats may include acceleration of loan terms, increases in loan interest, possible transfers of certain control rights, the enforcement of penalties, etc. Indirect costs stemming from these actions often relate to the consequential distress costs generated by lack of access to fresh funds, the costs of considering alternative sources of internal or external financing under time constraints, or the loss of bargaining power in the relations with other parties (Sarig 1998). Consistent with this, Rajan (1992) and Gorton and Kahn (2000) observed how loan rates and hierarchies of claims are calibrated also with the purpose of minimizing the bargaining powers of banks in future renegotiations. Each of these two groups of opportunistic strategies will be considered next.

11.5.3   *Project finance contracts discourage opportunism from input and debt financing providers*

A natural feature of PFCs is that all key providers (including lenders) subordinate substantial parts of their expectations to the completion of a common project by a legal entity that holds no other valuable assets under its property. As mentioned in the introduction, authors refer to this as the "community of interest" in project finance (Howcroft and Fadhley 1998). This commonality of interests around a single project bears positive consequences against the opportunistic strategies of both input providers and financers. In connection with these strategies, two aspects are to be considered: the first relates to the quality of the information that is available to parties during the bargaining as well as during operation phases; the second refers to the return value of expropriating actions implemented against a single project the success of which depends predominantly on the inputs from those potentially opportunistic parties.

In relation to the first aspect, PFCs provide higher incentives for parties to reveal information during the bargaining process. In PFCs, the allocation of a single project under a co-owned SPV provides incentives for parties to reveal information so as to reduce the likelihood of facing costly renegotiations in the future. In addition, as a consequence of the high risks it internalizes, the financing party will also request information for the assessment of a risk allocation system under which all foreseeable scenarios are considered. Furthermore, in PFCs the financing party has incentives to request and to reveal information not only about the solvency of its debtor – the SPV – but also about all input providers influencing the outcome of the project to be completed by the borrower.

The commonality of interests in PFCs also offers higher incentives for sponsors to reveal information during construction and operation stages. During operation, all sponsors are incentivized to pre-emptively request information so as to lower the costs of renegotiations on issues that had not been expressly regulated during the bargaining process. The community of interests in PFCs also provides incentives for sponsors to coordinate monitoring efforts so as to improve the enforcement of contractual provisions by turning observable information into verifiable information.

Moreover, close operative cooperation among contracting partners allows for informational benefits associated to the observable but unverifiable actions. Unverifiable information permits informal retaliations expanding self-enforcing margins as stated by Klein (1996). Informal retaliation, self-enforcement and low renegotiation costs allow for longer-term relational and more efficient interactions as described by Zheng *et al.* (2008).[31]

Besides, a single financing party also avoids the costs associated to collective action problems, including the duplication of efforts when implementing monitoring, renegotiating and enforcement actions (Carletti *et al.* 2007).[32] Information externalized by lenders provides certification benefits favouring minor investors *ex ante* and *ex post* contracting (Gatti *et al.* 2013).

The commonality of interests discourages both holdup threats as well as strategies based on hidden actions. In PFCs, the absence of a pool of independent business units ready to cross collateralize the project's risks implies that smaller expropriations may lead to larger increases in default risks, ultimately reducing the return value of opportunism. Return value concerns are also lower in the case of expropriations based on hidden actions in which parties calibrate their unobservable or unverifiable efforts focusing on their impact over distributable welfare (which itself depends on the partial output elasticity of efforts in the particular production function).

Particular opportunistic strategies of the financing party are also discouraged by the structural features of PFCs. In PFCs, the completion of a single project implies that all protective covenants are to be implemented around the peculiarities of the risks of that individual project. Therefore, unlike in corporate finance settings, in PFCs it is not possible that the financing party implements expropriating strategies based on the abusive enforcement of instruments, which may have been designed to prevent risks associated with other projects or based on the indirect costs generated and affecting different business units.

11.6 Project finance contracts mitigate conflicts between ownership and control

This section describes how PFCs mitigate the agency conflicts between ownership and control. In corporate finance contexts, informational asymmetries exacerbate the free cash flow problem of managerial indiscipline, whereas risk contamination threats intensify managerial risk aversion issues. Structural features of PFCs mitigate these conflicts by isolating cash flows in a dedicated company, by providing sponsors with efficient incentives to deliver monitoring efforts, and finally by resolving all key matters before the financing of the project begins, and thus eliminating any need for managers to take the relevant decisions.

11.6.1 Very large projects, managerial incentives and strategies under corporate financed structures

One disadvantage of funding large projects internally is that the administration of significant amounts of liquid assets may exacerbate the well-known free cash flow agency problem in management (Jensen 1986). Cash flows in excess of current needs may be used by managers to overinvest (instead of distributing dividends) and to grow beyond optimal size in a strategy known as "empire building."[33] Increasing company size allows managers to control larger sources of cash flow that can be used for their individual benefits. These benefits may include the consumption of perquisites and the possibilities of escaping the pressure from shareholders in relation to pay-out policies, salaries and other discipline sensitive matters.

Furthermore, managers may use unmonitored cash to mask poor results from managerial laxity away from market scrutiny. Among others, three aspects may be considered in relation to empire building managerial strategies when exceptionally large projects are completed under corporate finance structures: (i) the availability of free cash flow before and after completion, (ii) the possibilities for internal cross-subsidizing of cash flows, and (iii) the cost and effectiveness of monitoring and control over unique projects due to the presence of asymmetries and to the absence of market control.

Free cash flow and empire building problems may be exacerbated in the financing of very large projects due to the availability of free cash flow both before and after completion. During construction, long-term development processes are associated with uncertainties that induce prudent managers to take cash precautions in prevention of general eventualities (Damodaran 1997: 363). These cash provisions against contingencies can be more or less discretely administered by managers and used for camouflaging managerial laxities rather than to prevent eventualities. Also during construction, due to the material complexity of long-term projects, managers may also hide information and appropriate the benefits from new cost-saving technological improvements (Farrell 2003). After completion, during operation, capital-intensive projects may generate large amounts of liquid resources, which result in an exacerbation of the free cash-flow problem on its common form (Jensen 1986).

In corporate finance investments, the cash flows generated by very large projects may also be used for subsidizing managerial indiscipline in other business units. A distinctive feature of corporate structures is that the resolution of material incidents as well as the generation of progress information are natural competences of managers who operate under the supervision of individuals of the same organization, i.e. without the monitoring and control rigor from sponsors who are both input providers and risk-takers in the project.

Another distinctive feature of large projects that affects agency ownership and control is that these projects are often unique of their kind. From the singularity of these projects, some certain aspects are to be considered: first, these large projects are often protected by regulation on public services or they are designed to serve a single purpose that insures them certain monopoly power in a market of their own. Besides regulation and natural monopolies, exceptionally large and materially complex projects require large investments and technological efforts before completion that function as entry barriers against competitors. In addition, relative managerial performance evaluation methods may become difficult to implement without market references (Antle and Smith 1986). Inderst and Müller (2003) modeled how the capacities of managers to avoid market control by cross-subsidizing among different business units ultimately results in lower productivity for companies. All these features deprive managers from market disciplining pressure.

Besides the free cash-flow problem and empire building incentives, another source of discrepancies between ownership and control stems from managerial risk aversion. Under integrated financing structures, exceptionally large and risky projects may contaminate cash volatilities of companies, ultimately increasing their likelihood of default (Lewellen 1971; Leland 2007). Higher likelihood of default may deter poorly diversified managers from adopting the risky strategies that maximize value to shareholders. Aside of volatility, other features of large projects may affect the risk adverseness of managers. For instance, capital needs of large projects may consume internal financing resources ultimately affecting the smoothness of dividend distributions in the very short term (Easterbrook 1984).

In corporate investments, risk aversion may be hard to curve via compensation schemes. There is a rich body of literature dealing with managerial compensation schemes and how these can be designed to induce administrators to adopt optimal strategies (Grossman and Hart 1982; Jensen and Murphy 1999). Recent studies show that managerial risk aversion may be harder to prevent than was previously estimated in classic models. Parrino *et al.* (2005) evaluated the magnitude of investment distortions from risk aversion when companies take exceptionally large projects that affect expected bankruptcy losses. More recently, Milidonis and Stathopoulos (2012) have empirically observed a prevalence of risk averse behavior in dominance of compensation-based incentives.

11.6.2 Structural advantages of project finance contracts versus managerial indiscipline

PFCs mitigate the free cash-flow problem. The allocation of isolated projects in SPVs limits the sources of cash flow that may be used by administrators to disguise managerial laxity. First, in PFCs managerial indiscipline cannot be camouflaged with financial resources generated by other business units of the same company. Second, during completion, cash savings related to technological improvements as well as the cash provisions utilized for the prevention of unforeseen expenditures may be properly separated from regular cash flows, or even better, they may be kept beyond the reach of managers and in the hands of financing providers or of sponsors instead (Vinter *et al.* 2013: 225). Furthermore, in PFCs cash waterfall schemes may be used to synchronize cash flows with financing needs with little margin of error.

PFCs improve the availability of managerial information. By allocating projects assets in a separate legal entity, PFCs allow information on managerial discipline to be processed by a dedicated accounting system. The implementation of a bespoke information system allows for the inspection of cash flows and for the capturing of specific data reflecting the peculiarities of risks, needs and unexpected costs and benefits of a single project (Shah and Thakor 1987; Subramanian *et al.* 2008; Esty 2003). Besides, as a result from the commonality of risks that all parties take, in PFCs sponsors perceive a higher value from their monitoring and disciplining efforts. Unlike in corporate settings, in PFCs sponsors are equity investors but also specific input providers who cooperate directly in the material completion of the project. Sponsors are also insiders to the industrial sector of the project. As a result of this dual capacity, sponsors are qualified observers capable of detecting differences between formal information and the real status of a project (before technological cost savings as well as cost overruns are reflected by the accountancy). Moreover, due to their close operative and managerial interaction, sponsors may also incur lower costs for coordinating their monitoring actions, as described by Carletti *et al.* (2007) in corporate settings.

Project finance contracts also mitigate conflicts between managers and their principals by limiting and refining the scopes of empowerment of agents. In PFCs, the isolation of a single predesigned project under a single company liberates managers from the needs to take transcendental decisions. As mentioned in Section 11.2, in PFCs the three basic categories of decisions classically considered in literature (the investment problem, the financing problem and the dividend distribution problem) are either taken in advance or by the direct interventions of other stakeholders during the life of the project. In fact, due to the full outsourcing policies, in PFCs most of the cost-related contingencies fall under the managerial spheres of sponsors rather than under the competence of the SPV.

Essentially, in PFCs managers of the SPV are not expected to assume decisions beyond implementation of the project or beyond executive instructions from sponsors under the supervision of the financing party. Furthermore, because managers of projects are not expected to take any important decisions or identify alternative growth options, high-powered incentives are less frequently seen in project finance compensation schemes (Esty 2003).

11.7 Project finance contracts mitigate adverse selection problems with outside investors

The low number of well-informed investors prevents adverse selection problems in PFCs. This section considers: first, the essentials of the adverse selection problem between the company and outside investors in the financing of very large projects in corporate finance transactions; and second, how these problems are less acute in PFCs.

11.7.1 The nature of conflicts between controlling shareholders and dispersed financing providers

In corporate finance operations, informational asymmetries with external investors lead to the well-known adverse selection problems between external equity investors and the company (Myers and Majluf 1984; Myers 1984), and to a much lesser extent (in virtue of collaterals) between the company and debt providers. In this later case, the adverse selection problem is also referred to as the credit-rationing problem (Stiglitz and Weiss 1981).[34]

In debt, the adverse selection problem may be solved with collaterals from third parties, security interests, covenants and other credit protective mechanisms that may be used also as signaling devices (Chan and Thakor 1987; Manove *et al.* 2001: 739). In corporate finance transactions, the provision of collaterals and other sureties sufficient to cover the risks of very large projects may, however, impose costly financing and investing restrictions and consume much of the limited and valuable debt capacities of companies.

In equity, in the absence of collaterals, the adverse selection problem as a market failure may also be costly to solve. In order to shape their expectations, without trustable protections, dispersed equity investors can only rely on the signals that companies send to the market (Spier 1992; Spence 2002).[35] In corporate finance transactions, it is difficult for companies to recur to the open market, and issue collateralized debt (and signal to equity investors) without exhausting debt capacity; it is also costly to companies to seek equity financing without sending the message to the market that the shares are overpriced. Similarly, with limited sources of cash flows, it is not easy for companies to build internal sources in order to fund expensive projects without jeopardizing dividend distributions, ultimately affecting share value.

11.7.2 How project finance contracts avoid the costs of outside financing

PFCs reduce adverse selection problems both with equity and with debt financing providers. Adverse selection problems with creditors (i.e. with the single financing party) are mitigated by improving the quality of available information that allows for the enforcement of protective provisions. Risk aversion problems with equity sources are also alleviated in PFCs through raising funds almost exclusively from well-informed sponsors.

PFCs improve the access of creditors to information in many ways and through mechanisms that may not be implementable with dispersed debt holders in corporate finance transactions.[36] In PFCs, the relatively low number of key players allows for the coordination of managerial and monitoring efforts that can be directed by the financing party (Carletti 2004; Carletti *et al.* 2007). Moreover, in PFCs, the financing party holds a monopoly in the provision of debt for a single project; via a conditions precedent, the financing party also has a chance to describe the verifiable information that needs to be provided before the activation of the loan agreement and also during the life of projects.

Furthermore, PFCs allow for the design of specific and simplified governance systems around which the financing party may work with sponsors exerting disciplining influence when important decisions are taken. By relying on usual project finance covenants, the financing party may sustain long-term relational interactions with sponsors as stated by Webb (1991) and Klein (1996) without possible risk contamination hazards from other projects. Fundamentally, PFCs mitigate adverse selection problems in debt by allowing creditors to enforce pre-emptive provisions against the project and often also against key input providers in relation to their individual obligations.

On the other hand, adverse selection problems of equity sources are highly mitigated in PFCs due to the fact that equity holders are themselves the key input providers of the project where much of its endogenous risks are functions of their efforts. In their dual capacity, sponsors are not only better informed about the types of projects in which they invest, but they also can actively intervene on its management and control towards completion. Besides, it is regularly the case that, in PFCs, passive equity investors are large institutional investors capable of processing information obtained from lenders during the design stage of the project.

11.8 Concluding remarks

Unlike the case of corporate enterprises where reinvestment options are multiple and businesses are organized with a vocation of perpetuity, PFCs on the contrary, are employed for the completion of single and limited-life projects under the property of a special purpose legal entity.

This isolation of a limited-life project under a dedicated company permits that such a project might be assessed on its own merits, individual costs, risks and likely contingencies. Better information and separate incorporation also allows that all key aspects of projects are prevented by enforceable mechanisms that may be implemented by sponsors and by lenders as the ultimate risk-takers. The enforceability of these contractual arrangements dealing with all costs and foreseeable risks ultimately makes the allocation of projects under a SPV and its bankability under non-recourse schemes a practicable option. Consistent with this, three structural features of finance contracts are distinctive: first, the allocation of a project under a bankruptcy remote legal entity; second, the full distribution of costs and risks as well as the prevention of all contingencies via enforceable mechanisms; and third, the non-recourse nature of its financing.

This chapter has shown how these characteristics of PFCs allow for several benefits that are of great significance in the presence of exceptionally large projects and that may not be easily achieved under corporate finance settings. These benefits relate to the possibilities of allocating and isolating risks more efficiently; avoiding or discouraging opportunistic strategies and conflicts among stakeholders; and allowing information of better quality to be externalized in mitigation of adverse selection problems. First, remote allocation of the financing debt prevents risks from affecting stakeholders, thus avoiding distress costs and preserving debt capacities at the sponsors' level. Second, the completion of a project under a SPV avoids the debt overhang problem and it also impedes the implementation of both asset substitution as well as the asset dilution opportunistic strategies against creditors. Third, the financing of a single project and the identification of all debt sources also impedes debt dilution hazards. Fourth, the common allocation of the property rights and the subordination of individual's expectations to the completion of a project reduce the return value of expropriations, thus discouraging opportunistic strategies from input contractors as well as from debt providers. In addition, this commonality of interests provides strong incentives for sponsors to coordinate cross-monitoring efforts for collective discipline. Moreover, in PFCs, managerial-related conflicts (from free cash flow and managerial risk aversion) are highly alleviated by the fact that in PFCs all transcendental decisions are taken with the consent of creditors before the SPV is set up. Finally, PFCs allow the financing party to access information and to enforce risk pre-emptive mechanisms that, next to the fact that equity is fully provided by the sponsors, who are input providers to the project, mitigate adverse selection problems in a manner that is costly to replicate under classical corporate structures.

This chapter has focused on the basic benefits and the strategic advantages that are allowed by PFCs in relation to the different types of costs and conflicts that exceptionally large projects entail when financed under corporate settings. It remained beyond the scope of this analysis to examine all aspects relating to the agency conflicts among stakeholders within project finance organizations. The study of conflicts and opportunistic strategies within PFCs is a matter treated only by a few authors in academic literature. From the legal point of view, and as a way forward for later research, the consideration of these aspects is of great relevance for a better understanding of the environment in which parties design their contractual clauses. A more accurate comprehension of the internal dynamics of PFCs should also allow for an improvement on the ways in which existing default rules – or perhaps new specific statutory norms – are to be designed, and applied in this particular context.

Notes

1 The author wishes to thank Mariana Borsalino Migliore, Bobby Ray Fowler, Horacio A. Nicola and Désirée Wildt for their fundamental support. All errors are mine.
2 In 2007 PFC investments reached the yet unsurpassed peak of US$220 billion, before dropping to US$138 billion with the last financial crisis to return to almost pre-crisis levels of US$214 billion in 2011 worldwide (Gatti 2013: XV).
3 In the public sector, very frequently, project finance operations are designed under public-private partnership types of arrangements which have been informally standardized after the pioneering US Private Utility Regulatory Policies Act of 1978. These arrangements of variable formats are often derivatives of the early build-operate-transfer (BOT) or engineering-procurement-construction (EPC) formats. A second impulse for the use of project finance for public procurement came from the private finance initiatives (PFIs) of the Australian and British governments in the late 1980s and in 1992 in the case of Britain (Fabozzi and De Nahlik 2012: 485; Delmon and Delmon 2013).
4 According to Esty (2003), PFCs regularly include some 15 parties and up to 40 legally independent contracts defining their risk allocation structures. Larger contracts frequently involve up to several hundreds (exceptionally thousands) of ancillary covenants, which in most cases are formally independent instruments.
5 Some of the most remarkable ones include the articles by Esty (2003), Hart (2003), Dewatripont and Legros (2005), Martimort and Pouyet (2008), Bennett and Iossa (2006), and Corielli *et al.* (2010).
6 There is a small series of articles describing agency conflicts within PFCs. The main focus of their attention lies on the ways in which sponsors shirk efforts or implement opportunistic strategies, producing negative externalities to other input providers. From these arguments, normative considerations have been elaborated on the convenience of opting for integrated or for separated structures for the provision of public procurement goods. Hart (2003) initiated this trend of studies. He described the moral hazards among constructors and operators of privatized jails. See also Dewatripont and Legros (2005) and Blanc-Brude *et al.* (2006).
7 Projects can be of any industrial nature as long as they are capable of generating a minimum cash flow that should suffice to, in this order, serve the financing debt, cover completion costs and, if possible, also allow residual profits. PFCs may be structured to provide services to the general public or to off-takers contracted *ex ante*. In the cases of projects offering goods to the open market, solid marketing studies need to be included in the design stage for its bankability and before any risk is incurred. Consider an amusement park such as the Euro Disneyland or the Euro Tunnel projects (Finnerty 2007: 338 and 368).

8 Generally speaking, sponsors may be classified as industrial sponsors, public sponsors and financial sponsors. Industrial sponsors are the key input providers to the project and they influence the outcome of the project with their individual efforts. Public sponsors may be State agencies that provide some support to a project advancing public welfare interests. Financial sponsors are institutional investors, who free ride on the organizational efforts of other parties. They are usually specialized on the particular industrial sector of the project and take large risks, they expect high benefits and do not intervene in the evolution of the project. Unlike the financing party, sponsors may hold fixed or variable claims (i.e. from subordinated debt financing or from their equity contributions) that are always of the most junior hierarchies (Gatti 2013: 4). Throughout this chapter only the roles of industrial sponsors will be considered.

9 The life of PFCs may be divided into three phases or stages: the development or design phase, the construction and the production stages. The development stage is the phase in which the project is designed, key input providers to the project are identified, risks are fully allocated via enforceable mechanisms, foreseeable contingencies are put in place, and lending syndicates are formed. In this phase, financial and legal advisors, and often also State representatives, assist sponsors and lenders in the structuring of the project. The development phase concludes with the signature of the loan agreement (the "Financial Close" or the "Effective Date"). During the construction stage, cash is gradually injected into the SPV to be transformed into specific assets and sponsors as well as other input providers progressively deliver their material contributions towards project completion. In this period, exceptional warranties and collateral will be provided by the sponsors in relation to particular risks under their individual controls. This phase ends with the commencement of operations often referred as the "Commercial Operation Date." In the last phase of the project, the operation period, the project generates the proceeds to serve the financing debt and to reward inputs from sponsors whose compensations may have been delayed or subordinated; remaining wealth is distributed in the form of dividends. Once the project is functioning and generating revenues, project assets begin to have actual rather than future value, as much of the risks inherent to the construction and to its initial operations will now be dissipated (the levels and types of risk change from design and construction to market for the products and operating costs which at that point should have been hedged by different mechanisms). With assets having their own value, it is very common that projects are refinanced and some of the original investors (within the financing party or among passive sponsors) are substituted by investors with a lower appetite for risk. In the case of public works, it is a common practice that public agencies issue completion certificates that sponsors may sell at a discount value. For a good reference to the activities of project finance investment funds, securitizations and project finance CDOs see Gatti (2013: 212). In this period, once their presence is no longer determinant to the success of the project, sponsors may be allowed to discount their expected benefits including their equity shares and also their contractual claims which may have been delayed (Fabozzi and De Nahlik 2012: 15).

10 For instances, after the SPV failed to deliver its expected outputs, lenders may decide to remove some of the sponsors from their contractual roles as operators or managers of the project.

11 For a consideration of legal and strategic aspects of asset partitioning in corporate law see Hansmann *et al.* (2006).

12 For a good description of these arrangements see Finnerty (2007: 115).

13 Under the common strategy of preventing all foreseeable contingencies, in PFCs stakeholders also agree on the use of a series of hedging mechanisms that may be implemented to deal with financial risks affecting the project. Some may include

interest-rate, currency and credit default swaps coupled with more traditional forwards, futures and options, targeting certain risks selectively. The implementation of these hedging structures as well as of other credit enhancement mechanisms regularly includes the intervention of State support agencies besides the traditional insurance providers.

14 For an example of how managerial literature provides instruments for risks forecasting in the form of checklists see Fabozzi and De Nahlik (2012: 3).

15 Early studies on the costs of debt and capital structures following shortly after Modigliani and Miller (1958) only considered distress costs as including the expected losses from default. Only much later the concept of distress costs began to be studied on subcategories and dimensions. Ang *et al.* (1982) first analyzed empirical evidence of the administrative costs of bankruptcy procedures, Altman (1984) used a proxy methodology to assess the indirect costs of bankruptcy.

16 See for instance, Branch (2002) referring to economic and financial distress costs as bankruptcy-related costs elaborates the following classification: "(1) Real costs borne by the distressed firm; (2) Real costs borne directly by the claimants; (3) Losses to the distressed firm that are offset by gains to other entities; (4) Real costs borne by parties other than the distressed firm or its claimants."

17 When assessing the present value of financial distress costs, some authors also consider the values of betas of companies and market sectors as a measure of volatility. I am leaving aside this important consideration as I am focusing on the relationship between the project and the company that finances it. For a deeper discussion on betas as measures of volatilities see: Damodaran (1997: 107 and 293–95).

18 Both Static Trade-Off (Bradley *et al.* 1984) and Dynamic Trade-Off theories (Fischer *et al.* 1989) identify capital structure targets by comparing incremental bankruptcy derived costs with more linear tax benefits. The Pecking Order family of theories also considers financial distress costs as a fundamental element for selecting the sources of funding. Adverse selection-based models of capital structure (Myers and Majluf 1984; Myers 1984) choose external sources of funding by comparing the impact of financial distress with those from asymmetries of information. Agency cost-based models also elaborate their pecking order by marginally equating the cost of distress with the marginal benefits of debt in terms of managerial discipline. See Jensen and Meckling (1976); Townsend (1979). For a literature review including a brief introduction to modern capital structure doctrines see Frank and Goyal (2007).

19 The blurriness of the distinctions among the types and components of each of the categories of distress costs has resulted in some discrepancies on the empirical observations, which in any case always show some significant magnitudes: direct distress costs – such as litigation and judicial costs – have been found to be less significant than indirect ones. Weiss (1990) finds direct distress costs about 3 per cent to 5 per cent of the value of firms. Indirect costs, including loss of market share, and sales of assets under constraints (Shleifer and Vishny 1992), are known to be significant but also difficult to measure quantitatively (Hertzel *et al.* 2008). During the 1980s some studies found distress costs to be more substantial: in an extreme case, Altman (1984: 1077) measured indirect costs on some industrial sectors to be of 23.7 per cent of the firm's value. For a literature review on distress costs, see Cornaggia (2011).

20 Rational investors will choose among alternative sources of funding (internal or external equity debt) or by equating their marginal agency costs (Jensen 1986).

21 Esty (2003: 24) was one of the first authors to consider volatility as being one of the economic motivations for using project finance; Esty however did not consider the volatility caused by debt in capital structure but only the volatility resulting

from risk contamination from the presence of large risky projects under the corporate umbrella.

22 The volatility from debt in capital structure and its costs was one of the components of Modigliani and Miller's (1958; 1963) highly stylized fundamental models. In their seminal papers, these authors showed that in the absence of any frictions and other costs and incentives like tax benefit, the value of projects would not change with capital structure, even though debt, by itself, would mean higher default risk and higher interests.

23 Consistent to this, liquidity has been shown to be a determinant value for some types of mergers and acquisitions known as "liquidity mergers" (Almeida *et al.* 2011).

24 Risk-shifting incentives do not necessarily grow monotonically with leverage (Mao 2003).

25 See: Diamond and He (2012); Gertner and Scharfstein (1991).

26 An empirical survey on how covenants may reduce agency costs of debt in high-growth firms may be found in Billett *et al.* (2007).

27 Debt hierarchies systems in general are well described by Barclay and Smith Jr. (1995).

28 That is, an increase (decrease) of 1 per cent in the value of the company would imply an increase (decrease) of more than 1 per cent in the face value of the instrument.

29 Before Mao (2003) and (Diamond and He 2012), empirical studies from Titman and Wessels (1988) and Bradley *et al.* (1984) had found contradictory evidence on the relationship between the degree of leverage and underinvestment. More recently, Minton and Schrand (1999) made empirical observations on the impact of volatility, the cost of external capital and consequential debt overhang induced underinvestment.

30 Since creditors and minority shareholders have different types of claims, legal mechanisms protecting each of the two classes differ in nature and in the procedural requirements attached to them. Creditors will usually have an action based on contract law as soon as breaching is observed, but will be capable of triggering legal remedies against asset dilution usually only after an insolvency procedure has been opened (or at least, after insolvency becomes imminent). Minority shareholders, in contrast, will protect company value from asset dilution strategies as soon as their dividend expectations are seen to be illegitimately affected, i.e. in the same moment in which expropriations take place. Some examples of the many legal institutions protecting creditors are the 'Actio Pauliana' and their common law equivalent preventions against fraudulent trading or the regulatory requirements on legal minimum capital and their related rules on dividend distributions (Armour 2000; 2006). Legal systems also protect both creditors and minority shareholders by regulating the type and quality of the information that is to be externalized by companies. Examples of information-based protections are the regulation of accounting standards (Kraakman *et al.* 2005: 285) and the occasional necessary presence of gatekeepers and independent directors as qualified and neutral observers (Boot *et al.* 2006). Legal protections assisting creditors frequently relate to insolvency statutes, whereas minority equity-holders' protections are often based in the company norms dealing with delegated management systems. As it is the case with all legal remedies, the enforcement of these protective strategies greatly depends on the availability of verifiable information, which in exceptionally large companies may be scarce – particularly when hosting exceptionally large and materially sophisticated projects, and when controlling shareholders and managers acting on their behalves are the ones in charge of producing such information.

31 For a revision of early relational contracting models including literature review, see Hviid (2000).

32 On the problem of free riding in monitoring and multiple-bank lending, see in general Carletti *et al.* (2007).

33 For an empirical verification of over investment policies, including a literature review, see Richardson (2006). For a study of the distortions from perquisite consumption incentives over leverage ratios see Morellec (2004).

34 The adverse selection problem arises when, due to asymmetries of information, parties fail to know accurately or to rely on the types of their counter parties (Akerlof 1970). As a result, parties acting rationally will initially calibrate their strategies as if their counterparties were of the average type. As much as other contractors can anticipate this strategy, the parties of the best type who fail to signal quality will reject conditions and leave the market. The fact that good contractors are out of the market is anticipated by initial proponents who now adapt their original average offer to a new lower level. This again excludes another upper half of the market ultimately leading to a race to the bottom and to a collapse of the market. The magnitude of this market failure is determined by the capacity of both parties to screen or to signal their types reciprocally; the provision of collateral being the most common signaling mechanism (Spence 2002; Spier 1992).

35 In relation to companies seeking financing from equity sources, screening and signaling strategies may take many forms which may be more or less costly, depending on many factors (Leary and Roberts 2010). Some of most basic forms, however are simple and consist of playing with dividends, equity and debt in the open market. Consider the following examples of signaling with their impacts and their costs: First, shareholders may signal financial prosperity with dividends (Stiglitz 1969). Dividends are a luxury that bad firms cannot afford. Commitment to dividends have the corollary costs of depriving companies from valuable free cash flow (internal sources of funding) for other perhaps more valuable purposes. Fundamentally, in the case of the financing of large projects, once companies have committed to delivering dividends, they will become particularly vulnerable to the volatility of cash flow variations from very large business units. Furthermore, in relation to costly projects, commitment to issuing dividends in the short run may affect internal sources as large projects do not generate cash flows until the phase of operation, which may happen after years of construction. Second, companies may signal by playing with the issuance of equity (Myers and Majluf 1984): dispersed investors perceive that managers and shareholders who are asymmetrically (better) informed will issue equity only if they know that shares are overpriced by the market. Coherently, they may also understand that managers will buy if they are underpriced or with a good prospect of growing in their market value. Consequently, under this market dynamic, shareholders will lose value the more funds they raise from equity issuances. Besides the losses in monetary value, lowering the price of equity by selling shares to fund exceptionally expensive projects may pose a threat from institutional investors and competitors who may take the opportunity to increase their political power – or even to take over the company. Third, besides dividends and equity, shareholders may issue debt so as to signal that the company is financially healthy, far from distress costs and willing to take the risk of allowing senior claimants to control them. Debt capacity is however limited.

36 Shah and Thakor (1987) in an early paper while considering an optimal capital structure in PFCs stressed on the minimization of information costs as one of the main reasons why parties choose to place projects under a separate organization.

References

Agarwal, R. and Elston, J. A. (2001) 'Bank–Firm Relationships, Financing and Firm Performance in Germany', *Economics Letters*, 72(2), 225–32.

Akerlof, G. (1970) 'The Market for "lemons": Quality Uncertainty and the Market Mechanism', *The Quarterly Journal of Economics*, 84(3), 488–500.

Alam, Z. S. (2010) 'An Empirical Analysis of the Determinants of Project Finance: Cash Flow Volatility and Correlation', *Finance Dissertations*, Paper 18, Georgia State University.

Alchian, A. A. and Demsetz, H. (1972) 'Production, Information Costs, and Economic Organization', *The American Economic Review*, 62(5), 777–95.

Almeida, H., Campello, M. and Hackbarth, D. (2011) 'Liquidity Mergers', *Journal of Financial Economics*, 102(3), 526–58.

Altman, E. (1984) 'A Further Empirical Investigation of the Bankruptcy Cost Question', *The Journal of Finance*, 39(4), 1067–89.

Ang, J. S., Chua, J. H. and McConnell, J. J. (1982) 'The Administrative Costs of Corporate Bankruptcy: A Note', *The Journal of Finance*, 37(1), 219–26.

Antle, R. and Smith, A. (1986) 'An Empirical Investigation of the Relative Performance Evaluation of Corporate Executives', *Journal of Accounting Research*, 24(1), 1–39.

Armour, J. (2000) 'Share Capital and Creditor Protection: Efficient Rules for a Modern Company Law', *The Modern Law Review*, 63(3), 355–78.

Armour, J. (2006) 'Legal Capital: an Outdated Concept?', *European Business Organization Law Review (EBOR)*, 7(01), 5.

Barclay, M. J. and Smith Jr., C. W. (1995) 'The Priority Structure of Corporate Liabilities', *The Journal of Finance*, 50(3), 899–916.

Barnea, A., Haugen, R. A. and Senbet, L. W. (1980) 'A Rationale for Debt Maturity Structure and Call Provisions in the Agency Theoretic Framework', *The Journal of Finance*, 35(5), 1223–34.

Barnea, A., Haugen, R. A., and Senbet, L. W. (1981) 'Agency Imperfections, Problems, Capital Structure: A Review', *Financial Management*, 10(3), 7–22.

Bennett, J. and Iossa, E. (2006) 'Building and Managing Facilities for Public Services', *Journal of Public Economics*, 90(10–11), 2143–60.

Berkovitch, E. and Kim, E. E. (1990) 'Financial Contracting and Leverage Induced Over- and Under-Investment Incentives', *The Journal of Finance*, 45(3), 765–94.

Billett, M., King, T. and Mauer, D. (2007) 'Growth Opportunities and the Choice of Leverage, Debt Maturity, and Covenants', *The Journal of Finance*, 62(2), 697–730.

Blanc-Brude, F., Goldsmith, H. and Valila, T. (2006) 'Ex Ante Construction Cost in the European Road Sector: A Comparison of Public–Private Partnerships and Traditional Public Procurement', *Economic and Financial Report 2006/01 –* European Investment Bank.

Bolton, P. and Scharfstein, D. (1996) 'Optimal Debt Structure and the Number of Creditors', *Journal of Political Economy*, 104(1), 1–25.

Boot, A. W. A., Milbourn, T. T. and Schmeits, A. (2006) 'Credit Ratings as Coordination Mechanisms', *Review of Financial Studies*, 19(1), 81–118.

Borgonovo, E. and Gatti, S. (2013) 'Risk Analysis with Contractual Default. Does Covenant Breach Matter?', *European Journal of Operational Research*, 230(2), 431–43.

Bradley, M., Jarrell, G. and Kim, E. (1984) 'On the Existence of an Optimal Capital structure: Theory and evidence', *The Journal of Finance*, 39(3), 857–78.

Branch, B. (2002) 'The Costs of Bankruptcy: A Review', *International Review of Financial Analysis*, 11, 39–57.

Brown, D. T., James, C. M. and Mooradian, R. M. (1994) 'Asset Sales by Financially Distressed Firms', *Journal of Corporate Finance*, 1, 233–57.

Carletti, E. (2004) 'The Structure of Bank Relationships, Endogenous Monitoring, and Loan Rates', *Journal of Financial Intermediation*, 13(1), 58–86.

Carletti, E., Cerasi, V. and Daltung, S. (2007) 'Multiple-Bank Lending: Diversification and Free-Riding in Monitoring', *Journal of Financial Intermediation*, 16(3), 425–51.

Chan, Y-S. and Thakor, A. V. (1987) 'Collateral and Competitive Equilibria with Moral Hazard and Private Information', *The Journal of Finance*, 42(2), 345–63.

Chemmanur, T. J. and Fulghieri, P. (1994) 'Reputation, Renegotiation, and the Choice between Bank Loans and Publicly Traded Debt', *The Review of Economic Studies*, 7(3), 475–506.

Childs, P. D., Mauer, D. C. and Ott, S. H. (2005) 'Interactions of Corporate Financing and Investment Decisions: The Effects of Agency Conflicts', *Journal of Financial Economics*, 76(3), 667–90.

Corielli, F., Gatti, S. and Steffanoni, A. (2010) 'Risk Shifting through Nonfinancial Contracts: Effects on Loan Spreads and Capital Structure of Project Finance Deals', *Journal of Money, Credit and Banking*, 42(7), 1295–320.

Cornaggia, K. J. (2011) 'Financial Distress and Bankruptcy', in Baker, H. K. and Martin, G. S. (eds), *Capital Structure and Corporate Financing Decisions: Theory, Evidence, and Practice*, New York: John Wiley & Sons, Inc., 353.

Couwenberg, O. and De Jong, A. (2006) 'It Takes Two to Tango: An Empirical Tale of Distressed Firms and Assisting Banks', *International Review of Law and Economics*, 26(4), 429–54.

Damodaran, A. (1997) *Corporate Finance Theory and Practice*, New York: John Wiley & Sons, Inc., 876.

De Jong, A. and Van Dijk, R. (2007) 'Determinants of Leverage and Agency Problems: A Regression Approach with Survey Data', *The European Journal of Finance*, 13(6), 565–93.

Delmon, J. (2011) *Public–Private Partnership Projects in Infrastructure: An Essential Guide for Policy Makers*, Cambridge: Cambridge University Press.

Delmon, J. and Delmon, V. R. (2013) *International Project Finance and PPPs – A Legal Guide to Key Growth Markets*, Alphen aan den Rijn: Wolters Kluwer Law and Business.

Dewar, J. (2011) *International Project Finance – Law and Practice*, Oxford: Oxford University Press.

Dewatripont, M. and Legros, P. (2005) 'Public–Private Partnerships: Contract Design and Risk Transfer', *EIB Papers*, 10(1), 120–45.

Diamond, D. W. and He, Z. (2012) 'A Theory of Debt Maturity: The Long and Short of Debt Overhang', *NBER Working Paper Series* No. 18160.

Easterbrook, F. (1984) 'Two Agency-Cost Explanations of Dividends', *The American Economic Review*, 74(4), 650–9.

Eisdorfer, A. (2008) 'Empirical Evidence of Risk Shifting in Financially Distressed Firms', *The Journal of Finance*, 63(2), 609–37.

Esty, B. C. (2003) 'The Economic Motivations for Using Project Finance', *Mimeo – Harvard Business School*.

Esty, B. C. (2004) *Modern Project Finance: A Casebook*, New York: John Wiley & Sons, Inc.

Fabozzi, F. J. and De Nahlik, C. F. (2012) *Project Finance*, eighth edn, London: Euromoney Institutional Investor plc.

Fama, E. F. (1980) 'Agency Problems and the Theory of the Firm', *Journal of Political Economy*, 88(2), 288–307.

Farrell, L. (2003) 'Principal-Agency Risk in Project Finance', *International Journal of Project Management*, 21(8), 547–61.

Finnerty, J. D. (2007) *Project Financing – Asset Based Financial Engineering*, second edn, New York: John Wiley & Sons, Inc.

Fischer, E. O., Heinkel, R. and Zechner, J. (1989) 'Dynamic Capital Structure Choice: Theory and Tests', *The Journal of Finance*, 44(1), 19–40.

Frank, M. Z. and Goyal, V. K. (2007) 'Trade-off and Pecking Order Theories of Debt', in E. Eckbo (ed.), *The Handbook of Empirical Corporate Finance*, Amsterdam: Elsevier Science, 135–97.

Froot, K. A., Scharfstein, D. S. and Stein, J. C. (1993) 'Risk Management: Coordinating Corporate Investment and Financing Policies', *The Journal of Finance*, 48(5), 1629–58.

Galai, D. and Masulis, R. W. (1976) 'The Option Pricing model and the Risk Factor of Stock', *Journal of Financial Economics*, 3, 53–81.

Gatti, S. (2013) *Project Finance in Theory and Practice – Designing, Structuring, and Financing Private and Public Projects*, second edn, Amsterdam: Elsevier.

Gatti, S., Kleimeier, S., Megginson, W. and Steffanoni, A. (2013) 'Arranger Certification in Project Finance', *Financial Management*, 42(1), 1–40.

Gertner, R. and Scharfstein, D. (1991) 'A Theory of Workouts and the Effects of Reorganization Law', *The Journal of Finance*, 46(4), 1189–222.

Gorton, G. and Kahn, J. (2000) 'The Design of Bank Loan Contracts', *Review of Financial Studies*, 13(2), 331–64.

Green, R. (1984) 'Investment Incentives, Debt, and Warrants', *Journal of Financial Economics*, 13, 115–36.

Green, R. C. and Talmor, E. (1986) 'Asset Substitution and the Agency Costs of Debt Financing', *Journal of Banking and Finance*, 10(3), 391–9.

Grossman, S. J. and Hart, O. (1982) 'Corporate Financial Structure and Managerial Incentives', in McCall, J. (ed), *The Economics of Information and Uncertainty*, Chicago: University of Chicago Press, 107–40.

Hansmann, H., Kraakman, R. and Squire, R. (2006) 'Law and the Rise of the Firm', *Harvard Law Review*, 119, 1333–403.

Hart, O. (2003) 'Incomplete Contracts and Public Ownership: Remarks, and an Application to Public-Private Partnerships', *The Economic Journal*, 113(486), 69–76.

Haugen, R. A. and Senbet, L. W. (1981) 'Resolving the Agency Problems of External Capital through Options Resolving the Agency Problems of External Capital through Options', *The Journal of Finance*, 36(3), 629–47.

Hennessy, C. A. and Tserlukevich, Y. (2008) 'Taxation, Agency Conflicts, and the Choice Between Callable and Convertible Debt', *Journal of Economic Theory*, 143(1), 374–404.

Hertzel, M., Li, Z., Officer, M. and Rodgers, K. (2008) 'Inter-Firm Linkages and the Wealth Effects of Financial Distress Along the Supply Chain', *Journal of Financial Economics*, 87(2), 374–87.

Hoffman, S. L. (2009) *The Law and Business of International Project Finance*, third edn, Cambridge: Cambridge University Press.

Holmstrom, B. (1979) 'Moral Hazard and Observability', *The Bell Journal of Economics*, 10(1), 74–91.

Howcroft, B. and Fadhley, S. (1998) 'Project Finance: A Credit Strategy Based on Contractual Linkages', *The Service Industries Journal*, 18(2), 90–111.

Hviid, M. (2000) 'Long-term Contracts and Relational Contracts', in Bouckaert, B. and De Geest, G. (eds), *Encyclopedia of Law and Economics*, third edn, 46–72.

Inderst, R. and Müller, H. M. (2003) 'Internal versus External Financing: An Optimal Contracting Approach', *The Journal of Finance*, 58(3), 1003–62.

Jensen, M. C. (1986) 'Agency Costs of Free Cash Flow, Corporate Finance, and Takeovers', *The American Economic Review*, 76(2), 323–9.

Jensen, M. C. and Meckling, W. H. (1976) 'Theory of the Firm: Managerial Behavior, Agency Costs and Ownership Structure', *Journal of Financial Economics*, 3(4), 305–60.

Jensen, M. C. and Murphy, K. J. (1999) 'CEO Incentives – It's Not How Much You Pay, But How', in Jensen, M. C. (ed), *Foundations of Organizational Strategy*, Cambridge: Harvard University Press, 138–53.

Kalay, A. (1982) 'Stockholder-Bondholder Conflict and Dividend Constraints', *Journal of Financial Economics*, 10, 211–33.

Klein, B. (1996) 'Why Hold-ups Occur: The Self-Enforcing Range of Contractual Relationships', *Economic Inquiry*, 34(3), 444–63.

Kraakman, R., Armour, J., Davies, P., Enriques L., Hansmann, H. B., Hertig, G., Hopt, K. J., Kanda, H. and Rock, E. B. (2009) *The Anatomy of Corporate Law – A Comparative and Functional Approach*, second edn, Oxford: Oxford University Press, 231.

Kroszner, R. and Strahan, P. (2001) 'Bankers on Boards: Monitoring, Conflicts of Interest, and Lender Liability', *Journal of Financial Economics*, 62, 415–52.

Leary, M. T. and Roberts, M. R. (2010) 'The Pecking Order, Debt Capacity, and Information Asymmetry', *Journal of Financial Economics*, 95(3), 332–55.

Leland, H. E. (2007) 'Financial Synergies and the Optimal Scope of the Firm: Implications for Mergers, Spinoffs, and Structured Finance', *The Journal of Finance*, 62(2), 765–807.

Lewellen, W. G. (1971) 'A Pure Financial Rationale for the Conglomerate Merger', *The Journal of Finance* (Papers and Proceedings of the 29th Annual Meeting of the American Finance Association, Detroit, Michigan – December 1970), 26(2), 521–37.

MacKay, P. (2003) 'Real Flexibility and Financial Structure: An Empirical Analysis', *Review of Financial Studies*, 16(4), 1131–65.

Malitz, I. (1986) 'Evidence on Bond Issue Provisions On Financial Contracting: of Bond The Determinants', *Financial Management*, 15(2), 18–25.

Manove, M., Padilla, A. and Pagano, M. (2001) 'Collateral versus Project Screening: A Model of Lazy Banks', *RAND Journal of Economics*, 32(4), 726–44.

Mao, C. X. (2003) 'Interaction of Debt Agency Problems and Optimal Capital Structure: Theory and Evidence', *The Journal of Financial and Quantitative Analysis*, 38(2), 399–423.

Martimort, D. and Pouyet, J. (2008) 'To Build or not to Build: Normative and Positive Theories of Public–Private Partnerships', *International Journal of Industrial Organization*, 26(2), 393–411.

Mauer, D. and Triantis, A. (1994) 'Interactions of Corporate Financing and Investment Decisions: A Dynamic Framework', *The Journal of Finance*, vol. 49(4), 1253–77.

Milidonis, A. and Stathopoulos, K. (2012) 'Managerial Incentives, Risk Aversion, and Debt', *Journal of Financial and Quantitative Analysis*, Forthcoming, 1–43.

Minton, B. and Schrand, C. (1999) 'The Impact of Cash Flow Volatility on Discretionary Investment and the Costs of Debt and Equity Financing', *Journal of Financial Economics*, 54(3), 423–60.

Modigliani, F. and Miller, M. H. (1958) 'The Cost of Capital, Corporation Finance and the Theory of Investment', *The American Economic Review*, 48(3), 261–97.

Modigliani, F. and Miller, M. H. (1963) 'Corporate Income Taxes and the Cost of Capital: A Correction', *The American Economic Review*, 53(3), 433–43.

Morellec, E. (2004) 'Can Managerial Discretion Explain Observed Leverage Ratios?', *Review of Financial Studies*, 17(1), 257–94.

Myers, S. C. (1977) 'Determinants of Corporate Borrowing', *Journal of Financial Economics*, 5, 147–75.

Myers, S. C. (1984) 'The Capital Structure Puzzle', *The Journal of Finance*, 39(3), 575–92.

Myers, S. C. and Majluf, N. S. (1984) 'Corporate Financing and Investment Decisions when Firms Have Information that Investors Do not Have', *Journal of Financial Economics*, 13(2), 187–221.

Parrino, R. and Weisbach, M. S. (1999) 'Measuring Investment Distortions Arising from Stockholder-Bondholder Conflicts', *Journal of Financial Economics*, 53, 3–42.

Parrino, R., Poteshman, A. M. and Weisbach, M. S. (2005) 'Measuring Investment Distortions when Risk-Averse Managers Decide Whether to Undertake Risky Projects', *Financial Management*, 34(1), 21–60.

Pindyck, R. S. (1991) 'Irreversibility, Uncertainty, and Investment', *Journal of Economic Literature*, vol. 29(3), 1110–48.

Rajan, R. (1992) 'Insiders and outsiders: The Choice between Informed and Arm's-length Debt', *The Journal of Finance*, 47(4), 1367–1400.

Richardson, S. (2006) 'Over-Investment of Free Cash Flow', *Review of Accounting Studies*, 11(2–3), 159–89.

Sarig, O. (1998) 'The Effect of Leverage on Bargaining with a Corporation', *The Financial Review*, 33(1), 1–16.

Schwartz, A. (1989) 'A Theory of Loan Priorities', *The Journal of Legal Studies*, 18(2), 209–61.

Schwartz, A. (1997) 'Priorities and Priority in Bankruptcy', *Cornell Law Review*, 82, 1396–1419.

Shah, S. and Thakor, A. V. (1987) 'Optimal Capital Structure and Project Financing', *Journal of Economic Theory*, 42, 209–43.

Shavell, S. (1979) 'On Moral Hazard and Insurance', *The Quarterly Journal of Economics*, 93(4), 541–62.

Shleifer, A. and Vishny, R. W. (1992) 'Liquidation Values and Debt Capacity: A Market Equilibrium Approach', *The Journal of Finance*, 47(4), 1343–66.

Smith, C. W. and Warner, J. B. (1979) 'On Financial Contracting: An Analysis of Bond Covenants', *Journal of Finance and Economics*, 7, 117–61.

Spence, M. (2002) 'Signaling in Retrospect and the Informational Structure of Markets', *The American Economic Review*, 92(3), 434–63.

Spier, K. E. (1992) 'Incomplete Contracts and Signalling', *The RAND Journal of Economics*, 23(3), 432–43.

Stiglitz, J. (1969) 'A Re-Examination of the Modigliani – Miller Theorem', *The American Economic Review*, 59(5), 784–93.

Stiglitz, J. and Weiss, A. (1981) 'Credit Rationing in Markets with Imperfect Information', *The American Economic Review*, 71(3), 393–410.

Stulz, R. M. and Johnson, H. (1985) 'An Analysis of Secured Debt', *Journal of Financial Economics*, 14, 501–21.

Subramanian, K. V., Tung, F. and Wang, X. (2008) 'Law, Agency Costs and Project Finance', *American Law & Economics Association Annual Meetings*, Paper 77.

Tirole, J. (1986) 'Procurement and Renegotiation', *Journal of Political Economy*, 94(2), 235–59.

Titman, S. and Tsyplakov, S. (2007) 'A Dynamic Model of Optimal Capital Structure', *Review of Finance*, 11(3), 401–51.

Titman, S. and Wessels, R. (1988) 'The Determinants of Capital Structure Choices', *The Journal of Finance*, 43(1), 1–19.

Townsend, R. M. (1979) 'Optimal Contracts and Competitive Markets with Costly State Verification', *Journal of Economic Theory*, 21(2), 265–93.

Vanden, J. M. (2009) 'Asset Substitution and Structured Financing', *Journal of Financial and Quantitative Analysis*, 44(04), 911.

Vinter, G., Price, G. and Lee, D. (2013) *Project Finance – A Legal Guide*, fourth edn, London: Sweet & Maxwell.

Webb, D. (1991) 'Long-Term Financial Contracts can Mitigate the Adverse Selection Problem in Project Financing', *International Economic Review*, 32(2), 305–20.

Weiss, L. A. (1990) 'Bankruptcy Resolution – Direct Costs and Violation of Priority of Claims', *Journal of Financial Economics*, 27, 285–314.

Williamson, O. E. (1985) *The Economic Institutions of Capitalism*, New York: The Free Press, a division of MacMillan Inc.

Yescombe, E. R. (2014) *Principles of Project Finance*, Amsterdam: Elsevier.

Zheng, J., Roehrich, J. K. and Lewis, M. A. (2008) 'The Dynamics of Contractual and Relational Governance: Evidence From Long-Term Public–Private Procurement Arrangements', *Journal of Purchasing and Supply Management*, 14(1), 43–54.

Part IV

Corporate governance and corporate social responsibility

12 Corporate governance responses to environmental regulation and market-based instruments

Lars Hansson and Yanqiang Ding

12.1 Introduction

Business fundamentals in market economies all over the world, when all is said and done, are about profitability. However, the strategies for long-run competitiveness and business prosperity are more intricate today because of an increasing focus on sustainable development, with more and more demands and claims from consumers and governments on corporate social responsibility (CSR). Corporate governance has gradually been more and more integrated into external stakeholders' values, governmental regulation, and economic instruments. Sustainability and CSR reporting, covering economic, environmental, and social impacts caused by corporate activities, has expanded over the last two decades (Schaltegger *et.al.* 2006). Examples of this are the Global Corporate Sustainability Reporting (United Nations Global Compact 2013) and the Global Reporting Initiative. There are also online directories of corporate responsibility reports, such as the CorporateRegister. com.

It is in particularly notable when the World Business Council for Sustainable Development (WBCSD) addresses public policy options to scale and accelerate business actions for a sustainable world. It needs norms, standards, and codes of conduct, but also a "[b]udget reform and fiscal measures [which] move wealth into progressive practices and social inclusion, by pricing negative externalities and pollution, and discontinuing subsidies to harmful, obsolete practices. The prospects of higher carbon prices, pollution fees, and the loss of subsidies, stimulate the innovative capacity of business and consumers, and encourage the development of better alternatives" (WBCSD 2012b: 8). It is emphasized that "[g]overnments must make undesirable situations and their negative externalities sufficiently costly to trigger avoidance responses through innovation" (WBCSD 2012a: 9).

For the business community it is of fundamental importance to understand and thus anticipate how sustainability challenges lead to growing consumer demands for 'green products', as well as the growing influence that governmental environmental policies have on market demand and market supply. Business commerciality basics are increasingly affected by governments through regulatory approaches, 'green' taxes and subsidies in order to advance sustainable development. Law and regulation was a key constituent for industrial development throughout the twentieth century. At the end of the century, the regulatory framework was gradually complemented by market-based instruments (MBIs).

The theory of MBIs goes back to the work of Arthur Pigou, a British economist who developed the concept of market externalities a century ago (particularly in his renowned book *The Economics of Welfare*, published in 1920). Externalities were defined as those costs or benefits, i.e. negative or positive impacts on the well-being of third parties, that were not taken into consideration by producers or consumers on the market. If the externalities were negative, the market would lead to over-consumption of a product or service, and vice versa. If the government introduced a tax (often referred to as a Pigouvian Tax) corresponding to the marginal negative external cost, the market price would adjust to the right socio-economic cost, and thus the market would allocate resources in an efficient way. Consequently, if there were positive externalities, it would be relevant to subsidize for the extra benefits that the producer or consumer were not compensated for.

Most of the market failures today in the context of sustainable development are about negative externalities. However, MBIs today include much more than the 'green' taxes that were recommended by Pigou. The most obvious example is the trading with emissions allowances. Such schemes, which will be analyzed further in the chapter, do not generate any revenues to the state and thus cannot be labeled as 'taxes'. Despite this, they still give the same incentives in the context of corporate governance to reduce their emissions in a cost-effective way. However, new policies such as the EU scheme of trading carbon emission allowances that are gradually going to be auctioned on a market will have important similarities with a Pigouvian tax, although the price of the allowances is going to be set in a fundamentally different way. Other schemes that give incentive effects on the energy market, but no generation of revenues to the state, are green certificates and feed-in tariffs used to stimulate renewable energy. In the same way, deposit-refund systems give incentives for recycling. Fees and duties such as the Swedish airport fees and the Swedish maritime fairway duties are environmentally differentiated, but they do not generate additional revenue. There is a variety of similar examples which will not be covered here. It should also be mentioned that a growing interest in MBIs for gauging payments for positive external costs (payments for environmental services (PES)): has developed during the last ten years.

Environmental regulation (environmental standards) is often anticipated to be more environmentally effective, while MBIs are expected to be more efficient. This is something that textbooks in economics traditionally point out. However, there is a fundamental prerequisite for such a comparison. First, it is only applicable in situations where the environmental concern addresses the total amount of an emission or pollutant within a cap (geographic area) and not concerning the specific location of the emission or pollutant, i.e. an increase from one source will be compensated by exactly the same amount of reduction from another source. This means that a nuisance such as noise in most cases has to be regulated, as the postulation about interchangeability is not relevant. The same deficiency of interchangeability is also frequent when it comes to, e.g., toxics or hazardous substances in commodities or various additives in food, which means that it will often be more appropriate to reduce health risks and environmental dangers with preventative standards. Second, the emissions and pollutants must be possible to monitor, and the transaction costs for an exchange between polluters have to be 'reasonable'. If these conditions are not met, which is often the case, then MBIs can hardly replace regulatory approaches.

There are many interesting examples where the two environmental instruments – regulation and economic incentives – are enforcing each other. The most obvious examples of this are cap-and-trade programs. The total emission levels are regulated, at the same time as MBI approaches give flexibility to industry to allocate abatement measures to those who could reduce their emissions in the most cost-effective way. Even if there are no formal caps for individual companies and plants, green taxes are often used in order to attain specific reduction targets and as such a specific target can, of course, be regarded as equivalent to an overall regulatory standard.

The environmental effectiveness of a MBI is often different in the short-term perspective from the long-term perspective due to economic incentives encouraging the development of better technologies. This aspect of fiscal incentives is due to "avoidance responses through innovation," i.e. to diminish exposure to high costs for negative externalities (WBCSD, 2012a). The WBCSD accentuates that the efficiency of markets will stimulate the innovative capacity of business. Increased efficiency thus has the potential to reduce emissions and pollution beyond the initial reduction, which means an additional effectiveness.

Environmental regulation and market-based instruments stimulate research and development (R&D) for technological change. The impact of environmental regulation on industry was much in focus in the 1990s. Until then, the predominant view among economists as well as business people was that environmental regulation automatically gave a competitive disadvantage to industry. Step by step, this assumption became more contested. The initial debate was to a large extent provoked by an article of Michael Porter (1991) in which he addressed America's green strategy. The message was that environmental regulation triggers a new way of thinking, ensuing innovation of cleaner technologies, resulting in cost savings that, to a large extent, would off-set the abatement costs to reduce emissions. This statement, now known as the Porter Hypothesis, today has turned into a further argument for the use of MBIs because of its dynamic (innovative) effects. It is obvious that there is a large potential in a long-run perspective that governmental market interventions make production processes and products more efficient. Another and less obvious aspect of MBIs is that it is an instrument that could also be more effective than environmental regulation because of the dynamic effects regarding gradually reduced marginal abatement costs to reduce emissions and pollution.

The subsequent sections of this chapter are structured as follows: section 12.2 explores the concept of proportionality in environmental policy. A fundamental principle in policies aiming to attain sustainable development is a balancing of costs and benefits. The main conclusion here is that there is a lot of uncertainty about the costs for industry to comply with stricter environmental standards. Section 12.3 illustrates the general efficiency of MBIs. The conclusion of this section is that industry will have better information and incentives to pick the low hanging fruits, i.e. the cheapest measures to reduce emissions and pollution, compared with a regulatory agency deciding different emission standards. However, it is a well-known fact that industry also has problems to estimate the expected abatement costs. This is described in Section 12.4, where *ex-ante* and *ex-post* calculations of abatement costs are compared. The implications of these uncertainties about abatement costs is that the innovative capacity motivated by fiscal measures (e.g. MBI), as mentioned by WBCSD in Section 12.1, has the potential to increase the environmental effectiveness as compared to the outcome of emission standards, etc. This is analyzed more generally in Section 12.5, while a more specific case is described in Section 12.6. The specific case addressed here is the Swedish NOx charge, which illustrates the incentive to go beyond environmental regulation. The last part, Section 12.7, concludes that the merits of environmental regulation and economic incentives have to be analyzed on a case-by-case basis. The potential advantages of MBIs are based on the fundamental assumption that the total amount of an emission or pollutant is interchangeable between different plants within a cap (geographic area). There are numerous examples where the philosophy of interchangeability is not valid. In all these cases, environmental regulations are more appropriate.

12.2   The challenge to apply the concept of proportionality in environmental regulation

A fundamental principle for environmental regulation is the balancing of interests. In EU law, this is expressed by the concept of proportionality, which means that measures must be reasonable, considering the competing interests of different stakeholders. This means that any environmental concern must be balanced to what is regarded to be affordable. In the IPPC Directive (2008/1/EC) as well as in the Industrial Emissions Directive (IED 2010/75/EU), this principle has been addressed in the best available technology (BAT) reference documents, the so-called best available techniques reference document (BREF). In the Reference Document 'Economics and Cross-media Effects' some of the methods that can be used to balance economic costs against the environmental benefits are described.

The Reference Document on *Economics* (EC 2006: 52) points out a basic concept: "one can spend a euro only once." This means that in order to achieve highest environmental yield for each euro invested for environmental purposes, costs and benefits have to be balanced:

> The most explicit way to compare costs and benefits of a measure is to monetarise both and compare them in a cost benefit analysis (CBA). When the comparison shows that the benefits outweigh the costs, this indicates that the measure represents a worthwhile investment. If different alternative measures give positive results, the measure with the highest result is the one offering the highest overall value for money. However, such a cost benefit analysis requires a lot of data and some benefits are difficult to monetarise.

Comparison of costs and benefits in a socio-economic perspective is a principle. In practice, there has to be a more pragmatic view, which often means more focus on cost effectiveness: can we achieve what we want to attain at a lower cost compared with the alternatives (highest value-for-money). Such a focus is relevant when the benefit values are difficult to assess or sometimes not even relevant for monetarization. In other cases, the proportionality principle is more of a political decision based on the precautionary principle, where formal socio-economic proportionality and cost efficiency is not applicable. However, when it comes to many emissions and pollutants today, especially air pollution, damage costs per ton of emission are expressed in monetary terms.

The Sixth Environmental Action Programme of the EU is a good illustration of an integrated policy on air pollution that is based on economic principles. In the Clean Air for Europe (CAFE) Programme, the objectives are to develop, collect and validate scientific information on the effects of air pollution, including the validation of emission inventories, air quality assessments, projections, cost-effectiveness studies and integrated assessment modeling (COM (2005) 446 final). The ambition is to develop an integrated strategy to include appropriate objectives and cost-effective measures. The paradigm of proportionality based on a socio-economic perspective is obvious when the target is set (COM (2005) 446 final: 4–6):

> Concerning health impacts, currently in the EU there is a loss in statistical life expectancy of over 8 months due to PM2.5 in air, equivalent to 3.6 million life years lost annually ...
>
> In monetary terms, the damage to human health alone is estimated at between €189–609 billion per annum in 2020. In view of these costs, taking no further action is not an option ...
>
> The level of ambition chosen for this Strategy has been estimated to deliver at least €42 billion per annum in health benefits. These benefits include fewer premature deaths, less sickness, fewer hospital admissions, improved labour productivity etc ...

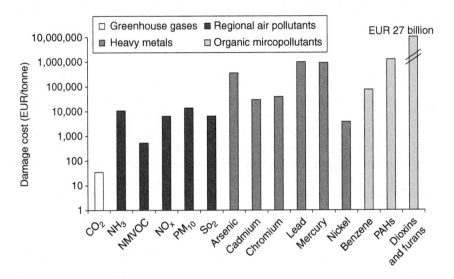

Figure 12.1 Estimates of the European average damage cost per tonne emitted for selected air pollutants

(Source: EEA (2011: 23).)

Note: the scale on the Y-axis is logarithmic

Attainment of these targets is estimated to cost approximately €7.1 billion per annum (representing about 0.05% of the EU25 GDP in 2020).

In Figure 12.1, the European average damage costs per tonne emitted for selected air pollutants are presented (EEA 2011). These values are mainly assessed by damage costs to health, but also damage to the environment. The cost of damage caused in 2009 by emissions, taken from the E-PRTR (information publicly available through the European Pollutant Release and Transfer Register (E-PRTR)), indicates that industrial facilities emissions related-damages were estimated as being at least EUR102–169 billion.

The quantified damage costs per unit of emission vary substantially between pollutants. Organic micro-pollutants are the most hazardous per tonne of emission, with estimated damage costs of EUR1–10 million. On the other edge of explicit damage costs is CO_2, valued at EUR34 per tonne.

Even if explicit values of pollutants, such as those used in the EU CAFE Programme, are applied in assessments based on the proportionality principle, there are still other challenges for the assessments related to the referred values themselves. The values are specific for different countries and regions. The EEA (2011: 24) illustrates this with the variation in national average damage costs per tonne PM_{10} emission across Europe, where the difference

Table 12.1 Estimates in three studies of abatement costs for PM_{10} reductions from cement kilns

Emissions mg/m^3 Limit value	Abatement cost (€ per ton clinker)					
	Ökopol (1999)		VDZ (2000)		Rabl (2000)	
	low	high	low	high	low	high
30	0.15	1.22	0.44	1.06	0.40	1.80
15	0.25	1.56	*	*	0.70	2.30

(Source: Adapted from Rabl (2000).)

Notes: *VDZ (2000) imply that such an emission limit is not realistic*

between countries with the lowest damage costs and the highest damage costs is 6–7 times.

Another challenge, which is more relevant for the present analysis of corporate governance responses related to the different types of environmental policy instruments – once the explicit values are integrated in the assessments – is to calculate what is 'optimal' or what is 'cost effective'. In order to be able to balance these costs and benefits, we have to find out what the abatement costs for industry to reduce their emissions and pollution are. There are a lot of uncertainties in these analyses.

A very typical case of such an uncertainty is briefly illustrated with cost calculations in Table 12.1, where three studies about abatement costs are presented for PM_{10} reductions from cement kilns that burn waste as fuel. Although just one of a vast number of similar calculations, it clearly illustrates the intrinsic challenge of environmental regulation. What is optimal? What is cost effective from a socio-economic perspective?

Calculations as those above were presented to the European Council and the European Parliament when they had to decide about a new Directive to regulate emissions from waste incineration. The abatement costs to reduce one kg of PM_{10} was calculated by Rabl (2000) to be in the range of 23 to 180€/kg. However, there were other calculations with divergent cost estimates. On the other end of the estimated costs to reduce PM_{10} emissions, Ökopol (1999) estimated that the indicated abatement costs for new plants to be in the range of 3 to 15€/kg. However, there is much more to add to this dilemma from a regulatory perspective. These ranges of abatement costs are just for one sector. Waste incineration and PM_{10} abatement costs, of course, have to be addressed in all sectors in order to attain cost efficiency.

Another illustration of the wide range of cost estimates is presented by Fischer and Morgenstern (2005). Figure 12.2 depicts the estimates from 11 major economic-energy models used for predictions of marginal abatement costs for the reduction of carbon emissions in the US. The analysis shows the significance of assumptions with respect to 'perfectly foresighted consumers', trade elasticities, cost estimates, mobility of capital, etc. If these conditions are not fully

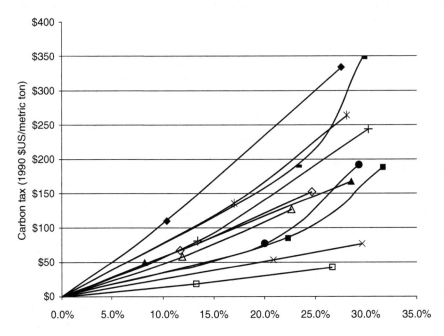

Figure 12.2 Eleven different models with predictions of marginal abatement costs for reduction of carbon emissions in the US

(Source: Fischer and Morgenstern (2005: 6).)

understood by industry itself, we can just imagine how much more difficult it must be for regulators to know what the relevant assumptions should be.

The two examples presented in Table 12.1 and Figure 12.2, together with a huge number of similar studies, show the difficulties today in assessing the 'true abatement costs' concerning the implementation of the proportionality principle in environmental regulation. In addition to this, there is another even more complex difficulty. The examples only illustrate the costs for an industrial sector and a market respectively. However, from a socio-economic efficiency point of view it is not just about the 'optimal' reduction of emissions in a specific industrial sector, it is about the 'allocation of responsibilities', i.e. to find out what the cost-effective reductions for specific companies and plants are. This is even more of a challenge when it comes to environmental regulation. The trade-offs between costs and benefits for specific stakeholders depend on factors that a regulatory authority really cannot know anything about. This lack of knowledge is of fundamental importance when it comes to understanding observed differences in dynamic outcomes of environmental regulations and MBIs.

Diverse optimal trade-offs for different stakeholders can be illustrated with the help of an advertisement in the Swedish magazine *LASTBILEN*

Figure 12.3 Advertisement for the reconstruction of trailers (*LASTBILEN* no. 11/1989)

(*The Truck*), published by the Swedish Road Hauliers Association in 1989 (Figure 12.3). The background for the advertisement was the following: the previous weight–distance tax for diesel vehicles had been changed a couple of months earlier to a weight–axle–distance tax, a tax construction that corresponded closer to the actual road maintenance costs. This change gave new incentives to reconstruct trailers.

The variable operating costs for wear-and-tear of roads differs significantly between cars and trucks. The costs are directly correlated with axle-weight loads (axle group numbers and types) in a non-linear way and distance traveled, which means that the costs for passenger cars are insignificant compared with trucks. The rule of thumb among highway engineers is that road deterioration is roughly proportional to vehicle axle weight to the fourth power, although one has to remember that it is lower for freeways and motorways (with a higher strengths standard) and higher for local roads, especially gravel roads (with a lower strengths standard). When the rule of thumb correlation is relevant, it means that doubling the weight on an axle increases the wear-and-tear on the roads by 2^4, or 16 times. Quadruple weight increases the cost about 250 times, etc.

When it comes to road cost responsibility, a heavier truck consumes more fuel than a lighter truck. This means that the heavier truck pays a higher tax through the fuel excise tax, and thus also pays more for additional external costs. However, the higher fuel consumption for heavier trucks is quite marginal, and does in no way correspond to the additional operational costs for wear-and-tear. While doubling the weight increases the marginal costs for wear-and-tear by 16 times, the corresponding 'externality tax' for externalities paid through the fuel tax typically is less than doubled. This is the reason why Sweden previously replaced part of the fuel tax for diesel vehicles by a weight–distance tax, and as mentioned above, in 1989, enhanced the tax into a weight–axle–distance tax. It gave commercial incentives to reconstruct trailers that corresponded to what was in the public interest. It is apparent that regulation was not an efficient alternative because the reconstruction of trailers was a socio-economic benefit only for some of the trailers, and that specific information about the trailers was known (or anticipated) only by the individual hauliers.

One of the most popular trailers in the 1980s was one with three axles and a taxation weight of 30 tonnes. The advertisement in *LASTBILEN* 1989 (Figure 12.3) informs about the possibility to convert such a three-axle trailer into a semitrailer with dolly, carrying the same weight. In different articles, as well as in some advertisements, the profits of reconstructed trailers were calculated (the example in Figure 12.3 is just one example among many other similar advertisements at that time). In this specific example the vehicle reduced the variable vehicle tax by SEK36,000 annually, while the capital costs only amounted to SEK21,000. The annual saving was thus calculated as being SEK15,000. These calculations were based on a 10-year write-off period and a distance per year amounting to 100,000 km.

The saving of SEK15,000 per year for the individual haulier was also a socio-economic saving of the same amount. The reason for this was that the tax reduction worth SEK36,000 corresponded to the reduced public costs for wear-and-tear of roads. The private capital cost of SEK21,000 corresponded to a similar socio-economic cost.

Does the calculation in the example above about costs and benefits to society of trailer reconstruction provide sufficient information to take legal proceedings fully in accordance with the proportionality principle? Should we regulate and thus make it compulsory to convert three-axle trailers into semitrailers with a dolly? The answer to this question is no. The reason for this statement is analysed in the following section.

12.3   The efficiency of market-based instruments

Socio-economic efficiency means that measures are undertaken only when the (marginal) benefits exceed the (marginal) costs. The general challenge with regulation is that it cannot in detail take into consideration the specific conditions of costs and benefits for all plants or, as in the case above, all hauliers. The annual profitability above, calculated to be SEK15,000, is only valid for the specific case given: capital costs calculated for a 10-year write-off period and a cost-saving based on 100,000 vehicle kilometres per year. If a regulatory approach is to be used with the purpose to reduce road wear-and-tear costs on a proportionality principle, i.e. to balance additional capital costs for hauliers with cost saving for the road administration, it is necessary for the

Table 12.2 The trade-offs between costs and benefits for a three-axle trailer being converted to a semitrailer with dolly (costs and benefits in SEK/year)

Write-off period	Economic calculation	Expected annual distance traveled (kilometers)				
		150,000	125,000	100,000	75,000	50,000
3	Cost	70,000	70,000	70,000	70,000	70,000
	Benefit	54,000	45,000	36,000	27,000	18,000
4	Cost	**52,500**	52,500	52,500	52,500	52,500
	Benefit	54,000	45,000	36,000	27,000	18,000
5	Cost	**42,000**	**42,000**	42,000	42,000	42,000
	Benefit	54,000	45,000	36,000	27,000	18,000
6	Cost	**35,000**	**35,000**	**35,000**	35,000	35,000
	Benefit	54,000	45,000	36,000	27,000	18,000
8	Cost	**26,250**	**26,250**	**26,250**	**26,250**	26,250
	Benefit	54,000	45,000	36,000	27,000	18,000
12	Cost	**17,500**	**17,500**	**17,500**	**17,500**	**17,500**
	Benefit	54,000	45,000	36,000	27,000	18,000

(Source: Hansson (1997: 36–9).)

Notes: **XX,000** = *profitable to convert a three-axle trailer to a semitrailer with dolly*

regulatory administrators to have specific information from all hauliers with respect to all their trailers. The reason for that is that the costs and savings differ between each and every trailer.

The annual capital costs for the conversion to more axles depend on the age of the trailers, which affects the write-off period. The benefits, i.e. cost savings for wear-and-tear, depend on the annual vehicle kilometre distance for each trailer. The specific conditions for social profitability are illustrated in Table 12.2. An older trailer, e.g. one with only five more years to write-off the investment cost, would cost SEK42,000 per year, whereas the benefits would amount to SEK36,000 for the same distance. In these circumstances, i.e. starting with an assumption of a distance traveled to be 100,000km, it is not profitable to convert the trailer. However, if the trailer was to be used for a distance of 125,000km per year, then it would result in a benefit of SEK45,000, and it would thus be profitable to convert the trailer.

The different outcomes in Table 12.2 point to the problems with a regulatory approach: how can a regulator attain the necessary specific information? What are the likely write-off periods for each and every trailer, which of course is based on more factors than the age of the trailer? What are the likely annual distances traveled for the same trailers? In addition to this information we also have to realize that this example is just for one type of trailer. There are a few more possibilities to convert trailers into other axle-combinations. Such assessments could, of course, only be made by those who are working on the hauliers market themselves.

The example above, highlighting the necessity to obtain adequate information as well as realizing the role of transaction costs, is a key issue in many

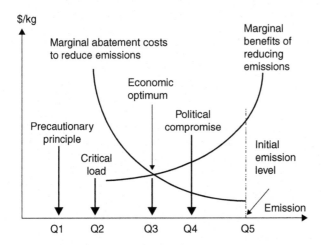

Figure 12.4 Emission standards based on the proportionality principle can be based on many criteria and compromises

cases where 'optimal reductions' of emissions or pollutants are considered. This issue is addressed in a more general way below. With environmental regulation, such as emission standards or a MBI, it is possible to attain emission reductions to comply with the proportionality principle. Although there are many examples where environmental target settings have been based on the proportionality principle backed up by socio-economic analyses (explicit benefit values > *ex-ante* calculated costs), there are never 'fine-tuning procedures' in order to obtain the theoretical optimum (by balancing step-by-step reductions with calculation of marginal benefits and marginal costs). In addition to this fact we can also notice that there are normally different views on how to understand the critical load concept and the precautionary principle, and how to balance such sustainability perspectives with industrial interests as well as equity aspects (Figure 12.4).

We have to be humble when it comes to how much we understand about the specific impact pathways, i.e. dose (exposure) – response relationship, which is essential in order to determine what is 'safe' or according to the 'precautionary principle' (not to mention the problems of non-linearity, thresholds and cocktail effects). What do we know about short- and long-term health and environmental effects caused by different levels of exposure to emissions and pollution? There are many late lessons from early warnings. A thoughtful analysis of the precautionary principle was recently published by the European Environment Agency (2013a and 2013b). One of the conclusions was the following:

> Precautionary actions can be seen to stimulate rather than hinder innovation; they certainly do not lead to excessive false alarms ... of 88 cases of claimed "false positives", where hazards were wrongly regulated as

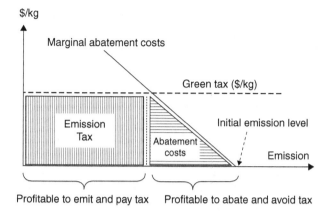

Figure 12.5 The trade-off between abatement and paying for pollution

potential risks, only four were genuine false alarms. The frequency and scale of harm from the mainly "false negative" case studies indicate that shifting public policy towards avoiding harm, even at the cost of some false alarms, would seem to be worthwhile, given the asymmetrical costs of being wrong in terms of acting or not acting based on credible early warnings.

(EEA 2013b: 39)

Whatever the background is for environmental target settings, the proportionality principle is not only about achieving an effective reduction (to reach the emission reduction targets, etc.), but also to achieve the reduction at the lowest total cost possible, i.e. a cost-effective reduction. In order to do that, we have to start with the low-hanging fruits, i.e. apply those abatement measures having the lowest costs, and then gradually continue with those measures having increasingly higher costs.

Is it possible to achieve the targeted reduction at the lowest total cost possible through environmental regulation? The empirical evidence is quite clear-cut about this. It is very unlikely, as some of the experiences presented in Sections 12.4 and 12.5 will demonstrate. This is a basic reason why today there is more and more focus on MBIs. With a 'green tax' or other market-based instruments the regulator does not need to gather detailed information from industry. The trade-offs are decentralized to industry (Figure 12.5).

If a company has to pay a 'green tax' for its emissions there is an option to pay the tax for all its present emissions, or to reduce its emissions and avoid paying a tax for that amount of emission reduction. The decision boils down to a 'simple' comparison of costs and savings for emission reductions: the company compares the (marginal) tax reduction with the (marginal) abatement cost for a (marginal) emission reduction. It should be noted that the marginal abatement costs are increasing for higher levels of emission reductions in Figure 12.5, in the same way as the marginal abatement cost-curve in Figure 12.2. However, the cost-curve slopes are 'opposite', as the x-axis in Figure 12.2 refers to *emission reduction*, while the x-axis in Figure 12.5 refers to *emission level*.

It is profitable to abate when the green tax exceeds the (marginal) abatement cost, as well as it is profitable to emit and pay for the emission when the green tax is lower than the (marginal) abatement cost. If the green tax is US$5 per kg emission, and the (marginal) abatement cost is US$3 per kg reduced emission, then it is profitable to reduce more emissions. If the (marginal) abatement costs on the other hand were US$7 per kg, then it is profitable to emit and pay the green tax for that.

The incentive effect is the same as above when a company has emission allowances that can be traded: the company compares the revenue from selling an allowance with the abatement cost for a (marginal) emission reduction, alternatively the cost for purchasing an allowance with the saving of an abatement cost for a (marginal) increase of its emissions. If the market price of an allowance is US$5 per kg emission, and the (marginal) abatement cost is US$3 per kg of emissions reduced, then it profitable to sell the allowances. If the (marginal) abatement costs, on the other hand, were US$7 per kg, then it is profitable to purchase allowances and emit more.

Both environmental regulation and MBI approaches require information about costs and benefits in order to attain adequate proportionality. When it comes to emissions and pollutants where it is relevant to apply total caps (which means that it does not matter how the reductions are allocated between industry and plants, as long as the total cap of emissions is not exceeded) there is an advantage of using an MBI approach: a regulator does not need specific information about individual plants in order to achieve cost effectiveness. On the other hand, an instrument like a 'green tax' can be expected to be much slower in its effectiveness. The tax level in practice has to be gradually adjusted in order to give 'the right incentives' to keep emissions within the cap, while environmental regulation by definition will manage this automatically.

The case above with the costs for road wear-and-tear (Table 12.2) was never regulated in Sweden (except for the maximum total weights). Cost effectiveness was attained through a MBI approach. In July 1989 the Swedish kilometre tax system for trucks and trailers was changed from a weight–distance tax to a weight–axle–distance tax. The tax difference between different weight–axle combinations (in principle) corresponded to the difference in wear–and–tear for road maintenance, calculated by the Swedish National Road Administration. This gave rise to new incentives for hauliers, and was thus the background for advertisements, such as the one presented in Figure 12.3. With a MBI linked to the true costs for road maintenance costs, there were private incentives to reconstruct trailers when there was socioeconomic profitability in doing so.

12.4 The *ex-ante* and *ex-post* calculations of abatement costs

In two classical articles (Porter 1991; Porter and Van der Linde 1995) it was stated, based on empirical observations, that "properly designed environmental standards can trigger innovation that may partially or more than fully offset the costs of complying with them." Innovation offsets could as well "even lead to absolute advantages over firms in foreign countries not subject to similar regulations" (Porter and Van der Linde 1995: 98). These statements are today known as the Porter Hypothesis.

The Porter Hypothesis was initially met with skepticism from a theoretical point of view, especially when it comes to the statement that properly designed environmental standards could trigger innovation that sometimes "more than fully offset the costs of complying with them" (Porter and Van der Linde 1995: 98). Would it be possible that there are potential win–win opportunities that for some reasons not have been realized? If so, we have to acknowledge that industry in such a case is inefficient. It could be argued that industry is irrational by taking for granted that there never will be any type of commercial benefits when emissions and pollutants are reduced. A well-known metaphor often used when economic rationality is questioned is the alleged reason why business people (or economists) never would make an effort to pick up a US$10 note on the ground: if it was a real note, somebody else would already have picked it up. Despite this metaphor, it is a reality that sometimes there are US$10 notes on the ground that receive no attention until something triggers a new way of looking at things.

One of the many intriguing examples of a win–win situation triggered by a new environmental policy approach is the BP commitment to reduce their CO_2 emissions. In 2002, the chief executive officer (CEO) of BP, Lord John Browne, gave a speech at Stanford Graduate School of Business, where he described the pledge of BP in 1997 to reduce the BP emissions by 10 per cent from the 1990 level by 2010 a target "broadly in line with the Kyoto targets, and based on the presumption that at some point in the future those targets or something similar would be converted into mandatory objectives" (BP 2002). The key instrument used by BP was a global internal emissions trading scheme that included 112 business units. This was in fact the first global trading scheme in the world (Victor and House 2006).

In his speech in 2002, Lord Browne mentioned that the target set was met seven years ahead of schedule. He also mentioned that BP met the target at no net economic cost: "That's a particularly noteworthy point, a positive surprise – because it begins to answer the fears expressed by those who believed that the costs of taking precautionary action would be huge and unsustainable" (BP 2002).

In the *Sustainability Report 2003* it is mentioned that BP achieved the reduction target and at the same time "gained $650 million in net present value through increased operational efficiency, the application of technological innovation and improved energy management" (BP 2003: 23).

Table 12.3 Marginal cost estimates and realization for compliance options

Industry estimates pre-1989	EPA 1990	Early allowance trades	Allowance trades 1995	Allowance auctions 1993–1995
$1,500	$750	$250	$170	$122–140

(Source: Burtraw (1996: 9).)

The BP experience is in no way unique. Empirical evidence often shows that *ex-ante* estimates of abatement costs are significantly higher than the *ex-post* experienced costs. An early example of the Porter reality is the experience of the US Acid Rain Program and the trading of emission allowances within a regulatory emission cap. The abatement costs were to a great extent lower than industry had calculated, and even a lot lower than the EPA predicted, based on the Porter Hypothesis. The costs for SO_2 reductions presented in Table 12.3 illustrate this.

Calculations of total annual costs over time show the same trend as the marginal cost estimates (Figure 12.6). Chan *et al.* (2012: 31) conclude that SO_2 emissions using the flexibility of emission allowance trading were reduced at a much lower cost compared with a traditional regulatory approach, and also at a lower cost than what had been predicted:

> More than twenty years later, the introduction of the national SO_2 allowance-trading program as part of the Clean Air Act Amendments of 1990 remains widely regarded as a landmark step in the worldwide history of environmental regulation. The program, while not without flaws, is viewed as a success by almost all measures. Certainly it demonstrated that broad-based cap-and-trade systems can be used to achieve significant emissions reductions, that firms can navigate and regulators can enforce the compliance requirements of such systems, and that giving the private sector the flexibility to pursue a range of abatement options can simultaneously protect the environment, stimulate innovation and diffusion, and reduce aggregate costs.
>
> (Chan *et al.* 2012: 31)

Another example of this divergence of *ex-ante* and *ex-post* costs is shown by Oosterhuis *et al.* (2006) in a report on *ex-post* estimates of costs to business of EU environmental legislation. Their study on differences between *ex-ante* and *ex-post* costs estimates are presented in Table 12.4. They conclude that their case studies:

> seem to confirm this mixed picture, with ex-ante overestimation of compliance costs occurring frequently, but not consistently. In many cases, the *ex-ante* estimates were about twice as large as the *ex-post* results. In some cases, however [...] much higher *ex-ante* / *ex-post* ratios were

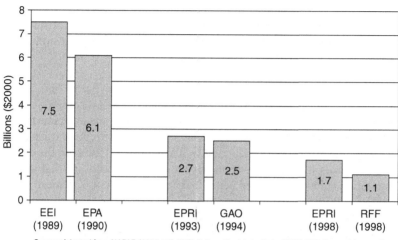

Source: Adapted from NAPAP (2005, 13). 'EEI': Edison Electric Institute; 'GAO': U.S. General Accounting Office (now: Government Accountability Office). Other abbreviations defined in the text.

Figure 12.6 Evolution of cost estimates for implementing the US Acid Rain Program (Source: Chan *et al.* (2012: 7).)

Table 12.4 Ratios of *ex-ante* and *ex-post* cost estimates of EU environmental legislation

Case study	EU Directive (Sector)	Ex-ante / Ex-post ratio	
		Upstream	Consumers
1	Large Combustion Plant Directive	2 (Germany)	6–10 (UK)
2	Integrated Pollution Prevention Control (IPPC) (Belgium Ceramics)	>1.2 (operational costs) ≈1.1 (capital costs)	
3	Ozone Depleting Substances	2.5 (1.4–125)	1.25
4	Transport (Netherlands)	2 (1.4–6)	
5	Packaging	—	—
6	Nitrates Directive (Agriculture)	≈2	

(Source: Oosterhuis *et al.* (2006).)

found. On the other hand, the IPPC case showed no large differences between *ex-ante* and *ex-post*, whereas the evidence in the packaging case is inconclusive.

(Oosterhuis et al. 2006: 14)

Ambec *et al.* (2013: 16–17) provide a 20-year overview of the key theoretical and empirical insights on the research about the Porter Hypothesis. They conclude that there are conflicting empirical results concerning the Porter Hypothesis. However, they still make the following conclusion based on their data:

> First, we find that the theoretical arguments for the Porter Hypothesis appear to be more solid now than when they were first discussed [as part of the heated debate in 1995]. On the empirical side, the evidence for the "weak" version of the Porter Hypothesis (that stricter regulation leads to more innovation) is fairly clear and well established. However, the empirical evidence on the strong version of the Porter Hypothesis (that stricter regulation enhances business performance) is mixed, but with more recent studies providing clearer support.

The short overview in this chapter of the Porter Hypothesis has had no intention to 'confirm' neither the weak nor the strong version of the hypothesis, although there are many case studies supporting the hypothesis. The reason instead is to show that there are important policy implications when it comes to using economic incentives as an option to regulatory approaches. Regardless of whether *ex-ante* estimates about abatement costs are larger (which is often the case) or lower (which sometimes happens) than the *ex-post* actual values, both situations make a case to use MBIs instead of environmental regulation. This will be further analyzed in Section 12.5. MBIs will not only be more efficient, they also have the potential to be more environmentally effective in a long-term perspective. This aspect is further analyzed in Section 12.6.

12.5 The potential effectiveness of market-based instruments

As shown above, various studies show that the observed abatement costs for the US Acid Rain Program were around 25 per cent of the calculated costs. This fact has implications not only for the efficiency of MBIs, but also the effectiveness compared with regulatory approaches. An intriguing example of this is the Swedish charge on NO_x emissions. Over time the marginal abatement costs dropped, as shown in Figure 12.7.

The findings about declining abatement cost-curves results from a survey of energy plants covered by the NO_x charge program during the period between 1992 and 1996. In addition to significantly declining marginal abatement costs, it is also noticeable that some of the reductions were attained at zero abatement costs. In addition to that, the level with zero abatement costs moved from 557kg per GWh in 1991 to about 300kg per GWh in 1996 (OECD, 2010: 160–1). One very interesting aspect of this is the following conclusion, once again a good example of the Porter Hypothesis:

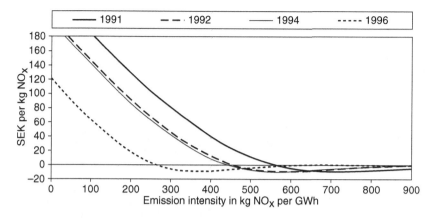

Figure 12.7 Declining marginal NO$_x$ abatement cost-curves
(Source: OECD (2010: 161).)
Notes: For 55 plants in the energy sector regulated by the Swedish NO$_x$ charge, 1992–1996

The introduction of the charge revealed opportunities to pick "low-hanging fruit" in abatement. Some of these opportunities existed also before the introduction of the NO$_x$ charge, but the charge, with its requirement to monitor NO$_x$ emissions continuously, made it possible for firms to discover and develop them to attain even lower emission intensity levels.

An important conclusion is that "taxes are an important driver for innovation" (OECD 2010: 161). However, it should be noticed that for two other sectors in the study – the pulp and paper sector and the chemical and food sector – no such shifts in marginal abatement costs over time were found. Such differences between sectors are often observed. The Porter Hypothesis is often observed, but it is not a universal outcome.

These innovative effects of the Swedish NO$_x$ charge, as well as the study about *ex-post* costs of EU environmental legislation, together with many more studies, show results that have very interesting implications: in addition to the well-known efficiency aspects of using MBIs, there is also an important potential of effectiveness (producing more than the desired result intended by environmental regulation) in a long-term perspective.

This might be considered as a surprising statement. When it comes to reducing emission levels, regulation is generally considered to be more effective, as the desired reduction will be attained within the decided time. With the incentives provided by MBIs, emission levels will go down in an iterative process, which in practical policy can be expected to take a much longer time. The first reason why we can anticipate an iterative process is the uncertainty about the right green tax level (MBI incentives) illustrated in Figure 12.5 in order to

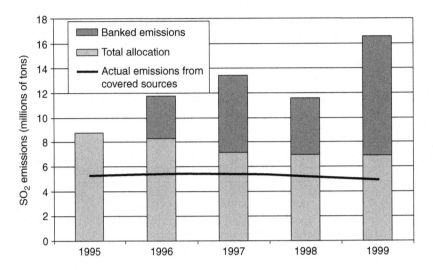

Figure 12.8 SO$_2$ emissions below the cap during Phase I of the emission trading program in the US Acid Rain Program

(Source: Braine and Feldman (2009: 6).)

attain the reduction target set with regulation as illustrated in Figure 12.4. If the green tax is set on a 'low level' the tax has to be increased after some time in order to further reduce the emissions. If the green tax is set 'too high' the reduction would go beyond the reduction target. However, there is a second and less recognized reason for the potential effectiveness of using MBIs: in a dynamic perspective, the incentives of environmental regulation and MBIs will be different.

Before we look closer at the dynamic incentives of MBI approaches, it is interesting to reflect upon experiences of the first years of the US Acid Rain Program, when trading with emission allowances was possible (Burtraw 1996; Burtraw and Palmer 2003). In the first phase of the program (1995–1999) SO$_2$ emission reductions from affected units were nearly two-times greater than that required by the regulation (caps). The reason for this was due to the possibility to bank emission allowances (Braine and Feldman 2009). The total amount of emission allowances and the actual emissions from the affected units are presented in Figure 12.8.

The total amount of SO$_2$ emission allowances in 1995 was 8.7 million tons. This quantity was the same as the total emissions in 1990. The cap for 1996 was reduced to 8.3 million tons, followed by a cap of 7.1, 7.0 and 7.0 million tons in the following three years. What happened then was that the actual emissions in 1995 only reached 5.3 million tons, much lower than the cap of 8.7 million tons. The same happened in 1996, the cap was set at 8.3 million tons, while the emissions were recorded at 5.4 million tons. The same happened for the following three years. Every year the emissions were below the cap. Why did this happen? Normally we would not expect industry to go (that much) below the emission standard. However, there was an incentive. Most emission allowances systems permit the purchase and/or sale of allowances. The US system also allows allowances to be banked for use in future years.

The incentive to bank allowances is an expectation that the future allowance price will increase, either through an increasing demand over time, or by a reduced supply of allowances during the forthcoming phases of the program. The empirical evaluation of the efficiency of allowance banking will not be addressed here. Instead, the main point here is to show that MBIs will not only be more efficient, but also that they can be more effective under certain circumstances, compared with environmental regulation. This is an example where there was a short-term additional effectiveness (reduction beyond the environmental regulation) due to the possibility of bank allowances. In the next section a long-term effectiveness of a MBI will be presented (see Figure 12.13).

In the US case it seems to be the expectations about the future reduction of caps that was the main reason for the observed effectiveness. An enlightening example of this is the nearly ten-fold increase in SO_2 allowance prices in 2005. During the period 2000–3 the price was in the range US\$130–220 per ton. In 2005, the price peaked around US\$1550. In the following three years, the price was reduced to the range of US\$179–740. The reason for this dramatic peak in the SO_2 price was that it gradually became evident in 2003 that the SO_2 cap would be reduced by two-thirds beginning in 2010. (See, e.g., Ellerman and Joskow 2003; Ellerman and Montero 2007; Mekaroonreung and Johnson 2012.)

The anticipated future reduction of caps and the possibility to bank allowances, and the actual price increase of SO_2 allowances when such a reduction became evident, are one reason for a dynamic effectiveness. Two more fundamental reasons for the potential dynamic effectiveness of a MBI are due to:

- the frequent *ex-ante* overestimation of compliance costs when it comes to environmental regulation, and
- the lack of information about specific abatement costs that differ for companies.

Although we in general know about overestimation of abatement costs, it is important to understand that it is not a universal fact. Therefore we do not know *ex-ante* when there are *ex-ante* overestimations. This is something we get to know much later, and only after measures such as environmental regulation have been undertaken. In addition to that, regulators do not know *ex-ante* about the specific abatement costs for different industrial plants – and then we also have to understand that in many instances companies do not really know it themselves. Even though the Porter Hypothesis appears

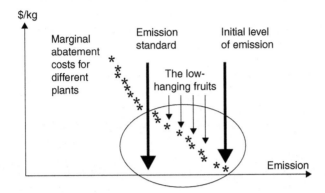

Figure 12.9 Emission regulation should try to pinpoint those emission sources with the lowest abatement costs

to be more solid today than 20 years ago (Ambec *et al.* 2013), the reality is still that there is an inherent uncertainty. A final example of a report that illustrates this is MacLeod *et al.* (2006), who reviewed 27 *ex-post* evaluations of the costs for environmental regulation. They found that the *ex-ante* cost calculations were overestimated for around half the cases being reviewed, while there also were frequent underestimates and occasionally some accurate cost assessments. In addition to this, the authors also discussed whether to include the opportunity costs for R&D resources in the abatement costs or not, something that can explain some of the differences between *ex-ante* and *ex-post* calculations.

With this background, the question is on what basis do regulators decide about emission standards, technology standards, etc. What we can observe empirically, however, is that standards are almost never set in such a way that they will pinpoint those industrial plants with the 'low-hanging fruits' (Figure 12.9).

In reality we know that environmental regulation is not in a position to pinpoint the low-hanging fruits. The abatement measures undertaken by industry look more like the illustration in Figure 12.10. This is the reason why trading with emission allowances has received more and more attention. The emission levels are regulated, but it is possible to trade with the allowances to emit. This means that the overall emissions target will be attained, but the reallocation of abatement measures will be a win–win situation compared with the initial allocation of commitments, benefitting both those industrial plants that abate less, and those that equally abate more.

The emissions trading in the US is a good example of the problems in facilitating Environmental regulation to pick the low-hanging fruits. With the flexibility of trading within a regulatory framework, it was calculated by Ellerman *et al.* (2003) that the abatement costs for SO$_2$ reductions during the period

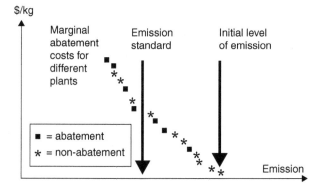

Figure 12.10 Emission regulation will lead to some measures to be undertaken with high abatement costs (high-hanging fruits), while other more cost-efficient measures with lower abatement costs (low-hanging fruits) will not be targeted

between 1995 and 2007 would have been US$34,925 million without trading. The total abatement costs with trading were calculated at US$14,875 million, which means a cost reduction of 57 per cent. It should also be noticed that this is an average for the whole period. During the second phase (from 2000 to 2007 in the calculations by Ellerman *et al.* 2003) the Acid Rain Program was extended. During Phase I, before the extension, the cost reduction was 33 per cent, while the cost reduction during Phase II increased to 62 per cent.

Another of the many examples of such win–win outcomes of a more flexible MBI mechanism compared with traditional regulation was the anticipated result of the EU Emissions Trading System (ETS). This trading scheme is based on the recognition that the flexibility of trading emission allowances offered the most cost-effective way for EU Member States to meet the EU's Kyoto Protocol obligations (European Commission 2005a: 6):

> The scheme should allow the EU to achieve its Kyoto target at a cost of between EUR 2.9 billion and EUR 3.7 billion annually. This is less than 0.1% of the EU's GDP. Without the scheme, compliance costs could reach up to EUR 6.8 billion a year.

Much of the expected cost effectiveness was due to predicted differences in initial abatement costs known by EU companies but not an EU regulator. Another important factor is that, for some sectors, there might be a marginal abatement costs drop over time, as illustrated in Figure 12.7. These reductions are seldom known about in advance, not even by the companies themselves. However, there are economic incentives to explore the potential benefits of going beyond the emission standards, to develop new technologies, or processes that reduce the abatement costs.

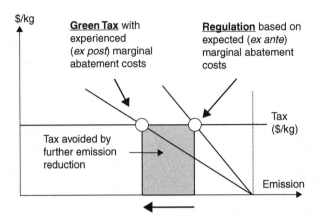

Figure 12.11 Emission tax avoided by reduction beyond the emission standard

The EU targets to reduce greenhouse gas emissions under the Kyoto Protocol were set at an 8 per cent reduction during the first commitment period between 2008 and 2012, compared with the base-year level of 1990. This reduction was overachieved: the average emissions of the EU15 declined by 12.2 per cent. In 2011 the EU15 emissions were down 14.9, and the EU27 emissions had been reduced by 18.4 per cent compared with the base-year level (EEA 2013c). If ETS offsets are considered, the emissions fell even more. During the second trading period of the EU ETS the cumulated surplus of EU allowances (EUA) continued to grow, and the EUA price dropped from EUR25–30 in 2008 to around EUR7 in 2012. In 2013, the price dropped to a low of EUR2.46, and subsequently the price has oscillated in the range EUR4–5. This is an indication that the abatement costs turned out to be lower than expected, although the global financial crisis in 2008 had a significant impact on the outcome. Then the experiences from the first trading period between 2005 and 2007 are a stronger indication of such effectiveness. After one year of trading the price of a EUA oscillated in the range EUR25–30. In May 2006 the European Commission released the first verified emissions data (European Commission 2006b). The market got to know that all the allowances had not been used, and it thus became obvious that it would be a much lower cost than expected to attain the reduction target during the first period. The price initially dropped to around EUR10, and in 2007 the price was below EUR1 by the end of the year.

A more obvious example of the potential effectiveness of a MBI is the Swedish charge on nitrogen oxides. The Swedish EPA (Naturvårdsverket 2003) summarizes the incentive effects in the following way:

> The evaluation clearly indicates that the cost per reduced NO_x unit is lower under the NO_x charge system than under the permit condition system. The incentive provided by the charge for further development of

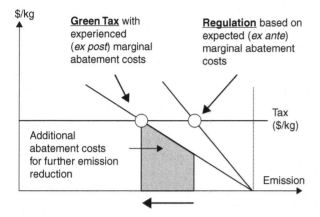

Figure 12.12 Additional abatement costs for a reduction beyond the emission standard

treatment techniques also remains after a given emission target has been achieved, which is not so with permit conditions.

The economic incentive is shown in Figures 12.11 and 12.12. With a green tax, a further reduction will immediately be rewarded through lower taxes paid for the emissions (Figure 12.11). At the same time the additional (average) marginal costs (depending on how the costs for R&D are calculated in this illustration) for the reduction are smaller than the tax avoided (Figure 12.12).

12.6   The Swedish NO_X charge: An example of an incentive to go beyond environmental regulation

The Swedish nitrogen oxides (NO_X) charge has been referred to above. In this section, the charge will be presented in more detail. It is an example of a MBI that has been both efficient and effective. It is also of interest because it gives a good empirical example as to what extent emissions were reduced below the permit conditions for the sectors covered by NO_X regulation.

In 1985 the Swedish Parliament decided that airborne emissions of nitrogen oxides had to be reduced by 30 per cent in 1995 as compared with the emission baseline level of 1980. The main approach to reduce emissions involved specific environmental permit conditions of maximum of NO_X emissions, quantified in maximum mg NO_X per megajoule (MJ) input of energy. Although the quantitative emission limits formally were set on an individual basis, it is obvious that many of these permits were 'standardized', such as a NO_X emission of 100 mg/MJ or 150 mg/MJ of energy input. In a report from the Swedish EPA (Naturvårdsverket 2003: 25) the challenges of NO_X regulation in the 1980s is addressed. The EPA analyzes the possibilities of specific regulation for different plants and processes in theory, but concludes that in practice governmental regulators did not have enough information in consultations and negotiations with companies. Thus, in practice it would not have been possible to attain cost-effective emission reductions. This reality was a fundamental reason why a NO_X charge was suggested in 1990.

In a Governmental Bill in 1990 (Proposition 1989/90: 141) about MBIs in environmental policy, a NO_X charge was proposed (taxes on carbon dioxide and sulphur had some time before that been proposed and decided by the Parliament, and were to take effect on 1 January 1991). The purpose was to reduce NO_X emissions in addition to the existing emission standards, with no intention to reinforce future emission permit conditions for companies.

The NO_X charge was decided to be SEK40 per kg emission when the new system was launched in January 1992 (SEK40 $\approx$ EUR4.55 in December 2013; in 2006 the charge increased to SEK50, about EUR5.70). The background for the level of the charge was calculation undertaken in a Governmental Committee (*Miljöavgiftsutredningen, Study on Market-Based Instruments in Environmental Policy*). A report by Carlsson (1989) came to the conclusion that a tax or charge of that magnitude would reduce NO_X emissions by 17–24 per cent. In the *Governmental Report* (SOU 1989/83: 247) the conclusion, based on the assumption that fewer plants were to pay the charge, the emissions were estimated to drop by 25 per cent. In the Governmental Bill (Proposition 1989/90–141: 22) it was estimated that the emission reduction would be one-third less in 1995 (four years after the introduction of a NO_X charge).

The NO_X charge is to be paid for emissions mainly from boilers, but also from stationary combustion engines and gas turbines, based on actual recorded data. To monitor emissions, it was necessary to invest in monitoring equipment (SEK250,000– 300,000, equivalent to around EUR30,000). Such equipment was quite expensive. Thus, it was from a proportionality point of view not considered to be relevant, to include small plants. The NO_X charge thus was initially decided to be paid for those plants producing at least 50GWh of useful energy per boiler. After some years the monitoring costs had dropped, and in 1997 the charge system was extended to include boilers producing at least 25GWh. To avoid competitive distortion on the market by excluding smaller boilers, it was decided that the NO_X charge had to be tax neutral, i.e. that the revenues were to be transferred back to the participating plants. The refunding was decided to be based on the total number of useful energy produced. This principle also had the effect that industry to a large extent accepted the charge.

In 2012, the total payments amounted to SEK674 million, while SEK668 million was refunded. This means that the costs for administration and monitoring were only 0.87 per cent of the revenue. All seven sectors covered by the NO_X charge have been able to reduce their emissions since the charge was introduced. The distributional effects with respect to net payers and net receivers, however, differ between sectors. The biggest sector of net

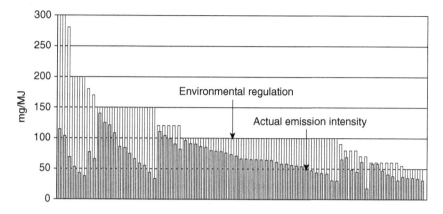

Figure 12.13 Environmental regulation and actual emission intensity for individual industrial plants covered by the Swedish NO$_x$ charge
(Source: Höglund-Isaksson and Sterner (2009: 22).)

receivers is combined heat and power, while the pulp and paper industry is the biggest sector of net payers. Nevertheless, it should be noticed that there are combined heat and power plants that are net payers, as well as there being pulp and paper plants that are net receivers.

Every year the Swedish EPA presents specific information about individual companies and plants and their performance not only for NO$_x$ emissions and useful energy produced, but also what type of boiler, etc. being used in the plant (Naturvårdsverket 2013). In addition to this, one appendix ranks all the plants according to kg NO$_x$ per MWh (the lowest relative emission is a plant with 0.018kg/KWh, while the highest emission value is 1.127kg/KWh). This transparency and comparison gives excellent opportunities for benchmarking of environmental performance.

When Parliament in 1990 decided to introduce the NO$_x$ charge in 1992, the emissions per input of energy were 160 mg/MJ. When the system went into force, industry had already reduced the emissions to 99 mg/MJ. Two years later, in 1994, the NO$_x$ emissions were down to 70 mg/MJ. At the same time, the specific NO$_x$ emissions per MWh of useful energy dropped from 0.50kg to 0.28kg. These reductions were much more than anticipated.

Höglund-Isaksson (2005) found that extensive emission reductions were achieved to very low or even zero or negative costs (see Figure 12.7). These reductions were mostly due to a trimming of the combustion processes.

The incentive effects provided by the NO$_x$ charge for further development of treatment techniques have resulted in emissions below the permit conditions for the sectors covered by NO$_x$ regulation (Figure 12.13). These reductions, different for different plants within each sector, show the additional effectiveness of the MBI used. Höglund-Isaksson and Sterner (2009) identify three measurements as indicators for the occurrence of innovations behind the observed additional effectiveness: distances to a technological frontier, cost savings in abatement for given emission intensity levels and invention activity levels measured as the number of patented technologies.

Sterner and Turnheim (2009) disaggregate average industry improvements with respect to the NO_x reductions in order to study how much of it is due to innovations by first movers, and how much is achieved by adoption and diffusion of technology. They found both factors very important: "Innovation has been rapid: the best firms have cut emissions in the order of 70 per cent. In spite of this, reductions have actually been even more rapid for the majority of firms so that the median firms have caught up with best practice" (Sterner and Turnheim 2009: 2996).

12.7   Concluding comments

The examples of MBIs addressed above, illustrating increased efficiency and effectiveness when compared with regulatory approaches, should not be misread. One should not read too much into the supremacy of MBIs when it comes to efficiency and effectiveness. In almost all cases there is more or less need for some type of regulation. The two most important cap-and-trade programmes referred to in this overview, the US Acid Rain Program and the EU ETS scheme, are based on a broad set of command-and-control regulations.

There are many cases where regulatory approaches initially were used, and then later industry was allowed more flexibility to attain the same reduction within the regulated framework. In the US, trading with emission allowances has been applied not only to SO_2 emissions that were described above, it was also used for NO_x emissions within the Acid Rain Program, the most well known of all emission allowance trading programs until much later, when the EU ETS was launched. Another US example is the Lead-in-Gasoline Program, where a refinery could use lead in its gasoline above the regulated quantity if they purchased emission rights from other refineries who were below their regulated levels. In addition to the most common application, which is allowance trading for air pollution, the principle of trading emission allowances has also been used for water quality trading (e.g. the Hunter River Salinity Trading Scheme in Australia). Moreover, it has been used for landfills (e.g. the Landfill Allowance Trading Scheme in the UK).

Most allowance trading programs have been adapted to make a stronger case for emission and pollution caps through the flexibility of trading with allowances. There are also many international allowance programs for extraction of resources, such as water or fishing. Another example is the management of geothermal aquifers (e.g. the management of Rotorua geothermal field, New Zealand). Offset-based approaches to nature conservation (e.g. biodiversity offsets and habitat banking) have even been introduced.

The relevance of using MBIs in the cases above is based on one very fundamental assumption: it is the total amount of a pollutant (or extraction of a resource) within a geographic area, which matters. This means that the specific location of the pollutant (or the place of extraction of the resource) does not matter. Therefore, emissions (and extractions) in different geographical locations are interchangeable with each other.

There are numerous examples of environmental regulation where the philosophy of interchangeability is not relevant: healthy drinking water quality, restrictions on additives and adulterants in food, safety and noise regulation, restriction of chemicals in products, acceptable pH levels in lakes, just to mention a few examples. In all of these cases, the use of MBIs seems to have a limited role.

MBIs have a potential of increasing efficiency and effectiveness in environmental policy when emission caps are set to reduce pollution or resource extraction. In some of these cases, the regulation is too blunt and MBIs can give further incentives to achieve targets in a cost-effective way while staying within the regulatory framework. In other cases the outcome can even be more effective with reductions going beyond the target reduction. The choice or combination of instruments such as regulation, trading with emission allowances, green taxes, and other fiscal incentive instruments has to be analyzed in each and every case, unbiased from expectations or preconceived views.

References

Ambec, S., Cohen, M. A., Elgie, S. and Lanoie, P. (2013) 'The Porter Hypothesis at 20: Can Environmental Regulation Enhance Innovation and Competitiveness?', *Review of Environmental Economics and Policy*, 7, Issue 1, Winter 2013, 2–22.

BP (2002) 'Beyond Petroleum. Business and the Environment in the 21st Century', Speech by John Browne, Group Chief Executive, BP: hosted by Stanford Graduate School of Business, 11 March 2002. London. Available at: http://www.bp.com/centres/press/stanford/highlights/index.asp (accessed 23 May 2014).

BP (2003) 'Defining our Path', *Sustainability Report 2003*.

Braine, B. and Feldman, B. (2009) 'Economics of Greenhouse Gas Trading: Reaching Environmental Goals Cost Effectively', International Emissions Trading Association (IETA), 4 November 2009.

Burtraw, D. (1996). 'Cost Savings Sans Allowance Trades? Evaluating the SO_2 Emission Trading Program to Date', *Discussion Paper 95–30-REV*, Resources for the Future, Washington, DC.

Burtraw, D. and Palmer, K. (2003) 'The Paparazzi Take a Look at a Living Legend: The SO_2 Cap-and-Trade Program for Power Plants in the United States', *Discussion Paper 03–15*, Resources for the Future, Washington, DC.

Carlsson, A. (1989) 'Effekter på energimarknaden av avgifter på svavel, kväveoxider och koldioxid' (Effects on the Energy Market From Charges on Sulphur, Nitrogen Oxides, and Carbon Dioxide); published in the Governmental Report *Ekonomiska styrmedel i Miljöpolitiken* (*Market-Based Instruments in Environmental Policy*), SOU 1989:84, Appendix 4.

Chan, G., Stavins, R., Stowe, R. and Sweeney, R. (2012) *The SO_2 Allowance Trading System and the Clean Air Act Amendments of 1990: Reflections on Twenty Years* *of Policy Innovation*, Cambridge, Mass.: Harvard Environmental Economics Program.

Ellerman, A. D. (2003) 'Ex Post Evaluation of Tradable Permits: The U.S. SO$_2$ Cap-and-Trade Program', Center for Energy and Environmental Policy Research.

Ellerman, A. D. and Joskow, P. D. (2003) 'Emissions trading in the U.S. – Experience, Lessons, and Considerations for Greenhouse Gases', PEW Center on Global Climate Change.

Ellerman, A. D. and Montero, J-P. (2007) 'The Efficiency and Robustness of Allowance Banking in the U.S. Acid Rain Program', *The Energy Journal*, 28, no.4, 67–92.

European Commission (2005a) 'EU action against climate change: EU emissions trading – an open scheme promoting global innovation', Information brochure (September 2005).

European Commission (2005b) 'Thematic Strategy on Air Pollution', *Communication from the Commission to the Council and the European Parliament*. COM (2005) 446 final, Brussels, 21 September 2005.

European Commission (2006a) 'Integrated Pollution Prevention and Control. Reference Document on Economics and Cross-Media Effects'. Available at: http://eippcb.jrc.ec.europa.eu/reference/ecm.html (accessed 16 January 2014).

European Commission (2006b) 'EU Emissions Trading Scheme Delivers First Verified Emissions Data for Installations', Press Release, IP/06/612 15/05/2006. Available at: http://europa.eu/rapid/press-release_IP-06–612_en.htm (accessed 30 January 2014).

European Environmental Agency (2011) 'Revealing the Costs of Air Pollution From Industrial Facilities in Europe', *EEA Technical Report*, no. 15/2011.

European Environmental Agency (2013a) 'Late Lessons From Early Warnings: Science, Precaution, Innovation', *EEA Report*, no. 1/2013.

European Environmental Agency (2013b) 'Late Lessons From Early Warnings: Science, Precaution, Innovation. Summary', *EEA Report*, no. 1/2013.

European Environmental Agency (2013c) 'Greenhouse Gas Emission Trends' (CSI 010/CLIM 050) Assessment published May 2013. Available at: http://www.eea.europa.eu/data-and-maps/indicators/greenhouse-gas-emission-trends/greenhouse-gas-emission-trends-assessment-5 (accessed 30 January 2014).

European Environmental Agency (2013d) 'Trends and Projections in Europe 2013. Tracking Progress Towards Europe's Climate and Energy Targets Until 2020', *EEA Report*, no. 10/2013.

Fischer, C. and Morgenstern, R. D. (2005) 'Carbon Abatement Costs – Why the Wide Range of Estimates?', 'Resources for the Future', Washington, RFF DP 03–42 REV.

Hansson, L. (1997) 'The Internalization of External Effects in Swedish Transport Policy – A Comparison Between Road and Rail Traffic', IIIEE, Lund, Sweden.

Höglund-Isaksson, L. (2005) 'Abatement Costs in Response to the Swedish Charge on Nitrogen Oxide Emissions', *Journal of Environmental Economics and Management*, 50, 102–20.

Höglund-Isaksson, L. and Sterner, T. (2009) 'Innovation Effects of the Swedish NOx Charge', *OECD Global Forum on Eco-Innovation*, OECD, Paris.

MacLeod, M., Moran, D., Aresti, M. L., Harrington, W. and Morgenstern, R. (2006) 'Comparing the Ex Ante and Ex Post Costs of Complying with Regulatory Changes', SAC Commercial, Edinburgh, and Resources for the Future, Washington, DC.

Mekaroonreung, M. and Johnson, A. L. (2012) 'Estimating the Shadow Prices of SO_2 and NO_x for U.S. Coal Power Plants: A Convex Nonparametric Least Squares Approach', *Energy Economics*, 34, Issue 3, May 2012, 723–32.

Naturvårdsverket (2003) 'Reducing NO_x Emissions. An Evaluation of the Nitrogen Oxide Charge' (The Swedish Environmental Protection Agency, a report in Swedish, with a six-page summary in English), Report 5335.

Naturvårdsverket (2005) 'The Swedish Charge on Nitrogen Oxides – Cost-Effective Emission Reduction', *Information Facts*, March 2005.

Naturvårdsverket (2013) '*Miljöavgift på utsläpp av kväveoxider från energiproduktion år 2012 – resultat och statistik*' (*Environmental Charge on Nitrogen Oxides From Energy Production in 2012 – Results and Statistics*); Dnr NV-06456–13, 2013-09-26.

OECD (2010) 'Annex A. Sweden's Charge on NO_x Emissions', *Taxation, Innovation and the Environment*, OECD Publishing. Available at: http://dx.doi.org/10.1787/9789264087637-9-en (accessed 20 January 2014).

Ökopol (1999) 'Economic Evaluation of Dust Abatement Techniques in the European Cement Industry', and 'Economic Evaluation of NO_x Abatement Techniques in the European Cement Industry', Reports (EC DG11).

Oosterhuis, F. *et al.* (2006) 'Ex-post Estimates of Costs to Business of EU Environmental Legislation', IVM, Institute for Environmental Studies, Vrije Universiteit, the Netherlands.

Porter, M. (1991) 'American Green Strategy', *Scientific American*, 264, 168.

Porter, M. and Van Der Linde, C. (1995) 'Towards a New Conception of Environment-Competitiveness Relationship', *Journal of Economic Perspectives*, 9 (4), 97–118.

Rabl, A. (2000) 'Criteria for Limits on the Emission of Dust From Cement Kilns That Burn Waste as Fuel', Centre d'Energetique, Paris.

Schaltegger, S., Bennett, M. and Burritt, R. (2006) '*Sustainability Accounting and Reporting*', Springer, Dordrecht, the Netherlands.

Sterner, T. and Turnheim, B. (2009) 'Innovation and Diffusion of Environmental Technology: Industrial NO_x Abatement in Sweden Under Refunded Emission Payments'. *Ecological Economics*, 68 (2009), 2996–3006.

Swedish Governmental Bill (1990) '*Om visa ekonomiska styrmedel inom miljöpolitiken*' (*Market-Based Instruments in Environmental Policy*), Proposition 1989/90:141.

Swedish Governmental Report (1989) '*Ekonomiska styrmedel i Miljöpolitiken*' (*Market-Based Instruments in Environmental Policy*), SOU 1989:84.

United Nations Global Compact (2013) 'Global Corporate Sustainability Report 2013'. Available at: http://www.unglobalcompact.org/AboutTheGC/global_corporate_sustainability_report.html (accessed 5 February 2014).

VDZ (2000) Verein Deutscher Zementwerke. Schneider, M., Hirth, G. and Magel, P. 'The economic effect of BAT on the production of cement'. Proceedings of VITO (2000). International workshop on economic aspects of BAT. Brussels. Available at: http://www.emis.vito.be/BBT/Workshop (accessed 25 January 2014).

Victor, D. G. and House, J. C. (2006) 'BP's emission trading scheme', *Energy Policy*, 34 (2006), 2100–112.

WBCSD (2012a) 'Changing Pace. Public Policies to achieve Vision 2050', World Business Council for Sustainable Development. Available at: http://www.wbcsd.org/changingpace.aspx (accessed 5 February 2014).

WBCSD (2012b) 'Changing Pace. Executive Summary', World Business Council for Sustainable Development. Available at: http://www.wbcsd.org/changingpace.aspx (accessed 5 February 2014).

13 The free market myth and its influence on corporate social responsibility

Constantijn van Aartsen

13.1 Introduction

We live in interesting and confusing times. On the one hand we are surrounded by authoritative rhetoric in favour of free markets, reductions in trade barriers and the value of competition. On the other hand we are witness to ongoing environmental issues, a persistent financial crisis and social destabilisation in various corners of the world. The link between economic development and environmental and social issues appears inevitable, but the question remains – where do we go from here?

Some argue that new innovations, further trade liberalisation, reductions in competitive barriers, increased competition and the adoption of corporate social responsibility (CSR) will result in considerable efficiency and productivity gains while simultaneously minimising the negative consequences of economic growth (European Commission (EC) 2011). Others argue that these measures will achieve exactly the opposite result and will further increase inequality and the unsustainability of the global economy, while doing little to promote long-term economic success (Doane 2005; Merino *et al.* 2010). The direction and outcome of this ongoing debate will influence the development and welfare of the human race for decades to come.

Currently, the most influential voice in this debate is represented by the parties favouring trade liberalisation, and free markets, a perspective that captures the dominant neoliberal policy approach of the last decades (George 1999). Adherents to neoliberalism emphasise the value and efficiency of free markets, private enterprise and the business community in creating jobs and satisfying human needs and desires (Peck 2008). In line with this, voters and consumers can express their dissatisfaction with unsustainable or exploitative practices and, through their actions in the marketplace, pressure corporations to include environmental, social and governance factors in their decision-making process (Van Aartsen 2013). To this end, neoliberal policymakers have emphasised the importance of voluntary CSR and consumer choice in promoting a sustainable shift in the global economy. This approach is logical, since the largest 44 corporations alone are responsible for 11 per cent of global gross domestic product (GDP) (Keys and Malnight 2011). Although it is rarely explicitly stated, evidence shows that neoliberal policymakers intend for the development of CSR to continue within a free market framework (EC 2011; Organisation for Economic Co-operation and Development (OECD) 2011).

While CSR is gaining traction, its success remains hotly debated (Horrigan 2010). Under current circumstances, corporations continue to take advantage of weak regulatory environments and resist the imposition of stricter environmental or social regulation (Fooks *et al.* 2011). Furthermore, the adoption of CSR remains limited to a relatively small number of front-running firms, of which only a few appear to have made full-scale commitments to social and environmental improvements (De Hoo 2011). Additionally, tax evasion practices and corporate crime are regular news items, negating the belief that CSR has transformed the landscape of corporate practice. Some argue that CSR has provided a tool through which corporations can cherry-pick profitable sustainable activities, rather than a mechanism for a sustainable global economy (Doane 2005: 24). Thus far, there is little evidence of a paradigm shift in corporate practice. There are many, however, who would find this a pessimistic perspective on recent corporate developments – a perspective that focuses on 'looking at the gap of where we are and where we need to be' and refuses to recognise that sustainable improvements do not happen overnight and will require the general adoption of a new sustainable mindset (Strandberg 2002: 5).

To shed further light on the debate concerning the value and success of CSR, this chapter examines the legal status of CSR within the globalised free market framework. The overarching question is how and to what extent free market theory influences the success of CSR. In answering this question, the chapter first examines the conceptual foundation of the legal framework for CSR and shows that CSR is subject to a dynamic internal debate (Sections 13.2 and 13.3). Noting that politicians and other policymakers are the most influential mediators for the outcomes of this debate, the chapter subsequently examines three decades of neoliberal dominance in policy circles (Section 13.4). Given that free market theory and neoclassical economic assumptions form the basis for neoliberalism, the chapter consequently studies the use of free markets as an organisational principle for the actual framework of CSR (Section 13.5). This analysis will reveal the contrast between the potential, conceptual legal framework for CSR and the actual quasi-voluntary legal framework for CSR (Section 13.6). Next the chapter will examine the success of the current framework for CSR and reveal that, while CSR is bringing progress, it is having little effect in tackling a considerable number of structural unsustainabilities in the global economy (Section 13.7). The chapter will then consider to what extent these shortcomings can be attributed to the use of the free market as the organising principle for CSR (Section 13.8). Section 13.9 offers a number of reflections on self-interest assumptions as a core principle of the free market theory. The chapter will conclude by examining whether free markets are a feasible basis for a sustainable framework for CSR (Sections 13.10 and 13.11).

13.2   Conceptual framework for corporate social responsibility

It is understood that corporations can contribute to economic growth, innovation and job creation (Harrison 2013). However, it is equally noted that they can undermine human rights, harm the environment and destabilise the societies in which they operate (Stephens 2002). Generally speaking, when profits are prioritised over ethics and fairness, environmental or social stability, then one can argue that corporations have disembedded themselves from the societies in which they operate. CSR legislation and practices seek to address this corporate social and environmental misalignment by pressuring or incentivising corporations to consider the environmental and social impacts of their operations.

The potential area of operation for CSR is very broad. At its most basic, the scope of CSR can be conceptualised as a series of social and environmental norms (Eijsbouts 2011) that are perceived to be absent or insufficiently present in business behaviour. These norms reflect ethics and fairness as well as environmental and social stability and include, for example, fair wages, non-exploitation of labour, fair competition, employee co-operation collective bargaining, environmental protection and customer protection. Corporate irresponsibility can be interpreted as a departure from one of these social norms. In the academic literature, these norms have been translated into a wide range of corporate issues, including but not limited to human rights, environmental standards, labour standards, consumer and client issues, supply chain standards, corporate governance elements, community development, corruption and anti-competitive business practices.

The interpretation of the extent to which CSR should be involved in or tackle these elements depends considerably on the point of view of the commentator as well as the academic field of study that is used to analyse the subject matter (Horrigan 2010; Van Aartsen 2013). CSR has developed as a tapestry to which a large number of authors have added their personal views and positions. While the concept of CSR is intuitively straightforward, i.e. reducing, changing and removing business practices that are harmful to society and the environment, there is no single technical definition of CSR that is universally agreed upon (Horrigan 2010). While some may view this discussion as largely semantic because the coherency of the concept is sufficient, the difficulty is that – without a universal definition – different actors and authors will use the same terminology in situations where the same terms are in actual conflict (Campbell 2007). To give one example, someone could argue that a 30 per cent reduction in CO_2 emissions is a concrete effort in sustainable practices. Another could argue that this is not sustainable, in the same way that a bomb that does 30 per cent less collateral damage cannot be considered 'humane'. To avoid this form of confusion, I have decided to adopt Campbell's definition of CSR:

> I view corporations as acting in socially responsible ways if they do two things. First, they must not knowingly do anything that could harm their

stakeholders – notably, their investors, employees, customers, suppliers, or the local community within which they operate. Second, if corporations do cause harm to their stakeholders, they must then rectify it whenever the harm is discovered and brought to their attention. Rectification could be done voluntarily or in response to some sort of encouragement, such as moral suasion, normative pressure, legal threats, regulatory rulings, court orders, and the like. This is a definition that sets a minimum behavioral standard with respect to the corporation's relationship to its stakeholders, below which corporate behavior becomes socially irresponsible.

(Campbell 2007: 951)

This negatively formulated definition of CSR is useful for a number of reasons. First, it embodies the core concept of how businesses can act responsibly. Second, it does not limit the field of action in the case of corporate irresponsibility to a certain response grounded in a specific field of study. Third, it grants no room for what Campbell refers to as sustainability's 'blind spot', where, for example, businesses may give to charity and engage in sustainable practices to achieve a high sustainability rating on the one hand, but, launder money for drug cartels on the other.[1] Even though CSR has proved an elusive concept to universally define, it can certainly be subjected to a comprehensive legal analysis.

13.3   The abstract legal framework for corporate social responsibility

The potential legal framework for CSR may be best visualised as an interconnected network between societies, businesses and the government. In practice it is a rapidly changing and dynamic framework and, while a snapshot of the current regulations is a helpful indicator of the current legal status of CSR, we shall later see that the current regulations only provide a partial overview of the potential legal framework for CSR. It is for this reason that we now evaluate the abstract legal framework for CSR.

From a corporate perspective, the abstract legal framework for CSR can be conceptualised by means of social, legal and economic licences to operate (Eijsbouts 2011). First, the *economic* licence to operate requires that firms remain sufficiently profitable to prevent their insolvency. Second, the *legal* licence requires that firms operate within the confines of the law. Finally, the *social* licence requires that firms maintain an adequate reputation of good behaviour or level of product stewardship to prevent societal outrage that could result in, for example, boycotts or protests. While these three different licences can be differentiated, it is necessary to stress their interrelatedness. If a firm receives social pressure following unethical business practices, then the negative impact on the social licence to operate may pressure governments to pass new legislation. Here we see that the social licence may influence the legal licence. Similarly, the social licence can affect the economic licence when consumers decide to boycott goods and services.

The interplay between these licences has resulted in an unusual tapestry of CSR legislation that can range from entirely voluntary (i.e. the absence of any form of regulation) to the hardest forms of law embodied in criminal and administrative law (Eijsbouts 2011). While accepting that the potential regulatory options available for CSR are broad, we will later see that in practice a number of factors have given rise to the current – largely voluntary – legal framework for CSR. A structural analysis of CSR will reveal why this is the case.

At the first level of analysis, CSR overlaps with a number of other fields of law and regulation. This is due to CSR's multidisciplinary nature and poorly delineated subject matter. Labour law, corporate governance, corporate law, transparency, reporting requirements and environmental regulations are examples of fields of law that have the potential to overlap with the issues falling within the scope of the norms underlying CSR. While it is understood that many elements contained within this field of law are indirectly linked to the purpose of protecting stakeholders, society or the environment, it must still be recognised that these fields have emerged out of a subject matter that is their own. As a part of this process, their development directly and indirectly influences the development of the abstract legal framework for CSR.

The second level of analysis considers that each field of study that influences CSR is in turn influenced by deeper elements that lie beneath the surface. For example, corporate governance will be influenced by economics and agency theory. Transparency requirements will be balanced by the need for secrecy on the one hand and demands for transparency by stakeholders on the other. Labour law is influenced by the twin needs of employee protection and the political desirability of a flexible labour market. The legislative branch (as a collective) mediates between these various needs and positions and ultimately decides if and how legal reform is implemented. This, of course, describes an ideal situation, free from external influence. In reality, lobbying by interest groups, such as non-governmental organisations (NGOs), corporations, etc. acts as an external influence on the mediation process of the legislative branch. The success of these lobbying activities depends not only on the influencer's level of access (Bouwen 2002: 368), but also on the ideological susceptibility of a given politician to the arguments presented by the lobbyists (Prummer 2011).

It is for this reason that the third level of analysis takes into consideration ideology in the legislative branch. The ideological worldview adopted by legislators and policymakers is a deep-structure factor that most influences the diverse patchwork of legislation for CSR. Even though a broad range of regulatory options for CSR are available and discussed, the use or non-use of various forms of law or regulatory tools is determined according to theoretical and ideological perspectives at the highest level of the legislature. Therefore, before we can understand the current legal framework for CSR, it helps to examine the dominant socio-political theory of the last few decades – neoliberalism.

13.4 Neoliberal conceptions of society and the economy

The political landscape is a complex and dynamic concept that is impossible to conclusively define and delineate. While political decisions require a certain level of consensus, discussion and compromise, it is still possible to identify dominant voices within the political debate. The last decades during which CSR has developed from a minor concept into a full-fledged field of study occurred during the currently ongoing period of neoliberal dominance.

Before exploring this dominant political perspective, it is important to note that neoliberalism is not a simple set of policies and that it cannot be construed as a black and white boundary where a policy or individual is 'neoliberal' (Peck 2008). Rather, it is important to understand '"neoliberalism" as a political project, an ongoing endeavour to create a marketized social reality and obliterate the boundary between economy and society by means of economic reasoning and action' (Vallentin 2012a: 15). While neoliberal policies are rarely discussed in these terms, it is likely that many readers will recognise the policies and principles outlined in the examination of neoliberalism below.

The elections of Margaret Thatcher and Ronald Reagan in the 1980s marked the beginning of the international neoliberal 'project' which, notwithstanding resistance, proceeded to gain dominance in many Western and particularly Anglo-American economic and political circles (George 1999). Neoliberalism is a socio-political theory that views free markets as the 'organizing and regulative principle underlying the state' (Lemke 2001) and holds a deep conviction that any form of market interference is in effect the exercise of government totalitarianism given that it impedes the economic (and therefore democratic) freedom of its citizens (Van Aartsen 2013). Using neoclassical economic conceptions of the individual, neoliberalism construes free markets as the most desirable form of organisation for every aspect of human life, including, but not limited to, education, healthcare and politics (Vallentin 2012a). The assumption is that the 'economization' of every aspect of daily life will provide 'superior if not the best possible solutions to problems in society' (Vallentin 2012b: 7). Unlike laissez-faire-ism, neoliberal policies aim to construct the conditions and stimuli for optimal free market behaviour and outcomes (Van Horn and Mirowski 2009). Whether this is found in individual conditioning through the use of competitive schooling, hierarchies and incentives, or the deregulation of financial markets to improve capital mobility, neoliberalism has spent the last 30 years politically, socially and legally reshaping the national and international landscape to favour free markets.

Although neoliberalism models human behaviour on the basis of the rational, self-interested market actor, it also realises that human behaviour can be irrational and regularly fails to reflect this ideal. As such, neoliberalism also seeks to implement policies to stimulate rational and self-interested (market) behaviour in individuals (Van Horn and Mirowski 2009). This social and cultural 'engineering' is a dynamic policy process that rewards the population for expressing those behaviours required for effective free market functioning. To the extent that neoliberal policies can stimulate and condition self-interested behaviour, free and competitive markets will arise in appropriate regulatory environments as a 'natural' expression of human behaviour.

The recognition that markets can fail to reflect the ideal is also reflected in the economics of regulation. According to Philipsen (2010: 205), '[t]he economic literature generally distinguishes between four kinds of market failure: (i) information problems; (ii) externalities; (iii) the presence of public goods; and (iv) market power'. It is generally recognised that regulation may be necessary to solve these market failures by means of, for example, environmental regulation (externalities), consumer protection (information asymmetry), competition law (abuse of monopoly power) and the regulated production/consumption of public goods. According to the public interest theory of regulation, it is in the public interest to intervene and 'correct' these market failures provided that measures are focused and do not cause further interference in free market functioning (Philipsen 2010: 205). As an aside, it is interesting to note that market failures, formulated as such, are failures in achieving external conditions for free market functioning, rather than failures that could result from potential shortcomings inherent to free market theory. Examining market failures from an economic perspective is, of course, not necessarily neoliberal. In fact, many forms of regulation can be used to solve these market failures. As Philipsen (2010: 207) comments, '[t]he type of regulation to be used depends very much on the specific circumstances of a market'. I would extend this remark and add that the form of regulation adopted to solve market failures is also highly dependent on dominant ideologies in the political arena. In the case of neoliberalism, Vallentin (2012b: 7) explains that 'neoliberalism is not about *laissez-faire*; it is a call for vigilance, activism and perpetual intervention. It involves a reconfiguration as opposed to a retreat of the state, which is to say that deregulation always involves re-regulation'. Rather than focusing only on non-intervention or minimal intervention with regard to the market failures outlined above, neoliberal regulation seeks to 'impose market rule' (Vallentin 2012a: 13) by means of policies that stimulate competition and economic activities.

In terms of social policies, neoliberalism rewards competitive behaviour to condition the population to more closely reflect the behavioural ideal required by free markets. A competitive society, construed from a neoliberal perspective, is concerned with individuals each gaining competitive advantage over the other. Conceptualised as such, economic inequality is a stimulus for innovation and economic growth rather than an adverse consequence of a predatory economy (Vallentin 2012a: 13). From a neoliberal perspective, state regulations, laws and rules that seek to interfere with market rule (or its consequences) are undesirable. From an organisational perspective, policies not centred on competition or economic growth (for example inequality reducing measures, environmental regulation) interfere with free market functioning and therefore, by definition, undermine innovation, productivity and competitive behaviour (or rather, undermine overall societal happiness, consumption and economic success).

Consequently, neoliberal policies create a social and economic framework for free markets. Economic policies generally advocate a minimal state, deregulated markets, flexible labour and capital markets, etc. and are theoretically expected to generate the highest free market returns. As a complement to the free market framework, social policies are designed to reward materialism, competitive behaviour and economic productivity. The combination of these policies is conceived to generate high levels of productivity, wealth and consumption that will in turn provide the highest levels of utility in a competitive society consisting of self-interested individuals.

In a democracy, according to neoliberal reasoning, economic freedom is an essential element for political freedom (Friedman 1962). This belief is reflected in the economic theory of public choice. Public choice views politicians and voters as 'self-interested actors interacting in a market environment. According to this theory, voters vote for the party that most embodies their self-interest and politicians succeed in elections by aligning their political point of view and their statements in a manner that coincides with the largest number of votes' (Van Aartsen 2013: 31). 'Naturally' competitive individuals living in a free market society can express their multitude of preferences effectively through market action. 'The freedom to express these preferences results in a political market governed by democratic choice. The conclusion is that free markets, whose forms are determined by society's collection of individual preferences, allows for the maximal expression of democratic choice' (Van Aartsen 2013: 31). Every yuan, euro or dollar spent represents an exercise of free will that, on an aggregate scale, will shape markets and influence businesses, governments, etc. to follow the will of the people, as captured by the will of the market. Conceptualising democracy in this manner renders any market interference as not only inefficient, but also inherently undemocratic.

The reasoning above leads to a number of policy outcomes that advocate market and business deregulation, promotion of capital and labour market flexibility, tax cuts for highest incomes, privatisation and reduction in public spending/austerity, an emphasis on self-regulation and competition, market liberalisation and free trade (WHO 2013; Monbiot 2013; Van Aartsen 2013). To give an indication of the influence of neoliberalism, it can be noted that these policy approaches are advocated, *inter alia*, by the economic policy advisors at the World Bank, the International Monetary Fund (IMF), the European Commission, the European Central Bank (ECB), the World Trade Organization (WTO) and the Inter-American Bank for Development (Martinez and García 2000; Hurt 2012; Kotz and McDonough 2010; Hooghe and Marks 1997).

This chapter has previously discussed the conceptual framework for CSR. Given that the development of CSR occurred during neoliberal dominance, is there evidence of neoliberal influence on CSR? To evaluate this, it is necessary to first look at the institutions that hold a dominant voice within the realm of CSR.

13.5   Dominant views on corporate social responsibility

The European Commission (EC), OECD and the United Nations (UN) are highly influential with regard to the legal development of CSR. To a considerable extent, these are the bodies that produce advice and guidelines that inform and determine the legislative outcomes of the debates that are internal to the field of CSR. To understand CSR in its current form, we need to consider the theoretical perspective through which these bodies view CSR. In other words, how do they perceive CSR and its place within the legal framework? Subsequently we can analyse these perceptions in terms of neoliberal influence and the actual legal framework for CSR.

13.5.1   The European Commission: 'A renewed EU strategy 2011–2014 for Corporate Social Responsibility'

The European Commission Communication on CSR is a non-binding policy document that is designed to give business, society and governments information on the Commission's perspective and wishes for CSR. The EU strategy for CSR states as follows: 'Corporate social responsibility concerns actions by companies over and above their legal obligations towards society and the environment. Certain regulatory measures create an environment more conducive to enterprises voluntarily meeting their social responsibility' (EC 2011). While it is not directly referenced, the European open and competitive single market is an important contextual element within which European efforts for CSR take place. Within this context '[t]he development of CSR should be led by enterprises themselves' (EC 2011: 7). In line with this, the European Commission views CSR as strictly voluntary, taking place in a realm of operation that extends beyond the law. It recognises that there is a role for public regulation to stimulate the voluntary adoption of CSR by corporations.

The benefits to the EU of businesses' participation in CSR are generic and include a significant contribution 'to the European Union's treaty objectives of sustainable development and a highly competitive social market economy' (EC 2011: 3). For businesses 'A strategic approach to CSR is increasingly important to the competitiveness of enterprises. It can bring benefits in terms of risk management, cost savings, access to capital, customer relationships, human resource management, and innovation capacity' (EC 2011: 3). The document also refers a number of times to the competitive value of CSR within the self-professed social market society (EC 2011). It is noticeable that the structural benefits of CSR are regularly presented in *direct* economic terms and combined with *indirect* social and environmental benefits.

According to the same document 'Public authorities should play a supporting role through a smart mix of voluntary policy measures and, where necessary, complementary regulation, for example to promote transparency, create market incentives for responsible business conduct, and ensure corporate accountability' (EC 2011: 7). This smart mix of policy measures and complementary regulation is frequently referred to as 'meta-regulation' (Parker 2007), and is generally designed to facilitate or incentivise the adoption of social and environmental goals in corporate decision-making. It is supporting legislation that does not directly interfere with market functioning and corporate decision making.

13.5.2 Organisation for Economic Co-operation and Development – OECD Guidelines for Multinational Enterprises

The 2011 OECD issued its *Guidelines for Multinational Enterprises* (OECD 2011) that state: 'The Guidelines provide voluntary principles and standards for responsible business conduct consistent with applicable laws and internationally recognised standards' (OECD 2011). While the document does not refer explicitly to CSR, there is no doubt that it focuses on responsible business conduct (OECD 2011: 3). Even though the *Guidelines* themselves are binding on Member States, it is clearly stated that CSR consists of voluntary acts undertaken by corporations that promote social and environmental goals that are not strictly required by law (OECD 2011). The *Guidelines* also indicate that public authorities can provide a meta-regulatory environment to promote responsible business conduct. The form of such an environment is described as follows: 'The ability of multinational enterprises to promote sustainable development is greatly enhanced when trade and investment are conducted in a context of open, competitive and appropriately regulated markets' (OECD 2011: 14). Appropriate regulation is unspecified, but, given the reference to open and competitive (free) markets, it is not an unreasonable assumption that appropriate regulation would reflect the economics of regulation and stimulate competition and economic activity rather than interfere with market functioning (as examined in Section 13.4). As we can see, the OECD (similar to the EC) emphasises the value of voluntary CSR, within a free market context.

13.5.3 United Nations Global Compact

Launched in July 2000, the UN Global Compact is a leadership platform for the development, implementation and disclosure of responsible and sustainable corporate policies and practices. Endorsed by chief executives, it seeks to align business operations and strategies everywhere with ten universally accepted principles in the areas of human rights, labour, environment and anti-corruption. With nearly 8,000[2] corporate participants in over 140 countries, the UN Global Compact is the world's largest voluntary corporate sustainability initiative. (UN 2011: 2)

The United Nations Global Compact is an international initiative started by the UN to promote the adoption and dissemination of best practices, information and policies regarding CSR. As well as requiring that business participants adhere to its ten universally accepted principles, the Global Compact also requires each participant to issue a yearly *Communication on Progress* regarding the implementation of these principles (UN 2011). As indicated by the quote above, the Global Compact is a voluntary initiative.

The Global Compact document, written by law firm Latham & Watkins LLP, on 'The importance of voluntarism' indicates that while voluntary initiatives are not a substitute for effective regulation, they can 'play an essential role in the drive to encourage business to embrace corporate responsibility and business ethics' (Latham & Watkins 2009: 1). The document further notes that: 'Voluntarism can assist in embedding universal principles of ethical globalization in markets and economies', that it 'can foster competition among organizations to be better corporate citizens' (Latham & Watkins 2009: 2) and can 'help identify material objectives and drive long-term business success' (Latham & Watkins 2009: 3). Additionally, it notes that voluntarism 'should never be a substitute for effective regulation' (Latham & Watkins 2009: 1). The document clarifies that voluntary CSR, as promoted by internal and external (meta-regulatory) drivers, can play a helpful role in promoting ethical business practices in globalised (free and open) markets (Latham & Watkins 2009). It also notes that voluntary CSR can help companies 'build brand equity', 'foster relationships with local communities', 'inspire their employees' and 'find new revenue sources' (Latham & Watkins 2009: 3). Voluntary CSR can also 'limit the risks and costs of corporate responsibility' and 'help bridge regulatory gaps' (Latham & Watkins 2009: 2–3). On the whole, the UN Global Compact places primary emphasis on the benefits of the implementation of the 'ten principles'. Secondary emphasis is placed on the competitive, social, and economic benefits for companies participating in CSR.

13.5.4   *Insights from the dominant views on CSR*

The perspectives offered by the OECD, EC and the UN Global Compact are highly influential within the theoretical landscape for CSR. The general consensus on the appropriate legal form for CSR (voluntary) among these bodies effectively limits the active sphere of CSR reform to the realm of meta-regulatory nudges and voluntary initiatives within a free market context. It is worth noting that the EU and OECD countries are home to the vast majority of multinational corporations. As such, the *OECD Guidelines* and *EU Commission Communication* form the basis for an 'actual', rather than an abstract, legal framework for CSR.

Each of these institutions emphasises the value of free markets and does not make a suggestion that their operation should be interfered with. Rather, CSR should be viewed as a complementary practice to promote sustainability within the free market framework. To this extent, it can be stated that – similar to neoliberal thinking – CSR currently appears to be organised around the principle of the free market. We can look for further evidence of this in the actual legal framework for CSR.

13.6 Practical legal framework for corporate social responsibility

Keeping in mind the potentially broad range of regulatory options, we are now able to formulate a general legal framework for CSR as it currently operates. As noted earlier, the current legal framework for CSR is a reflection of the opinions of dominant policymakers and institutions such as those discussed above as regards the appropriate role, binding nature and scope for CSR. As noted earlier, these opinions and decisions are influenced by lobbying groups such as corporations and NGOs. Under the current legal framework for CSR, the overlap with other fields of law which touch on social and environmental issues are not to be considered a part of the actual legal framework for CSR.

Therefore, at the first level of approximation, the current legal framework for CSR can be characterised as voluntary given that CSR practices generally extend to socially and environmentally desirable business practices that go beyond the scope of the law. The absence of strict legal requirements within the approaches to CSR adopted by the EU, OECD and UN Global Compact has strengthened the perception of CSR as a 'voluntary' business practice. However, if we look closer we can see that the interconnectedness of the various licences to operate drives firms to adopt ethically sound practices, even if they are not legally required to do so (Eijsbouts 2011; Parker 2007).

These drivers (licences) are complemented by the use of meta-regulation. As advocated in particular by the European Commission and the OECD, these smart policy mixes consist of measures and complementary regulation which are designed to facilitate or incentivise the adoption of social and environmental goals in corporate decision-making (Parker 2007). An example of meta-regulation would be to require and/or enforce the accurate reporting of non-financial information, even if the disclosure of non-financial information was not a legal requirement. As Parker (2007: 213) explains, meta-regulation:

> can also entail any form of regulation (whether by tools of state law or other mechanisms) that regulates any other form of regulation. Thus it might include legal regulation of self-regulation (e.g., putting an oversight board above a self-regulatory professional association), non-legal methods of 'regulating' internal corporate self-regulation or management (e.g., voluntary accreditation to codes of good conduct, etc.), the

regulation of national law-making by transnational bodies (such as the EU), and so on.

If one considers the use of meta-regulations in combination with social pressure from consumers and NGOs, and the interrelatedness of the licences to operate then, at the second level of approximation, CSR can be considered 'quasi-voluntary'.

Despite its quasi-voluntary (hereafter also referred to as voluntary) nature the absence of formal corporate law requirements related to CSR has meant that corporate governance has emerged as one of the primary vehicles for the adoption of ethical and social standards in corporate decision-making (De Hoo 2011). If one agrees with the premise that CSR should be voluntary, then linking CSR and corporate governance is logical. If a corporation's actions occur at the expense of society, the economy at large or the environment, then a failure in the internal structures of the corporation may be at the heart of the problem. Assuming that no laws are broken but that harm still occurs, then the voluntary integration of ethical norms and values into corporate governance structures provides an attractive means to promote CSR. One can argue that this reasoning lies at the basis of the proliferation of Codes of Conduct and similar voluntary corporate guidelines, standards, etc. at the national, international and individual business level (Chatterji and Listokin 2007).

In light of this analysis the current legal framework for CSR can be conceptualised as a quasi-voluntary framework that promotes and incentivises the adoption of extra-legal social and environmental standards within the boundaries of the free market.

13.7 The impact on discourse and success of quasi-voluntary CSR

Having provided a general overview of the legislative and conceptual framework for CSR, it is now time to ask what the impact is of this 'quasi-voluntary' approach and whether it has been successful in tackling issues related to corporate unsustainability. While most businesses do not engage in what is generally considered socially irresponsible behaviour, there is significant evidence that CSR is failing to tackle many of the deeper unsustainabilities at the heart of corporate practice and the economic system. This evidence will be discussed below. Furthermore, the general consensus that CSR should be quasi-voluntary has considerable implications for the scope of debate for CSR practice and legal reform.

Please note that there are many businesses, individuals, NGOs, politicians and governments that are making concrete commitments and efforts to support sustainable practices. There are many who want a stronger legal framework for CSR or are making the most of the current framework. Nevertheless it must still be asked whether quasi-voluntary CSR is actually working. This section should not be misinterpreted as a negative reflection on those dedicating their efforts to a sustainable future within the current framework for CSR.

13.7.1   Limited scope for discussion of regulatory reform

In terms of the internal debate on CSR, the mutual support of dominant institutions for voluntary CSR within a free market context is a decision that, in lieu of the consideration of broader regulatory options, normalises quasi-voluntary CSR. The effect of this is that quasi-voluntary CSR within a free market framework is made to appear natural and inevitable, relegating proponents for stronger regulatory options for CSR to the fringes of the discussion.

This effect is strengthened almost inevitably because CSR practitioners seek to provide solutions within the framework advocated by the dominant policymakers, seldom desiring or able to engage in discussions concerning the validity of the framework itself. Instead, practitioners are compelled to evaluate the success and progress of CSR as well as proposals for CSR activities within this 'normalised' free market framework. In doing so, practitioners are implicitly consenting to and further normalising the free market framework for CSR. We can see evidence for this in the discussions concerning the 'business case' for CSR.

The dominant approach within the academic business literature on CSR has been to analyse and promote what is known as the 'business case' for CSR – where businesses can do well (financially) by doing good (ethically) (McWilliams *et al.* 2006). For CSR proponents seeking to promote the inclusion of social and environmental factors in a business environment, the most straightforward method to do so within a voluntary framework is to indicate that CSR-related actions and policies are profitable (Van Aartsen 2013). A reflection of the prominence of the business case is that the benefits of CSR are regularly couched in economic terms, as mirrored in the positions of the European Commission, the OECD and the UN Global Compact.

Elaborate theories have demonstrated potential cost savings, reputational benefits, efficiency improvements, innovative developments, etc., resulting from voluntary adherence to stricter environmental and social standards. Despite this, an oft-quoted meta-analysis by Margolis *et al.* (2007) found no conclusive link between businesses engaging in CSR and financial performance. Furthermore, the meta-analysis found a potential reverse correlation between financial performance and CSR expenditure (Margolis *et al.* 2007). In other words, the idea that businesses can do well by doing good is still missing a concrete factual link. This supposition remains tenuous and may even be inversely dependent on business success, where businesses with better financial performance are more likely to engage in CSR practices.

Despite this fundamental 'missing link' between the success of CSR in theory and in practice, few want to face the implications of this shortcoming on the sustainable value of quasi-voluntary CSR. It is still referred to in the *EC Communication on CSR* (2011) and few would be pleased to admit that CSR efforts may not be having as large an impact as they would hope or like. Without this link, an ongoing focus on the business case and the market value of quasi-voluntary CSR is a form of wishful thinking that renders the adoption of extra-legal social and environmental standards secondary to profit motives (MacLeod 2005), while simultaneously creating an illusion of normality and success which limits discourse and controversy, thereby blocking meaningful reform.

13.7.2   *Limited participation and doubts concerning the quality of reporting*

The EU currently leads on CSR, boasting the largest number of companies providing non-financial reports. But this progress cannot necessarily be equated with the achievement of sustainability goals. Although '2,500 European companies publish CSR or sustainability reports ... this is still only a small fraction of the 42,000 large companies operating in the EU' (EC 2011). Similarly, the UN Global Compact, as the largest CSR initiative in the world, has attracted only 10,000 business participants[3] – out of over 60,000-plus multinational corporations and their '800,000 subsidiaries and millions of suppliers' (Maguire 2011).

Even though the number of business participants is increasing, research shows that participation and non-financial reporting do not necessarily give a reliable indication of actual sustainability performance. Research by Arnold suggests that: 'there seems to be a greater focus on benchmarking of reporting activity rather than on benchmarking the results achieved by the companies in the particular areas of concern' (Arnold 2008: 26). Furthermore, the scale and structure of the information reported may be so comprehensive that stakeholders are confused rather than informed by the report (Arnold 2008: 25).

Additionally, CSR reporting seems to fail to take into account gross irresponsible behaviour by firms that is unreported or buried. HSBC, for example, notes on its website that 'As a global organisation, we have an impact on countries right across the world. We ensure our business is sustainable by taking a long-term view; valuing our employees; addressing the direct and indirect impact we have on the environment and investing in the communities we serve'.[4] Nevertheless in 2012, they paid a $1.9 billion dollar fine for laundering money for drug cartels.[5] Following the emergence of these practices they promised in 2010 to implement appropriate safeguards to prevent these sorts of actions. Despite this, in 2013 a whistleblower at HSBC stepped forward with evidence that the bank is currently still laundering money for terrorist groups (Halasa 2013). While this issue still requires a formal legal decision, it does make it appropriate to question the value or semantic accuracy of sustainability reporting by companies engaged in gross violations of perceived or actual social and/or environmental standards. Although these issues are frequently presented as a small number of 'bad apples', the grossly irresponsible behaviour related to persistent exploitative labour practices (Apple, Lidl, Gap, H&M (Mishkin 2013; Paige 2013)), LIBOR, forex, and ISDAfix manipulation (RBS, HSBC, Deutsche Bank, JP Morgan Bank, Citibank (Smythe 2013; *The Economist* 2013)) or continual safety violations (BP (Mouawad 2010)) indicates a level of systemic violation that CSR is not currently equipped to deal with. CSR may even contribute to the issue by obfuscating actual corporate social performance. While many companies and employees will not be involved in such behaviour, it would be wrong to treat such violations as fully isolated incidents.

13.7.3 *Unsustainable production and emission patterns*

Many products are still produced unsustainably and planned obsolescence practices remain largely unchanged. Since 2000, overall CO_2 emissions by OECD countries have decreased only marginally, largely due to the impact of decreased consumption following the financial crisis (OECD 2013). While there are positive shifts related to supply chain analyses and product lifecycle assessments, their scope of operation is only partial. The overall lifetime of a good is rarely considered as a factor for sustainable practice (Cooper 2005). The focus is rather on the minimisation of resources required for production. Regardless of these improvements, the prevalence of planned obsolescence practices represents a significant barrier to achieving a sustainable economy.

Under planned obsolescence – whether it is overtly stated or not – consumption and sales are promoted by designing products, e.g. a lightbulb to last for only a limited duration. Even though we can produce goods with more replaceable components that will also last significantly longer, standard economic incentives currently point in the wrong direction and make it profitable for firms to develop products which must be replaced after a relatively short period of time. As Cooper (2005: 57) notes 'planned obsolescence, the deliberate curtailment of a product's life span, has become commonplace, driven by, for example, a need for cost reductions in order to meet "price points", the convenience of disposability, and the appeal of fashion'. One could also argue that companies must currently participate in planned obsolescence to remain competitive and register continuous growth. Thus far, CSR and other regulatory choices, have failed to provide a long-term solution to this catch-22 problem. Abandoning highly unsustainable planned obsolescence practices would significantly reduce consumption and have a severely detrimental impact on economic growth and employment under current economic models.

13.7.4   Tax evasion and illicit capital flows

Other elements not successfully tackled by CSR include tax evasion and illicit outflows of capital. While it is considered normal behaviour for companies to seek to reduce their tax payments, this practice currently constitutes an enormous social externality. Despite the efforts of CSR proponents to strengthen the moral compass of corporate Practice, Global Financial Integrity (GFI) estimated that, in 2009, illicit capital outflows (as a result of mispricing, etc.) resulted in the illegal transfer of US$1.3 trillion from developing to developed countries (Kar and Curcio 2011: i). According to the 2010 GFI report: 'The proceeds of commercial tax evasion, mainly through trade mispricing, are by far the largest component [of illicit outflows], at some 60 to 65 percent of the global total' (Kar and Cartwright-Smith 2010: 1). In Europe it is estimated that the EU loses approximately 1 trillion euros in taxes annually due to corporate tax evasion (Baker 2013). Furthermore, a 2012 study found that, in the run up to 2010, the global super-rich had placed at least US$21 trillion dollars in tax havens.[6] The rise of CSR appears to have done little to stem the tide of the financial 'grey' area, which is frequently used to avoid liability for illegal money transfers, and tax evasion.

The sums and profits involved with illicit capital practices are large enough to ask whether any economic actors would voluntarily forego the benefits of this legal grey area. The following quote from Devinney (2009: 49) indicates that voluntary CSR approaches may fail to understand the nature of corporations: 'A potentially naive assumption underlying CSR is that firms are guided by society and do not deliberately manipulate that society for their own benefit. It is the natural vice of corporations that they gravitate toward solving problems from which economic rents can be claimed'. Ultimately, a corporation is guided primarily by its bottom line and, as the business case for CSR demonstrated, social and environmental concerns do not overrule this self-interested behaviour that resides at the heart of modern corporations (Chatterji and Listokin 2007).

13.7.5   Reflections on the current framework for quasi-voluntary CSR

Politicians have collectively and independently determined CSR's quasi-voluntary structure, but seem resigned with regards to the significant issues left unchallenged by the current approach to CSR. At this point it is important to recall that, while the dominant consensus on CSR appears to exclude mandatory inclusion of social and environmental standards, in theory there is a full spectrum of regulatory options available. These options range from corporate law, criminal and administrative law to self-regulation, transparency requirements and even a reliance on good business conduct (Eijsbouts 2011). However, despite the environmental and social issues which the global community faces and which remain unaddressed by CSR politicians during this period of neoliberal dominance have made an overall choice to follow neoliberalism and use free markets as the organising principle for quasi-voluntary CSR.

While some argue that neoliberalism is no longer a significant policy factor, and that its influence has waned over the years, we can find many examples which refute this. Iceland's collapse followed neoliberal financial deregulatory reforms (Wade and Sigurgeirsdottir 2012) – neoliberal reforms for which it received much praise from the international business and political community right up until the moment of financial collapse (Wade and Sigurgeirsdottir 2012). More recently, these policies are being applied throughout the Eurozone with little success to speak of in terms of economic growth (Van Aartsen 2013). According to Sizemore (2013) the implementation of neoliberal policies has even resulted in Greece being downgraded to an emerging market. In similar fashion, the success stories of the economic development in, for example, India, China, Taiwan and South Korea are also contrary to international trends on the best policies and approaches to economic development (Hausman and Rodrik 2003). Regardless, the influence of neoliberalism remains strong.

Despite contrary examples and evidence of neoliberal failures, neoliberalism itself has proven highly resistant to criticism. Its adaptive nature has meant that its forms and expressions have regularly changed around the core belief in the superiority of free markets, rendering consistent criticism difficult. What remains constant, however, is that neoliberals consider free markets to be infallible. Market failures are not caused by inconsistencies or shortcomings of free market theory and assumptions, but are rather a consequence of the failure of governments, individuals and societies in fulfilling their supporting role for free markets (see Section 13.4). It is for this reason that dominant policymakers seldom consider whether free markets are actually a feasible organisational basis for CSR and a sustainable economy. It is for this reason that we now turn to consider how free market constraints have affected CSR.

13.8 Quasi-voluntary CSR operating within free market constraints

Free market proponents remain strongly opposed to stronger forms of regulation to implement the social and environmental standards related to CSR. Rather than compelling old markets to shift to sustainability through assumedly 'ineffective' state action and regulation, it is considered preferable to educate consumers and allow them to vote with their dollars to induce companies to compete to develop more sustainable products (as explained in Section 13.4). A neoliberal would argue that this is democracy in action, combined with a healthy dose of sustained economic growth during the (necessary) transition to sustainability. This transition is assisted through non-interventionist meta-regulatory options: The language used in the OECD's *Guidelines for Multinational Corporations*, the EU's *Commission Communication on a renewed strategy for CSR 2011–2014*, and the documents released by the UN Global Compact support this view.

By surrendering the development of quasi-voluntary CSR to free markets and corporations, we see that this allows corporations to determine the direction and development of CSR. Indeed, the EC's (2011) *Communication on CSR* states that: 'The development of CSR should be led by enterprises themselves'. This reveals that corporate freedom (or rather, economic freedom) is one of the intentions behind quasi-voluntary CSR. In using this freedom, Levy and Kaplan believe that multinational corporations 'have sought to shape the meaning of CSR in ways that deflect its radical potential, by stressing voluntarism rather than legal obligation or public accountability' (Levy and Kaplan 2008: 6–7). This freedom has also allowed corporations to selectively use CSR where it is profitable and can be used as a competitive tool. Devinney (2009) notes that corporations have influenced the development of legislation to structure it in a way so that it constitutes a barrier to entry for new and foreign competitors. Structuring legislation in such a manner undermines the emergence of new competitors, protecting the vested corporate interests that have already been established. The 'grandfathering' in the European Emissions Trading Scheme that grants larger permits to established firms also constitutes a similar barrier to new competition (Castree 2009). Mining companies have used their CSR activities to justify and lobby for standards that granted them an 'oligopolistic lock' since these standards 'imposed disproportionate costs on smaller rivals' (Devinney 2009: 53). Fooks *et al.* (2011: 1) reason that CSR is 'a form of corporate political activity' since 'CSR strategies can enable access to and dialogue with policymakers and provide opportunities for issue definition'. Although one perceives that the true purpose of CSR is to embed social norms into corporate activities, the current voluntary approach allows firms to decide if and how these social norms are embedded.

Although corporations have not always been designed solely to generate economic returns, the general rise of shareholder primacy during the neoliberal era has globally driven the institutional development of firms in this direction (Ireland 2005). Since corporations are increasingly institutionally designed to propagate self-interest and maximise profit, if they integrate CSR they are inclined do so for their own benefit – an economic model which emphasises aggressive competition and self-interest necessitates this. Although there exist partial exceptions to the profit motive for corporate actions, such as the business judgment rule (Branson 2001) and the 'enlightened shareholder model' (Harper Ho 2010) now adopted in the US and UK respectively, the current legal framework for CSR, with its soft nature, in practice still allows firms in most situations to continue prioritising profits over social norms. The emphasis on the business case for CSR guarantees this since businesses are advised to engage in CSR for profit motives.

The Margolis *et al.* (2007) meta-analysis discussed above suggested that large corporations which have higher profits are more likely to participate in CSR, implying a reverse causality for the link between CSR and corporate financial performance. The relevance of this is that the most profitable firms will be most able to participate in CSR and use it as a competitive tool to influence legislation and restrict the emergence of new competitors and/or the performance of other competitors. The European Commission's *Communication on CSR* notes that it is important for the EU and national governments to 'facilitate the better integration of social and environmental considerations into public procurement [...] without undermining the principle of awarding contracts to the most economically advantageous tender' (EC 2011: 11). Although they note that public procurement should not discriminate against small and medium-sized enterprises (SMEs), the reality is that large firms, due to their economies of scale and low cost of capital, are 'the most economically advantageous' and remain the most likely to receive government projects. This grants corporations further access to governments and policymakers, paving a way for them to influence and limit the agenda, potentially allowing them to use CSR 'to shape government policy' (Fooks *et al.* 2011: 3). Furthermore, Steurer (2010: 7) notes that within the current free market framework for CSR 'If economic instruments are employed in the context of CSR they are not concerned with taxes that are statutory for all, but rather with tax breaks and subsidies'. Subsidies, of course, are contrary to the concept of a free, open and efficient market as advocated by free market proponents.

Another crucial element that undermines 'free' market functioning, especially in the US context, is a hyper-commercialised and deregulated media. One of the most powerful tools for raising public awareness is the media, but McChesney (2011: 3) notes for the US context that 'as the control in each [media] market became concentrated among one or two or three owners, and as ownership concentrated nationally, all media came to reflect the interests of owners and advertisers, rather than diverse interests of any community'. Chomsky (2002: 29) states more poignantly that: 'The [global] media are a corporate monopoly'. Although the media certainly plays an informative role in highlighting corporate malfeasance and the need for CSR, there may be a selection bias stemming from their corporate ownership:

> most of [the media] attracting the largest audiences are owned by a few transnational companies and serve a commercial purpose, selling audience eyeballs to advertisers. Not surprisingly, content that empowers citizens and reports critically on government – and particularly corporate – power is rare. What media cover least [...] is their own concentrated ownership and hypercommercialism.
>
> (McChesney quoted by McManus 2009: 233)

Corporate media ownership and media reliance on opinion leaders such as politicians and corporate PR representatives may result in a selection bias that prevents mass media from being independent from corporate interests. In *Rich Media, Poor Democracy*, McChesney blames neoliberalism's market fundamentalism for the current commercialisation of news and corporate bias in mass media (McManus 2009). The corporate influence on media and journalism undermines the social licence and the 'not quite voluntary' nature of the current legal framework for CSR. Media firms rely heavily on advertising for income; they will be reticent to criticise the large corporations that, through advertising, have become their primary source of income. According to McChesney (2001: 2) 'neoliberal policies [...] invariably [...] call for communication media and communication markets to be deregulated. What this means in practice is that they are re-regulated to serve corporate interests'. The larger the corporation, the more money it can use for advertising and the more likely it is to have more positive or less negative media coverage. Media bias favours profits at the expense of a well-informed public, a public that must be well informed to maximise the effectiveness of quasi-voluntary CSR.

These examples and general arguments run contrary to the free market reasoning and rhetoric that justifies a voluntary approach to CSR. What we do see is that these policies favour actors that are most capable of political, economic and monetary competition. This does not disregard that the vast majority of corporate employees are well intentioned and considerate of the society and environment. There will be many who are passionate about CSR and the ethical and social norms which form part of its conceptual basis. However, what we have seen above provides evidence that the implementation of quasi-voluntary CSR by corporations acting within a self-interest oriented free market framework has regularly taken place for less than altruistic reasons. This insight invites us to critically analyse neoliberal self-interest assumptions.

13.9 Reflections on self-interest

Self-interest is an idea that has taken hold of Western political, social and economic thought for hundreds of years (Sears and Funk 1991). In line with this idea it is understandable that self-interest as an organisational basis for human behaviour has proven very attractive and has been largely unquestioned. Other reflections of self-interest in organisational design are revealed in corporate legal theories relating to shareholder primacy, and enlightened self-interest models and, at a practical level, in the use of bonuses and other incentives to stimulate and reward 'correct' behaviour (Hansmann and Kraakman 2000). These theories and models appeal to an individual's material self-interest to achieve (theoretically) optimal and efficient results. As discussed above, neoliberalism has also adopted self-interest as the norm for human behaviour and used social policies to promote competition and market-oriented behaviour. As Peck notes while commenting on the neoliberal leaning Chicago School of Economics 'A Chicagoan [...] looks continuously for new ways to introduce the market system of rewards and penalties' (Peck 2008: 17). This economisation or marketisation of as many aspects of life as possible is designed to integrate self-interested market behaviour into as many social, political and economic interactions as possible.

Self-interest assumptions, however, have not been adopted without critique (Miller 1999). A number of authors over the years have argued that self-interest theories are self-fulfilling and are creating the results that they purport to be a natural state of affairs (Miller 1999). The organisational design of institutions and laws reflects the perspective of human nature held by its designers (Ferraro and Pfeffer 2005). Consequently, actors must adapt to the behavioural assumptions that underlie these systems in order to succeed. Free market systems are based on the assumption that individuals are self-interested and therefore, individuals operating under free market conditions are rewarded socially or materially for expressions of self-interest (Ferraro and Pfeffer 2005). While the intention is to promote efficient and competitive behaviour, the unintended consequences may be more destructive than is generally assumed.

Studies have suggested that the degree of individual expression of self-interest is a form of learned behaviour and that human behaviour cannot be accurately replicated through pure self-interest principles (Ferraro and Pfeffer 2005). Even though the self-interest conceptualisation is widely held, research shows that people are also concerned with procedural fairness, the impact of collective outcomes over personal outcomes, and whether laws and policies reflect personal values rather than merely promote individual material well-being (Miller and Ratner 1998). Furthermore, it was found that individuals who are highly self-interested are more prone to corrupt and free-riding behaviour (Ferraro and Pfeffer 2005). At a global level, these undesirable behaviours may be reinforced through neoliberal social policies and the use of free market theory as an organisational principle.

The discussion on neoliberal theory revealed that governments play a significant role in structuring economic and social interactions. In the case of neoliberalism, this restructuring has occurred to favour and promote free markets and competitive behaviour. As such, what some would call 'free markets' are in fact markets that are structured to favour the most competitive individuals and institutions in our societies. By extension, neoliberalism reconstructs societies to favour those who are the most self-interested. It is worth noting that neoliberalism narrowly interprets self-interest as a form of rational egoism motivated by the materialist desires of the individual (Van Aartsen 2013). This individualist approach to self-interest (as opposed to a potentially alternative form of enlightened collective self-interest) is reflected in neoliberal restructuring. Having said this, organisational models of self-interest, of course, do not preclude collective outcomes *per se*. It is not uncommon that when a majority or large group of people demand a certain form of environmental regulation that it is indeed passed.

The shortcomings of self-interest assumptions have not gone unnoticed in economic circles. However, the implication of these insights has thus far not resulted in a fundamental reform of traditional, neoclassical economic theory. Self-interest critiques have, in particular, emerged in the field of behavioural economics and the related field of behavioural law and economics. As behavioural law and economics scholars Jolls, Sunstein and Thaler (1998: 1471) note '[e]conomic analysis of law usually proceeds under the assumptions of neoclassical economics. But empirical evidence gives much reason to doubt these assumptions; people exhibit bounded rationality, bounded self-interest, and bounded willpower'. Rather than reforming economic theory, Jolls *et al.* (1998: 1475) explain that '[b]ehavioral economics is a form of economics, and our goal is to strengthen the predictive and analytic power of law and economics, not to undermine it'. Behavioural economics has an empirical focus and seeks to improve the accuracy of predictions regarding human behaviour. In doing so, the focus is not to understand human behaviour but to find a more accurate description with which traditional (neoclassical) economic models can be updated (Berg and Gigerenzer 2010). This is confirmed in Jolls, Sunstein and Thaler's (1998: 1474) statement that 'behavioural economics allows us to model and predict behavior relevant to law with the tools of traditional economic analysis, but with more accurate assumptions about human behavior, and more accurate predictions and prescriptions about law'. Berg and Gigerenzer (2010) criticise behavioural economics for being an elaboration on neoclassical economics rather than a new empirical discipline. They reason that 'the dominant method in behavioural economics can be better described as filtering observed action through otherwise neoclassical constrained optimization problems with new arguments and parameters in the utility function'. Abrams and Keren (2009: 2018–19) agree, noting that behavioural law and economics 'sees departures from rationality not as passing occurrences, but as the products of flawed decisional heuristics, which are pervasive but potentially corrigible'. While there are departures from this approach in the behavioural law and economics scholarship, the dominant part still remains within the neoclassical frame of thought (Abrams and Keren 2009). While the insights from behavioural law and economics would seem to challenge neoclassical/neoliberal self-interest assumptions regarding the individual, their application to improve economic modelling has neutralised their radical potential. Rather than arguing that economic models are incomplete and should be reformed because they do not reflect human behaviour, a converse argument is made that human behaviour is imperfect and policies should incorporate/ameliorate these imperfections to achieve greater coherence in the application of economic models. This resonates closely with neoliberal desires to implement policies to condition human behaviour such that it more closely reflects the behavioural ideals contained in free market theory.

The institutionalisation of self-interest in association with free market oriented social and economic policies is in inherent conflict with achieving sustainability through quasi-voluntary, free market CSR. One can argue that we are relying on an egocentric and destructive side of human nature to serve the public good, while seeking to correct for negative behaviour by further institutionalising self-interest norms that contribute to the underlying unsustainability and corruption in the first place. In other words, the use of free markets as an organisational principle stimulates self-destructive behaviour, even as it attempts to distort and 'correct' natural human behaviour. This behaviour, as we have seen above, stimulates corruption and free-riding behaviour and appears antithetical to the concept of CSR. In light of these insights, it should be understood that quasi-voluntary CSR structurally places self-interest and profits above the social and environmental norms that should form the legal foundation for CSR. Whether intended or not, this is a consequence which flows naturally from CSR being subsumed within the general free market framework.

Neoliberal restructuring towards a competitive society occurs at the expense of those less able to compete, such as the poor and vulnerable or those who are less productive (or rather, less profit-maximising and self-interested). Conversely, if we look at global trends, such as rising wealth and income inequality (Walton and Seddon 2008), environmental degradation which primarily affects the poor (United Nations Water 2011; Hutchings and Reynolds 2004; International Union for the Conservation of Nature 2007), increases in chief executive officer (CEO) pay (Smith and Kuntz 2013), banks which are 'too big to fail' and 'too big to jail' (Shaughnessy 2012), we see that the 'free' market system has proven hugely beneficial to those most able to compete – large corporations and institutions, and wealthy and powerful individuals (Merino *et al.* 2010). In an economy marked by neoliberal policies and the organisational value of free markets the strongest and most capable of economic, political and financial competition are guaranteed to succeed over all other actors.

13.10 Corporate social responsibility, free market reflections and the performance of neoliberal policies

It is important to recognise that few would make the argument that the globalised economy is actually a free market economy. However, there is a general supposition that the globalised economy, through further liberalisation (and neoliberal) policies will approach more and more closely the free market ideal. How well have the past 30 years of neoliberal dominance fared in reshaping the global economy in the image of free markets?

Vitali, Glattfelder and Battiston note in their 2011 study of the control network of global corporations that 'transnational corporations form a giant bow-tie structure and that a large portion of control flows to a small tightly-knit core of financial institutions. This core can be seen as an economic "super-entity" that raises new important issues both for researchers and policy makers' (2011: 1). Their analysis finds that almost 40 per cent of the economic value of global multinational corporations is 'held, via a complicated web of ownership relations, by a group of 147 [corporations] in the core, which has almost full control over itself' (Vitali *et al.* 2011: 6). Of this core, 75 per cent are financial institutions including Barclays PLC, JPMorgan Chase & Co, Deutsche Bank, Goldman Sachs, Morgan Stanley, Lloyds, ING and others. Vitali, Glattfelder and Battiston also note that '[s]ince many [transnational corporations] in the core have overlapping domains of activity, the fact that they are connected by ownership relations could facilitate the formation of blocs, which would hamper market competition' (Vitali *et al.* 2011: 6–7).

The success and failure of this economic super-entity is intertwined – competition amongst each other is not in their financial interest. In light of this information, the free market concept is not only inaccurate, but may even be harmful by continually reinforcing the misrepresented state of the global economy. Financial manipulations by members of this entity contributed to and exacerbated the financial crisis, cost taxpayers billions in subsidies (bailouts), distorted prices and led to a considerable number of other direct and indirect externalities (Taibbi 2013). The alignment of interests within the entity is also likely to have resulted in more difficult access to factors of productivity for 'outsiders', or easier access to factors of production for 'insiders' – creating potentially significant barriers to entry in the process. Looking at the interconnected global economy as a whole, it seems conceptually more related to a collusive network than to a 'level playing field' where 'individual' corporations are 'competing' fairly for profits. But what about the overall success of neoliberal policies and the free market as an organising principle?

> Friedrich Hayek, Milton Friedman and their disciples – in a thousand business schools, the IMF, the World Bank, the OECD and just about every modern government – have argued that the less governments tax the rich, defend workers and redistribute wealth, the more prosperous everyone will be. Any attempt to reduce inequality would damage the efficiency of the market, impeding the rising tide that lifts all boats. The apostles have conducted a 30-year global experiment, and the results are now in. Total failure.
>
> (Monbiot 2013)

First to note is that neoliberalism has contributed to greater levels of inequality. According to the UN Conference on Trade and Development's *(UNCTAD) Trade and Development Report 2012* 'over the past three decades, income inequality increased dramatically, particularly in developed countries, reaching levels not observed since the 1920s' (UNCTAD 2012: 37). Second, the economic performance during the period of neoliberalism compares 'unfavourably with those achieved during the post-war boom' (Kotz and McDonough 2010: 6; Palley 2004: 6). The *UNCTAD Report 2012* notes that for a selection of developed countries[7] the average corporate income tax rates dropped from roughly 47 per cent to 31 per cent and 'did not lead to a rise in gross capital formation (GFCF) in developed countries from the 1990s onwards' (UNCTAD 2012: 131). The reduction in taxation reflected unfavourably on public and private investment. For developed countries, 'investment rates were not lower – but indeed often higher – in the first three decades of the post-war era, even though taxes on profits and top incomes were higher than after the widespread fiscal reforms implemented subsequently' (UNCTAD 2012: 130). Furthermore, UNCTAD notes that 'Mass unemployment has accompanied growth and development the past few decades', never falling much below 6 per cent in developed countries (UNCTAD 2012: 143). It is highly questionable how neoliberalism and free market theory have gained dominance despite their policies having resulted in increasing inequality, poorer economic growth, greater unemployment and decreased investment in the economy. Monbiot notes 'unequivocally that [neoliberal] policies have created the opposite outcomes to those they predicted' (Monbiot 2013).

It must also be remembered that the economisation or marketisation of society, as desired by neoliberalism, requires that:

> [N]ature's amazing cycles of renewal of water and nutrients are defined into nonproduction. The peasants of the world, who provide 72 per cent of the food, do not produce; women who farm or do most of the house-work do not fit this paradigm of growth either. A living forest does not contribute to growth, but when trees are cut down and sold as timber, we have growth. Healthy societies and communities do not contribute to growth, but disease creates growth through, for example, the sale of patented medicine.
>
> (Shiva 2013)

Excessive economisation has a destructive tendency. The *UNCTAD Report* showed that the past three decades of free markets as an organisational prin-ciple has been economically unsustainable. Furthermore, by stimulating and rewarding self-interest, free markets have created greater levels of corruption and free-riding behaviour, indicating that they are socially unsustainable even as they seek to engineer human behaviour. Finally, we have seen that, despite the efforts of many passionate practitioners, quasi-voluntary CSR has failed to tackle structural unsustainabilities in the global economy. It is time to move beyond quasi-voluntary CSR within a free market framework.

13.11 Conclusion

This chapter first discussed the conceptual legal framework for CSR to demon-strate that corporate departure from social and environmental norms results in corporate disembedding from society. It showed that this can be addressed by means of a wide range of regulatory options, ranging from entirely volun-tary activities to the hardest forms of law. Sifting through some of the issues

in the debate on the definition for CSR, the chapter opted for a negative definition of CSR to set a minimum standard for responsible corporate behaviour.
Subsequently it was shown that, despite definitional issues, CSR can certainly
be subjected to an abstract legal analysis to indicate the scope of the potential
legal framework for CSR.

This abstract analysis revealed that the interconnected nature of the economic, social and legal licences to operate is given legal form according to
dominant perspectives and decisions made within the political landscape.
After identifying and discussing neoliberalism as the dominant socio-political perspective in the political realm, the paper subsequently analysed the
OECD Guidelines, the European *Commission Communication on CSR* and
the UN Global Compact for indications of neoliberal influence. Evidence of
neoliberalism was found in the support of each of these institutions for voluntary CSR under free market conditions. Having identified free markets as
the organising principle for CSR, the chapter found that the current legal
framework for CSR is appropriately described as a quasi-voluntary framework assisted by meta-regulation. Under this legal framework, the most obvious method to promote CSR is to advocate the business case for CSR and
argue that businesses can do well by doing good.

Nonetheless, it was shown that quasi-voluntary CSR has failed to tackle
structural unsustainabilities in the global economy and that the emphasis on
the business case for CSR normalised the adoption of CSR under free market constraints. This form of CSR stifles discussions for reform and does not
solve issues related to, for example, planned obsolescence, high emissions,
limited participation and dubious non-financial reporting.

Rather, quasi-voluntary CSR has allowed self-interested firms to use CSR
as a tool to gain advantage and stifle competition. It has resulted in the corporate selection of the degree and method of implementation of social and
environmental norms. In effect, the business case and the operation of CSR
within a free market framework has resulted in the social and environmental norms underlying CSR being placed secondary to profit motives. It was
shown that businesses have in fact used CSR to undermine what could be
called 'free market functioning'.

This result can be expected from the institutionalisation of self-interest
assumptions regarding human behaviour. Despite the scientifically revealed
inaccuracy of these assumptions, the use of free markets as an organisational
principle under neoliberal dominance has increased the 'economisation' of
daily life and stimulated self-interested behaviour. This has occurred despite
the rise of behavioural (law and) economics. Insights from psychology and
sociology have indicated that this institutionalisation of self-interest norms
is likely to increase the prevalence of corrupt and free-riding behaviour. This
alluded to the inherent destructive effect of using self-interest centred free
markets as an organisational principle for CSR.

Self-interest analysis was used to support the argument that neoliberal
restructuring around free market principles created conditions which favoured

the most politically, economically and financially competitive actors in society. Conversely, those who are less able to compete are considerably more disadvantaged in free market systems. In looking at the success of free market reorganisation, it was found that an economic 'super-entity' at the core of the global economy encapsulates roughly 40 per cent of global corporate value. Organisations owned by this entity benefit little from internal competition and are more likely to benefit from collusive practices. This entity is the most financially, economically and politically competitive actor in the global economy and shatters the myth of a 'level playing field' and a competitive globalised economy.

Finally, it was shown that the economisation of every aspect of life is inherently destructive towards natural and social capital. This destructive nature of free markets was further reflected in their inability, even after three decades of prominence, to create superior economic conditions. This realisation was further echoed in the social unsustainability of the use of institutionalised self-interest, and the failure of quasi-voluntary CSR and other forms of law to tackle structural unsustainabilities in the global economy. We can conclude that, despite all the rhetoric praising their success and value, free markets do not exist and, if they did, their self-destructive tendencies would render them unsustainable.

This returns me to the question I originally posed in the introduction to this chapter – where do we go from here? The heart of CSR lies in the value of its underlying social and environmental norms. It is this element that has generated interest, support and passion among politicians, consumers, businesses, employees and NGOs. CSR's current failures can be strongly attributed to the failure of free markets. It is now time to collectively determine a strong legal framework for CSR that embodies and protects social norms, and does not rely on the self-destructive nature of the free market.

Notes

1 BBC (2012) 'Senate Report: HSBC allowed drug money laundering', BBC, 17 July 2012, available at: http://www.bbc.co.uk/news/business-18866018 (accessed 14 February 2014).
2 This figure is now over 10,000 businesses.
3 UN Global Compact website, available at: http://www.unglobalcompact.org/AboutTheGC/index.html (accessed 14 February 2014); http://www.unglobalcompact.org/HowToParticipate/Business_Participation/ (accessed 14 February 2014).
4 HSBC website, Sustainability section, available at: http://www.hsbc.co.uk/1/2/about-us/sustainability (accessed 14 February 2014).
5 BBC (2012) 'HSBC to pay $1.9bn in US money laundering penalties', BBC, 11 December 2012, available at: http://www.bbc.co.uk/news/business-20673466 (accessed 14 February 2014).
6 BBC (2012), 'Tax havens: Super-rich "hiding" at least $21tn', BBC, 22 July 2012, available at: http://www.bbc.co.uk/news/business-18944097 (accessed 14 February 2014).

7 Australia, Austria, Belgium, Canada, Finland, France, Germany, Greece, Ireland, Italy, Japan, the Netherlands, Norway, Portugal, Spain, Sweden, Switzerland, the UK and the US.

References

Abrams, K. and Keren, H. (2009) 'Who's afraid of law and the emotions?', *Minnesota Law Review*, 94, 1997–2074.

Arnold, M. F. (2008) 'Non-Financial Performance Metrics for Corporate Responsibility Reporting Revised', European Academy of Business in Society, School of Management, Cranfield.

Baker, L. (2013) 'European Union Loses 1 Trillion Euros Each Year To Tax Dodging', *Huffington Post*, 12 April 2013. Available at: http://www.huffingtonpost. com/2013/04/13/eu-tax-dodging_n_3070298.html (accessed 14 February 2014).

Berg, N. and Gigerenzer, G. (2010) 'As-if behavioral economics: Neoclassical economics in disguise?', *History of Economic Ideas*, 18(1), 133–66.

Bouwen, P. (2002) 'Corporate lobbying in the European Union: the logic of access', *Journal of European Public Policy*, 9(3), 365–90.

Branson, D. M. (2001) 'Rule That Isn't a Rule-The Business Judgment Rule', *The Valparaiso University Law Review*, 36(3), 631–54.

Campbell, J. L. (2007) 'Why would corporations behave in socially responsible ways? An institutional theory of corporate social responsibility', *Academy of Management Review*, 32(3), 946–67.

Castree, N. (2009) 'Crisis, Continuity and Change: Neoliberalism, the Left and the Future of Capitalism', *Antipode*, 41, S1, 185–213.

Chatterji, A. and Listokin, S. (2007) 'Corporate social irresponsibility', *Democracy: A Journal of Ideas*, 3, 52–63.

Chomsky, N. (2002) *Media control: The spectacular achievements of propaganda*, 7, New York: Seven Stories Press.

Cooper, T. (2005) 'Slower consumption reflections on product life spans and the "throwaway society"', *Journal of Industrial Ecology*, 9(1–2), 51–67.

De Hoo, S. (2011) 'In Pursuit of Corporate Sustainability and Responsibility: Past Cracking Perceptions and Creating Codes', Inaugural Speech, Faculty of Law, Maastricht University, 20 October 2011.

Devinney, T. M. (2009) 'Is the Socially Responsible Corporation a Myth? The Good, the Bad, and the Ugly of Corporate Social Responsibility', *Academy of Management Perspectives*, 23(2), 44–56.

Doane, D. (2005) 'The myth of CSR', *Stanford Social Innovation Review*, 3(3), 22–9.

Eijsbouts, J. (2011) 'Corporate Responsibility, Beyond Voluntarism – Regulatory Options to Reinforce the Licence to Operate', Inaugural Speech, Faculty of Law, Maastricht University.

European Commission (2011) *Communication from the Commission to the European Parliament, the Council, the European Economic and Social Committee and the Committee of the Regions: A renewed EU strategy 2011–14 for Corporate Social Responsibility*, COM(2011) 681 final, Brussels. Available at: http://eur-lex.europa. eu/LexUriServ/LexUriServ.do?uri=COM:2011:0681:FIN:EN:PDF (accessed 14 February 2014).

Ferraro, F. and Pfeffer, J. (2005) 'Economics Language and Assumptions: How Theories can Become Self-Fulfilling', *Academy of Management Review*, 30(1), 8–24.

Fooks, G. J., Gilmore, A. B., Smith, K. E., Collin, J., Holden, C. and Lee, K. (2011) 'Corporate Social Responsibility and Access to Policy Élites: An Analysis of Tobacco Industry Documents', *PloS Med*, 8(8), 1–12.

Friedman, M. (1962) *Capitalism and Freedom*, Chicago: The University of Chicago Press.

George, S. (1999) *A Short History of Neoliberalism*, Presented at the Conference on Economic Sovereignty in a Globalising World, Bangkok: 24–26 March 1999.

Halasa, M. (2013) 'Is anybody listening? HSBC continues to launder money for terrorist groups says whistleblower', *Huffington Post*, 28 August 2013. Available at: http://www.huffingtonpost.com/marni-halasa/is-anybody-listening-hsbc_b_3831412.html (accessed 14 February 2014).

Hansmann, H. and Kraakman, R. (2000) 'End of History for Corporate Law', *Harvard Law School John M. Olin Center for Law, Economics and Business Discussion Paper Series*, Paper 280.

Harper Ho, V. E. (2010) '"Enlightened Shareholder Value": Corporate Governance Beyond the Shareholder-Stakeholder Divide', *Journal of Corporation Law*, 36, 59.

Harrison, J. D. (2013) 'Who actually creates jobs: Start-ups, small business or big corporations?' *Washington Post*. Available at: http://www.washingtonpost.com/business/on-small-business/who-actually-creates-jobs-start-ups-small-businesses-or-big-corporations/2013/04/24/d373ef08-ac2b-11e2-a8b9-2a63d75b5459_story.html (accessed 14 February 2014).

Hausman, R. and Rodrik, D. (2003) 'Economic Development as Self-Discovery', *Journal of Development Economics*, 72(2), 603–33.

Hooghe, L. and Marks, G. (1997) 'The Making of Polity: The Struggle Over European Integration', *European Integration online Papers (EIoP)*, 1(004).

Horrigan, B. (2010) *Corporate Social Responsibility in the 21st Century – Debates, Models and Practices Across Government, Law and Business*, Cheltenham, UK: Edward Elgar Publishing.

Hurt, S. R. (2012) 'The EU–SADC Economic Partnership Agreement Negotiations: "Locking in" the Neoliberal Development Model in Southern Africa?', *Third World Quarterly*, 33(3), 495–510.

Hutchings, J. and Reynolds, J. (2004) 'Marine Fish Population Collapses: Consequences for Recovery and Extinction Risk', *Bioscience*, 54(4), 297–309.

International Union for the Conservation of Nature (2007), 'Species Extinction – the Facts'. Available at: http://cmsdata.iucn.org/downloads/species_extinction_05_2007.pdf (accessed 14 February 2014).

Ireland, P. (2005) 'Shareholder primacy and the distribution of wealth', *Modern Law Review*, 68(1), 49–81.

Jolls C., Sunstein C. R. and Thaler, R. (1998), 'A behavioural approach to law and economics', *Stanford Law Review*, 50, 1477–9.

Kar, D. and Cartwright-Smith, D. (2010) 'Illicit Financial Flows from Africa: Hidden Resource for Development', Global Financial Integrity.

Kar, D. and Curcio, K. (2011) 'Illicit Financial Flows from Developing Countries: 2000–2009 Update with a focus on Asia', Global Financial Integrity.

Keys, T. and Malnight, T. (2010) *Corporate clout: the influence of the world's largest 100 economic entities.* Available at: http://www.globaltrends.com/features/shapersand-influencers/66-corporate-clout-the-influence-of-the-worlds-largest-100-economicentities (accessed 14 February 2014).

Kotz, M. and McDonough, T. (2010) 'Global Neoliberalism and the Contemporary Social Structure of Accumulation', *Contemporary Capitalism and its Crises: Social*

Structure of Accumulation Theory for the Twenty-First Century, Cambridge: Cambridge University Press.

Latham & Watkins LLP (2009) 'The Importance of Voluntarism', *UN Global Compact*. Available at: http://www.unglobalcompact.org/HowToParticipate/Business_Participation/the_importance_of_voluntarism.html (accessed 14 February 2014).

Lemke, T. (2001) 'The birth of bio-politics': Michel Foucault's lecture at the College de France on neo-liberal governmentality', *Economy and Society*, 30(2), 190–207.

Levy, D. and Kaplan, R. (2008) 'CSR and Theories of Global Governance: Strategic Contestation in Global Issue Areas', *The Oxford Handbook of CSR*, Oxford: Oxford University Press.

MacLeod, S. (2005) 'Corporate Social Responsibility within the European Framework', *Wisconsin International Law Journal*, 23(3), 541–52.

Maguire, M. (2011) 'Issues in Brief – The Future of Corporate Social Responsibility Reporting', *The Frederick S. Pardee Center for the Study of the Longer-Range Future*, January 2011.

Margolis, J. D., Elfenbein, H. A. and Walsh, J. P. (2007) 'Does it Pay to be Good? A Meta-analysis and Redirection of Research on the Relationship Between Corporate Social and Financial Performance', Working Paper, Harvard Business School.

Martinez, E. and García, A. (2000) 'What is 'Neoliberalism'? A brief definition', *Global Exchange*, Available at: http://www.csom.umn.edu/labor-education-service/programs-courses/documents/What_is_Neoliberalism.pdf (accessed 14 February 2014).

McChesney, R. W. (2001) 'Global media, neoliberalism, and imperialism', *Monthly Review*, 52(1), 1–19.

McChesney, R. W. (2011) 'Corporate media versus democracy', *Ciberlegenda*, Issue 02.

McManus, J. H. (2009) 'The Commercialization of News', *The Handbook of Journalism Studies*, New York: Routledge, 218–36.

McWilliams, A., Siegel, D. S. and Wright, P. M. (2006) 'Corporate Social Responsibility: Strategic Implications', *Journal of Management Studies*, 43(1), 1–18.

Merino, B. D., Mayper, A. G. and Tolleson T. D. (2010) 'Neoliberalism, deregulation and Sarbanes-Oxley: The Legitimation of a Failed Corporate Governance Model', *Accounting, Auditing & Accountability Journal*, 23(6), 774–92.

Miller, D. T. (1999) 'The Norm of Self-Interest', *American Psychologist*, 54(12), 1053–60.

Miller, D. T. and Ratner, R. K. (1998) 'The Disparity Between the Actual and Assumed Power of Self-Interest', *Journal of Personality and Social Psychology*, 74(1), 53–62.

Mishkin, S. (2013) 'Foxconn admits student intern labour violations at China plants', *Financial Times*, 10 October 2013. Available at: http://www.ft.com/cms/s/0/88524304-319f-11e3-817c-00144feab7de.html (accessed 27 May 2014).

Monbiot, G. (2013) 'If You Think we're Done with Neoliberalism, Think Again', *The Guardian*, 14 January 2013. Available at: http://www.theguardian.com/commentisfree/2013/jan/14/neoliberal-theory-economic-failure (accessed 14 February 2014).

Mouawad, J. (2010) 'For BP, a History of Spills and Safety Lapses', *New York Times*, 8 May 2010. Available at: http://www.nytimes.com/2010/05/09/business/09bp.html?pagewanted=all&_r=0 (accessed 14 February 2014).

OECD (2011), 'OECD Guidelines for Multinational Enterprises', OECD Publishing. Available at: http://www.oecd.org/daf/inv/mne/48004323.pdf (accessed 14 February 2014).

OECD Factbook (2013). Available at: http://www.oecd-ilibrary.org/sites/factbook-2013-en/09/02/01/airqty_g1.html?contentType=&itemId=/content/chapter/factbook-2013-70-en&containerItemId=/content/serial/18147364&accessItemIds=&mimeType=text/html (accessed 14 February 2014).

Paige, J. (2013) 'Bangladesh Clothing Workers Still Exploited, Five Months After Factory Fire, Panorama Investigation Finds', *The Independent*, 23 September 2013. Available at: http://www.independent.co.uk/news/world/asia/bangladesh-clothing-workers-still-exploited-five-months-after-factory-fire-panorama-investigation-finds-8833102.html (accessed 14 February 2014).

Palley, T. I. (2004) 'From Keynesianism to Neoliberalism: Shifting Paradigms in Economics', *Neoliberalism – A Critical Reader*, London: Pluto Press.

Parker, C. (2007) 'Meta-regulation: legal accountability for corporate social responsibility', *The New Corporate Accountability – Corporate Social Responsibility and the Law*, Cambridge: Cambridge University Press, 207–37.

Peck, J. (2008). 'Remaking laissez-faire'. *Progress in Human Geography*, 32(1), 3–43.

Philipsen, N. J. (2010) 'Regulation and Competition in the Legal Profession: Developments in the EU and China', *Journal of Competition Law and Economics*, 6(2), 203–31.

Prummer, A (2011), 'Political Networks, Ideology and Lobbying', Department of Economics, European University Institute. Available at: https://political-economy-breakfast.wikischolars.columbia.edu/file/view/Lobbying.pdf/254806764/Lobbying.pdf (accessed 14 February 2014).

Sears, D. O. and Funk, C. L. (1991) 'The Role of Self-Interest in Social and Political Attitudes', *Advances in Experimental Social Psychology*, 24, 79.

Shaughnessy, H. (2012) 'Too Big to Indict, HSBC, Barclays and UBS Set Ugly Precedent', *Forbes*, 11 December 2012.

Shiva, V. (2013), 'How Economic Growth has Become Anti-Life', *The Guardian*, 1 November 2013. Available at: http://www.theguardian.com/commentisfree/2013/nov/01/how-economic-growth-has-become-anti-life (accessed 14 February 2014).

Sizemore, C. (2013) 'Greece Downgraded to "Emerging Market", But Will it Ever Emerge?', *Forbes*, 20 June 2013. Available at: http://www.forbes.com/sites/moneybuilder/2013/06/20/greece-downgraded-to-emerging-market-but-will-it-ever-emerge/ (accessed 14 February 2014).

Smith, E. B. and Kuntz, P. (2013) 'CEO Pay 1,795-to-1 Multiple of Wages Skirts U.S. Law', *Bloomberg*, 30 April 2013. Available online at: http://www.bloomberg.com/news/2013-04-30/ceo-pay-1-795-to-1-multiple-of-workers-skirts-law-as-sec-delays.html (accessed 14 February 2014).

Smythe, C. (2013) 'Big Banks Sued for Manipulating Forex Rates', *The Independent Online*, 4 November 2013. Available at: http://www.iol.co.za/business/international/big-banks-sued-for-manipulating-forex-rates-1.1601432#.Unj_xvmkqj8 (accessed 14 February 2014).

Stephens, B. (2002) 'The Amorality of Profit: Transnational Corporations and Human Rights', *Berkeley Journal of International Law*, 20(1), 45–90. Available at: http://scholarship.law.berkeley.edu/bjil/vol20/iss1/3 (accessed 14 February 2014).

Steurer, R. (2010) 'The Role of Governments in Corporate Social Responsibility: Characterising Public Policies on CSR in Europe', *Policy Sciences*, 43(1), 49–72.

Strandberg, C. (2002) 'The Future of Corporate Social Responsibility', Strandberg Consulting, VanCity Credit Union. Available at: http://www.corostrandberg.com/pdfs/Future_of_CSR.pdf (accessed 14 February 2014).

Taibbi, M. (2013) 'Everything is Rigged: The Biggest Price-Fixing Scandal Ever', *Rolling Stone Politics*, 25 April 2013.

The Economist (2013) 'The FX is in – Are Foreign-Exchange Benchmarks the Latest to be Manipulated By Bankers?', *The Economist*, 12 October 2013. Available at: http://www.economist.com/news/finance-and-economics/21587824-are-foreign-exchange-benchmarks-latest-be-manipulated-bankers-fx (accessed 14 February 2014).

United Nations (UN) (2011) 'United Nations Global Compact – Corporate Sustainability in The World Economy', *United Nations*, New York: United Nations. Available at: http://www.unglobalcompact.org/docs/news_events/8.1/GC_brochure_FINAL.pdf (accessed 14 February 2014).

United Nations Conference on Trade and Development, Development and Trade Report 2012 (UNCTAD) (2012) United Nations, New York and Geneva. Available at: http://unctad.org/en/PublicationsLibrary/tdr2012_En.pdf (accessed 14 February 2014).

United Nations Water (2011), *Policy Brief – Water Quality*. Available at: http://www.unwater.org/downloads/waterquality_policybrief.pdf (accessed 14 February 2014).

Vallentin, S. (2012a) *Neoliberalism and CSR: Contradictions and/or Converging Forces?*, Public and Private Regulation of CSR Conference at Copenhagen Business School. Available at: https://conference.cbs.dk/index.php/workshopCSR/CSR2012/paper/viewFile/1557/616 (accessed 14 February 2014).

Vallentin, S. (2012b) *Neoliberalism and CSR: Overcoming Stereotypes and Embracing Ideological Variety*, Paper presented at the 28th EGOS Colloquium in Helsinki, Finland, 2–7 July 2012, SWG 10: The Changing Role of Business in Global Society.

Van Aartsen, C. W. (2013) 'CSR in Times of Neoliberal Hegemony', Maastricht University, Master's thesis.

Van Horn, R. and Mirowski, P. (2009) 'The Rise of the Chicago School of Economics and the Birth of Neoliberalism', in Mirowski, P. and Plehwe, D. (eds), *The Road from Mont Pèlerin – The Making of the Neoliberal Thought Collective,* Cambridge: Harvard University Press, 139–78.

Vitali, S., Glattfelder, J. B. and Battiston, S. (2011) 'The Network of Global Corporate Control', *PloS one*, 6(10), 1–36.

Wade, R. H. and Sigurgeirsdottir, S. (2012) 'Iceland's Rise, Fall, Stabilisation and beyond', *Cambridge Journal of Economics*, 36, 127–44.

Walton, J. K. and Seddon, D. (2008) *Free Markets and Food Riots: The Politics of Global Adjustment*, Oxford: Wiley-Blackwell Publishers.

WHO (2013) 'Trade, Foreign Policy, Diplomacy and Health – Structural Adjustment Programs (SAPs)', World Health Organization. Available at: http://www.who.int/trade/glossary/story084/en/index.html (accessed 14 February 2014).

Part V
Comparative conclusions

14 Comparative and concluding remarks

*Michael Faure, Niels Philipsen and
Guangdong Xu*

14.1 Background

As we made clear in the Introduction (Chapter 1), this book is the result of
a conference that was held in May 2013 in Beijing. This conference constituted a follow-up to an earlier conference held in Beijing in May 2012, which
resulted in a book with the same publisher.[1] Whereas the first volume largely
(and relatively broadly) focused on issues related to economics and regulation
in China, the second conference, and hence this book, provided a more narrow focus by concentrating on law and finance and more particularly on the
role of law and regulation in sustaining financial markets.

As we equally made clear in Chapter 1, this book is the result of collaboration between various partners in China and Europe, especially the Research
Center for Law and Economics of the China University of Political Science
and Law (CUPL) in China, and the Maastnicht European Institute for
Transnational Legal Research (METRO) in the Netherlands. A law and economics approach was used to address the different law and finance topics
discussed in this book. It was logical and appealing to use this methodological
approach, since it has more particularly been the economic approach to law
that has examined the question to what extent legal instruments and institutions can contribute to the development of financial markets and, more generally, to economic growth.

14.2 The relation between legal institutions, financial markets and economic growth

The role of legal institutions and its relationship to financial markets and economic growth is a fascinating topic for China. Many have looked with mixed
emotions (varying from envy and admiration to confusion) at the Chinese
economic model. Even in times where the world economy has plunged into a
global financial crisis, China seems to have been relatively untouched by this
phenomenon and continues its annual economic growth at between 7 and
9 per cent. However, one of the issues that the contributions in this volume
wanted to address is whether it suffices to merely focus on those – admittedly

fascinating – growth numbers without looking at a number of deeper questions, e.g. relating to the sources and foundations of this economic growth, and the costs incurred for this economic growth. Indeed, one of the questions addressed in this volume in a critical way, *inter alia* in Chapter 4 by Xu and Gui, is to what extent this Chinese growth model can be considered sustainable in the long run. Moreover, it also merits analysis to what extent the economic growth miracle observed in China can be attributed to institutions and more particularly to legal rules and regulations. The traditional assumption in economic theory, especially following the path-breaking work by Douglas North, is that institutions are crucial for developing economic growth. However, it is less clear how one should interpret that starting point in the case of China, where institutions apparently play a different role from those in Western societies like the US or Europe. Moreover, if institutions do at all play a role in stimulating economic growth in China, questions can again be asked about the way in which institutions in China attempt to reach economic growth and about the sustainability of those efforts.

It is to some of those questions that the contributions in this book attempt to provide answers by examining particular legal instruments and institutions, especially in relation to their ability to stimulate (financial) markets in a broad sense. That is, the contributions focus e.g. on how institutions can stimulate the financial system, but also on how they can stimulate competitive market forces. Insights regarding the way in which institutions and instruments can fulfil these roles are obviously crucial for China and for other legal systems, including Europe and the US. The various chapters in this book attempt to examine how the relationship between legal rules, institutions and instruments on the one hand, and financial markets on the other hand works, the basic idea being that those insights may also lead to a fine-tuning and potential improvement of those legal rules, instruments and institutions.

14.3   Different approaches

As we made equally clear in Chapter 1, a variety of research approaches was followed by the contributors to this volume. In many chapters a *positive approach* was adopted to examine to what extent legal rules have particular effects on the functioning of markets. Some contributions went a step further and provided *policy recommendations*, indicating how particular legal rules may be better able to stimulate the functioning of the market mechanism. For example, Faure and Ma in Chapter 9 argued in favour of some criminal enforcement of the Anti-Monopoly Law in China, which could potentially improve the way in which the Anti-Monopoly Law can contribute to stimulating an effective competitive environment on the market in China.[2]

In some contributions a *comparative law and economics* approach was applied. These contributions compared, for example, various national regulatory regimes (notably in the EU, the US and China) to look at the comparative efficiency or effectiveness of particular rules and institutions with respect to either the goal set by the legislator or the economic goal of improving social welfare. In some cases this led to recommendations to improve institutions in one of the legal systems. In Chapter 10, for example, He used experiences from the compensation for victims of disasters in the US and, more particularly, the way in which insurance markets play an important role in this respect to formulate specific recommendations for China.

14.4 Different topics

The number of topics that could be dealt with when examining the question how law contributes to the functioning of (financial) markets is potentially huge. This book covers a wide variety of topics. The advantage of this rather broad approach is that it allows comparisons of how various legal rules can stimulate the functioning of markets in a more or less effective manner. However, to facilitate understanding, we have managed to take advantage of relationships between contributors' topics and divided the chapters in separate parts dealing with specific related issues.

14.4.1 Law, financial development and economic growth

The chapters included in Part I dealt with the important topic of law, financial development and economic growth, and thus went to one of the conference's core questions – addressed also in the well-known *Doing Business* studies published by the World Bank – on the relationship between particular institutions and economic growth.

The first chapter of Part I, Chapter 2 by Nicolas de Sadeleer, could not be presented at the Beijing conference in May 2013, but was added to the volume at the editors' request in light of the topic's relevance, namely economic governance in Europe. De Sadeleer shows how – as a result of the financial crisis, but in fact already preceding the 2008 crisis – various European institutions issued rules aiming at economic governance, all with different shapes and contents, but sharing a common goal to reinforce fiscal discipline at the EU Member State level with a view to achieving macroeconomic stability and sustainable public finances. A crucial issue, as De Sadeleer shows, is the division of competences between the Member States and the EU and the instruments possessed by the European institutions (more particularly the European Commission) to achieve compliance with the budgetary obligations to which the Member States have agreed. De Sadeleer shows that, as in any federal system, a crucial issue is how the central level (*in casu* the EU) can avoid free riding by Member States through an effective enforcement mechanism.

The second contribution in Part I, Chapter 3 by Shouji Sun and Jiye Hu, provides an innovative contribution to the law and finance debate by showing the importance of the financing of the pension system in different countries and the effects this financing system may have on the financial stability of a State. Sun and Hu test the legal origins hypothesis, stressing that for example the financing system in the Netherlands (which basically consists of a system where current generations save for future pensions) has provided a better financial stability; than so-called pay-as-you-go (PAYG) systems, in which the current generation has to finance the current pensions. Interestingly, the authors cast doubt on the legal origins hypothesis, arguing that the classic story of La Porta, Lopez-de-Silanes, Shleifer and Vishny, being that the common law would be better for economic growth than the civil law, cannot be generally upheld when examining how countries fared during the financial crisis. They argue that there were substantial differences between different legal systems that all had a civil law background, such as the Netherlands, Greece and Chile. Sun and Hu show that it is not the legal origin, but, so they hypothesise, rather the financing of the pension system (which is more effective in the Netherlands and Chile than, for example, in Greece) which can explain why particular countries (like Greece) suffered more than others (e.g. the Netherlands) under the financial crisis.

The third chapter in Part I (Chapter 4) addressed the effects of financial regulation in China on economic growth. In this chapter Guangdong Xu and Binwei Gui point at an apparent paradox, being that on the one hand China is now the second largest economy in the world (even passing Japan), but on the other hand a system they refer to as financial repression. That repression more particularly consists of severe controls *inter alia* on interest rates, precisely in order to stimulate investments. Xu and Gui show that the repressed financial system acts as a double-edged sword for economic growth in China. On the one hand, financial repression could arguably promote China's economic growth by lowering the cost of capital, thereby encouraging investment and production. On the other hand, evidence shows that financial repression endangers China's economic health by damaging its economic efficiency, slowing job creation and distorting the country's economic structure. In the short term, the pro-growth effects of financial repression may outweigh its anti-growth effects, and the overall influence of financial repression may therefore be beneficial to economic growth. However, such a scenario can hardly be expected to last into the long term.

This topic of the way in which government can, via various regulatory tools stimulate economic growth (also via price controls) is further developed in Chapter 5 by Tao Xi and Jianwei Chen on law, money and prices. In this chapter, the authors offer a theoretical framework to analyse the main endogenous factors that influence the money supply in China, such as commodity prices, asset prices, exchange rates, foreign exchange reserves, household deposit rates and enterprise loan rates. Proceeding from the objectives of maintaining currency value stability and economic growth, as stipulated in Chinese (monetary) law, and taking the perspective of risk prevention, Xi and Chen provide some policy recommendations. For example, the authors argue that China should carefully manage the relationship between its money supply and the development of the real economy, the fictitious economy and the international economy. They also recommend China to adjust its industrial structure, balance the relationship between investment, consumption and savings, and coordinate the balance between its domestic economy and the international economy.

The contributions to Part I of the book have added to the well-known literature on law and economic growth. In fact, they have taken the debate further, for example, by showing that, differently than some literature had assumed, legal origins as such are no guarantee of economic growth (Sun and Hu). This highlighted the argument that it may be short-sighted to simply focus on economic growth as a proxy for economic success. Indeed, as a result of the largely investment-driven government policy, gross domestic product (GDP) in China may have systematically grown, but that does not guarantee that this type of investment-based growth equally leads to welfare in a broader sense, i.e. sustainable development.

14.4.2   The role of financial regulation

The chapters in Part II all focus on financial regulation and how various types of regulatory instruments can (positively or negatively) affect the functioning of financial markets, this being the central question of this volume.

In the first chapter of Part II, Chapter 6 by Niels Philipsen, attention is paid to the way in which the services provided by an important stakeholder in financial markets – auditors – are regulated. Philipsen shows how, since the late 1980s but more particularly after the scandal involving Arthur Andersen and Enron, the markets in which large audit firms operate have fundamentally changed, leading to a *de facto* oligopoly of a small number of worldwide operating accountancy networks active in auditing large and quoted companies. In addition, regulators in various jurisdictions now look at auditors with increasing suspicion and have consequently imposed more serious regulatory requirements on them. Most of those requirements, as discussed by Philipsen, aim to avoid conflicts of interests between auditors and the firms they are supposed to audit, thereby promoting independence and quality of audit services. One aspect equally examined by Philipsen, which has so far received less attention in the literature, is that many audit firms are exposed to high liability claims. The European Commission has provided a Recommendation allowing EU Member States the option to limit auditors' liability in various ways. Limiting auditors' liability has also been proposed as a solution to deal with the lack of competition in the audit market. Philipsen discusses this option and an alternative, namely allowing outside ownership via a deregulation of legal form and shareholding restrictions. Although debates on these topics have largely taken place within the EU and US, Philipsen shows that they are undoubtedly also relevant to the Chinese context, where professional services, including those provided by auditors, are generally subject to increasing regulatory requirements, and where many accounting scandals have also taken place.

The second chapter in Part II (Chapter 7) deals with the important issue of enforcement of regulation in securities markets. Tianshu Zhou shows that China relies on a mix of private and public enforcement in its securities markets, both, however, have their particular strengths and weaknesses. Zhou argues that, also in a transitional economy like China, private enforcement should be regarded as an important instrument to solve problems in securities markets. However, private enforcement in China is underdeveloped. According to Zhou, private enforcement can be improved, for example by a better allocation of judiciary resources, by introducing more investor-friendly legal institutions and by allowing better access to data on judiciary decisions.

The last chapter in Part II, Chapter 8 by Wenjing Li, deals with another topical subject: the importance of the so-called shadow banking system in China. This chapter is partially linked to Chapter 4 by Xu and Gui, who examined the consequences of financial repression in China on economic growth. One of the effects of the financial repression in China is that a substantial part of the financing of economic activities, as Li shows, does not take place via the regular banking system, but via a so-called shadow banking system. Li explains that the development of this market for shadow banking is, understandably, partially the result of the heavy regulatory controls that push stakeholders to look for alternative sources of finance in the shadow banking system. Li, moreover, shows that this system of shadow banking in China should not be compared to, for example, traditional money lenders that are active in developing countries. In fact, even some of the major State-owned banks are engaged in shadow banking, showing that the shadow banking system is now effectively playing an important role in China's economy. That again, so Li argues, raises important questions concerning financial stability and sustainability.

14.4.3   *Design of financial instruments*

Part III of this book consists of three chapters that examine design issues relating to financial instruments and financial markets.

Chapter 9 by Michael Faure and Jingyuan Ma addresses the role of China's Anti-Monopoly Law (AML) in regulating competition on the financial market. Faure and Ma more particularly focus on one aspect of this law, namely its enforcement. They question whether the current, merely financial, penalties incorporated in the AML constitute an effective deterrent to price fixing and hardcore cartels. Faure and Ma argue that it could be examined whether China would, in the long run, have an interest in following the US model where serious breaches of antitrust law (such as price fixing) can give rise to criminal liability and non-monetary sanctions, more particularly imprisonment.

The next chapter, Chapter 10 by Qihao He, deals with the question how particular financial instruments, such as insurance, but also other instruments (like bonds) could be used to finance the consequences of disasters. He points at the fact that scientific evidence indicates a serious likelihood that the incidents of disasters may increase, also as a result of climate change. This raises, also for China, the question of how compensation for the victims of those disasters could be financed. The author discusses various theoretical models, more particularly based on first-party insurance with a role for the State as reinsurer of last resort, and shows how those models have success- fully been applied in the US to provide compensation even in cases of so- called catastrophic risks. Given that China already is and may in the future increasingly be exposed to disasters with serious financial consequences, He argues that the development of the analysed financial and insurance instru- ments may be a prudent choice for Chinese policymakers as well. According to He, a good choice may be a mandatory multi-year insurance in which pre- miums sufficiently reflect risks.

Chapter 11 by Federico Wesselhoefft deals with project finance contracts (PFCs). Wesselhoefft explains how an intricate web of various contractual relationships emerges whereby parties often create special financing vehicles merely for the purpose of being able to finance a variety of complex projects. Those contractual arrangements and corporate vehicles play a fundamental role in the practice of project financing and yet much still needs to be investi- gated about the way in which these financing mechanisms function and oper- ate. Wesselhoefft provides a law and economics analysis of the basic benefits and strategic advantages that are enabled by PFCs. Wesselhoefft does so in relation to the different types of costs and conflicts that exceptionally large projects entail when financed under corporate settings.

14.4.4 *Corporate governance and corporate social responsibility*

Part IV of this book deals with the important issue of corporate governance and, more generally, the role and task of corporate social responsibility (CSR).

The first chapter in Part IV by Lars Hansson and Yanqiang Ding (Chapter 12) provides an analytical overview of the complex variety of regu- latory and market-based instruments that can be and are in fact used by differ- ent policymakers to provide incentives to stakeholders, particularly corporate actors, to internalise environmental externalities. One of the crucial tasks of corporations, also within a framework of CSR, is obviously the protection of the environment. However, as is powerfully argued in the subsequent chap- ter by Van Aartsen, the current paradigm in corporate law and governance, through its focus on and promotion of self-interest and individualism, pro- vides little scope for corporations to spontaneously follow corporate environ- mental responsibility. That is why Hansson and Ding argue that instruments will be necessary to cure the market failures caused by environmental exter- nalities. The traditional dichotomy between *regulation* (often referred to as a 'command and control approach') versus market-based (also called eco- nomic) instruments is carefully explained. The authors show that the major theoretical advantage of market-based instruments (such as green taxes and emission trading) is that they provide better incentives for cost internalisation and environmental innovation. Hansson and Ding provide supporting data, from Sweden and other sources, showing how the implementation of market-based instruments has been able to reduce emissions more effectively than a traditional regulatory approach based on command and control.

As already indicated, Chapter 13 by Constantijn van Aartsen adopts a strong stance against structural shortcomings in capitalist and market-based perspectives on corporate governance and CSR. By focusing too one-sidedly on ideological perceptions of self-interest and market mechanisms, policy-makers have created a broader economic paradigm in which, individual material gain and self-interest is inherently, structurally, and organisationally granted a higher priority than sustainable outcomes. Van Aartsen argues that a radical paradigm shift is necessary whereby the traditional self-interested view of corporate law, corporate governance and CSR should be left behind in favour of an approach which builds on and promotes the social and ethical norms underlying theoretical discussions of CSR. This radical shift would create an enabling environment for economic stakeholders to become more aware of and more able to act upon their CSR. According to Van Aartsen, the need for this paradigm shift is one of the lessons that can be drawn from the recent financial crisis, which (so he argues) is a precise, even unavoidable, consequence of the relentless pursuit of self-interest.

14.5   Comparative conclusions

14.5.1   On mutual learning

Looking more broadly at the various chapters presented in this book, there are undoubtedly some conclusions and trends that can be identified. A first point is that many of the chapters show, as is often the case in comparative legal studies or comparative law and economics that there is a lot of scope for mutual learning between legal systems. The type of inter-institutional comparison provided in this volume can provide useful insights into legal systems that are interested in improving the effectiveness of the instruments, and institutions they use. This type of mutual learning was present in numerous chapters in this book (for example in Chapter 6 by Philipsen on the regulation and liability of auditors, and in Chapter 9 by Faure and Ma on criminal enforcement of competition law).

Within this volume, much of the mutual learning related to the case of Europe and China, whereby many contributors (explicitly or implicitly) examined how experiences in Europe could provide useful insights for policy developments in China. For example, the contribution by Hansson and Ding analysed whether market-based instruments (like taxation or emission trading) could be useful tools for environmental policy in China. However, many contributors warned that mutual learning does not necessarily entail blindly copying institutions and approaches found in one legal system and applying it to another. It is well known that legal transplants may provide considerable benefits, but insights gained in one country need to be adapted and tailored to the institutional environment of the receiving country. Otherwise the important legal rule could act as a 'Fremdkörper' that cannot find its place in the hostile environment in which it is introduced. Questions on the effectiveness of legal transplants were asked *inter alia* by Zhou concerning the tendency in China to copy US institutions in the control of its securities markets. More particularly, the US tendency to rely on private litigation may not always be suitable for the Chinese context where, to put it mildly, the necessary conditions with respect to an independent judiciary with good expertise may not always be fulfilled.

14.5.2 On the role of law and regulation

As we already indicated above, various chapters provided interesting insights with respect to the relationship between legal institutions and economic growth. Sun and Hu largely defend the thesis that it is not so much the legal origin that matters for economic growth but rather the financing and structure of pension funds. Also Xu and Gui showed that regulation may indeed play a role in stimulating economic growth in China, but that the long-term efficiency of the way in which this is stimulated (via a strong investment-based policy) can be doubted. Another consequence of the financial repression was identified by Li with respect to shadow banking. To some extent the development of shadow banking could be seen as an application of the famous Coase theorem. Indeed, the experience with shadow banking in China shows that when regulation creates inefficiencies that inhibit the development of efficient solutions, parties may via bargaining (in this case between providers of capital and entrepreneurs) develop alternatives to circumvent inefficient regulation.

A question that is closely linked to whether law is necessary for economic growth is to what extent government intervention in the form of regulation is necessary at all. That is, for example, an issue which is at the heart of the contribution by Wesselhoefft, who describes the often inventive solutions that private parties have developed to stimulate project financing. Wesselhoefft shows that the market has been able to develop highly complicated financial devices (such as special purpose vehicles (SPVs)) especially designed to provide financing for the development of complex projects. Wesselhoefft shows how parties acting in the market not only have been able to deal with the transactional difficulties of these arrangements, but also how these private parties usually manage to circumvent the application of potentially distortive default law and regulation. Again, the market has apparently looked for various answers to particular questions and needs that have arisen in the market.

This touches upon classic dilemmas in law and economics and regulation theory, i.e. to what extent can and will, solutions be developed in a satisfactory way via the market or whether regulatory intervention by government is necessary. The traditional answer provided in economic theory is obviously that such a government intervention is needed only to the extent that there would be a market failure, as is also pointed out in Philipsen's chapter. However, some of the complex topics discussed in this book (varying from the regulation of pension funds to monetary policy and economic governance) equally show that it is not only on the basis of the classic paradigm of market failure that governments will decide to intervene. The latter is particularly important in China where, for example in competition policy, but also in many other domains the government certainly did not only see its task as having to control market failures. Other values, like the protection of the economic order, market integration or (again within the particular case of China) the maintenance of the socialist market economy, are in some cases explicitly mentioned as policy goals as well. Hence that shows that one needs to be somewhat careful when analysing the need for regulation merely within the classic market failure paradigm of the capitalist economy. In the case of China, that may certainly be a too narrow perspective. However, even for Western countries, Van Aartsen argues that a free market approach, e.g. to corporate law and corporate governance, central to his chapter, may be a too narrow focus, given the shift in expectations that society has as far as the functioning of corporations is concerned.

14.5.3   *On choosing the right instruments and institutions*

By taking a broad approach towards the topic of law and finance, we allowed contributors to this book to focus on a variety of crucial issues dealing with instruments and institutions within financial markets. Hence, important topics could be addressed in this book, such as the optimal financial instruments to compensate victims of disasters (see He's Chapter 10), the role of monetary policy in promoting economic growth (see Xi and Chen's Chapter 5), economic governance in the EU in the light of the financial crisis, and the debt crisis (see De Sadeleer's Chapter 2), but also the question how the lack of competition in the market for auditors can potentially be addressed by limiting liability and relaxing legal form and shareholding requirements (see Philipsen's Chapter 6).

Furthermore, regulation should not automatically be equated with government regulation. Van Aartsen explicitly pleaded for using the private regulatory mechanism called CSR to induce corporations to take their responsibilities towards stakeholders other than shareholders seriously. Similarly, Hansson and Ding showed that in the environmental arena regulation should not necessarily be the classic government regulation in the form of command and control, but could also take the form of more flexible market-based instruments (MBIs).

14.5.4   *On policy recommendations*

The contributors to this volume have used a variety of different economic approaches, which together show the richness and variety of the economic approach to regulation and institutions. As already indicated, some engaged in mostly descriptive, positive approaches, i.e. using economics to explain the effects of particular regulations. Other contributors went beyond the more positive approach and provided normative policy recommendations. Traditionally, economic scholars have been careful in formulating policy recommendations. However, even though one obviously always needs to remain careful, it may for the particular case of China be important indeed to take this next step by pointing the policymaker explicitly at some of the implications of economic theory for policy reform, provided of course that policymakers would wish to be guided by economic theory in their decision making. The advantage of this more normative approach is that in that case concrete policy recommendations are provided following the theoretical analysis. Hence, for example, Hansson and Ding provided clear recommendations on implementing their 'eco-logics' in environmental policy, He formulated policy recommendations regarding the role of insurance in covering catastrophic disasters, Xi and Chen provided some policy suggestions in relation to Chinese monetary policy and Li equally recommended targeted regulation of the shadow banking sector.

14.5.5   On empirical studies

One important feature of many of the contributions to this book is that, as is now more generally the case in law and economics,[3] the results of empirical studies have been incorporated in the analyses. For example, Sun and Hu provided an empirical analysis of the effects of various models of financing a pension system, and Xu and Gui empirically analysed the effects of repressive financial regulation. Using existing empirical evidence, Zhou examined to what extent private and public enforcement are effectively used in regulating securities markets in China. Hansson and Ding also backed up their plea in favour of the use of MBIs in environmental policy with empirical studies showing the positive effects of those instruments *inter alia* in the case of Sweden.

This tendency, i.e. to increasingly incorporate the insights from empirical studies into law and economics analysis, should certainly be welcomed and even be encouraged. Empirical studies can be considered as a necessary tool in addition to theoretical law and economics. Simply said, empirics allow a 'reality check' to back-up or reject the hypothesis that has been developed on the basis of theoretical studies.

14.6   The way forward

This book is the second in a row in the long-standing collaboration between METRO and CUPL. In the introduction to this book, the editors already made clear that this publication and the preceding conference could only be realised thanks to the contribution of many. Here we would like to repeat our gratitude to those mentioned there. We hope that the chapters in this book have provided a modest contribution to the important question how legal instruments and institutions can stimulate the effectiveness of (financial) markets.

At the same time, we realised that only examples from a few sectors could be discussed and that, moreover, there are still many more issues to be further explored and examined, both theoretically and empirically. China can be considered a wonderful laboratory for those interested in policy analysis. Many new developments are taking place legal borrowing and legal transplants occur on a daily basis; and legal reforms are the order of the day. Moreover, adequate datasets are increasingly available that allow empirical testing of the effects of particular policy changes. This book should therefore certainly not be considered as a final answer, but as one stepping stone towards futher research projects that will equally analyse the fascinating case of economic regulation in China.

Notes

1 Faure, M. and Xu, G. (eds) (2013) *Economics and Regulation in China*, London: Routledge.
2 For more examples, see subsection 14.5.4.
3 See Klick, J. 'The Empirical Revolution in Law and Economics', Inauguration Address, Erasmus University Rotterdam, 2013.

Printed in the United States
by Baker & Taylor Publisher Services